'Carter writes as if he has ADD, careering through his life on oil rigs in exotic locations. He won't win the Booker, but his yarns burn with anarchic energy . . . in a word, irrepressible.'
—*Herald Sun*

'This is one of the most split-my-sides-laughing memoirs I think I have ever read . . . that blows along like the North Sea.'
—*Northern Star*

'Not so much a thriller as a driller, *Don't Tell Mum* is our tip for Bloke's Book of the Year (BBOTY).'
—*Sunday Telegraph*

'What you have here . . . is that rare situation of somebody who not only has a story to tell but the ability to tell it. Carter's anecdotes are told with great good humour and perfect timing.'
—*The Age*

'Ever wondered what happens to the boys from the movie *Jackass* when they grow up? They become oil rig workers. Shit happens, so some of the stuff that Paul Carter and his friends get hit with probably isn't their fault – although sitting at the top of an oil rig derrick during a thunderstorm is probably inviting God to hit you with something. Otherwise most of the madness and mayhem, interspersed with the occasional car or motor-cycle accident and totally over the top practical jokes, are clearly all down to Paul. As for the chain-smoking monkeys, pool-playing ferrets and bar-tending orangutans . . . if the humans are crazy the animals should be too.'
—Tony Wheeler, founder of *Lonely Planet*

'Great two fisted writing from the far side of hell.'
—John Birmingham, author

'This is a book for blokes . . . Carter is a kind of modern day Indiana Jones . . . a natural storyteller.'
—*Sunday Tasmanian*

'A unique look at a gritty game. Relentlessly funny and obsessively readable.'
—Phillip Noyce, film director

SMOKING MONKEYS, DRILLING RIGS, BIO-DIESEL BIKES
AND OTHER STORIES

SMOKING MONKEYS, DRILLING RIGS, BIO-DIESEL BIKES

AND OTHER STORIES

THE COMPLETE PAUL CARTER

ALLEN & UNWIN

This edition first published in 2011

Don't Tell Mum I Work on the Rigs... copyright © Paul Carter 2005
This is Not a Drill copyright © Paul Carter 2007
Is That Thing Diesel? copyright © Paul Carter 2010

All rights reserved. No part of this book may be reproduced or transmitted in any form or by any means, electronic or mechanical, including photocopying, recording or by any information storage and retrieval system, without prior permission in writing from the publisher. The Australian *Copyright Act 1968* (the Act) allows a maximum of one chapter or 10 per cent of this book, whichever is the greater, to be photocopied by any educational institution for its educational purposes provided that the educational institution (or body that administers it) has given a remuneration notice to Copyright Agency Limited (CAL) under the Act.

Allen & Unwin
Sydney, Melbourne, Auckland, London

83 Alexander Street
Crows Nest NSW 2065
Australia
Phone: (61 2) 8425 0100
Fax: (61 2) 9906 2218
Email: info@allenandunwin.com
Web: www.allenandunwin.com

Cataloguing-in-Publication details are available
from the National Library of Australia
www.trove.nla.gov.au

ISBN 978 1 74237 907 4

Set in 11.5/14.85 pt Bembo by Midland Typesetters, Australia
Printed in Australia by Griffin Press

10 9 8 7 6 5 4 3

The paper in this book is FSC certified. FSC promotes environmentally responsible, socially beneficial and economically viable management of the world's forests.

CONTENTS

FOREWORD ix
DON'T TELL MUM I WORK ON THE RIGS 1
THIS IS NOT A DRILL 175
IS THAT THING DIESEL? 353

FOREWORD

I sat down this morning to write you a note—a thank you note—to introduce this compendium. My memories are random and punctuated with idiocy and violence, with all the things oil men do. These moments are not ghostly or ethereal as memories sometimes are, but clear and sharp like Japanese steel. So for what it's worth . . .

'Buy me a doggy. Please, Daddy' . . . I'm interrupted.

My child looks at me and Lola's huge blue eyes tear down my barely adequate sensible defences. Multiple questions flash like inkblot test cards in my mind: Who's gonna take it for walks, pick up its poo, wash it, feed it, medicate it? The final card flips . . . breasts, no wait . . . yup, it's breasts . . . sorry.

A week later it's a pony. I say 'NO', but the look of deep blue disappointment plays havoc with me for hours. We settle on a goldfish . . . Patches is dead within a week. A formal service is held with the entire cast of Lola's all-singing, all-dancing cuddly toy ensemble. She's desperately serious, but as soon as Patches is below ground Lola spins her little face in my direction and joyfully asks for a squirrel.

We're in Perth, in love, in the middle of a white hot Australian summer. My wife Clare is nine months pregnant with our son. Our front lawn is dead; everything not under shade is dead. I turned off our reticulation months ago after our local council decided water is more valuable than oil. Clare wanders about in the heat like a giant lost penguin in a dress. Her poor body is distended in a way that hurts to watch; she is Godzilla to my Tokyo. My son is going to be huge.

It's early January, and Lola and I are in the supermarket. My bachelor days are a distant memory as I wander down aisle 12 looking for shampoo and thinking about the good ol' days (and the fact that I haven't washed my hair in twenty years). I'm happy to be where I am now, mind you. If I think hard about the past, I can get back to the reality of male-shared bachelor accommodation, when your house mates are a drill crew, the house is in the third world and you're fresh out of both legal and illegal addictive stimulants. I used to look back on those days the way women look at babies, or men look at breasts, but not anymore.

The shampoo finds its way into my hand, and I wander back into the line of fathers doing the Saturday morning shop. Lola is helping. She has purpose in her stride and a large bag of chips under her arm. 'Where are you going, little brown mouse?' I ask her.

She fires a furrowed look. 'I have chips,' she says with authority. Apparently, we're headed in the right direction. Lola manoeuvres around adult giants like an expert winger in a test match, throwing backwards glances to make sure I'm still there.

'Where are you going with the chips, little brown mouse?' I amble on behind her.

'I'm going to put them in the toilet.' Lola announces her intentions and bolts off towards a 'Staff Only' door.

I intercept and pick her up, lifting her into that folding seat thingy at the front of your standard shopping trolley, but she does the go-rigid thingy that kids do when they don't want to get strapped into the kid's seat in the family car. So I give in and stick her in the trolley with the shopping. That was my first mistake.

An hour later I'm almost done. This is my first family grocery shop, and I feel like I'm in control, even though Lola is randomly grabbing items off shelves. It's keeping her quiet so I can concentrate on getting all the stuff on the list my wife gave me this morning, and I couldn't care less if we pay for ten plastic spatulas and a dozen boxes of pink jelly.

We hit the end of the shortest queue and slowly plod towards the cash register. At least it's a human-operated checkout and not a machine. As soon as the small Chinese lady on the till eyeballs Lola her hands shoot up: 'You got problem wiff yo kid.' I look down as Lola spins her head around to look at me and all I see is a thin white string dangling from her mouth. My eyes scan down to her hand and I zoom in on what appears to be an open pack of giant cigarettes.

'Oh shit.' The tampon is expanding so I grab her forehead and pull the string, while shoppers lean in to get a good look. It pops out like a tennis ball the dogs been playing with for a week. The woman behind me calls me a bad father, so I launch into her while Lola, unfazed at all this, casually climbs out of the trolley right under my distracted nose and bolts for the front door. My second mistake.

'Yo kid, Mister. She gone.' I turn to see her disappear through the front doors. This is it—this is me losing my child. Adrenaline has me clearing the checkout in one leap. I come around the corner full tilt, looking like I'd just robbed the bank, and there she is standing outside a chocolate shop holding the chips again. She sees me coming and bolts back into the supermarket, under the turnstile past a dozen slow-moving pensioners, down the cosmetics aisle and through the 'Staff Only' doors, laughing all the way.

I skid to a stop in the loading bay wildly searching, my head on a swivel. There's a teenage kid with spots and a beanie holding onto a pallet jack in the corner who stops chewing his gum when I yell at him: 'Little girl, this big, green jumper, curly hair, which fuckin' way?' He points to the opposite corner.

I wonder what our son will be like as I profusely apologise to the beanie-clad kid who is now helping me to clean up the chips Lola has spread all over the floor. She watches us and then slowly pees on the floor. I have forgotten the 'Code Brown' kit bag for such accidents—my third mistake—and I'm about to have another one of these! Clare and I are struggling over the name. I want a simple hard geezer's name—Ray, Sid, Eddie, you know. He needs to be strong, so he can deal with me later on in life while I enjoy a heavily medicated Reagan-style slide into chronic dementia.

It's all the questions that do my head in. 'Lola, you're big enough to tell Daddy when you need to go to the toilet.'

'Why?' she asks.

'Because you don't pee in your pants.'

'Why?'

You can see the pattern forming here. And so it goes all the way to bedtime. 'Brush your teeth, please Lola.'

'I don't want to brush my teeth.'

'If you don't brush your teeth, they will all rot and fall out, and you won't be able to eat any more ice cream.'

'Why?'

'Brush your teeth.'

'I don't want to brush my teeth.'

Right about here Clare and I reach task saturation. I gladly walk off, happy in the knowledge that Lola is off to poke Lego up her arse instead of brushing her teeth. Clare goes the extra mile and gets the task done, every time.

FOREWORD

I sit back down to finish my thank you note in my shed and, of course, get distracted . . .

There's a 2001 Kawasaki W650 that whispers quietly across the concrete at me. I wander over with a spanner, tinker for hours and sometime later find myself asleep under it. I remember, as I suddenly wake and slam my head into the swing arm, that you make your own luck. Fate, synchronicity, karma, whatever you want to call it, will play its part.

My life has been blessed so far, so I must have done something right in a past one. I have a wife who loves me, and a son who gathers momentum to enter our utterly confusing and dangerous world. And then there's Lola—my riotous three-year-old daughter—waiting to grin back at me and instantly break my heart when my key hits the lock at the end of the day.

It's been six years since my first book was released. I hope I have made people laugh—laugh out loud. In my 42 years on this good earth I have learnt a fraction of what I should know, but I will say this . . . get yourself a motorcycle. It doesn't matter who you are or what you do, motorcycles will leave you altered, somewhat less subdued. The better you get the more you can take, and once you know you can handle a bike in the middle of everything mother nature—and short-sighted motorists—can throw at you, you exude a special quiet confidence. People who know you will sense a change but never quite put their finger on it.

If a bike can't set you free today, then work on it again tomorrow.

Paul Carter

DON'T TELL MUM I WORK ON THE RIGS

SHE THINKS I'M A PIANO PLAYER IN A WHOREHOUSE

TENSION LEG
PLATFORM
LAND RIG
JACK-UP RIG
DRILL SHIP
DRILLING &
PRODUCTION
FIXED
PLATFORM
SEMI-SUBMERSIBLE RIG

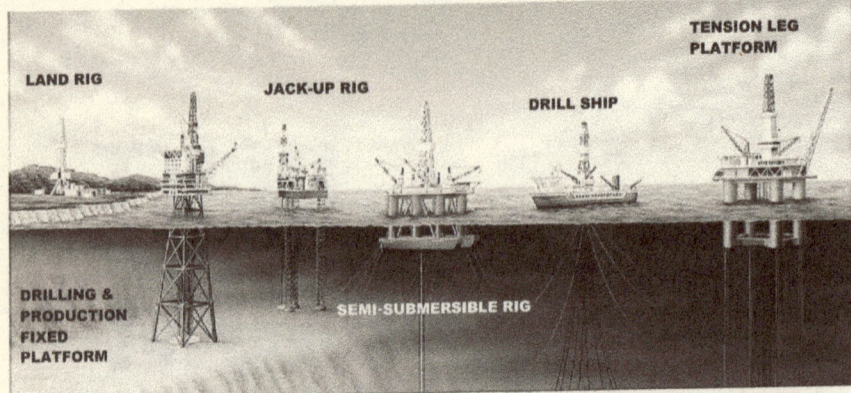

There are many different types of drilling rigs with multiple variations on their capabilities and adaptability to the environment in which they are drilling in. I have not gone into the technical aspect of this industry. But so you have a basic overview this page gives a rough idea of the different rigs that are out there and their most obvious components.

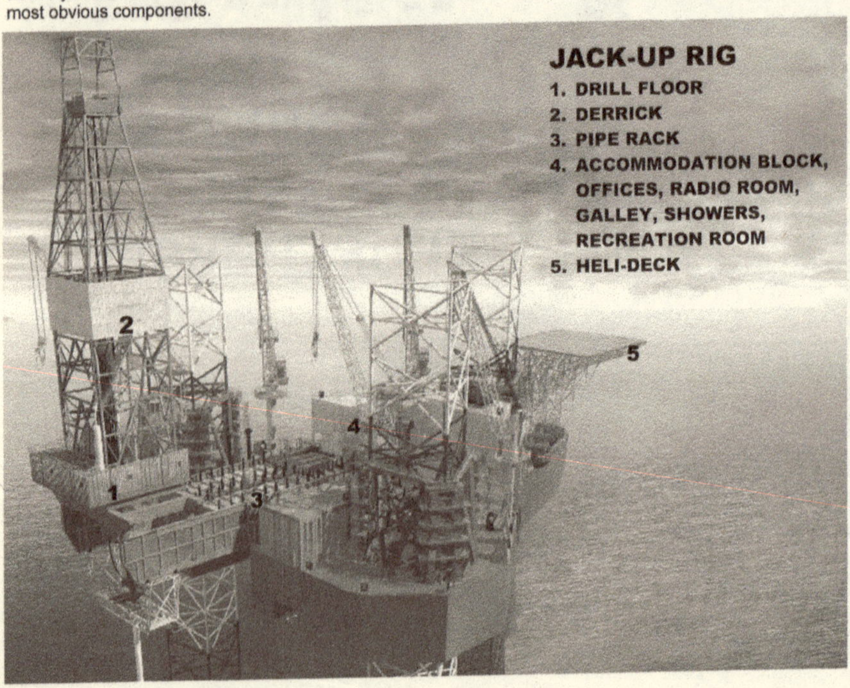
JACK-UP RIG
1. DRILL FLOOR
2. DERRICK
3. PIPE RACK
4. ACCOMMODATION BLOCK, OFFICES, RADIO ROOM, GALLEY, SHOWERS, RECREATION ROOM
5. HELI-DECK
2
5
4
1
3

CONTENTS

PROLOGUE 7
1. ACHTUNG SPITFIRE, 1969–87 9
2. POOL BALLS, 1987–94 20
3. PACK-A-DAY MONKEY, 1994–95 30
4. SATURATION, 1995–96 44
5. KILLER MOUSE, 1996–97 55
6. THE DEVIL'S BUSINESS, 1997–98 67
7. THE HOBBIT HOUSE, 1998–99 77
8. WHERE YOU FROM?, 1999–2000 92
9. BARREL FEVER, 2000–01 102
10. THE DARKEST CONTINENT, 2001 110
11. GOBBING, 2002 127
12. RIG UP, RIG DOWN, 2002 135
13. LEGLESS IN RUSSIA, 2003 141
14. THE GHOST OF A FLEA, 2004 154
15. AH MENG, 2004 164
EPILOGUE 173
ACKNOWLEDGEMENTS 174

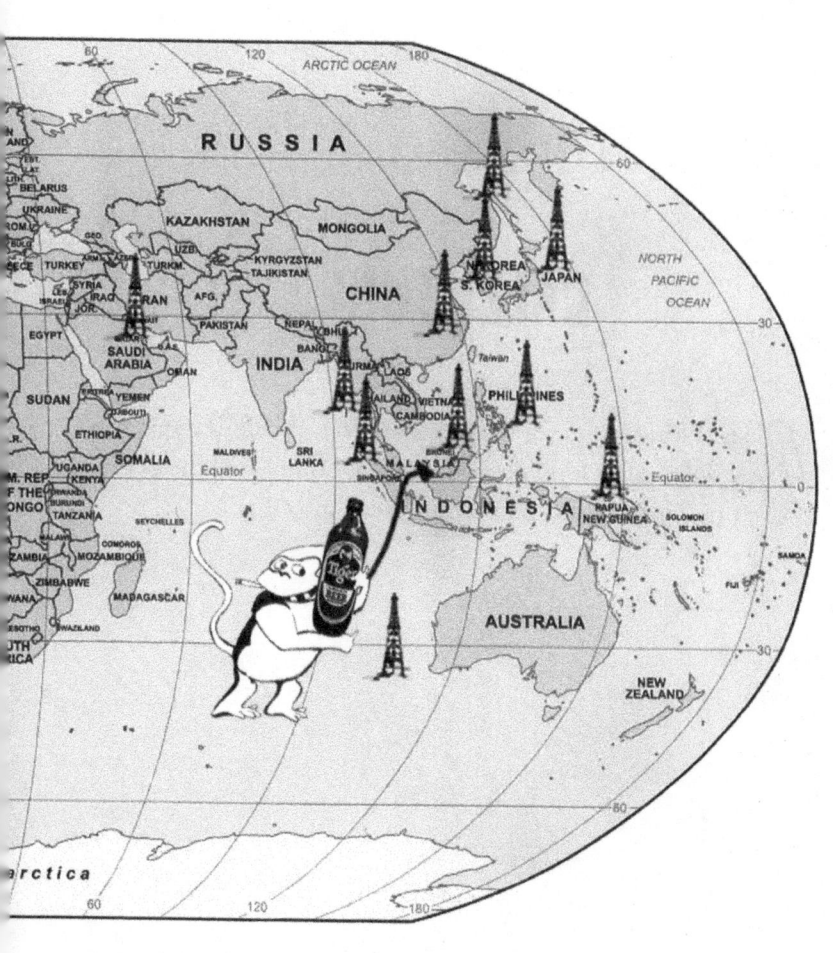

CALENTURE

A name formerly given to a tropical fever or delirium suffered by sailors after long periods at sea, who imagine the ocean to be green fields and desire to leap into them.

PROLOGUE

The man sitting next to me looked panicked; I tried to hold on, beads of nervous sweat forming on my forehead. My knuckles went from white to blue, I bit into my upper lip. About halfway through the take-off climb, the inevitable happened: my backside let go. I yelped in complete horror as two piping-hot spurts of poo shot down my trouser legs . . . I'd just lost my arse on a commercial airliner . . . oh my God.

I fumbled at the seatbelt, my IV bag dangling from my mouth. The man next to me ran away as I hobbled down the fuselage towards the nirvana of a business-class toilet. Kicking off a metabolic chain reaction, within minutes I had the rest of my crew frantically scurrying towards toilets in immediate and imminent danger of crapping all over the place. And all because some guy in logistics didn't check the bottled water on the rig. What were we thinking, that eight grown men with dysentery could clench all the way from Port Moresby to Singapore? But it was either that or we take the 'death by local hospital' option.

I locked the toilet door, catching my reflection in the mirror as I pulled down my pants and surveyed the horror. I looked so bad for a second I thought I was in there with a pale sweaty stranger. It was one of those unbelievably embarrassing moments in life when you just wish you could go back in time and be ten years old and life was just an endless romp in the park. How did this happen? How in hell did I let this happen?

It was a long flight . . . There's some kid out there in the front row who's going to be disturbed for a while, and that's just because of the smell. I wasn't coming out of that toilet. It gave me time to ponder just how I got to this auspicious point in my ridiculous career path to rapid bowel movement oblivion.

In point of fact it all started when I was about ten but there was no park to romp in . . .

1 ACHTUNG SPITFIRE, 1969–87

I was born in the UK to a German mother, an English father, an older sister and a cat called Brim. Brim was an overt snob who would only drink his milk after I had popped any bubbles that floated on the surface. My father would inevitably end up walking by these goings-on and step on the edge of Brim's saucer, sending milk directly up his trouser leg.

My early life was not happy; I don't recall any memories of Dad that make me smile, just overwhelming fear. Brim and I would regularly jostle over the best hiding places, while my father, with his milk-stained trousers, would look for us.

My father was in the Royal Air Force, a navigator. He was a 'children are seen and not heard' kind of dad, and so my sister and I lived a disciplined life. In all our family photos we look like we are having our picture taken for a police line-up.

These should have been the times when life was just an endless romp in the sun and tomorrow didn't matter, when parents were neither a fear nor a worry but something so dependable you would look for that peace of mind in adult life and marry it.

For the Christmas holidays, I was sent to visit my respective grandparents, one year with the Germans, the next with the English. Every year the standard holiday war movie would play on or around Boxing Day, and every year it was something like *The Great Escape* or *The Dirty Dozen*. Throughout the movie, my English grandfather would cheer and clap and when it was over he would pull out his medals and tell me war stories. My German grandfather, on the other hand, would curse and cringe at every standard scene of a single American soldier gunning down countless Germans without once reloading his weapon. When the movie was over, he would crack open a bottle of Schnapps and get blind drunk.

Needless to say we never got together to have nice family dinners with my grandparents.

I think I was around six when I saw *The Magnificent Seven*, the first movie I remember seeing. It had a profound effect on me. My father was away a lot so I took all my male cues from TV. After that movie I wanted to be a cowboy. Just like Steve McQueen.

Then one day, after I had been a cowboy for some months, my father returned from service in Canada with a real Western gun holster. The belt went from just under my nipples to the top of my bellybutton and the holster itself was almost as long as my right leg. All my cap guns just dropped straight through it so I replaced them with my drink cup. It was one of those kiddies' plastic cups with a screw-down lid, it had Charlie Brown on it, but when it was wedged down into the holster all you could see was gun leather and a blue cup handle.

I would parade around the street quick-drawing and slurping cordial. My mother called me 'The Milkshake Sheriff' and wherever she took me the holster came along, Church, Sunday School, the local pool.

The Milkshake Sheriff made only one real enemy in town, a huge Old English sheepdog named 'Benny'. He would spot the Sheriff strutting across the park, bound up, and with one paw knock him down and start shagging him. I hated that dog.

A few years later on a visit to my German grandparents I sat down to watch the post-Christmas movie and this time it was *The Great Escape.* There was Steve McQueen again. I loved it. By the end of the movie my grandfather was hammered on Schnapps as the Germans lost again and I was ready to trade the holster for a motorbike.

I tooled around the neighbourhood on my pushbike, trying to jump it over people's back fences. I would try to appear surly and indifferent. Looking through one of my mother's magazines one day, I found an article on Steve McQueen. It said he was a man who liked fast bikes and fast women. So I tried to find fast women, but at the age of ten I misunderstood what that meant. I started with the babysitter . . . 'So, you like Fisher Price music baby?' She sent me straight to bed with a firm 'There'll be no Starsky & Hutch for you Mister'.

My mother was a saint; she made up for my father's insanely strict parenting routine with boundless love and affection. One day she got the strength to leave. My sister and I were bundled into the back of the Mini and that was that. Dad ended up leaving the Service and spent the rest of his working life as a directional driller on the rigs; coincidentally my mother ended up working for a major oil company and that led to our eventual emigration to Australia. One of the strange things about the drilling industry is that it is global but very small, and every now and again I run into some old drilling hand who knew my father.

Mum moved to Aberdeen, Scotland, and my sister and I went to a new school; home life, although devoid of the luxuries of my father's house, improved a great deal. We didn't have any money for the kinds of things a ten-year-old boy wants, but we loved each other and Mum made me the man of the house, or rather man of the tiny rundown council flat. I could get away with murder.

When I was fourteen I suddenly started getting bullied at school. His name was Athel, he was thick and had been held back a year because of it. Athel didn't like my glasses. Mum could not afford to take me to an optometrist so I had National-Health-black-one-size-fits-all nasty grown-up glasses; I looked like a midget Michael Caine.

After Athel was finished I had to tape them together.

My mother's solution to Athel was that I should get a big stick. Instead I talked her into getting me an air rifle. (I had been mildly obsessed with guns since I was five, when I was given a pair of Star Trek pyjamas that came with a phazer gun water pistol.)

The idea was simple. Athel had a gang of boys who kept jumping me and beating me up. He cut the tyres on my bike with a flick knife, and told me he was going to cut my pecker off. So I was going to kill him with my new rifle. It had worked in the war movies . . .

I stole wooden pallets from the loading bay of a nearby supermarket and constructed a hide-out overlooking Athel's backyard. I lay there for hours with my BSA .22 air rifle in hand. I knew Athel stole his father's cigarettes and hid near the shed to smoke them. All I had to do was wait. And sure enough out he came, so I let him have it. The pellet hit him square in the forehead, sending him backwards into the shed door. His screams soon had his father over him, but Athel's sniper-in-the-tree-line story and bleeding head quickly became unimportant as his father realised he had been smoking. Then it was Athel's father who was screaming. I looked on in mute fascination. Athel was not dead, and that's a good thing; he never bothered me again.

Life, as they say, comes down to a few moments. That was one of them. My glasses were never a problem again. A few years after shooting Athel I joined the Gordon Highlanders 2nd Battalion ACF. Thanks to my father I was already totally indoctrinated into the military system—he would check that my toys and clothes were always stowed where they should be, and my room was freakishly tidy—so the military was no surprise. The drill sergeant was scary to the other lads, but compared to my dad he was just a man who yelled a lot. I knew he couldn't hit me. The Highlanders was a great experience, and I managed to fulfil all my childhood firearms needs.

Not long after the Athel incident my mother came home and said she had met a really nice man through her new job with the oil company. His name was John and she wanted to bring him home so my sister and I could meet him. I was happy if she was happy, and my sister was about to move in with her boyfriend so she was happy. John turned out to be great. He was totally relaxed and also treated me like a grown-up, so I didn't give him any shit and he was happy too.

With home life steady at last, I started spending more time hanging around Mum's office or at the workshop talking to the offshore guys when they came in on a crew change. Mostly Americans at that time, they would congratulate me on my polite manners and shove everything from Buck knives to Zippo lighters in my pocket. John would get back from a rig and tell me stories about the strange places he worked in, and always brought me back something cool.

Mum's boss was a larger-than-life character, Jessie Thomas Jackson—JT. A big man in his fifties, impeccably dressed, he, unlike many adults, always shook my hand and despite my mother's protests let me hang out in his giant office. He was remarkably good to me. He would let me drink Coke from his little fridge. I would sit on his massive leather couch, awe-inspired, gazing at the array of rig memorabilia on the shelves.

Sometimes he would look at me over his glasses the way grown-ups do and say, 'C'mon over here Pauli.'

I would run up to his big wooden desk.

'How'd you like to do some work for me?'

'Yessir.'

'Okay whad'ya say you wash ma car for me 'n clean up the inside too, how'd that be?'

Off I'd go and an hour later JT would wander down the front steps of the office, his hands buried in his pockets rattling the change about. He'd take a minute to survey the silver Mercedes. 'Damn good job son.' In his big hand was a twenty-pound note. That was way more than any other neighbourhood kid got for washing a car.

On one occasion he let me drive his Mercedes to the shops and back. 'Don't tell your mom you drove okay buddy.'

In the years Mum worked for JT he always took time to chat to me or walk around the workshop with me and 'bullshit to the boys'. Both JT and his wife June looked after their people in a way I have never seen again. They had us over for dinner many times. He had changed the course of our family's future for the best by employing my mother.

JT was still going offshore well into his seventies. I would have liked to thank him as an adult but I never took the time and sadly he died in 2002, the last of his generation. The oilfield is run by the corporate machine more than ever now, lawyers backed by engineers who have never seen a rig. The human side is gone, the bottom line rules, and it's every man for himself.

Outside my crew I don't trust anyone. Not in the office, and especially not the client.

These days it leaves the older guys who remember the rigs when they were still wild, seething. They speak up on occasion, usually at a critical moment during the meeting before the main meeting which proceeds the really big meeting where we talk about what we're going to say when we have the really really big meeting with the people in Houston joining us via satellite speaker phone (that's the meeting where no-one makes a firm decision because of the consequences of getting sued for making a decision). 'Aw fuck all this horse shit' the old guys say, when the bureaucracy gets ridiculous and the legal implications of opening your mouth has you more concerned about losing your job than actually solving the problem. And for the tiniest of moments everyone in the room is reminded of the qualities that made these men pioneers when the drilling game was in its infancy.

A year after Mum and John got together, JT offered John a job. Then when the company decided to open an office and machine shop in Australia, he asked John if he would like to transfer there, with permanent residency sponsored by the company. John and my mother jumped at the opportunity. I was fifteen and again life changed dramatically for the better.

Perth was a great place to discover Australia. I loved going to the beach, I started surfing, everyone was so nice . . . so many girls wearing so much less than they do in Scotland.

The next three years were a total blur: I didn't do well at school, I was far too busy discovering my first girlfriend, first beer, first motorcycle, and the fact that everyone had a pool in the backyard. Unlike rainy Scotland, barbecues didn't start and end in the garage. Fruits and vegetables were big, days were long and hot, and neighbourhoods were large and well planned with wide streets and clean footpaths. We had a house with a huge backyard; Mum installed a spa in the middle of the back patio. She planted endless flowers and ferns that flourished around the steamy pool. Within a year our house and especially the back patio looked like a tropical oasis. John got a big 4WD and the two of them went exploring on weekends, and often flew off to Asia on long weekends. For some reason they trusted me to 'look after things' while they were away. I was in teenage heaven. Just after my eighteenth birthday Mum and John got married. John asked me to be his best man; it was a special day, in a great new country.

I left school early, I wanted money, I wanted rigs, I wanted to fly in a helicopter, and say Gawd-damn a lot. I wanted to wear one of those gold company cigar rings. (What can I say, it was the 1980s.) But most of all I wanted an adventure. It's hard to get a rig job if you don't know someone, harder still if you're eighteen and green. I didn't want to ask John, I had to do it myself, but all I could get was a porter's position in a swanky hotel downtown. I'd answered an ad in the paper and they hired me. I was punctual and polite, but lost the job because I was caught having sex with a guest by a room service attendant.

A brief stint as a waiter followed but that too was doomed. The head chef was young; we would regularly hide in the back alley smoking joints and drinking wine. One night during the pre-Christmas rush of corporate dinners, we took things too far. Fran, one of the waitresses, was a law student who looked down her nose at having to wait tables. To rattle her cage, I hatched a plan involving the chef, the biggest tomato he could find in the cool room, some raw steak and a meat cleaver. Fran could not stand the sight of blood, and whenever one of the chefs nicked a finger she would run, covering her mouth and honking about hygiene and food. So I cut the tomato in half, pushed my white shirt cuff over my hand and dropped the tomato down inside the hole where my hand should have been. With some strips of steak hanging over the edges and lots of tomato sauce, it looked gruesomely real. Fran came through the double doors into the kitchen doing her balancing act, both arms full of dirty dishes. I spun around, waving my gory stump at her. She froze, turned white and made the long fall, straight down, face first into a banquet trolley of half-eaten food scraps.

Some years later I was living with three mates in a nice house not far from town. Pete, Phil, Iain and I got along perfectly well. There was never an argument or any of the standard scuffles you get with shared accommodation. The house was old but by no means run-down; we had a pool and a massive yard to grow drugs in. The back porch was huge, coming out of the house from two sliding doors then dropping down five feet to a surrounding rose bed that not only provided a natural balustrade of rose bushes but cover for our dope. Looking back now, it stands out clearly as the easiest time in my life.

Friday night was a ritual; it was my turn to fill the beer fridge out the back and provide dinner. We would sit around on the back porch in our underwear, everyone also wearing an obligatory funny hat, smoking joints and drinking beer, recalling the day's activities and planning the weekend.

One typically hot still Perth summer night when it was my turn to cook, I waited until everyone was sufficiently stoned and then called 'The Winged Wok'. Our Chinese takeaway food arrived and as we started peeling the cardboard lids off the steaming hot aluminium containers, someone farted. That may not seem overly funny, but when you've been smoking Pete's special Denmark Death blend it's bloody hilarious.

Iain roared, throwing himself backwards on the back legs of his plastic IKEA chair. But the legs snapped off, leaving him rocking precariously on the edge of the porch, so then he lunged forwards grabbing at the tablecloth, which dumped thirty dollars of piping-hot Chinese and a fruit bowl full of grass into his crotch. The high-pitched scream made us all grit our teeth as we watched him disappear over the side.

We peered down over the edge of the porch at him, sitting in amongst the roses which Pete's mother had pruned the previous weekend, covered in sweet-n-sour and dope. Iain didn't look up. We stopped laughing and jumped down to help him up, but he was frozen still, with his arm grasping his right thigh where the pruned stump of a rose bush was protruding through it.

'Oh fuck . . . call an ambulance.' I tried to scrape off the Chinese food and dope covering Iain's leg.

Phil grabbed the phone.

'Yes . . . he's in shock, I think,' Phil said, trying to sound normal. 'You better bring a hacksaw or something, okay, okay.'

'Where the fuck is Pete?' I yelled.

Pete came running up with his camera. 'Okay . . . put his hat back on.'

'You fuckhead!'

'I'm okay boys,' said Iain quite calmly. 'There's no pain.'

'That's 'cause you've been smoking this shit all night,' said Phil, scooping up a handful of greeny-orangey goop.

The camera flashed, making Iain blink.

'Someone's pulling into the drive.' Pete panicked. 'Hide the dope!' But his paranoid attempts at hiding the dope only had him smeared in it from head to toe.

The paramedics took one look at us and asked, 'Has the patient taken any drugs or alcohol . . . other than what he's lying in, gentlemen?'

In what seemed like seconds they had Iain on a gurney with the rose branch still through his thigh, sticking up under the sheet.

'He looks like he's got a boner,' said Pete.

'Can we come too?' asked Phil, but they slammed the ambulance doors and were gone, sirens blazing.

I suggested we follow them and so we all piled into my Holden, still in our underwear, liberally covered in Chinese food and marijuana.

'I'm still hungry,' Pete was eyeballing a McDonald's drive-through. So then we stocked up on burgers and munched our way to Fremantle Hospital, Pete dipping his chips in the greeny-orangey goop.

Not surprisingly the hospital staff wouldn't let us in but they did accept a burger, which Phil insisted they pass on to Iain as soon as he felt up to it.

2 POOL BALLS, 1987–94

After writing countless letters to drilling contractors I finally landed a job, as a roughneck (labourer) on a land rig drilling core samples for Western Mining. The job meant moving to a tiny town north-east of Perth, about twelve hours by car, but I was happy because I got what I wanted. So I packed up my old Holden, the boys wished me good luck, and with just enough money for petrol, I made for the rig.

Leinster is the middle of nowhere. A mining community of about ten thousand, it is 376 kilometres north of Kalgoorlie, the nearest large town and centre of Western Australia's mining industry. I was assigned a staff house on the edge of town, sharing with Craig, a geologist from Brisbane. Craig and I got on very well. He too had recently arrived and we found a lot of common ground to occupy our leisure time.

We decided to throw a party for my birthday, only about ten people showed up, but we had a good time. I drank too much scotch and tried to spot some hash with a hot knife over the stove, but ended up passing out on the kitchen floor. That's when two of the guys who were electricians decided to go out to their trucks and get as much gaffa tape as they could carry then tape me naked to the kitchen floor. I came to thinking I was a paraplegic. Everyone spent the next hour laughing at my attempts to pull the tape off my body. We're not talking about a small piece of plaster here—by the time I was tape-free I didn't have any body hair left either.

Craig gave me a big joint 'for the pain', so I did manage to calm down, then half an hour later, I had the munchies like never before. But as usual we had no food. Luckily, the camp chef had made me a birthday cake earlier and had even saved me a slice during the feeding frenzy that occurred while I was taped to the floor. Of course, it was the best cake I had ever tasted but I was still starving. Looking into the fridge the way you do when you're stoned at two in the morning, hoping that by some miracle you're going to find a whole barbecued chicken hidden in the back, I saw nothing but beer and mouldy half-eaten TV dinners.

Then the camp chef told me that when he was making the cake, he had cracked some eggs into a tea cup, and suggested I fry them up for a sandwich. Like a man possessed I grabbed the tea cup from the fridge, threw the eggs into the big frying pan, lit the gas plate and started frying. But nothing was happening. The eggs wouldn't cook. I checked the gas, it was on; I turned it up. Still the eggs just sat there, refusing to cook. Hungry, half-naked and still sore from pulling every last hair from my body, I ran into the living room and complained, 'My eggs won't cook.'

By this time the party had reached stupor stage and no-one felt inclined to help me. Craig, however, managed to haul himself off the couch and make the long trip to the kitchen. But when he got to the stove he started laughing. Craig had discovered why my eggs wouldn't cook. 'You're trying to fry apricot halves Pauli.'

One of the guys at the party was called 'Riff'. Riff tried to play an electric guitar solo while standing on the coffee table, but it broke, sending him into the lap of our large neighbour who became disturbed and began punching him. Riff used his guitar as a shield and ran outside. I followed to calm him down and we talked in the driveway for a while. Riff was the town garbage man and needed an offsider to help him with his Saturday run. I needed the money so I applied and he agreed.

The next day Riff arrived with his flatbed truck. Walking up to the passenger door, I thought that my massive hangover was affecting my vision because I couldn't see him inside, but then I realised the whole cab was thick with smoke from the bongs he had chain-pulled on the way over. I got in, holding my breath, and wound down the window.

'Keep it up mate,' said Riff. 'Unless you want two million flies inside after the first stop.' He shoved the bong back in his mouth and flicked his lighter.

We drove to the first camp, where bulging, black plastic bin liners that had been sitting in the desert heat for days were lined up outside the camp kitchen port-a-cabin. I pulled at the first of a dozen bags, but the knot at the top came off in my hand like melted cheese. Rancid garbage and thousands of blowfly maggots spilled down the sides.

'You're gonna have to shovel those into the truck mate,' yelled Riff from the cloud inside the cab.

So I tied my shirt around my head, leaving just a tiny slit to see through, and shovelled for the next forty minutes. Billions of flies followed my every move, determined to get into my ears, nose, eyes, mouth—it was infuriating, not to mention disgusting. Riff did the next one, his long hair and stoned bliss making him oblivious to the marauding flies. And so the day went on, driving from camp to camp, one of us shovelling garbage while the other smoked bongs.

After the last camp we drove out to a remote site where a deep trench had been dug for the garbage to be dumped into, burned and covered up. By now I was quite stoned too and finding everything quite funny. Riff backed up the truck to the edge of the trench, and I staggered out, climbed into the back and shovelled out the revolting mass. When I'd finished Riff hooked up the forty-four gallon drum of petrol and hand pump which he had tied to the back of the truck then handed me the pump and climbed back into the cloudy cab. The pump wasn't working. I cranked the handle but no fuel came out, so I kicked the drum over on its side, letting all the petrol pour into the trench, then rolled the empty drum into the trench thinking, 'Job well done'.

Riff grinned at me through his dirty hair as I climbed back in the cab.

'I need a lighter,' I told him.

'I'll drive over there,' he said, raising a finger off the steering wheel pointing nowhere in particular. 'And you light the rag on this stick and chuck it in the trench, from a safe distance mind.' His eyes were so red he looked demonically possessed. He pulled another cone and handed me his lighter.

I jumped out with the stick and walked back to the trench, a black cloud of flies swarming around my head. Then following Riff's instructions, I lit the rag and threw the stick, but it fell short of the trench, teetering on the edge. So I wandered up and kicked it over.

All I remember is the sound, and getting punched in the whole body. The trench exploded in a fireball that people saw from the town miles away and the drum went into a low orbit. My shirt was on fire, and I started rolling around in the dirt screaming. Riff came running and helped put me out. My fringe was gone, so were my eyebrows, but I was okay. Then Riff was laughing. 'The whole fuckin' drum,' he kept saying, over and over again. We drove back to town, not a fly in sight.

The work was hard at Leinster but I enjoyed the vast open country. Time passed quickly. The rig was mounted on the back of a huge truck and I learnt the do's and don'ts fast. Des, the man in charge, treated his crew well and we respected him. But while work was hard, life's lessons were sometimes even harder.

On one occasion, I had a few days off during a blisteringly hot summer and Craig and I were driving down the main street when he suggested a beer in the Wet Mess, one of the two bars in town. Except this was the bar for the wild men.

'No way . . . I'll get raped,' I protested, but Craig was already getting out of the car and heading towards the bar, chuckling at me.

It was early afternoon so there were only four hall-pack truck drivers shooting pool inside. They were all Maori, two of them had tribal tattoos covering one side of their faces. All stood over six feet and looked like they'd been genetically engineered to crush small buildings. They nodded hello as we walked in. Everything was concrete—the bar, the stools—beer was served in plastic cups, and the windows had heavy bars instead of glass. We decided to play pool on the other table, and Craig paid the deposit for two cues and a tray of balls. (This was normal practice because every weekend they got demolished in a brawl.)

An hour rolled by and soon the four truck drivers started getting rowdy. They suddenly broke out in a vicious fist-fight, all four trading blisteringly hard punches. We panicked . . . but there was only one way out of the room, past them.

The fight spilled over on top of us, I made for the door but ran straight into one of the fighters, then his elbow ran into me. It was painless, really. I'd never been hit hard before, not hard like that. My brain went numb, lights out. I was on the floor, my nose wasn't working, tears were streaming down my cheeks. I could vaguely see the back of one giant bent over the pool table, his right arm swinging up and down, delivering his fist into the tabletop. I could feel the vibrations in the floor as he pounded on the felt. Then as quickly as it had started it was over, and they were gone. The barman was also gone, having locked the bar door and the steel grille between the roof and the bar counter behind him. My nose was smashed; blood flowed into my mouth and down the front of my shirt like two GT racing stripes. I got up slowly, and that's when I saw Craig. He looked dead.

Flat on his back in the middle of the pool table, he was covered in dark red blood, bubbles formed in the middle of his face. I didn't recognise him. The big trucker had shoved a ball in Craig's mouth, balled up another one in his fist and beaten Craig's face into a pulp. He had lost all his teeth, his jaw looked broken, as did his nose.

I carried him out to the car and struggled to get him inside. His blood spilled down my back as I positioned him. My head was spinning. I caught my reflection in the window—I looked like I'd just murdered someone.

The tyres shrieked to a stop in the doctor's driveway. Craig was unconscious, slumped forwards against the seatbelt, his head hanging down with a series of bloody saliva strings connecting his face to his crotch. A young woman was at the door, telling me that her father the doctor was in Perth for a wedding and she was unable to help me. The nearest medical help was a two-hour drive to Leonora. I ran back to the car.

Craig had a pulse, and was making a rhythmical gurgling sound so I knew he was sort of breathing. I floored the car as much as I could, regularly checking his pulse and trying to light bloody cigarettes with the car lighter. Finally I began passing signs to Leonora and felt triumphant just getting him there alive. The doctor lived in a modest whitewashed house and he had the flying doctors on final approach for the main street within an hour.

The plane's large rear doors swallowed up my friend in superfast time, its departure sandblasting everyone in red prop wash as it vaporised down the main street and into the afternoon's dust-bowl sky. The doctor explained that Craig was stable but would need facial surgery and new teeth and his jaw was going to take more than a month to reset. He gave me a shot of anaesthetic, then he straightened my nose: shoving a wooden tongue depressor between my teeth and bracing my head between his knees, he quietly said, 'Now this is going to hurt'. It did.

During my drive to town, I had managed to cook the head gasket on the car, but luckily the doctor lived next door to a used-car yard so I just traded it for a Ford ute that had 'Killer Deal' painted across the top half of the cracked windscreen. I drove back to Leinster slowly, with my face a mess, bruised and swollen, squinting into the sunset on the straight desert highway through the 'Killer Deal' windscreen.

Six weeks later the four men had been fired over the incident and charged with grievous bodily harm, and all four were in

Perth waiting for their day in court. Des asked me to drive to Kalgoorlie and pick up Craig at the hospital. He'd organised a new company truck and suggested that we go from the hospital to the car dealer, and from there Craig would drive the new truck back to Leinster. I decided to drive Craig's Toyota Hilux to get him; it was old and slow but more reliable than my 'Killer Deal' ute.

I left at daybreak and by early afternoon I was sitting in the hospital waiting for Craig. The doctor walked him into the room, one arm around his shoulder. Craig had lost a lot of weight but that was insignificant compared to his face. Four bolts protruded through the skin, all joined with tensioning wire that formed a square around his mouth. Anything he ate had to go through a blender first. I felt so sorry for him. He had to return in a month to have the bolts removed but at least he could go back to work in the meantime.

I told him the plan, but he just wanted to have a beer. So we picked up the new truck and agreed to stop at the last pub on the way out of town. Craig didn't say much but he did have his jaw wired up, with a straw jammed in one side of his mouth, and a cigarette in the other, so there wasn't much room for conversation. We stuck to two beers each—Craig sucked his—and as we walked out to the cars he unexpectedly turned and hugged me.

'Thanks mate,' he said and smiled with his eyes.

We had a convoy plan but minutes later I was crawling along in his crappy old Hilux and he was disappearing fast into the distance in the brand new Landcruiser. At least it was dusk, my favourite time in the bush.

It was easy to drift off in your mind on the long straight road, with ten minutes to the next corner and no radio, just the wind blowing hot against your skin. The desert stretched into the burning orange horizon in all directions. I felt lucky, I didn't miss the city at all. I paid more attention to the road as I took the solitary corner, but was still driving in a state of boredom. Heat haze distorted the road ahead, but I knew instantly that something didn't look right.

It was the new truck, lying on its side . . . I was looking at its black chassis. My heart jumped, I floored it but the Toyota just blew smoke and grumbled at me. My mouth went bone dry as I pulled up next to the truck; I prepared myself for the worst.

There was a thumping sound coming from inside the cab. Then I saw a massive tail. It belonged to a wounded kangaroo, a huge red wounded kangaroo. Craig had hit him mid-hop and sent the beast through the windscreen into the cab. Somewhere underneath its bulk was my friend. It was kicking against the dashboard fighting for breath, and I had no chance of moving it. I didn't know if Craig was dead or alive—Do I go back to town? Get help? Do I try to move the roo?

I tried to get to Craig, but the kangaroo's tail was too strong and likely to thrash me into the broken windscreen. I couldn't see Craig, only angry kangaroo. So I went for the shotgun in the Hilux, but could only find one rat-shot shell in the glove box.

My hands were shaking so much I was worried I'd hit Craig so I jammed the end of the barrel up to the roo's head and shot it point blank. But it was much heavier than me; I couldn't move it. Craig's feet were now visible so I sat on the road, one foot either side of the windscreen. With sweat stinging my eyes, the roo's blood tasting sweet in my mouth, one of Craig's feet under each of my armpits, and using my legs for leverage, I pulled him through the windscreen and out from under the dead roo. He popped out onto the road, on his back; I had cut him on small bits of glass left in the windscreen frame.

Scrambling up, I saw Craig's face and it filled me with horror, my mouth filled with vomit. The bolts that were around his mouth had caught in the kangaroo's hide and were now in the middle of his face, with big chunks of bloody fur stuck to them. Once again he was unrecognisable.

There was a pulse, however, and he was alive so once more I strapped him in and drove back to town. The same doctor who had waved us goodbye was still on duty. He looked whiter than his coat when I came tearing into the hospital's main entrance covered in blood. Another six weeks later, Craig took the bus back. His good looks were gone but in his ever-positive style, life took on a new precious zest, even when he catches people staring. He just wasn't supposed to die young.

3 PACK-A-DAY MONKEY, 1994–95

I spent a little more than a year working in Western Australia's goldfields when a friend of John's rang me out of the blue and offered me a job. The oilfields were booming then, with jobs available just about everywhere. I hopped from one company to another, working mostly in Asia. My twenties went by so fast I got whiplash.

In that first year working offshore my initial attempts at fitting in were fumbled. Then I got lucky and found myself standing on the drill floor with Erwin Herczeg. Erwin had done it all; run every kind of pipe, on every kind of rig, on three continents, in more than a dozen countries. His reputation was impressive to say the least, but he never bragged about it nor belittled anyone with 'been there done that'. As luck would have it, he took me under his wing and I learnt from the master. Erwin imparted his knowledge in a steady, patient way and I retained just enough to keep my limbs intact and my sanity preserved. I looked forward to any job that he was on, and I took every opportunity to work with him.

While my working life was on track, my social life became bizarre. When I got off a rig, I'd stand in front of the big board at Changi International Airport in Singapore and choose a flight to wherever. I had money burning a hole in my pocket and no financial sense, so I'd take off and fuck around in Tunisia for a month, returning broke to a rig with only some obscene Polaroids and one too many drunken stories.

After a couple of years rig-hopping around South-East Asia with different crews, I landed a job on Erwin's crew, based at Brunei. By now I had gained more experience and I really wanted to work with Erwin, but before I started in Brunei I took a break at home. Mum and John had some news. After nine years in Australia, they were being transferred to Songkhla, Thailand.

I dropped my mother at the airport, and Perth became a lonely place. That night I went into a new bar where a friend was working, ordered a beer and pondered. Miles away in my head, I thought about tracking down my father, perhaps spending some time with him because we hardly knew each other, I decided to make some calls the next day. Then I noticed a young woman behind the bar. She was fit looking, about five four, with short cropped black hair, bright red lipstick and a black T-shirt. I could tell straightaway that she was no ordinary woman. She had more attitude than most of the rig crews put together. I asked my friend who she was. Ruby turned her head and I called her over.

She had a great walk, purposeful, feminine. I was riveted. Somehow she managed to suggest all at once a mix of sexuality, combustible rage and poetic sensitivity. 'Hey,' she said and smiled, then someone else called her, but walking away she looked back just long enough to give me a 'Hey you . . . kiss my arse' kind of look.

I felt like I'd been shot in the heart. Unfortunately I was due to leave Perth in a few days so I promised myself I would get to know Ruby when I came back.

Brunei is a small sovereign state on the island of Borneo, located pretty much in the middle of the South China Sea. It's a beautiful place, free of most of the problems that corrupt other South-East Asian countries. The locals on the crew were hospitable beyond belief, hard working and cooperative without the ego-driven hardline attitude of the Western crews I was used to.

The staff house in Brunei was located in a small village on the coast. I shared with Drew, the base manager, who was a pleasure to live with, and our home life was clean, comfortable and quiet.

One day our neighbours came back from a trip into the jungle to visit relatives who still lived in an old-style 'long house'. They had a baby makak monkey with them. Someone had killed his mother with a blow gun and on retrieving the body discovered the infant still clinging to her. He looked pathetic, sitting in a bird cage on their front porch, just skin and bone and so small you could sit him in your hand. When Erwin, who regularly came through and stayed at the house, saw the monkey he took pity on the little creature, and before long the monkey was ours, acquired in exchange for some company caps and T-shirts.

We named him Joe and he quickly became a very cool pet. By the time he was fully grown, he stood at about one-foot tall, with brown eyes and dark grey hair. For all intents and purposes he thought he was one of us. After his first year he developed a taste for beer, speed-metal music and headbutting the bathroom mirror. Unfortunately Joe also enjoyed the odd cigarette. This wasn't a worry at first, but then he started turning into a pack-a-day monkey, and, because he couldn't figure out how to light up, he would steal your lit cigarette, perch on top of a cupboard, coughing and smoking, and then discard the butt rather carelessly. We soon became very concerned about him burning down the house, especially if he'd had a few beers.

Joe only became a problem when he hit monkey puberty and started masturbating ten times a day. You'd be watching TV, glance over and there he was, on the couch, feverishly batting off through clenched teeth and a menagerie of high-speed facial expressions. He spent most of that time outdoors for obvious reasons. That pissed him off, so he took it out on the postman, and anyone else he didn't know who came to the house. At one point Joe got pretty bad, everything from verbal abuse up to, and including, throwing shit.

It was during Joe's puberty that the Shell drilling manager decided to drop by unannounced; he had never been to the staff house before and took us completely by surprise. A charming character, always keen to have a chat over a beer with anyone from a roughneck to the company owner, the drilling manager was one of those rare people with lots of power who knew how to handle it properly. On this day his wife came along too. She was typically Dutch, tall, blonde and stunning.

Brunei is a fairly strict Muslim country. Any women you see are always wearing a traditional 'baju kurung', and are totally covered up, exposing only their faces. I had been there for over a year, Drew three years, and Erwin had been in and out longer than anyone. We hadn't seen the female form in some time. Neither had Joe; in fact he had never seen a woman wearing Western clothing.

We'd been standing at the bar chatting for a while when Joe came in. He jumped up on the bar and stood level with Mrs Drilling Manager's breasts, his eyes like saucers, mouth open, staring from my chest to hers and then back to mine. In one lightning move he grabbed her right boob, just as she finished saying 'Ooh what a lovely monkey, what's his name?' Then she was screaming. Her wineglass shattered on the floor as Joe deftly made his way up her arm onto her shoulder while she pirouetted around waving her arms as if she was being attacked by an invisible swarm of bees.

Sufficiently aroused, Joe leapt onto the ceiling fan and, doing about ten revolutions per minute, commenced masturbating. While Mrs Drilling Manager was readjusting her bra and regaining her composure, we tried everything to get him down—all kinds of tempting treats, Cuban cigars, my best single malt, the only copy of *Juggs* in circulation in the country. But the little bastard was on a mission. So we did the only thing left to do . . . we turned up the fan.

This particular fan was huge; it looked like someone had bolted a B-52 propeller to the ceiling. No-one had ever set it higher than five on the dial, which was enough to pin three grown men to the floor, their cheeks rippling like skydivers. It turned into a test of Joe's determination: he was a tiny masturbating astronaut in a centrifuge, we hit ten on the dial, furniture began rattling across the floor . . .

'*Go for it little man,*' cried Drew. Joe was a blur of teeth and fur.

Finally he flew off, slamming into the far wall, unharmed but dizzy. I watched him really enjoy a smoke. The drilling manager was folded up laughing on the couch, his wife next to him with the molestor's little hand prints all over her top.

Joe's apposing thumbs allowed him to do a lot more than just fiddle with himself. He would regularly stand in front of the stereo, twisting dials and prodding buttons, and every now and again music would blast out sending him wild. He would run off to look for his stick, come back and bash the stereo until the music stopped. Usually the music only stopped because we used the remote to turn off the stereo, but it was still a victory to Joe.

It took me six months to teach him to pee in the toilet and not hit the rim. This was finally done by getting him to stand on the front rim, facing the upright seat and leaning forwards so his hands rested on the cistern, thereby achieving the right angle, much like a human male does when trying to pee with an erection.

Joe and I had one of our greatest battles in the toilet. I had returned home from a job offshore to an empty house; Drew was on annual leave, Erwin was offshore. Joe had been home alone, though we had installed a dog door for him to come and go, and three days a week a lady from the village came to clean the house and feed him.

I was tired and filthy when I walked in. I dumped my bag in the laundry, stripped off and threw all my clothes in the washing machine, and proceeded naked straight to the bathroom. In a slow exhausted trance I closed the door, took a shower, shaved and then sat on the toilet and was thumbing through *Sports Illustrated* when Joe burst into the house through his dog door. He knew I was home and ran from room to room looking for me. I called out and in the inch gap between the tiled floor and the bottom of the door I could see his little feet standing on the other side. Joe put his head against the floor and stretched out one hand under the door. I dangled some toilet paper just beyond his reach and he tried to grab it. But our little game didn't last long.

Joe jumped up onto the door handle. The bathroom door was, I think, someone's front door at one time and had a big old-style lock and key made of heavy brass. Before I realised what was happening, Joe had turned the key and locked me in.

I had that same awful feeling you get when you're about to board a plane and remember you left the iron on. Joe started bashing the key against the door and chattering excitedly to himself. Realising how much trouble I was in I jumped over to the gap at the bottom of the door and tried to coax him into giving me the key. But he wouldn't.

The door was made of solid timber and opened towards the inside, so I had no chance of breaking it down. There was no window, and no-one was due to come to the house for another two days. I pulled the shower curtain off the rail and slid it under the door, hoping Joe would get tired of bashing the key against it and drop it on the curtain, then I could pull the curtain back and get the key. But no, he wandered off and left me sitting on the bathroom floor.

I visualised spending the next forty-eight hours there, crying myself to sleep in the bathtub wrapped in a towel. I could hear the guys saying, 'Grown man gets locked in the toilet for two days by a monkey, what an idiot.' I plotted revenge: 'I'm going to skin that little bastard and turn him into a toilet seat cover when I get out of here.'

After three hours of failed attempts at escape that included taking the heavy porcelain cover off the toilet cistern and bashing it against the door, and pulling a steel downpipe off the ceiling so I could start tunnelling—through the roof if necessary!—I finally figured it out. I straightened a metal shower-curtain ring and used it to knock out the pins in the door hinges. It took ages but eventually I got the pins out, removed the door and staggered into the hall.

Joe was sitting on the couch with the key next to him. He waited just long enough for me to see him then bolted outside, giving me a week to cool off before returning home, where the bathroom key was now nailed to the door.

Later that year the village started preparing for the annual 'Hari Raya' celebrations, but because it fell on the same day as the Chinese New Year, something that happens only every fifteen years, the party atmosphere was intensified. I decided to go over the border into Malaysia and get some beer, returning with enough alcoholic supplies to keep Erwin and myself amused for the evening, and a big box of firecrackers.

We sat on the porch, got drunk and lit the firecrackers which went off with a hell of a bang. I decided to blow up a coconut. The whole area around our house was littered with coconuts which fell from the palm trees, and I found that the older ones were perfect because the gap at the top where they had grown on the tree was big enough to push a firecracker inside. The resulting explosion was massive. I would light the fuse with a cigarette and bowl them down the dirt road where they vaporised in huge balls of white shrapnel—great fun.

Joe had been locked in the house but somehow got out. Just as I let go of a lit coconut, he passed me, running after it down the road. He thought it was a game. I took off after him and the bouncing coconut, but didn't close the gap in time. Joe jumped on it just as it went off—BANG—he flew off into the jungle. I screamed. We found him straightaway, but his fur was scorched, his body totally limp. I pressed him against my ear, listening for a pulse. He was gone.

I was devastated. I had stupidly blown up my monkey with a coconut, and we're supposed to be more advanced than they are? Have you ever tried explaining yourself to one of them?

The next day I buried him with his favourite toy, a can of his preferred beer, a pack of cigarettes and the bathroom key.

To get my mind off Joe's demise I was sent on a HUET (Helicopter Underwater Escape Training) course. Every two years all personnel who work on offshore installations have to go through HUET. It's a two-day intensive course in how to crash. Supposing you survive the impact, and let's face it, auto rotation aside, lift versus drag and rotation is all good until the rotors stop turning. If that happens a helicopter will drop like an anvil with a tractor tied to it, HUET is designed to imprint the correct egress method to save your life. It's also fun, and all done in a fantastic simulated environment.

There's a scale copy of a helicopter hanging over a giant pool, with wave machines, smoke machines, powerful fans, fake debris, everything you need for a good crash. The crew is strapped into the chopper with four-point harnesses, wearing inflatable life jackets equipped with lights, whistles, compressed air canisters, and of course your EPLT (Emergency Personal Locator Transmitter). If you're working in an area where the water temperature is cold, then as well as all the gear you have to wear a survival suit. That's basically a really thick, all-body condom that reeks of sweat and rubber.

The EPLT is a wonderful device, about the size of a pack of cigarettes, that transmits your position, accurate to within ten square metres on the global emergency frequency. So, should you find yourself bobbing about alone in the middle of the North Atlantic whistling 'I am Sailing' to torchlight, one of the most important bits of kit is your EPLT. I wish I had one for my car keys sometimes! Some years ago, an offshore worker finished a contract drilling job and stole his EPLT, taking it back to the United States as a keepsake. A few months later his son found it and activated it, and within the hour he had choppers and police cars swarming on his suburban home.

The compressed air canister, or spare air, is vital too. It gives you time to make your escape from the crashed chopper. Many helicopters are capable of making an emergency landing on water, like the Sikorsky SN series which has an underside that looks just like a boat, and most can inflate big pontoons to float and stabilise the aircraft in the water. However, helicopter engines are on their rooves, and depending on the sea conditions and how badly they crashed, they can overturn easily. And if that happens they sink, rather like an anvil with a tractor tied to it. I know of only three occasions where everyone got out unharmed from a submerged inverted helicopter that was ditched at sea.

HUET is designed so you can practise escaping from a rapidly submerging upside-down fuselage. They simulate all this very well: first the pilot calls 'BRACE' and you adopt the brace position, then you wait for the impact with the water, take a big deep breath as the fuselage fills up with water fast, stay still as it rolls over, and hey presto you're sitting there strapped in upside-down.

If you're next to a window, you pull out the rubber lining from the frame around the perspex window and punch it out with your elbow, then release your four-point harness, climb out the window, being careful not to snag your 200-pound beer gut on the edge, pull the cord on the life jacket, and float leisurely to the surface of the pool. If you are unable to hold your breath any longer, then by all means use the spare air canister. If your life jacket fails to inflate, then just follow your bubbles to the surface. You have to do it three times from different seats in the aircraft, so you get used to opening combinations of different hatches, doors and windows. Oh and all this can happen in the dark.

We did the HUET course once in Asia. The entire crew was hungover, and two guys swallowed so much pool water they vomited as we rolled over. I watched them disappear in the dim light into a cloud of barf. The guy next to me released his harness before he jettisoned his window and so lost any leverage he had to open it, instead opting to kick me in the head until he couldn't hold his breath any more. I just sat there upside-down with the spare air in my mouth. I could make out Ambu, who had inflated his life jacket inside the aircraft and was now pinned to the floor. To my right it looked like an impromptu rugby scrum, four guys were attempting to use one small door at the same time, and one of them was trying hard to suck air out of his radio transmitter. My air ran out just as they lifted the whole thing back out of the water, with everyone still inside and Ambu still trying to figure out how to deflate his life jacket. The giant pool was littered with bits of gear and vomit. Jack the HUET senior instructor and safety diver was always great and showed superb patience but that day I think even he was tested. His relief when we finished HUET and moved on to sea survival, where we were joined by two pilots, was short lived. Every time they mentioned 'dangerous flying situations' we would yell out 'Hi-Jack' and wave at our instructor.

During my Brunei stint, I went back to Perth for a few months' time off. I rented a small house near the city, purchased a second-hand car, and put the jungle, the rig, Joe and Asia out of my mind, at least temporarily. Ruby was right where I left her. We talked and effortlessly fell into a fast friendship. But my romantic thoughts were shot down quickly. Ruby was direct: 'You're just not my type. Sorry mate.'

Over the next three years, however, Ruby and I became very tight. She could raise hell partying from Friday night 'til Monday morning, come home and go straight to work looking like the front cover of the latest 'single white female and proud of it' magazine, whereas I looked like I needed a heart-lung bypass just to get to the front door.

Living in the jungle of Brunei puts you in touch with life at its most primitive. It's not for the sensitive products of Western society. In the jungle, you have to kill something if you want to eat. In the jungle, there is always something trying to eat you. Competition is incredible. There are thousands of links on the food chain. I always thought the jungle would smell like boiled Kings Cross, but it doesn't. It smells great, and the jungle floor is always clean—because the moment something slows down it's eaten.

While I was in Brunei, the oil company was spending money on training and team building, positive activities for guys like me who were isolated for long periods of time. One of these team-building exercises for the upper management was held in the Brunei jungle. A few of us 'commoners' also got to be involved. It was fun explaining to upper management that there was no shower or cold beer. They thought it would be a piece of cake, like one of those 'outward bound' courses. You should have seen their faces drop when the team leader said, 'If you boys want to eat, you're going to have trap and kill something.'

The upper management guys were not used to the thought of having to kill for food. For most of them, hunting and gathering meant rolling down the car window and grabbing a burger, which they could do without too much trouble.

The upper management exchanged blank looks until finally one of them took charge. The idiot actually tried to lure a monkey from its branch with a fucking banana. Then he attempted to beat it to death with a rock that he cleverly hid behind his back. Of course, the monkey, with a lifetime of guerilla warfare experience, promptly retaliated by getting his mates to systematically piss all over the manager. Wherever he went, it was open season and for the next hour all you could hear was whooping and chattering from the canopy as the monkeys had a laugh at his expense.

At the end of the day everyone was shattered. Their beds were simple 'A' frame hammocks, slung a couple of feet off the ground. One guy was freaked about having to spend the night in the bush, so he popped a couple of sleeping tablets. His hammock sagged during the night and he woke up to discover that half the jungle had crawled and slithered into his shorts—even his bites had bites. He screamed like a madman, rolling on the ground and fishing madly in his crotch.

It was great to see these arrogant men who enjoy throwing their weight around in the business world so wonderfully far out of their depth. Standing around in the jungle, bunched up, paranoid and alienated, businessmen look as out of place as a 50-foot pyramid of severed heads in Taylor Square.

Surprisingly, most of the businessmen really enjoyed the jungle experience. They learned new things about themselves, like how not to beat a monkey to death, and dropped a few pounds in the process. Although, as soon as they got back to Singapore, it was beers and dinner and 'Thank God that's over'.

In the oil business, like most industries, it's the accountants and lawyers who call the shots, and these people make decisions that ultimately put crews in situations that affect lives in ways they could not possibly comprehend. How these team-building exercises were supposed to help them make better lawyers and accountants I don't really know. A wise man once said, 'The road to hell is paved with lawyers and accountants.'

4 SATURATION, 1995–96

Shell launched a massive 'work over' campaign during my second year in Brunei. A work over is basically an existing producing well that needs a service. The rig simply retrieves the old pipe and runs a new pipe back in the hole (the completion string). Any special items on the string other than the pipe itself are referred to as 'jewellery'. These can be any number of things, from down-hole motors to mandrels and radioactive sources for survey purposes.

In the work over, part of the new 'string' was a down-hole titanium gauge. This was very expensive jewellery. Our one-of-a-kind-specially-made-don't-fuck-this-up-titanium gauge was getting picked up off the supply vessel. Because the seas were a bit rough that morning the crane was using the whip line. But the whip line promptly snapped and there went the we-only-had-one-of-those-you're-in-big-trouble-now gauge into the sea.

Usually there is a back-up for every conceivable thing that could go wrong. But this jewellery was one-off, and replacing it was not an option. There was simply no time to specially make a replacement gauge, let alone the mammoth cost of airfreighting a 30-foot long hunk of metal halfway around the world. This was going to be a retrieval, using a crane barge and a saturation dive crew.

Saturation diving is very dangerous; the men who do it are a breed apart, a group within the group on a rig. It's rare to see them on a rig these days as more oil companies are utilising ROV's instead. A ROV is a Remote-Operated Vehicle, basically a submersible with mechanical arms that can perform all manner of tasks on sub-sea equipment. The ROV is piloted from the rig via a cable tethered to the sub—it's like playing a really cool computer game.

I have met a few 'sat' divers and the things they told me raised the hair on the back of my neck. Most of the horror stories involved the hyperbaric chamber, where the crew goes to decompress after a job. The chamber sits on the deck of the rig, a cramped metal tube-like container with only one small round window. Its internal atmospheric pressure matches the depth pressure that the dive crew had been working at. They have to stay in there for days, as the nitrogen in their blood slowly escapes, totally relying on the support staff to bring them food, monitor their progress and take care of their lives.

One 'sat' diver came to grief in the toilet. He was unfamiliar with the old hyperbaric chamber they were using. He went to the toilet, located in the only separate section in the chamber, sealed the hatch and did his business. Flushing the loo in a hyperbaric chamber is a complicated affair, especially when you're knackered after a long job. You have to operate a number of levers and valves that seal the toilet and then the poo is sucked out into a container. This process happens in a fraction of a second—your poo equalising to atmospheric pressure instantly. This diver got the levers back to front and ended up with his bum creating a seal around the toilet while his insides were sucked out in a millisecond, killing him instantly. Another guy decompressed too fast and the expanding airspace between his fillings and his teeth had him rolling about in agony on the deck as his teeth exploded.

Our 'sat' divers arrived within twenty-four hours of the gauge going down but in that time the weather had turned nasty and all operations were shut down until it was safe. The divers had been briefed on the job and knew what could and couldn't be done in Brunei. Although it's a Muslim country, expat workers are allowed to bring in one litre of alcohol each. The eight-man 'sat' crew followed procedures to a tee, but the weather was against them so they settled into the only decent hotel in the village to wait it out.

Two days went by with no change. Late at night on the second day the divers got really bored. There was no night life in the village, of course, so they each drank their allocated bottle of scotch and made their own fun. When a 'sat' crew is on stand-by, and there's nowhere to go, no women to chase, or bars to demolish, the make-your-own-fun scenario usually ends badly. These include some of the more amusing near-death by misadventure stories you hear. For our boys Brunei was not a fun-rich environment, with a distinct lack of things or people to fuck with, so they went for the biggest thing in town . . . the mosque.

Boltcutters easily breached the main gates. Access into the main building, via an open window, was even easier. At the top of the big tower in the middle, they found what they were looking for. Years ago the *Koran* was belted out from the tower via a megaphone and an open book, but these have been replaced with a time-delay tape deck. The prize sighted, the divers exchanged tapes. They also changed all the padlocks they could find on their way out with the locks from their offshore kit bags. The 5 a.m. call to prayer was not a good one; most of the village was head-down-arse-up as Johnny Cash's 'Burnin' Ring of Fire' wailed over the rooftops. The religious police got involved, and it took hours for the locals to get in and turn off the tape. The divers were lucky they only got kicked out of the country with 'Religious Offender' stamped over their passport photos. We never got our gauge back.

I went to see my parents in Thailand and had a great time. Mum showed me just about every side of Songkhla from the best local restaurants, hotels and temples, to umbrella factories and the boot camp where they take teenage girls from the kampong and teach them how to shoot a bizarre array of inanimate objects out of their genitals, including bananas, ping-pong balls, even a blowgun. They can open bottles, smoke a cigarette, draw a picture, solve a Rubik's cube, all with the holiest of holies. It's a sad place, where innocence is burned alive for a quick profit from a drunk tourist.

Mum was going to the orphanage on the edge of town twice a week to teach the kids English and she took me into the building where they try to look after the HIV-positive babies. Born into death, they didn't stand a chance. It shook me like never before and tears ran down my cheeks—we're useless to them. I walked out ashamed of my ignorance, my easy life, and how lucky I have been.

I also experienced 'Songkran', the Thai water festival. I had no idea it was a special day as I walked to the market. An old woman opened her front door, babbled something at me and hurled a bucket of water at my face. So I walked home, completely bamboozled, changed into dry clothes and re-emerged on the main street only to get hammered with water bombs by a truckload of teenage boys. Home again I learnt about 'Songkran'—the Thai new year celebration where people throw water at each other as a symbol of purification—and returned to the main street prepared, with John's large fire extinguisher in my big backpack. Looking like a wannabe 'Ghostbuster', I was ready to join the fun.

One morning I woke to the screams of my mother and ran to the kitchen in my underwear. She had seen a big snake go under the fridge, but she told me not to worry as John had made a 'snake stick'. This was a two-metre long steel pipe, about an inch in diameter, with a sharpened U-shaped prong welded to the end. With this high-tech device I was somehow supposed to get said snake out from under the fridge and onto the front lawn where it would remain perfectly still while I cut its head off.

I took the stick from my mother who said she would be upstairs phoning John in case I stuffed up. I stuck the stick under the fridge and poked about towards the back. The two-metre cobra, who was perfectly cool and happy under there, took the stick away from me and chased me out to the front lawn, where I'm sure he hoped I would remain perfectly still so he could cut my head off.

Then Mum screamed from the upstairs balcony, 'Oh my God Pauli, there's another one behind you.' The cobra's mate that no-one had noticed was making her way around behind me.

They had trapped me. With nowhere left to go, I climbed up the 'Spirit House' in the centre of the front lawn. About two metres high, the Spirit House is a small model temple that most

Thais have in the garden. Every morning, a glass of water and some food and sometimes flowers are placed by the Spirit House as an offering to Buddha. I knocked all that stuff off as I scrambled up. The cobras circled for a bit then began climbing too.

Thankfully John's foreman arrived in a truck. He took one look at me, perched on the Spirit House in my undies then casually walked up, picked up both snakes, smiled up at me and put them in a bag, waving as he drove off. I climbed down and spent the rest of the day recovering upstairs with Mum.

For the next twelve months I fluctuated between the 'work over campaign' offshore and the new well getting drilled deep in the jungle. Each offered up its own unique issues, but never got remotely dull or repetitive.

One hot and humid morning during the monsoon season in Brunei, we got the call to go immediately to the heliport and catch a flight to a land rig deep in the rainforest. We were going out to replace a crew who had been there for way too long. There is supposed to be an industry cut-off point for time spent on remote closed-in locations like that, but I have yet to see that implemented properly. This crew had broken all the records; they had been there for months.

Anyone who has spent a significant amount of time in the jungle will eventually either love it, and not want to leave, or hate it, and end up flipping out. On this occasion the crew consisted of locals who were completely at home in the jungle, so they were fine. The crew chief, on the other hand, was a Texan on his first job in South-East Asia, which is quite an adjustment, let alone the jungle. I was told on leaving the base that he had stopped talking a few days previously, and had spent the last twenty-four hours locked in his cabin.

The jungle can suffocate your mind. Over time a man can start to slip mentally without realising it. I had to replace the Texan immediately before he degenerated to the point when the medic had to give him a shot, put him in a straightjacket and send him home where he would be told to sit up straight, suck the drool back in and try to get a new job. I was looking forward to getting out there—I always felt completely safe in the jungle, much more so than on a Sydney street—and most of the previous six months I had spent offshore, so the prospect of working in the bush again was exciting.

The land rig was 150 kilometres north of our base, and the pilot was planning to shut down and stay there for an hour to refuel and get something to eat. That would give me enough time to talk to my disturbed American colleague and get him safely on the chopper for home. My boss's departing words were, 'Make it quick, and no fucking about okay?' And off we went.

Life is fragile enough without the occasional hint of death that lands in your lap. Enough time had passed since my last hint and I had lapsed back on my laurels, confident in the illusion that I was indestructible. My illusion dissolved just after take-off. It was only supposed to take forty minutes, over the jungle, down a valley, over a small river, and there it was, a hole in the canopy, a green tube illuminated by floodlights, with lots of noise, Diet Coke and cigarettes. I was already there in my mind, telling stupid jokes and catching up with the boys, but no.

Within ten minutes of take-off our chopper, a twelve-seater Sikorsky, was enveloped in dense low cloud, and it was obvious that there were not going to be any spectacular panoramas that day. So I talked to the crew, or rather screamed at the crew over the noise of the turbine, and tried not to notice the violent turbulence or succumb to my once well-hidden paranoid fantasies that had us all screaming as the rotor blades shattered and we began to make that fall into the abyss. I have always hated old choppers. I'm not fond of most choppers but old bouncy choppers really shit me to tears. They carry too few personnel to attract more than a passing nod when they crash, as they do quite regularly.

Every time I read *Upstream*, an oilfield newspaper, there's an article like this:

> Bumfuck Nowhere: all nine passengers and crew died yesterday when a twelve-seater Sikorsky helicopter operated by Doom Air crashed in a really big ball of flames shortly after take-off from Bumfuck Nowhere regional airport. Witnesses said the helicopter fell for, oh wow, ages before vaporising into the jungle at 1592 miles an hour.

So I just sat there and went to a happier place in my mind, which progressed into lurid thoughts of naked cheerleaders playing with a giant beach ball . . . Perhaps that had more to do with the way a chopper vibrates. I kept looking out the hole where the window should have been into the murk, when suddenly the aircraft shook and threw us all over the place as it became caught in a massive monsoon storm. These can appear out of nowhere in the jungle. Hot steamy air races across the jungle canopy and collides with cold offshore sea air, and a very big storm ensues. I was getting worried and could see the same look on all the faces around me; we were flying through one of those 'Dr Frankenstein . . . it's time' electrical storms. Lightning cracked down through the rain, vaporising all the moisture around us, the sonic boom making everyone jump in unison.

The pilot tried to drop out of the weather, falling fast for a few hundred feet into clearer air. When we were only about fifty feet above the tree tops, skimming over the canopy, we rose up sharply and started popping in and out of the low cloud like a confused pigeon. This went on for fifteen minutes, up and down, up and down. Every time we popped into clear air there was nothing but jungle as far as you could see. The pilot came on the speakers in our headphones, and in a calm Louisiana drawl said:

'I don't know if you boys have noticed, but I'm having a little trouble eyeballing the rig. We have lost some instruments and need to do dis approach by line-of-sight, and I've got a master caution light on my fuel, so I would appreciate it if y'all could yell out if you see da rig, okay fellas.'

Before he had finished speaking all eight men were craning their necks in all directions, desperately looking for the rig, but it was like trying to find a pin in a sea of broccoli.

Many of the chopper pilots who work in the oil business flew in the Vietnam War and possess a kind of 'dynamic lethargy' that makes them very calming to fly with. Our pilot radioed the rig and asked them to release red smoke, which allowed us to vector in on its exact position, touch down and disembark. We arrived to a muddy location and a disturbed crew chief. I was just happy knowing I didn't have to make the flight back.

The crew chief, John, was indeed locked in his cabin. I banged on the door and eventually I heard the key turn in the lock. I kicked off my muddy boots, put them on a piece of cardboard by the door and stepped inside. It was a standard port-a-cabin, twenty by twelve feet, with two small beds at either end, two lockers, and a table and chair between them. It was in a real mess; rubbish everywhere, dirty plates and empty cans littering the floor. There was no window; it was dark inside, the only light coming from a lamp that was angled right down an inch from the desk. Big moths whizzed in and out of view, occasionally crashing into the desk lamp. I tried the main overhead light but there was no bulb.

John was sitting on his bunk in his underpants, just staring at the floor. He had not shaved in a few days and looked like he needed a good meal. I told him to get dressed and start packing up his gear. Walking over to the desk, I saw what looked like little piles of insect body parts, wings and heads in one, legs and mush in the other, and a razor blade and tweezers sat under the desk light.

'John, you're on this chopper mate. It's going as soon as it's refuelled and they've done some minor repairs,' I lied.

He just looked up at me and grunted 'Okay'.

I sat on the bed opposite him, wondering where to start cleaning up, as it was now my cabin. John was getting his gear slowly, pulling his towel off the hand-rail by his bed. Then I sensed movement by my feet. Looking down directly between my bootless feet in the dark, I focused on what looked like a very hairy human hand crawling towards my right foot. It was the biggest spider I had ever seen.

Adrenalin shot through my body, and soon I was airborne grabbing the first thing I saw—my boot. This thing was a monster, the size of a cricket ball with legs, so I proceeded to bash it to death with my safety boot. Whereupon John proceeded to bash me over the head with his safety boot. Apparently, it was his pet, and John had been locked up in his cabin at night catching bugs and feeding this thing for weeks. He named it 'Walter' and he and Walter had become firm friends.

Most of Walter was now decorating the floor and the heel of my boot. John and I lay on the floor, he was crying and my ears were ringing and blood was running down my forehead. He was still crying when the medic sedated him and put him on the chopper. The storm had blown itself out. I watched the chopper disappear through the green tube in the jungle canopy, my head throbbing in time with the rotor blades, but it would heal, unlike John's.

5 KILLER MOUSE, 1996–97

We settled in and started the job.

I loved being back in the jungle. I loved the smells and the sounds, and its intense green presence. At night floodlights illuminated the site attracting every type of nocturnal creature. During the monsoon season moths the size of dinner plates would whiz around the rig doing acrobatics that occasionally ended with someone catching one in the head, the impact knocking off their hard hat and leaving them looking like they'd just come off badly in a custard pie fight.

Monkeys would get braver every day, eventually hanging around the rig like groupies after a concert. I would leave my former-little-shop-of-insect-horrors cabin and pass a dozen monkeys all eyeballing me. 'Hey buddy . . . got a smoke?' they would chatter. I would have a pocket full of nuts, always something, which I'd throw to gain safe passage, remembering from my experiences with Joe that pissing them off was dangerous.

All the guys on my crew were locals. My derrickman, Ambu, is an Iban, a descendant of the headhunters who originally ruled the jungles of Borneo. His grandfather lopped off his fair share of heads during the Japanese occupation in the Second World War. Ambu has the 'bamboo' tattoos of a headhunter around his throat but says he only took a few heads in his forty years in the jungle. I always had time for Ambu. His ability to work in any condition made him invaluable on a job. He is not afraid of anything because he has his power. His power is a thin leather belt decorated with teeth and charms made from lead fishing weights. As long as Ambu wears the belt, he cannot die. Remember *The Lone Ranger*? Well, talking to Ambu was like having a conversation with Tonto.

'Come . . . we go.'

'Come . . . we eat.'

'Ambu . . . cannot die.'

Born and raised in the jungle, Ambu possesses the intimate knowledge that only a lifetime of living there can give you. Nothing in the jungle follows the rules as we understand them. Dogs don't chase cats, cats don't chase mice. Monkeys don't ask for bananas, they want cigarettes. Ambu, for example, arrived at the workshop in the village once with two dogs in tow. One was a big shaggy dopey-looking thing with a perpetual drool problem and the other was a small scruffy multicoloured guy who walked under the bigger dog. I asked if they were his dogs. Ambu pointed at the big one and said, 'She's Kuching . . . She my dog . . . The other one is Kuching's dog . . . His name Arnap.'

'Your dog has a dog?' I asked.

Ambu nodded. 'She bring him home one day.'

It was on this job that I got my first taste of Ambu's amazing skills in the jungle and his ability to bullshit as well. We were shut down, waiting for another service company to fix an equipment failure. Everyone was bored brainless and sitting around in a small clearing at the edge of the site. Ambu pipes up, 'I can make the mouse kill the scorpion.'

Ambu was known for his little statements, so I said, 'Okay Ambu, off you go.'

'You wait . . . I bring to you.'

'I'm coming with you,' I said.

'Come . . . we go.'

He was excited to have me tag along and promised to show me something only a few white men have seen. I had to bring a roll of gaffa tape, a flashlight, a painter's mask, my sneakers, a small wood saw, goggles, gloves and rags. Stuffing all this and some water into a backpack, I grabbed a walkie-talkie from the radio room and we set off.

Ambu took off like someone does in the supermarket when they can't find the bread. I was lost after five minutes. I could hear the rig, but the jungle was so dense I had no idea where it was. The canopy blocks out a lot of light but that didn't stop Ambu from moving fast between the trees. Climbing around the rocketship fenders of a massive moss-covered tree, I found a beaming Ambu. He grabbed the backpack and pulled out the saw then plunged it into the centre of the trunk, as if stabbing an enemy with a sword, turning his head to spread a betel-nut smeared grin at me. That's impossible, I thought, the tree was not a tree, but something else entirely. I looked more closely. It had once been a tree, a long time ago, until a strangler vine crept up and slowly but tightly coiled itself around the trunk, spiralling from the base all the way up to the canopy. Over the years, the vine, like a vegetarian python, had throttled the life out of the tree and eventually the tree rotted away to nothing, leaving a hollow tightly coiled rope tube to the sky. Ambu cut a neat hole in the vine, tipped the contents of the backpack on the floor, pointed at them and said, 'Put on'.

The gloves were taped to my sleeves, the rags were wrapped around my head and taped to the mask and goggles, my collar was taped to the rags around my head, and everything was taped to everything else. With the flashlight in my top pocket, I climbed in. The darkness made it easier to cope with the slimy insect-riddled walls, but it was still revolting. My goggles steamed up quickly so I took them off, and by the time I was halfway up sweat had soaked through everything and I was wet down to my undies. When it got too tight to keep going, I pulled the saw from my belt and cut my way through. Finally I was at the top and able to stick my upper body out.

At first all I could do was pull off the rags to get some air onto my face. I felt instant relief, like letting go of your end of a fridge on house-moving day. I was sitting in the jungle canopy on the roof of a world untouched by man. It was breathtaking. I felt like I did when I walked into the Sistine Chapel and looked up at Michelangelo's panels. I was awestruck, my senses overloaded with the beauty of it, despite the vines digging into my bum and the bizarre crawling monsters spewing out of the vine tube. You see the jungle is the wrong way around. All the things that make plants grow and help sustain life in the jungle from slime to great apes, come from the canopy. It's so dense that it traps all the sunlight, water, everything. If you want bugs at home you kick over a rock, here you climb a tree.

Ambu was shouting something from below. I had been up there too long; Ambu had already found his scorpion and was eager to go and find the mouse. The climb down the vine was much more fun than climbing up—just imagine getting sucked down a giant vacuum cleaner hose.

I was too tired to go mouse hunting so Ambu walked me back to the rig and went on his own. It took him until the following evening to find the right mouse. We were sitting in the clearing, smoking and drinking coffee, when he turned up with a metal garbage can lid, some tongs from the kitchen and a metal ammo box. He made a little circle of rocks in the centre of our clearing, up-ended the bin lid and placed it on top of the rocks. We all fell silent and crouched down to watch the show.

Ambu flipped open the ammo box lid and using the tongs pulled out a big black scorpion. Everyone backed up a few feet, it looked so evil. The scorpion was placed in the centre of the bin lid, its pincers were raised and its curved tail, with the poisonous stinger, hovered over its body. Big enough to cover your hand, it could kill a man in a few minutes. Then from a small cardboard box in his pocket Ambu produced a tiny mouse and dangled it by the tail over the scorpion. It was just a little ball of fuzz with a pink tail, no bigger than a golf ball.

'So you're saying that puny thing is gonna kill the fuckin' scorpion?' one of the boys asked.

Ambu nodded and waited for the boys to start placing bets.

The kitty was up around a hundred bucks when he dropped the mouse in the lid. The scorpion went for it, but it was like a forklift truck and couldn't turn fast enough to grab the mouse, who just ran around the scorpion in ever-decreasing circles until it was directly behind the tail. The scorpion could only turn in its own space, it just wasn't fast enough. The mouse ran up the scorpion's tail, and, hanging on to it, started biting through the tip. In less than a minute, the stinger and poison sac were bitten off, then the mouse ran down the scorpion's back and bored its teeth into the scorpion's head. The mouse hung on, staying out of the pincers' reach, until the scorpion lay dead.

Ambu collected his money, then announced, 'You want to see the scorpion kill itself?'

We were all mesmerised by then. 'Yeah sure Ambu.'

So he lit a small fire under the lid and tossed another scorpion in. As the heat slowly started cooking the poor thing alive, it could no longer alternate legs to stand on, and speared itself in the belly, dying instantly. I had no idea there was a creature that given no choice would kill itself.

The next trip home to Perth became my last. Ruby had decided to move to Sydney and asked if I'd go with her to help her find a flat and get settled in. I was happy to go as I had never visited the east coast before and a few weeks later we arrived in Sydney.

It didn't take long for Ruby to find a flat she could afford and she also found work in the first week, pouring beers in a bar in town. I was due back in Brunei in a month which gave me time to look around. Sydney was a change of pace from Perth, and I loved it. I decided to make it my new home on my next crew change.

I looked up my friend Barry who pushed tools on a Brunei rig and was home having some time off. He introduced me to his sister Louise, a successful businesswoman running her own advertising agency, who was as much fun as her brother without the spontaneous loud outbursts. It was then that Louise first raised the possibility of being creative for a living. She saw my paintings; I had been painting for years in my spare time, but never showed them to anyone. She loved them and invited me to her office to meet John, the company's creative director. We all got along so well that whenever I was back in Sydney I would drop in to the office and talk with Louise and John. Eventually, over about twelve months, this turned into work. For an hourly rate I would sit with John in the studio and brainstorm concepts, think up 'tag lines' for print advertisements and write 'copy' for all kinds of things. I loved advertising, the whole process, from an initial idea to walking down the street or opening a magazine, sometimes months later, and seeing something you worked on. It gave me a lot of satisfaction.

For me Sydney can be a cage with golden bars; it's easy to fall into a complacent stupor. I've even caught myself becoming interested in architecture! If I'm not careful I will soon have the mind of a backpacker. In Sydney, if you can get past the day-to-day living stuff—you know, can't find a parking space I can competently drive into, there's no credit left on my phone, and the dog's just been sick on the dash—life is easy, especially after spending months on a rig.

I did miss Perth for a while, but when I returned to finish packing up all my belongings to send over to Sydney I saw Perth differently. It was close to Christmas, and deserted, because everyone had gone somewhere else for the holidays. It looked just like a clean giant version of Bondi with no people. I spent the whole time playing 'spot the locals'. No people, no cars, no-one open for business. Preparing for the holidays in Perth is rather like sorting out the household after a thermonuclear weapon has gone off. You're going to need everything from stockpiles of petrol to one thousand rolls of toilet paper.

I hired what seemed like the only vehicle left in Western Australia and thoroughly enjoyed driving down Perth's deserted streets. On those rare occasions when someone did pull up behind me and the lights turned green, they would patiently sit there and wait for me to leisurely push in the clutch, slide the stick into first gear and peel off without a care in the world. In Sydney you'd better be riding the clutch and completely in sync with the traffic lights so that your car is already moving as they turn green. If you're not, the bastard in the car behind you will be battering the horn and spitting all over the windscreen as he screams his pre-emptive road rage verbal attack.

During my last week in Sydney it rained constantly, turning Ruby's small street into a river. One night Louise was having a party at her house in Balmain, following a dinner in a harbourside restaurant. I was having an absolute ball. She really knew how to entertain friends and family, and it made me not want to go back to the jungle village and deal with the boys.

At the end of the night I jumped in a cab and set off through the rain back to Ruby's flat, near Kings Cross. The flat was on the top floor of a renovated Victorian two-storey building. The tin roof, however, was as old as the rest of the external structure and had rusted through. I was sitting on the toilet, reading the sports page from the weekend paper, when I heard a loud crack.

During that rainy week, water had accumulated in the space between the rusty tin roof and the renovated ceiling. I looked up, registered what was about to happen, and immediately started weighing up the odds of wiping first and running . . . or just clenching and running. I made a grab at the toilet roll but the whole ceiling split through the middle, dumping what felt like tonnes of cold water and gyprock on my head. Ruby just laughed when she got home. We had to use an umbrella to go to the toilet for the next few days.

A week later I was standing on the drill floor in the pouring rain telling the story to Erwin; Ambu came up to relieve the derrickman.

'I go up stair now,' he said and grinned.

The derrickman is the guy who works up in the big tower that juts out of every rig rather like an industrial Eiffel Tower. It's a tough job in bad weather and inherently dangerous. Working in the derrick is all about timing; everything that the driller does affects what everyone else on the drill floor does, especially the derrickman as he's got nowhere to run. His only escape device is a static line tethered from the top of the derrick to the main deck below. Usually set at a tragic angle, this line, called a 'Geronimo' or a 'Tinkerbell line', has a handle that you grab and hold onto as you ride the line down to safety, controlling your rate of descent by moving the handle braking lever.

While he's up there, one of the derrickman's jobs is to 'stab' the pipe. This routine process involves the roughnecks on the drill floor lining up the pipe at waist level with the last joint of pipe sticking out of the rotary table. They need the derrickman to help line up the pipe so it's straight from the top end, therefore enabling them to screw the threads together. The derrickman releases the 'stabbing board', a pivoting plank like a diving board, then walks out to the very end and, wearing a safety harness called a 'belly buster', leans out at a horrific angle to make sure the pipe is lined up straight. So basically the derrickman spends a fair bit of time dangling off a board ninety feet above the drill floor. Having a good head for heights is a bonus.

The rain was coming in hard, but Ambu was unfazed as he made his way up to the derrick. The derrickman whose shift was finishing, Jake, is as funny as Ambu and comes from the same part of Borneo. The two of them have been working together for twenty years. He also speaks English like Tonto.

Jake arrived on the drill floor looking pissed off.

'What's up?' asked Erwin.

'Aw fuck . . . I lose my teeth,' Jake was pointing at his mouth. He chews tobacco constantly, which involves a fair amount of spitting, and while leaning out on the stabbing board he lost his false teeth down the pipe. That made three sets so far for the year, the last pair going down the toilet when Jake got seasick during a storm on our last offshore job. It looked like we were in for another set.

The wind picked up a few hours later, and horizontal rain lashed the drill floor. The difference between rain at home and rain in the jungle is the difference between shaking off your brollie and looking like you just got flushed down the toilet. But nothing short of a typhoon will stop the job. The sky flashed as if taking a giant photo, and we all blinked as the thunder cracked down on our heads.

We had a couple of hundred joints still to run in the hole, and all I could think about was the end of my shift and a warm bed to crash in. Another flash and bang . . . lightning hit the derrick. Everything shorted out, followed by a few seconds of darkness and then the emergency battery lights came on. The driller gathered everyone; we all looked okay. I ran over to the intercom, thumbing the talk button.

'Ambu . . . Ambu . . .'

I ran into the middle of the drill floor and craned my neck back, scanning the inside of the derrick . . . but I saw nothing.

'Get a man in a riding belt up there now and another up the ladder.'

Then we heard him coming down in the tiny emergency elevator. Everyone froze and watched its slow descent to the drill floor.

The door flew open and out stepped Ambu, his hair standing straight up. He had one hand in his mouth.

'PPPPaul . . . My teeth are hot . . . My teeth are hot.'

I pulled off a glove and put the tip of my finger on one of his teeth. His fillings were hot, and so was the zipper on his coveralls. For once, he looked really frightened.

'Okay . . . Go and have the medic check you out. Ambu, got your belt on mate?'

Ambu was not hurt because he had his power belt on, at least that's the way he tells it.

After the jungle stint and we all got back to the base in one piece, I took a break, opting to go and visit my father. It had been a long time, and I was a little nervous about seeing him again.

The drive from our village to the capital of Brunei was a smooth journey for the most part. At the time, the Sultan was constructing a freeway that was to cut through the jungle, connecting all the small villages dotted from the southern-most point to the capital Bandar Seri Begawan in the north. Eventually there would be new sealed roads from every village, all flowing into the main artery like a concrete Amazon River. But for the moment I was driving on a potholed single lane road that was losing its battle against the jungle which threatened to swallow it.

The staff car was a clapped-out fifteen-year-old Mazda that struggled to sit on eighty, but I was in no hurry. Glancing in the rearview mirror, I saw an ancient Greyhound bus looming up on my tail. I moved over to the left so the driver could pass safely, and the bus began to overtake me, kicking up dust and diesel fumes into my open window.

I was about to start cranking up the window when I heard what sounded like the biggest belch ever. Looking directly at me from only a few feet away was a buffalo. He had been unceremoniously hog-tied, up-ended and slid on his side into the luggage bay of the bus between the front and rear wheels, with two of the sliding doors left up as his head was too big to fit in. We looked at one another for a moment, his big eyeball registering mine, and then he was gone.

6 THE DEVIL'S BUSINESS, 1997-98

Twenty-four hours later I was on the London Underground going from the airport to the city where I was hooking up with Steve, an old friend, in Leicester Square to talk rigs and life, love and failed relationships—poor man's therapy with too much beer and a hot bacon and eggs vindaloo by morning. The Tube is always crowded and noisy; Londoners, much like Parisians or New Yorkers, are tolerant of their personal space being invaded daily. On the other hand I was totally uncomfortable, having arrived from a lush wild land where just seeing more than a dozen Westerners in a week was extraordinary. In the middle of a typical smelly tunnel, the rattle of the overcrowded peak hour train stopped. The lights flickered and went out, a few mumbled complaints wafted around. How British, I thought. Anywhere else and someone would be lying stabbed on the floor. The train driver's voice came over the speakers. 'British Rail would like to apologise . . . for everything.'

Steve has an odd way of looking at the world, but he's also fun. I asked him how he copes with being thrust back into his inner-London 'normal' life after living on a rig for months, often in a rough country. He pondered it for a few seconds then replied in his cockney accent, 'Well me old son, I get owme from Eathrow . . . Straight down the boozer . . . Get abowt ten pints-o-lager down me neck 'n go down Piccadilly at five in the mornin' wiv a packet of bird seed 'n a cricket bat . . . I fackin' ate pigeons . . . no wot I mean?'

The next day I was on a platform at Paddington station waiting for a train to my father's place. I was hungover from my evening with Steve, and had the worst case of jitters since that chopper got lost in the jungle. I hadn't seen my father for many years.

To my initial horror I saw him do a whole menagerie of things that I do. His mannerisms, his voice, the way he walks when he's pissed. If you haven't spent any time with your father and then suddenly spend a week with him as an adult, it's confronting. But we had a fantastic time and at least I know what's going to happen to me when I get older. If I make it to old age, I'll check out the way I checked in . . . fat, bald and dressed badly, with a mild boob fixation.

During my Brunei stint I found myself back in London, enroute to Aberdeen and the North Sea. A job had come up out of the blue, and I would have been a fool to refuse.

The North Sea is an oilfield icon, the centre of the drilling industry where historic breakthroughs have occurred, as well as some of its worst disasters. It is one of the roughest seas on Earth, but is also capable of producing six million barrels a day.

Since its initial boom with the 'Forties Field' in the 1970s, it has become a sea-borne exercise in maritime gridlock. It's unbelievably crowded waters, sprouting platforms in all directions, ebb and flow on a mammoth scale and it has become a white-knuckle obstacle course of freighters, rigs, tankers and commercial fishing boats.

I was standing-by in a hotel in Aberdeen, but a two-day wait turned into a four-day wait and on the fifth day the job was cancelled; the North Sea was not to be for the moment. Hanging around had given me a chance to look up some old friends so it wasn't a total disappointment, and I had a day in London on the way back to Brunei.

Steve was away, which was probably a good thing, so I decided to have a look at one of London's lesser known evils. This city has produced some of the most amoral and unsavory characters ever recorded—even worse than Steve! As a boy I had read about Sweeney Todd, who was running around at about the same time as Burke and Hare and Jack the Ripper, and it scared the piss out of me. Eighteenth-century London was a black pit of evil and Todd, born in 1748, was its most damned offspring. He came from a typical gin-fuelled broken home, and was already in prison at fourteen where he learned, amongst other things, like how to survive, the barber's trade. At nineteen he was released and eventually saved and stole enough to open his own shop. And so the Demon Barber of Fleet Street went to work.

Todd had one barber's chair in the centre of his tiny shop, and another identical chair fitted to the ceiling of his tiny basement. He invented an ingenious pivoting system whereby he could switch chairs simply by pulling a lever. Todd would lock the shop door, slit the throat of his customer, pull the lever, and in a few seconds the victim would be in the basement and the empty chair on the basement ceiling would be waiting on his shop floor for the next punter. Todd would then scarper down to the basement to finish off the victim in a killing frenzy that would put a Great White to shame. Then he robbed them, skinned them and dissected them.

To further the evil, Todd started a relationship with a woman called Lovett who ran a pie shop not far from his barber shop. And when his nefarious basement became full, he transported the remains of his victims via ancient underground tunnels to Lovett, who ground them up and sold them to hungry locals as veal and pork pies. If they were alive today, they would probably be in the real estate business.

I was curious to see Todd's shop but more interested in the location. It was on Fleet Street near Temple Bar, where The Strand and Fleet Street meet, right next door to St Dunstan's Church. Temple Bar was already a London landmark when Todd set up shop. It is the location of a huge Masonic edifice which was originally erected by the Knights Templar, who used St Dunstan's Church. It was this which I had come to see.

Some years earlier I became a Freemason. A great deal of older guys in the oil world practise Freemasonry. Sweeney Todd's shop was a vital connection to the Lodge that I was curious about and keen to discuss at a meeting.

Freemasonry has made the jump out of the Dark Ages, and removed the shackles of its shady misplaced reputation, one it acquired in the years preceding the Cold War. It is a noble and studious organisation, and I have learned a great deal in my time at meetings, not just history or Templar lore but about myself also. There are Masonic Lodges in almost every city in the world, and, should I find myself in a strange place with no contacts, I can call the Lodge and always meet the most interesting characters. Yes, it does have secrets and signs, handshakes and formalities; they are part of a history that goes back centuries and have been kept alive for tradition—something I respect in a world where moral values are traded for anything and everything every day.

On my way back to Brunei after visiting my father, I quickly lost my rose-coloured glasses. My flight stopped briefly in Singapore, where two-thirds of the passengers got off and were replaced by Indian and Pakistani workers. All the construction and hard labour in Brunei is carried out by imported workers. They arrive in droves to dig ditches and haul bricks for ten cents an hour.

One of the two Indian men next to me nudged me and pointed at his embarkation card. It's the card that you have to fill out in flight for the immigration people at the other end: Where have you been? Where are you going? Where do you live? Got any drugs? etc. I was filling out my card when the Indian guy saw his opportunity to get his filled out for him. Going from the grunts and nudges, I guessed he could not read or write English.

I smiled and said, 'Please wait while I finish mine.'

So he slides his card over the top of mine while I'm writing, tapping with a manky (dirty) finger on the tabletop.

'Okay mate give me your passport.' I filled it out for him . . . Mr Barney Rubble of Number 1 Credibility Street, Toy Town. He was most impressed and babbled something at his mate sitting on my other side, who grinned and slid his card and passport under my nose. Seymore Butts took his papers back without saying thank you then disappeared towards the back of the plane, returning moments later with half a dozen passports in each hand, that he dumped on my table without looking at me. He settled back into his in-flight movie, blowing his nose on his sleeve for the umpteenth time: he had a bad head cold and blew his nose on everything except a tissue.

I picked them up and dumped them in his lap. 'No way,' I said, shaking my head.

They landed back on my table again.

'Fuck off.' I grabbed them and threw the lot towards the front.

When the passports flew off he screamed, blowing snot down the front of his shirt. Barney took off to retrieve them while Seymore pressed the call button, glaring at me through the snot. The flight attendant arrived, looking flustered, as most of the passengers at the front of her section had just been hit in the head with snotty passports and had pressed their call buttons. Eventually we all calmed down and tried hard to ignore each other.

The meal cart arrived. 'Beef or fish?' the flight attendant asked and faked a smile.

'Beef please,' I said.

'There's no more beef.'

'Then why did you give me a choice?' I asked.

She gave everyone else the fish. Barney and Seymore practically inhaled their mini-meals, both belching loudly afterwards. My meal arrived, but as I was peeling off the metal lid Seymore leaned over me to talk to Barney and sneezed into my food. I had had enough. I stood up on the seat, stepped on Seymore's head on the way out and found a vacant seat at the back where I tried to relax for the landing.

But it occurred to me that the arrival would be a circus if I didn't get out ahead of Barney and Seymore—they were going to be pointing at me in the queue and I was going to be in trouble. I was going to have to get out ahead of them and make a fast exit from the airport.

Luckily I didn't have any check-in luggage, just my small grip bag and, as everyone made a civilised exit from the plane I broke out into a run. I was first through immigration and customs—nice one—and even had time to savour a backward glance at Barney and Seymore who were brandishing their papers.

There was a strange air in the office the next day. I asked what was going on and was told that one of our people had been diagnosed with testicular cancer following a standard work medical. (He beat it eventually, but endured more than a year of intensive treatment and trauma.) I was due for my medical that week so the news wasn't comforting.

After my checkup the doctor handed me a pamphlet titled 'Testicular Cancer and You'. He said, 'Have a read of that Paul, and familiarise yourself with the self-examination methods.'

'Why? Is there something wrong with my nuts doc?'

'No, no, it's just so you know.'

The doctor had given the pamphlet to everyone on the crew to read as a precaution, even the Iban guys who can't read too well, and just pointed at the pictures and laughed. I stuffed it into my pocket and forgot about it.

A week later I was sitting in the tool pusher's office on the rig, staring at the drill floor through the window. I found the pamphlet on testicular cancer in my pocket, lit a cigarette and started reading. There was a quick guide to checking yourself with cartoon images showing you exactly what to do. The cartoon showed a naked bloke, bent over and scrutinising his ball sac which he was stretching out with his left hand. His right hand was reaching around the back, shining a flashlight flush up against his nuts, the idea being that you illuminate your balls and look for any abnormalities. The pamphlet also had pictures of abnormalities, like those skin cancer booklets that have pictures of melanomas, so you know what to look for.

I looked up at the windowsill and there sat a two-foot long black metal 'Maglite'. It's the Rolls Royce of flashlights, the ones security guards bash you on the head with. It was two in the morning, everyone on night shift was on the drill floor . . . I thought, why not, so I dropped my coveralls, grabbed the Maglite, bent over and lit myself up. Everything looked okay, then I noticed my bits were making shadow puppets on the wall in front of me. Distracted by this, and I have to say mildly amused, I didn't hear the tool pusher walk in.

'Boy . . . what in the fuck are you doin' wid my flashlight?'

I dropped it into my undies and in one superfast move pulled up my coveralls and spun around to face him. But my gear only went halfway up because the Maglite hit my crotch, something they don't warn you about in the pamphlet. To his credit the tool pusher listened patiently as I tried to explain and wiped his Maglite on my sleeve. An hour later, the whole drill crew was lined up checking themselves.

Working in Brunei was a pleasure and three years went by too quickly. My time was up, a new project was forecast in the Philippines, and the 'grapevine' had me going. In the meantime I didn't want any of the postings the company offered, as that involved going to areas I had already worked in or places that were too dangerous. So I settled on the best gig up for grabs, in the Middle East.

There was plenty of oil work for me, hopping up and down the Persian Gulf from Oman to the UAE (United Arab Emirates) and on to Saudi Arabia. At the time, the world was in flux; working in oil gives you a finely tuned sense of change, and it was clear that there was something going on. Guys would sit around and debate constantly, and not just the usual small stuff, a coup or tribal conflict, but something much bigger. The last time the walls whispered like that, the Gulf War kicked off within a year. The drilling just goes on regardless. I met a guy who was working on a land rig in Syria at the time. He was happy to work there because everyone got extra danger money. From the drill floor he could see the coalition forces light up the night sky. One day the crew saw an American F-16 fighter jet crash nearby, and a few hours later the downed pilot showed up asking to use the phone.

I spent most of my time in Saudi, and had no problems moving around the region, thanks to my excellent history and having lived in Brunei without any problems for years. Saudi Arabia is ruled by a tribal monarchy and governed by Sharia (Islamic law). It is definitely not just another traditional country going through a change. The stakes in Saudi are way higher. It controls one-fourth of the world's oil reserves, therefore it can directly affect the supply of oil to the rest of the world. Saudi Arabia is the most prized ally of the United States, whose interest in Middle East politics goes well beneath the surface, and both countries protect their energy fiercely.

This relationship started in 1933 when the Saudi ruler Ibn Saud granted a massive oil exploration contract to the Standard Oil Company. This evolved into Saudi Aramco, the power brokers who have 260 million barrels of oil and 225 trillion cubic feet of natural gas in their back pockets. On top of that Saudi Arabia is the keeper of the Muslim holy cities, Mecca and Medina, and the spiritual home of 1.3 billion Muslims worldwide—that's equal to the population of China. The Saudis have the best-trained, best-equipped military force in the Middle East, and, with the US as their best buddy, who's going to fuck with them? Perhaps themselves; Saudi Arabia is in a cultural maelstrom, where enormous wealth and power meet uncertainty and fear, where tribalism and customs meet mobile phone consumerism. As the oil-rich Saudis wrestle with their small quiet land that we rarely hear about, the Westerners who know the inner politics, hold their breath. After the September 11 attacks on the World Trade Center, they shit their pants. Saudi Arabia is the birthplace of Osama bin Laden and fifteen of his hijacker pals.

Men sit in think tanks for months, turning over all the scenarios, so we can maintain our suspension of disbelief that nothing's going to happen again. I wonder what's going to happen in fifty or eighty years when the oil starts to dry up . . .

My time in the Middle East was short. I was in and out, because the walls echoed of war and upcoming turmoil. I opted to get out and go back to Asia, working for myself on a day-rate basis. Freelancing was more lucrative but the work was sporadic and often spontaneous. The phone would ring at ten o'clock at night, and the flight would depart at six the following morning; most jobs started in just that way. As fate would have it, after a few months my old employer phoned and asked if I would 'day-rate' on the Philippines project. I agreed and found myself back with my old crew again.

7 THE HOBBIT HOUSE, 1998—99

Manila is a mosh pit with an airport. The city is in perpetual gridlock, and travelling just a few miles can take hours, unless you have a skilled local driver. The trick is to treat the traffic like a bad dog—don't show any fear, because like bees and dogs Manila traffic can smell fear. Drive fast, don't look both ways, is a popular technique in Asia; along with, if I don't see you, you're not there.

Five of us were in the car getting thrown around all over the place. I'd been up all day in Sydney then got the late-night call, did the high-speed pack, rushed to the airport, flew shitty economy for eight hours, arrived in Singapore, went straight to the job briefing, back to the airport, flew really shitty economy for five hours to Manila, and was finally sitting in an overcrowded jeep on a congested downtown freeway. The air is around a million parts per million carbon monoxide and we're all smoking. Needless to say I was exhausted, my trick neck had popped out of its socket, but that pain was a welcome distraction from my back pain. I felt like a bag of broken china. I was so tired that potholes, fumes and noise aside, I slept regardless, my head rag-dolling from side to side.

At one point during my deep slumber, our driver hit a bottomless pothole sending my face into the dashboard.

'Aw fuck!' I sat back, holding my nose, blood running from both nostrils. I angled the rearview mirror to face me and poked at my front teeth. 'Fuck . . . my tooth is chipped . . . fuck.'

As I nursed my smashed face, we progressed up Roxas Boulevard at the rate of your average tectonic plate. The static traffic encourages local kids to wander up and down the lanes selling just about *anything* to motorists. A boy appeared next to me with a wooden box suspended by a rope around his neck. I looked into the box and there, lined up neatly, were a dozen black three-foot long rubber double-ended dildoes.

'Back-massager,' the boy said, flipping one around his back and pulling it to and fro as if he was drying his back with a towel.

'No thank you,' I said and smiled.

Peter, who was in the back, grabbed one and tied it around his head so the two bell-ends jutted out above each eye. '*We mean no harm to your planet*,' he proclaimed with a straight face to the people in cars around us, who looked on in mute fascination.

Ambu thought that was great and also tied one around his head. Then they proceeded to bash each other over the heads with them all the way to the hotel, finally stuffing them into their offshore bags as we pulled up in the hotel entrance.

The job was high profile and despite the logistics of travel we were well looked after. The hotel was five star, with gold taps, butler service, the works—which made a nice change from the whorehouses we usually ended up in. After checking in, I watched a porter cart off Ambu's bag, across the expansive marble lobby with one foot of black-rubber penis wobbling in time to his efficient walk.

Peter and I were in the elevator on our way up to our rooms when a Japanese family got in. Peter is truly an animal. He takes tremendous pleasure in embarrassing me, and we had just departed the second floor when he rocked over on one leg and let go with the biggest fart I have ever experienced. And it was an experience because not only was there the expected olfactory-audible result but the looks on the faces of that poor family is something I'll never forget. Mum and Dad went bright red, exchanging inner screams, as Peter finished off. My ears popped. One of the two children screamed and buried his head in his mother's skirt, the other child started crying. I was as red as the parents, and mouthed the words best fitting Peter's abilities: 'You bastard.'

He grinned and looked at the crying child and said, 'Hey . . . there's a monster in here. I can smell him.'

We all held our breaths to the top floor but the damage had been done and those children would never be the same again.

The next morning the rig phoned, all choppers were cancelled because of bad weather. 'Hurry up and wait.'

I spent the day with Tommy, the driver. He's a speed addict and made no attempts to be discreet about it. He did, however, get me from A to B faster than any bus or taxi could.

'I drive car like the wind yes,' he said through clenched teeth.

Tommy also talked almost as fast as he drove the car. I heard all about his battered past and underprivileged siblings doing the hard yards in the provinces. He explained in high-speed pidgin English how he had been too high to sleep the night before so decided to clean his flat at two in the morning but got caught up in finding out just exactly how much toilet paper you can suck off the roll with a new vacuum cleaner.

Tommy was good at his job, but he was also armed. I was more than a little conscious of him being on drugs with a gun in his pants. Then again, almost everyone in Manila is armed, and some bars even have a little booth like a cloak room where you have to 'Check your weapon' before entering.

I asked him to show me the real Manila, he did. At one point we drove into a ghetto backstreet lined with garages. It was like stumbling onto the set of *Night of the Living Dead*. All the junkies staggered out of the darkness with bloody bandages on their arms and legs. Tommy explained that heroin is cheaper and easier to get than a needle, so in desperation they slash into an open vein and rub the dope into the wound.

He also took me to his local cockfight arena. Cockfighting, like not getting run over, is a national pastime. The birds are bred to fight, so imagine a vicious chicken. The pit is lined with clear plastic that is splattered with blood, because the birds fight to the death. Small curved blades, each about 3 inches long, are tied to the bird's legs so the fights are short. There was lots and lots of betting going on. It took some time to get my bet down as everyone was yelling at everyone in Tagalog (the Filipino language) and I had to point a lot and do a pantomime of 'Rocky'. But I ended up winning 500 pesos on a particularly violent chicken who, with his huge puffed-out plumage, looked a bit like Tina Turner.

Tommy dropped me off at the hotel and said he expected us to be standing-by for a few more days as the weather forecast was really bad. Filipinos tend to be a little blasé about bad weather. Of the seven thousand islands that make up their beautiful archipelago, not one escapes the average thirty-three typhoons a year. On top of that, the Philippines has seventeen active volcanoes and regularly experiences earthquakes that would send your hardened Californian tremor veteran under the nearest door frame.

The next day was miserable. Monsoon rain streaked down through the smog turning Roxas Boulevard into a river; no adventures today. Peter came by all excited about a bar he had discovered the night before. He really wanted me to go with him that night, but I told him that I had seen it all, every weird sick gimmick that any Asian bar had to offer. Peter assured me I had never seen anything like this, but he wouldn't tell me what it was. Coming from a man who still does fart tricks at forty-five years of age, it didn't capture my imagination.

We watched an in-house movie and ordered room service for lunch. When the room service guy arrived at the door, he looked a bit pale. I asked him if he was okay, and he said there was a hurricane going on outside then opened up the thick floor-to-ceiling drapes to reveal a horrific storm.

'I'm worried about my family,' the room service guy said.

'Fuckin' hell,' said Peter and opened the balcony door, but the wind snatched it out of his hand and slammed it back against the wall.

Wind and rain blasted in almost knocking over the little room service guy. All three of us pulled the door shut, and just as I closed the latch we watched a palm tree sail past the balcony. Our hotel had double-glassed doors and thick walls, one of the few buildings in the area that wouldn't fall down if you pissed against it. But half of Manila is a shanty town, and a lot of people would be left homeless.

I went back out on the balcony, the wind was so strong it was creating a dead air vacuum that wanted to suck me out into the vortex. I gripped the handrail and looked over. The storm sent bits of corrugated tin and debris in a procession past the hotel. The palm trees were bent over almost touching the ground, and the streets were now awash with stalled cars and blown-off rooftops.

That night Peter returned to my room pleading with me to go with him to the bar he was obsessed with. The weather had died down but still no choppers for at least the next twenty-four hours.

'All the boys are coming except you. C'mon we'll get loaded... have a good time.'

I gave in. Tommy arrived to drive us through the rain to Manila's red light district, Makati. Peter told Tommy to drop us on the main strip, and then led us down a side street to an old timber and brick building. Its neon sign flickered in big pink broken letters 'The Hobbit House'.

We went in through two saloon style doors that opened into a large room with a big bar at one end. It took me a moment to take it all in; we just stood there. The place was entirely staffed and run by dwarfs and midgets, it looked like every tiny person in Asia had a job there. Peter was right. I hadn't seen anything like it.

'Hey, where's Ambu?' I asked.

'He's still outside... Fuckin' great place, huh?' Peter was right at home.

Ambu was talking to Tommy who had parked the car, and they were still standing on the main street. I went to get them, as we walked up the side street Ambu froze. He peered at the entrance where two midgets were now standing. 'How far away are they?' he asked.

At the bar stood a driller, Paul, who I hadn't seen in a few years. He was a big man in his forties, and he roared when he saw me then picked me up and hugged me. Paul was drunk, and more than a little upset over his recent divorce, as I learnt over the next hour.

A midget prostitute in heels and a boob tube was walking on the bar. She sauntered up to Paul and me, stopped in front of us, leaned a hand on my shoulder and at eye level said, 'You buy me drink.'

'Err . . . some other time.' I didn't know what to say.

Paul was laughing. 'You think that's funny, check him out brother.' Paul was pointing at Ambu, who, having recovered from his initial shock, was chasing a midget wearing black velcro coveralls, a neck brace and a kid's crash helmet.

'You pick him up 'n throw him against that wall,' Ambu said with excitement as he ran past towards one corner of the bar which was padded and covered with velcro from floor to ceiling.

We did shots of Tequila and Paul was in the middle of another bitter divorce story when the little guy in the crash helmet ran past. Quick as a flash Paul grabbed him by the ankle and, a beer in one hand and the upside-down midget dangling in the other, continued his story.

'Anyway, I said, "You take the kids bitch and I'm not givin' you shit".'

I interrupted him, 'Mate,' and nodded at the poor midget; all the blood had rushed to his face.

'Oh yeah,' said Paul and, in a kind of drunk hammer-throw manoeuvre, spun around and sent the midget flying end over end into the wrong wall.

Everyone booed and threw food and drinks at us.

The night degenerated further into full-blown drunkenness. I managed to escape with Tommy, who was as drunk as me, and woke up outside my hotel room door, a porter shaking my shoulder.

'Sir . . . Sir.'

I looked at my watch, it was two in the morning. 'My card key won't work.'

He bent down and took it from me. 'You're in the wrong hotel, Sir.'

They were very understanding and organised a taxi to take me to the right hotel where I promptly threw up.

It took two days for me to feel normal again, the weather had cleared up and our chopper was set for an early departure. Our flight to the rig was going to take two hours, with a refuelling stop on one of the bigger islands called Busuanga.

Sparsely populated, Busuanga is a lush green paradise, spectacular from the air. While the chopper refuelled we had just enough time to wander to a small shack where a woman made the best noodles I had ever tasted. Eating them was done by holding the bowl under your nose and pretending to use chopsticks while actually slurping down your food with lots of loud noises. It's considered bad manners to eat Western style, i.e. with cutlery, but belching, farting, picking your nose/teeth/bum, smoking, spitting, shouting and kicking the pig that's under the table are all perfectly fine.

At the time, the Philippines wasn't the safest place to be; there was an extremist group creating havoc in the southern islands. The group operating where we were was called the 'Abu Sayyaf' and specialised in K&R (kidnap for ransom), usually of tourists who would finish up beheaded on TV.

Oil workers have to have very complex insurance policies that cover everything from acts of God to getting snatched by extremists. K&R happens a lot in the oilfields, especially in South America, Africa and parts of Asia. The extremists know they will get paid the insurance money and so prefer to grab oil people, whose insurance costs go up as more and more get kidnapped.

This cost eventually finds its way to the oil companies who countermeasure by hiring third-party security specialists. They are tasked with providing close protection and defend the rig and its personnel. Depending on who you're working for and where, these people vary from thugs with guns, to mercenaries, to ultra-professional ex-elite forces personnel who tend to be of medium build and height, are quiet and organised, and for all intents and purposes look like my accountant. Except they can perform complex mental calculations while constructing a shape charge to breach a hotel fire door that's been welded shut, and drop someone at 500 yards with open sights or a toothpick at three feet. And, of course, they can maintain control of half a dozen shit-scared rig pigs.

Despite all this, the rig was a pleasure to work on and it was great to be back with the crew.

One of the drillers was a Frenchman who thought it was great fun to try and aggravate me by attacking the monarchy.

He would bound up and yell across the drill floor in his thick French accent, '*Hey Paul . . . Fuck your queen . . . ha ha ha ha ha ha.*'

Or he would page me, and the speakers located in every room on board would chime: 'Bing . . . Bong . . . Paul, pick up . . . Line one please.'

And I would dutifully jump to the nearest phone, 'Paul speaking, hello.'

'*Fuck your queen . . . ha ha ha ha ha ha.*'

Then my new French friend, who I now called 'Frog One', progressed from verbal attacks to practical jokes, starting with the old styrofoam-cup-dipped-in-a-grease-bucket-and-carefully-stuck-on-your-hard-hat-when-you're-not-looking trick. I walked around with half a dozen cups on my hat, the boys grinning at me. 'What?'

So I retaliated with the Fork in the Redwing. This is a good one . . .

First you take a fork and place it inside a safety boot, on its back so the prongs are facing up. Redwing boots are preferred as they are big, heavy and fairly high with two looped leather straps that you hook your fingers through to pull them on. This requires some effort: you have to really push until your foot reaches a point of no return and finally it slips down into the heel. If there is a fork laying there, you end up with the fork's prongs lodged behind your big toe. If you try to pull off the boot, your toe gets stabbed. The only way out is to cut through the steel toecap and pull out the fork through the sawn-off toe, wrecking the boots. It takes ages to saw off the toe, especially because you have to hobble all over the place looking for the hacksaw that's been hidden by the bastard who put the fork in your boot.

'Fuck you,' the French driller yelled down the phone.

'Fuck your president,' I replied calmly.

He got me back a week later. We had to go on stand-by in town and wait while the rig finished drilling out the next well section. So we all got in the personnel basket, which is a big metal basket for transferring people from the rig to a vessel such as a boat. The crane operator picked us up, swung the boom over the side and instead of setting us down on the deck of the crew boat dunked us into the sea, waist deep, for ten minutes. I looked up, dumbfounded, and then saw the Frenchman giving me the finger from the crane 200 feet above us.

I could just make out his mouth, 'Fuck you'. He was ecstatic.

The crew, on the other hand, was really pissed off. We were soaked, as was all our gear, and the ride to town was going to take twelve hours.

A week later we arrived back on the rig and I was prepared for an awesome payback. While in town I picked up two big bottles of food dye. When Frog One finished his shift, I found his new boots and emptied the food dye into them. After a twelve-hour shift in the tropics, your feet are soaked, as is the leather inside your boots and they are often still wet when you start your next shift. He came out in the morning, checked his boots . . . he knew I had arrived the night before, but there was nothing unusual and so he began work.

Twelve hours later I heard a scream by the boot rack. He was going to have one green foot and one blue foot for weeks.

'Paul, pick up . . . you bastard . . . English pig.' He was on the PA so I answered.

'Good evening Frog One.'

'Fuck you . . . I get you back you bastard.'

I thought I got away clean but a week later I was on another job in another part of the world when one of the roughnecks ran up to me.

'What happened? Sit down,' he said then took off my hard hat and burst out laughing.

'What the fuck are you doing?' I protested.

Frog One had soaked the black foam inside the sweat band of my hard hat with red food dye. As I sweated it ran down my face and looked like I was bleeding. And I had a red band around my bald head for weeks.

The Philippines offered up a lot of surprises towards the end of my two years there. The Abu Sayyaf had become a real problem for expat personnel. We continued staying at the same hotel, the staff were very nice and efficient, and would try to get you back if you got kidnapped. However, we could no longer stray too far from the hotel as the terrorists had begun a hardline bombing campaign: detonating devices in shopping malls, outside churches, in the international airport, in rubbish bins in crowded streets. And there was the regular decapitation of some kidnapped tourist splashed over the papers and TV.

Standing-by in the hotel one day, I ran into Dangerous Dave, an American ex-army man; if Dave was any more laid back, he'd be dead. After four consecutive tours in Vietnam, Dave just doesn't sweat the small stuff. I think that's the way he's been since the early 1970s; he can recall the most horrific moment and still smile afterwards. I liked Dave; he never acted dangerous, but wouldn't tell me how he got his nickname. We would chat for hours in the hotel bar; Peter would join us but only until Tommy was ready to drive him to the Hobbit House.

After one particularly enjoyable session with Dave, I wandered up to my room and fell into a deep sleep, only to be woken by a nauseous feeling. I hadn't had that much to drink, but I felt like I might throw up, so I sat up in bed, turned on the bedside light and rubbed my head. The curtains were moving, but it didn't register. I got up and felt dizzy. The curtains were definitely swaying from side to side. I stepped out onto the balcony, hundreds of car alarms shrieked below and I realised that the whole building was swaying. It was an earthquake. Shit.

I tried to remember what to do. I grabbed my wallet and passport, threw on a hotel bathrobe and took off down the fire stairs. Passing the lift door I could hear people crying out from the long shaft below. Taking three stairs in one step I made it from the top floor to the lobby in record time, blasting through the side door into the crowded lobby. The hotel manager was reassuring a throng of guests that the hotel was built on those rubber shock absorber things that let the building move rather than fall down.

'They have been used in America for some years, and I can assure all of you that our hotel is built to withstand . . .'

Crack.

He stopped as the massive chandelier above us began to break free of the roof.

Everyone scattered. I jumped over the reception desk, hitting the floor at the same time as the chandelier. But there wasn't a huge explosion of breaking glass as everyone expected, more of a thump. The whole thing was made of some kind of safety glass and it basically just bounced about for a while, a bit of an anticlimax really.

I found Dave in the lobby examining the shatterproof chandelier.

'Pretty cool,' he said and smiled.

I bummed a smoke from him and suggested we have a drink. 'I'm not going back up to my room just yet.' The quake was over, but the whole aftershock thing was playing on my mind. 'Let's sit out the front,' I said, 'Then if there's another one we can just grab our drinks and run across the street and watch the hotel bounce.'

We had just sat down when the petroleum engineer from the oil company came bounding up to our table. In her late forties—I can't remember her name I must have blanked it out—she was a nightmare, the only aggressive Vietnamese woman I ever met. She worked in the office south of Manila and had been staying in the hotel waiting for her flight home in the morning. Dave kept his disdain for the woman to himself; always a gentleman, he just smiled and sipped his whiskey. She was in a state over the quake but suddenly digressed into giving Dave a hard time about his company's equipment failure on the rig, something Dave was totally uninvolved in.

'Hey,' I said. 'He's been standing-by in town for the last week, talk to his back-to-back on the rig in the morning.' ('Back-to-back' is the man on the rig who does your job when you're not there.)

She put her hands on her hips and glared at me, not sure what to say.

'Okay, bye bye then,' I said and glared back.

There was a short burst of high-speed Vietnamese then she spun on her heel and stormed off.

'What did she say?' I asked Dave.

'You don't want to know,' he said, watching her walk off. Then he added, with a smile, 'Could have sworn I shot her in the war.'

My jaw dropped.

'Just kidding,' he said.

Dave told me stories about the war. He had seen a lot and I guess his number just wasn't supposed to be up then. He talked about Saigon, the good times he had. I asked if he ever went back after the war.

'Sure,' he said then explained how it just made him feel old as the few former girlfriends he managed to find had all turned forty and had bad backs.

Dave was not a grumbling veteran; if anything, I had to really push him to talk about the past. He always painted an intriguing picture of Vietnam—his backbone stiffening at the memory of long gone combat—and I hoped to go there and see it for myself one day. Once again synchronicity put me there on my next campaign.

I took a break in Sydney, riding my motorcycle all over the place, exploring. Stopping for a drink one night I watched a stunning young woman walk into the bar and in one fluid movement peel off her jacket and hurl it on top of a giant fridge.

Her name was Pia, and she was as bright and funny as she was beautiful. I spent the rest of my time in Sydney with her. I was so caught up I missed my departure flight back to work for the first time in ten years. She was all I could think about for the next month. I was in Singapore, preparing the tools for Vietnam, mundane stuff, and I phoned her every night, feeling unable to wait a month to get back to Sydney. When I did get back, the time passed way too fast.

Pia's family were superbly hospitable. We would spend weekends together and I was completely at home in their company. For the first time it hurt me to have to go offshore, and I realised how hard it was to have a family and work in the oil industry.

That was a bad moment. If this was true love then I understood the agony but not how to deal with it.

8 WHERE YOU FROM?, 1999–2000

I arrived in Vietnam without incident, even my flight was comfortable. However, I then had to hang around the airport for two hours, waiting for a colleague to arrive from the United States. John was a Texan, he sounded nice on the phone, it was his first trip overseas, and I had been assigned to babysit him until he got to the rig.

In the past young men in the oil industry were pulled like magnets to the neon lights and semi-naked teenage prostitutes of Vietnam, often on the way from the airport to the hotel, only to end up in trouble, handi-vacced of all documentation, money, jewellery, vital organs, and they haven't even seen the rig yet. This is done in all manner of slippery ways, my favourite being the 'Titty Mickey': this involves some kind of powerful God-knows-what sedative applied to a nipple, said nipple is then thrust into the face of Western John Doe who thinks, 'Super', and two minutes later he's face down.

I found a comfy place to sit with a good view of the arrival hall. I always travel in jeans and an old T-shirt, trying not to look like anything but a backpacker fast approaching his use-by date. I couldn't have missed John: he was six feet plus, well built, in his late twenties, wearing a Stetson and the obligatory hubcap-sized belt buckle; he had the confident cowboy-boot stride of a man who knows how to rope a barmaid; his Halliburton alloy briefcase was covered in oil company stickers, and his Rolex and puzzle ring twinkled 'MUG ME' across the airport.

As I approached he looked at me the way you would if a stranger asked for loose change. I talked him into waiting inside the airport while I got us a taxi—one look at Big Tex and the price would quadruple.

We dumped our bags in the boot, I told John to keep his briefcase with him, and if possible to sit on it. The taxi was an old Chevy with no airconditioning. As we got in he wound down his window and laid his ten-thousand-dollar arm on the sill. I tried to explain why that wasn't a good idea, and the taxi driver also suggested he wind up the window, but John just spat his wad of chewing tobacco out the window, gave me an ambiguous grin and said, 'Aw hell no-one's gonna fuck with me old buddy.'

I smiled back and locked my door. Ho Chi Minh City is full, to the smog-filled tune of six million people. We coursed down tree-lined Phan Dinh Phung Boulevard, past French villas, with their wrought-iron gates green with age, then went deeper into the heart of 'Old Saigon' which is local jargon for the city's increasing decline into drug trading and prostitution. To get to our hotel we had to drive through a seedy part of town, navigating through a few million people on scooters, and before long the wide boulevardes gave way to narrow backstreets.

Amputees scuttled up to our car, begging for change. Street kids pounded on my window. The driver yelled at them, 'Bui doi (dust of life), no good.'

John was throwing US coins out the window, much to the dismay of the kids who threw them back as no-one trades in coins, only paper money. In this grim sanctuary for panhandlers John got nailed. Two young men on a scooter roared up, the pillion jumped off and held a machete under John's throat, while a third came from nowhere and stripped him of everything—all in a few seconds. There was nothing any of us could do, with John sitting there, the blade rammed against his throat pushing him up until his cowboy hat was pushed down over his eyes. In a plume of blue exhaust smoke they were gone, and so was John's passport and offshore pass. Oh well, I thought, that put me on the job alone.

The driver turned around, shaking his head at John, and said, 'We go embassy now.'

'Hotel first, then you take him to the embassy,' I instructed.

John was in shock, he wanted to get out of the car and chase them, but they had long gone. 'You're lucky they didn't take your arm off,' I said.

The next day I left John at the US Embassy and continued on to the industrial area of Bien Hoa, once a massive US air base during the war, and from there to Vung Tau, a crowded town where all the supply boats gather to feed the rigs. I found my hotel near the harbour and phoned the rig, explaining that John wasn't going on the job and there was no-one else obtainable at short notice. They understood so I stood-by in the hotel waiting for the rest of the crew to arrive later that day.

The crew members were flying in from all over the place, arriving one by one at the hotel. Erwin and Ambu, amongst others, were involved, and I was stoked to be with them again. I left a message for the crew to meet me in a bar nearby, and there we stayed for the next three days, waiting for the rig to finish delayed operations.

On the second day Damian came down to the bar and sheepishly stashed a pink shopping bag under the table. Another one of the guys grabbed it and pulled out a skipping rope.

'I'm fed up with jogging around the heli-deck,' explained Damian.

'You can't skip,' said Erwin.

'I can . . . I can even do the crossover thing.'

'Go on then Leon Spinx.' I handed him the rope.

It wasn't any old skipping rope mind you, this one had an elasticised rope and weighted handles. Damian stood in the middle of the rundown bar, directly underneath a huge ceiling fan. I was about to say something but Erwin winked at me, and I thought, what the hell, it could be funny, so shut my mouth.

Damian swung the rope in an 'I could have done this for a living' confident way, only to wrap it over the centre of the fan which then snatched it from his hands, whipping the rope at head height around the bar. Damian hit the deck, hands over his head. Everyone stopped laughing and took cover when the momentum of the fan stretched out the elastic rope, sending it swinging in our direction. The helicoptering handles began smashing glasses on the bar as the fan started to come out of the roof. It eventually fell, landing on top of Damian, who just got up and walked out, but refused to speak to us for days.

The afternoon of the third day finally found us walking over the grassy airstrip towards the chopper on our way to the rig. The small airport was still riddled with thirty-year-old bullet holes, and everywhere you looked brass casings littered the ground. From the air, however, we got a much better idea of just how much ordnance was dropped on South Vietnam during the war.

The huge craters left from the bombing had never been filled in, just overcome. Rickety bridges had been constructed over any that landed on roads, the rest were now ponds.

'Fuck . . . they shelled the shit out of this place,' Damian said with his camera pressed up against the chopper's perspex window.

The rig was nasty, with cramped dirty rooms and old smelly toilets. I had a shower after we arrived, that is to say I stood under a nozzle that jutted out of the wall dribbling water on my head. The TV room wasn't much better; you never know what you're going to find when you walk into a rig TV room, CNN, BBC, Discovery Channel, naked prom queens cavorting in jello. Then it was off to the galley for something to eat. The crew had renamed it 'Chucks', the food was bad, even now when I burp I can taste it. I shuffled along in the queue, my aluminium tray in hand, playing 'Spot the Con' with Erwin.

Spot the Con passes the time while you're waiting for your gruel. There are a reasonable number of ex-convicts working in the oil industry. You can usually pick them by their rough jail-house tattoos, and the way they protect their food: the ex-con is the guy who looks at everything except what he's eating without making eye contact.

I got to the service window and found a three-hundred pound, sweaty, bald Chinese guy glaring at me over the bain-marie. Had he been wearing a black one-piece suit and a bowler hat, he would have looked exactly like 'Odd Job' from the Bond movie *Goldfinger*. I asked him to identify the various grey reconstituted meat food products bubbling in front of me. He began rattling off the menu as Erwin leaned in and started doing his best Sean Connery, but Odd Job had obviously heard the joke about who he looks like before and let fly with some high-speed abusive spittle-ridden Cantonese.

Dinner was foul, it had all the texture of a boiled shoe and even less flavour. I went to bed miserable, pulling back my threadbare sheets to reveal a cockroach that resembled a bronzed soap bar with legs. I thought, I will dream and escape to wide rolling hills and quiet walks with Pia, wake up happy and refreshed if Ambu doesn't snore, rig up and start the job. The sooner it's over the sooner I'm home.

The Vietnamese crew was great to work with, the job was going well and we would have all the pipe run in the hole and be back on the beach in two days—nice one. I started my second shift at night; a nasty storm was blasting the rig and the seas had really picked up. It was raining hard and the rig was moving around a lot. This makes the derrickman's job even harder; Ambu was up there doing his best. The driller on the other hand didn't see it that way. An American with no patience and a short temper, he got fed up around three in the morning, told the assistant driller to take over, and stepped out from behind the brake.

The brake is a large metal lever jutting out of the floor at the driller's feet. It can be locked down into place via a chain and, as the name suggests, the brake stops the movement of the top drive, and in turn the up or down movement of the pipe which is being made up (screwed together) on the drill floor.

The assistant driller took hold of the brake while the driller came over and told all the Vietnamese roughnecks to step back. The local roughnecks are small people and we were running a 13⅜-inch casing, a big heavy pipe.

With the movement of the rig and the small people trying to line up the free joint hanging in the derrick it was all too heavy with too much movement. The driller got hold of the loose joint of pipe, swinging about in the derrick in a manly kind of vertical head lock, and started heaving and pushing it over the static pipe sticking up in front of him. Finally the two pipes looked lined up, separated by only six inches and the driller's beer gut hanging over the inside rim of the static pipe.

The driller had his back to the assistant driller, who let the loose pipe down and they lined up, slamming together with a loud metallic clang.

The driller staggered back but at first none of us realised what had happened. His arms were doubled over his belly, then he straightened up, dropping the contents of his abdomen on the floor at his feet. He had disembowelled himself, and was dead within seconds.

Because of the weather it was out of the question to get a chopper and send his body home, so the medic taped him up in bin liners and put him in Odd Job's cool room. The chopper we were expecting was a Bell-type 212, the same model used in the war and luckily someone realised the driller, a really tall man, well over six feet, was too big to lie on the floor as his feet would stick out the doors. The seats were welded to the chopper so moving them was impossible too. Then we hit on the solution: we moved him into Odd Job's freezer, taped him to a plastic chair and froze him in the sitting position. When the chopper finally arrived for him, the roughnecks gathered around his rigid body strapped into the seat and had a group photo while he began slowly defrosting.

Back in Vung Tau after the job the crew amused themselves with a shocking TV show that can best be described as 'Cambodian Idol', featuring poor lonely people with no legs singing on stage—all the contestants had some kind of prosthetic appendage. Erwin and I opted to go and visit the Cu Chi Tunnels, 70 miles north in the Tay Ninh Province. There is a visitor centre there where you can see, according to the Vietnamese information posters, why America failed to bring US-style democracy to Vietnam. For five dollars you get a guided tour of the famous tunnels, a subterranean maze of Vietcong guerrilla caves, and for a dollar a round you can shoot a surplus Soviet-made AK-47 or an old M-16 at a paper water buffalo. If you're a good shot you win a Vietcong hat.

At least some money is coming into the country by turning the remains of war into a tourist attraction. More than half of Vietnam's current population was born after 1975 so there is little interest in the conflict from locals. We had beers in a bar called 'Apocalypse Now'. Erwin told me how he got a role as an extra when Michael Cimino shot *The Deer Hunter* in 1978; later at home I got the digitally remastered DVD and sure enough there was Erwin. We kicked on to a few more bars, having a good time, until a group of drunk American businessmen called us 'oil trash' and shoved Erwin. We were not dressed like oil trash, we didn't draw attention to ourselves, or look for trouble. He ignored them until an olive bounced off his head. I had never seen Erwin really go off before: he waded through them like a Jedi master, and we got arrested.

The Vietnamese police are not to be fucked with. They cuffed us both and took us to the station, where we sat and waited, cuffed again to a huge old wooden bench. Metal loops jutted out of the middle, creating an armrest as well as a solid place to attach the handcuffs. Both your wrists were cuffed with the metal loop running through the chain, so you had to sit with your hands to one side. An hour later the bench was almost full. I had a small local guy sitting next to me on the right, Erwin was next to him, and he was next to a prostitute and two very quiet Europeans. The only vacant seat was on my left. Three police officers crashed through the metal doors, struggling to subdue a massive American. He looked like a biker, with a long greying beard, shaved head and tattoos up and down both of his massive arms. He roared obscenities at the police, who flayed about at the end of his hulk, until finally he got tired and they cuffed him to the seat next to me, but only by one hand.

I tried hard not to make eye contact or even a sound but after a moment the biker grabbed my shoulder in his paw and twisted me around. 'DID YOU FUCK MY WIFE?' he spat out through brown teeth, veins bulging on his melon head.

'No . . . no I didn't.'

He let me go, leaned forwards and looked down the bench. 'DID ANY OF YOU MOTHERFUCKERS FUCK MY WIFE?'

Everyone froze. Then Erwin leaned forwards, looked him in the eyes and said, 'What does she look like?'

The biker was on top of me in a second, trying to get to Erwin with his free arm. The whole bench came down, and soon the police who brought the biker came in.

'He started it,' I said and nodded towards the biker thrashing about at the end. So they stun-gunned him until he pissed his pants, unconscious.

My flight back to Sydney was just as smooth as the trip in, unusual for me. Pia was going to visit relatives in rural New South Wales and invited me to go with her. We spent two weeks on a fantastic farm located in a picturesque valley; they had motorbikes I could take off on, and rifles to shoot tin cans with. Pia spent the days painting and in the evenings we would go for long walks.

One day a bull arrived in a big truck. He was a prize bull and everyone hoped he would father lots more. After a few days, however, it became apparent that the prize bull was gay, opting to ignore all the best looking cows and bash down a fence made of telegraph poles to try and hump another bull, who ran away, seeking refuge in the paddock where the farmhouse was located. We woke early the next morning, the whole house rocking from side to side. Not another fucking earthquake! I jumped out of bed and ran out the front, grabbing a banana on the way so I could have breakfast and watch the house bounce. Standing on the front porch was the 'straight' bull; he was having a scratch against the wall and moving the whole building. He really was a big animal.

'Where's your boyfriend?' I said in his ear. He wandered off unimpressed.

9 BARREL FEVER, 2000–01

My phone rang in the car on the way back to Sydney. There was a job in Papua New Guinea on a land rig in the highlands and my flight departed the following morning. Again it was a cakewalk. I'm on a roll, I thought. But not for long.

The rig was right up in the mountains, deep in the jungle. Locals wandered up every day in grass skirts, carrying muskets, their faces painted. Now and again they would take a pot shot at the rig. The location was still being set up, the area having been cleared using high explosives, otherwise known as 'instant wood chipping'. In every ancient tree, wise and proud, were generations of evolution buried deep, which is vaporised 'cause it's fast and cheap. Even though they plant another tree, somewhere else, to make up for the one they destroyed, I feel a twinge of guilt, because essentially I'm a cat-loving pacifist who ought to care deeply about the environment. On the other hand, I represent people who would squeeze schoolchildren to death if they thought some oil would come out.

To summarise my political opinions about oil, greed and the environment, both then and now:

- I firmly believe that when politicians aren't kissing babies they're stealing their lollipops.
- There is no oil in schoolchildren.
- Everyone in oil is a lying weasel . . . except me.

Lots of guys in the oil industry have bucked against the system until the system has hardened them into balls of frustration and that's all they've got left. The environmentalists and the oil companies each have their propaganda machines vilifying each other, but inevitably most of the time we fall back reassured that the entire planet is nothing but two feet of top soil surrounding a huge ball of oil. In PNG you can exploit the locals; you can do whatever the hell you want with government backing and your own armed security. Sometimes the oil companies do go into overkill . . . fear of the locals overwhelming the rig has the security personnel asking if they can mine the perimeter, and after compromising decide instead to use two hundred bear traps from Canada. (At the time I wondered if they got the traps from the same company that supplies the clubs for bashing baby seals.) But mostly, we do need the heavy security, as proven not so long ago in Banda Aceh, at the top of Sumatra's long finger, where the local people tore a rig to pieces.

The first time an attack happened I thought, all these guys with guns is a bit much isn't it? Like using mercenaries to discipline naughty schoolchildren or hiring Jamie Oliver to help Pol Pot eat people in Cambodia. But I was thankful for their presence on more than one occasion. Most prevalent in my mind is a drill floor in Columbia. At the time Bill Clinton was 'fighting the drug war' but using the DEA choppers to ferry men and equipment to and from the rig. So apart from getting its dope from Columbia, America gets quite a bit of oil there as well.

The rig was a bit close to the other major cash crop in the region. As a result some unlucky third-generation farmer got his straw-thatch hut, goat, wife and crop napalmed. Naturally he's angry and finds the rig, levels his weapon at it and has a go. The alarm went off; a horn and light flash which meant run fast into a safe room, lock the door and wait for the security staff to give you the all-clear. Just before the alarm sounded a thirty-foot mushroom cloud exploded in the jungle near the rig. It turned out another murderous farmer/local gunman had fired a Rocket-Propelled Grenade at the rig and missed, the RPG passing directly between the cross members of the derrick. The security staff took a back bearing and hunted the man down. He was in two body bags in the cool room within the hour. I asked why two bags and was told that they had used hot loaded strung buckshot. This is a solid projectile that's been cut in two, hollowed out in the centre, with six inches of wire coiled inside and the two heavy ends spinning around the wire. It cut trees down; from the top of the rig you could see a cleared tube through the jungle.

On the highlands rig we managed to avoid life-threatening locals, same politics, though, but this time PNG got the last laugh. We had just finished powering up our tools and checking everything when one of the rouseabouts came up carrying a case of bottled water. We all grabbed one each and guzzled it down. Anywhere in this part of the world it's second nature to be wary of the drinking water: I have even been caught out with bottled water when I put ice in it and fell sick because of the ice.

After only half an hour or so I felt ill. One by one the crew began to disappear, doing that hurried clenched run of a man about to have a rapid bowel movement. My turn came, I took off across the deck, there was no warning, everyone was in the toilet blaming the bottled water. I went to the medic who examined the case of water still sitting out on the deck. He realised what none of us did, the bottles had been filled with God-knows-what and re-sealed. Small beads of superglue had been applied to the ringseal that attaches to the cap, so we got the loud crack as we unscrewed the caps, giving us the okay to gulp down a litre each.

The medic looked worried. He explained that the necessary medication to deal with this was not on the rig yet so he was going to get some immediately from the supply base in Port Moresby by chopper. He was still on the phone organising this when our condition progressed from regular diarrhoea to red hot violent uncontrollable I-can't-leave-the-toilet diarrhoea.

The medic ditched Plan A and organised an emergency chopper to get us to a hospital, as he feared we had all contracted dysentery. In a situation like this you're given the choice of going to a local hospital and having the wrong procedure performed by someone who can't speak English, or flying to the nearest Western hospital, first class if necessary, and having your bits sewn back on or whatever you need, assured in the knowledge that you probably won't die. I chose the get-out-of-PNG option, thinking stupidly that I could clench all the way to Singapore. Three of the others chose possible death by bowel movement in a local hospital.

We boarded the chopper with our IV drips inserted and towels shoved down the backs of our coveralls. Transferring directly to the first flight to Singapore, I was in business class next to a large happy-faced German man whose expression dissolved into horror when he saw the IV. We took off . . . so far so good. But about halfway through the take-off climb my backside let go. I yelped in complete terror—I'd just lost my arse on a commercial airliner . . . oh my God.

Two scalding squirts of piping-hot poo shot down both trouser legs. I feverishly pulled at my seatbelt and, grabbing the IV in my fist, hurtled down the fuselage towards the virtual heaven of a business-class toilet. The flight attendant looked sympathetic as I shot past and thankful, I'm sure, that my trousers were tucked into my boots. Slamming the door I spun around, gripped the IV bag in my teeth, pulled down my coveralls, disconnecting the IV bag from the needle, and sat down just in time for round two of the most embarrassing experience of my entire life.

I think that over the next hour I must have shat my own bodyweight, and then the projectile vomiting started. I don't know if you've ever been violently sick in an aircraft basin, but in case you haven't, don't, because it flies straight back out and all over you.

By this time I didn't know if I should sit or stand, eventually opting for the more comfortable vomit-on-your-own-genitals-position. I refused to come out, naturally, no matter how much my colleagues begged. 'Piss off, find your own.' They had to tag-team it, using the other toilet opposite me all the way.

When we did finally get to Singapore, the aircraft pulled up short of the terminal, a staircase on wheels arrived at the back door and an ambulance was standing-by. We debussed to the appalled looks of our fellow passengers, a few children screamed at me as I made my way down to the back as if walking on hot coals. Inside the ambulance were wheelchairs fixed to the floor with little curtains around them and potties underneath. Everyone hurried to a chair and, not bothering with the curtains, we made a horrid chorus as the driver hurried, windows down, to Changi Hospital.

An Indian doctor was waiting wearing his turban and pleasant bedside manner. We wheeled into his waiting room.

'Gentlemen, I'll be needing a stool sample from each of you please.'

'There's some on my foot,' said Jack.

'There's some of yours on my foot too,' I said.

The poor doctor slid the potties out from under our chairs while we sat there, occasionally twitching, one by one going off to get cleaned up. The good doctor was bent over a microscope, then he sat back in his chair, spoke into a nurse's ear and turned to talk to us.

'We know what kind of parasite you have all ingested, so now we can administer the right medication.'

'Can I have a look?' I asked. I wanted to see what had done this to me. The boys curled upper lips and scowled at me as I wheeled over and craned my neck over the microscope. Swimming about in a frenzy were lots of tiny monsters looking like an underwater scene from *Jurassic Park*.

'Oh my God.' I felt like a victim in an alien movie.

'Yes . . . that is in your bowel,' he said, the calm way a doctor does.

'Give me the fuckin' shot.'

The upside of having had Amoebic Dysentery, apart from not dehydrating to death on an airliner, is that I haven't had to run to a toilet in years as the body builds up an immunity to parasites. The downside was, for months afterwards, I would be at a party or just standing around in the workshop, and when someone cracked a joke, everyone else burst out laughing, but I was sprinting to the toilet to check.

And I was scared to fart for a year.

There was a directional driller who I regularly ran into, a New Zealander by the name of Maurice. A good-looking man in his early forties, Maurice was very good at his job and very good at getting in all kinds of shit when he wasn't drilling. He was well respected by everyone, even when he got loaded and wild at company functions. Maurice needed a warning posted on his forehead, or explicit instructions for party holders to lock up their wives and daughters and organise a team of men with restraints to capture him in case he kicked off, as Maurice had no concept of fear, or of consequences.

Maurice told me about his farm in New Zealand and his dogs that he hunted wild pigs with. The best of the pig dogs were Chaos and Razor and from what I heard they, like their master, knew no fear. Maurice pulled a tattered photo from his wallet one day and showed them to me. I didn't know what to say. Chaos looked like a Staffy crossed with a rhino, and Razor was basically just a monster. Apparently, Razor, in his youth, got hold of a massive pig in the mountains; the pig mauled him so badly he lost most of his jaw. Had he belonged to anyone else Razor probably wouldn't have made it out of the woods that day, but Maurice being Maurice carried the big dog home and drove him straight to the vet. The vet recommended Razor be put down, as without teeth he was unable to survive. Maurice, however, wasn't ready to give up and so had a dentist make, from scratch, a full set of surgical-steel teeth to be placed in the dog's reconstructed jaw. While Razor was waiting for his new teeth, Maurice had to puree all his food and handfeed him, but the dog sank into a deep depression, kicked to the bottom of the pack in the farm's canine hierarchy; he was inconsolable. Until he got his new teeth. The result, much to Razor's delight, was terrifying. And he knew it. You could tell by the way the dog was grinning. He looked like he had a mouth full of chrome crab claws. Razor immediately ascended to the top of the food chain. These days, the wild pigs do a big double-take and run away.

10 THE DARKEST CONTINENT, 2001

Christmas was only a few weeks away, and my heart was broken. Pia ended it for a reason I had to accept, the oldest one in the book of failed oilfield relationships: I was away too much. I was completely intoxicated with Pia, the sun rose and set with her. When she left I was crushed. I moped around the house for weeks and weeks. The phone and doorbell would ring, I never answered it. Eventually the money started to run low, so I reached out looking for a gig but there was nothing going on.

Walking through town one Saturday night I ran into a friend, and he asked where Pia was, but for some reason, I couldn't say the words. I just said she was doing her own thing. He offered to buy me a drink so we wandered into a seedy-looking first-floor bar in Kings Cross called Barons. Hearing his news distracted me and I started to relax and enjoy myself. We had a few more drinks and talked about grabbing some dinner when someone dropped a coin into the jukebox and set off all my triggers at once. It was our song. I felt suddenly empty, as though I had just given too much blood.

He was recalling a skiing holiday in Aspen but I was hunched over my beer, unable to stop myself from crying.

He stopped talking. 'What's wrong Pauli?' he leaned in; the bar was getting crowded and noisy.

'I love Pia,' I said, speaking into my glass, too embarrassed to look him in the eye.

'I love beer too, Mate, but I'm not going to cry about it.'

Christmas was only days away when I was approached with an offer to work in Nigeria for six months. I had heard so many bad reports about West Africa over the years that my immediate reaction was 'No thank you', but with a depressing Christmas looming and the lack of work in Asia, not to mention my state of mind, I phoned back.

I contacted everyone I knew who had worked in Nigeria and developed a morbid curiosity about the place. Once my gear was packed I was eager to go, and get away from Sydney before Christmas found me bah-humbugging my way through a bottle of scotch. The company emailed asking if I could stop over in Paris to discuss some 'logistical issues'. This was unusual, but I agreed as Mum and John were only a short train ride from Montparnasse Station and I could stay with them for a night.

I left Sydney very quietly. Ruby and Tony, good friends who kept my head up regardless of how much I pissed and moaned about my lack of a normal life, were there to wave me off. I was so depressed, but when I finally found my way to the seat on the aircraft and started thumbing through the in-flight magazine, my mood lifted for the first time in weeks.

No matter what Africa had to offer, I knew it was a better option than skulking around the house over the festive season looking like someone just shat on the turkey.

The flight was your standard economy-class nightmare exercise in confined space anxiety management, with a couple of infants screaming so loud that dogs 35 000 feet below us could hear them. I ate the mini-meal with the mini-plastic cutlery, watched the mini-TV trying not to get the headphone cord in my mini-mashed potatoes, while the overweight flatulent pensioner next to me made a concerted effort to have the whole cabin smelling like cabbage before the flight attendants had cleared away the trays. I'm sure everyone else in that section felt the same way. We were locked in, unable to escape because of the tray tables and the mini-food carts that effectively block your path to cleaner air and a mini-toilet where one could have a few mini-moments of relative solitude, or a claustrophobic panic attack, whatever gets you through today's budget air travel. Just think of the frequent mini-miles, not the deep vein thrombosis that will have you dropping dead on a beach on your first day.

Charles de Gaulle International Airport sucks. I had been through there on a few occasions and it was always a pain. Eventually I found myself standing in a heaving sea of tired passengers with methane intoxication, all jostling for a good spot near the luggage carousel. I could hear the two children from the flight still breaking the sound barrier and making people on the other side of Paris cringe and cover their ears. (It's not that I dislike children, I love them, and I totally understand it's the air pressure in their little inner ears causing them pain, and that they are too young to clear their sinus passages and equalise the pressure; it can be very painful, like flying with a bad head cold. I just don't have any experience with kids. Even with my sister's three boys, I am told I handled them like rabies-infected carrier monkeys. She made me change a nappy. I have seen men cut limbs off, all kinds of nasty accidents on the drill floor, but a nephew's shitty nappy made me gag and resemble someone trying to deal with an untidy parcel filled with a mixture of nuclear waste and velcro. But, as I've been told before, it's different when it's your own kid's poo, right?)

My taxi pulled up outside our Paris office and I was greeted by a friendly receptionist, who politely showed me into the manager's office. He was affable and smiled too much, and while he was offering me coffee I saw the 'poor bastard' look in his eye. The logistical issues turned out to be remarkably silly, almost comical if they were not so serious.

On arrival in Lagos, after going through customs and immigration, I was to look for my driver; he would be wearing green company coveralls and holding up a sign with my name on it. I would approach and speak this sentence and only this sentence, 'It's hot here, just like Australia.' The driver, upon hearing that, was to answer, 'Just as hot, but no kangaroos.' If he didn't say that, it meant that he had murdered the real driver, stolen the company car and was planning to drive me out of town, put two in the back of my head and make off with my stuff.

I was curious as to who thought up the dialogue, because it was bloody stupid. The French manager, puzzled at my sarcasm, said he constructed the sentences. I only hope one day I can see him arrive at Kingsford Smith, walk up to his driver and say, 'Bonjour, the potato is on the suitcase.' He didn't get it, and went on to emphasise that this was a vital protocol as two men had been killed exactly that way only a few months earlier. So with my ridiculous cloak-and-dagger routine committed to memory, I walked off to spend an enjoyable evening with Mum and John.

We had a fabulous dinner and a special wine; we sat and talked until late about the entire goings-on in our lives. I ate too much *fois gras* and hoped my Nigerian driver wouldn't shoot me as I padded up the stairs to brush my teeth and sleep off John's three bottles of Château de Carrier Monkey. Mum cried at the train station the next day, and gave me her standard 'Don't forget your safety' line. But she and John knew the rigs well after thirty years in the business so it was pointless trying to gloss over where I was going.

The flight to Lagos was a carbon copy of the Paris flight, except I was the only white person. Babies screamed, the food was small and tasteless. Instead of a smelly pensioner I sat next to a middle-aged Nigerian woman who enjoyed telling me that Lagos Airport is the most dangerous airport in the world, and I should be very careful indeed. That's no problem, I thought, I'm just going to walk up to a complete stranger and come out with the dumbest line imaginable, and hope he doesn't blow my brains out for two hundred dollars in traveller's cheques, a Mars Bar and some dirty underwear.

I could smell Nigeria before I could see it. Then on our final approach I looked down and saw a mess that resembled a Manila shanty town after a typhoon, with extra shit and heavy on the random people with big guns.

Everyone disembarked, that is to say, everyone just got up and rushed the cabin crew, who flung the door open and let the passengers trample over each other in a bizarre scramble to get out. I thought, perhaps the flatulent pensioner from yesterday was on this flight? But when I rounded the last corner of the terminal I understood why: eight immigration booths and one guy on duty.

He spotted me a mile away at the back of the official queue-jumpers' queue, his eyes immediately bulging. You could almost hear the 'KA-CHING'. They told me in Paris to arrive looking poor, no jewellery etc., so I was looking lower than whale shit,

German grandfather, Berlin, 1942.

My father, 1957.

English grandfather, London, 1943.

Erwin teaching his crew, one job at a time.

Waiting for a chopper, Africa, 2003.

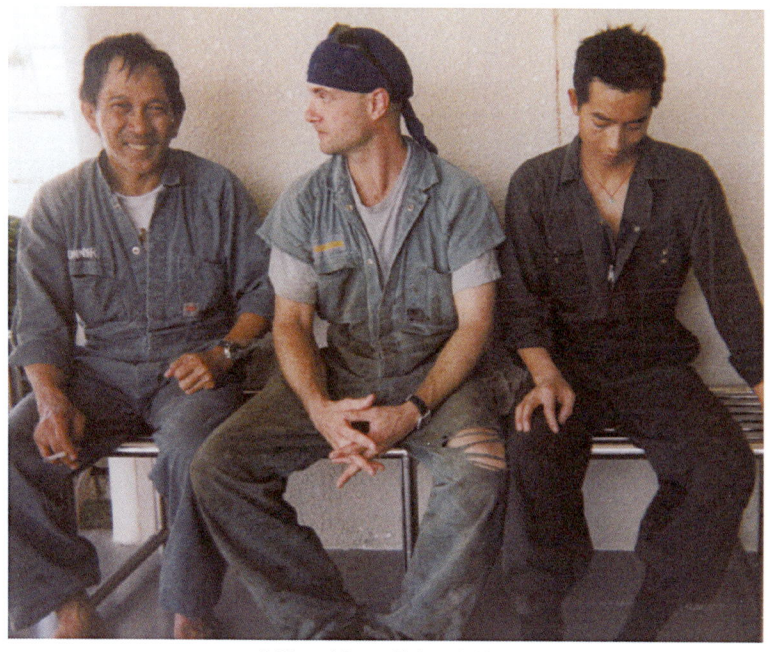
Still waiting, China, 2004.

The offshore workhorse Sikorsky SN-61.

Brunei, our home for three years.

Derrick, looking up from the drill floor (stabbing board on left).

Derrick from the outside with drill pipe racked back in stands.

Drill floor during a typhoon.

Close protection, Nigeria, 2003.

The walkway to the drill floor is aptly named.

Damian discussing confined space anxiety management with Joe, during a visit to Brunei, 1994.

Local visitors, Brunei.

Ah Meng, Singapore.

Live gas well flow test mishap, Philippines, 2001.

Anti-pirate devices, Nigeria.

and if you saw me at home you would cross the street to avoid me. But I could not disguise white skin; a bribe was definitely in order. I hoped they took traveller's cheques.

After dealing with him and his two mates in customs I was officially in Africa. Passing through large wooden doors I was suddenly confronted with a mass of black faces, all staring straight at me. Then just behind the front row of the crowd I saw the sign 'Mr Pauli'. Practising my line under my breath, I walked up to the fit-looking man in green coveralls who bore the sign and said in a loud confident voice, 'It's hot here, just like Australia.'

He gave me a blank look, then flashed a huge bent-toothed grin and said, 'I am de driva.'

Cocksucker, I thought, what do I do now? Leaning in, with lots of eye contact, I repeated, 'IT'S HOT HERE, JUST LIKE AUSTRALIA.'

'Oh yes sa, BUT NO HOT KANGAROOS.'

Close enough.

'I am Oscar de driva.'

'How do you do Oscar, now get me fuckin' out of here.'

'Very good Mr Pauli follow me, I have caa with aircon-dishanings.'

Oscar was only twenty-one and had already managed to father four kids. He had been working since he was eleven and looked it. His English was good, I especially liked his accent. He hoped we could talk a lot and perhaps I could help him learn to read and write. He was in the middle of asking questions about what it was like to live in a free Western democracy and sleep with white women when I became distracted by a large sign on the side of the road.

Fifty feet square in size it read, 'Welcome to Port Harcourt'. Most of the letters had long since fallen off, and the whole thing was riddled with bullet holes and covered in brown stains that suggested some strange explosion had occurred involving lots of hot coffee. Two huge black vultures perched on the top of the sign and a third was on the ground with his head buried inside what turned out to be the chest cavity of some unlucky Nigerian.

My jaw slowly dropped, as I tried to take it in. That summed up Port Harcourt perfectly.

Oscar flashed me another bent grin, palmed a pistol from under the seat and said, 'First time in Nigeria? No wahalla, you are always protected sa.'

Christ, for a second I thought he was going to point that gun at me, and I would be joining the vulture picnic, the second course in an ever-increasing pile of dead idiots. So I played it cool, only making him stop once so I could throw up.

Guns are as common a sight in Nigeria as mobile phones are in Sydney. In this respect the Nigerians put even the Americans to shame—but no wait, guns don't kill people, people kill people right? Oscar de driva always had his mobile phone and his gun on him. I thought Nokia should develop a camera/gun, or a phone/gun, or even a gun/phone/camera . . . there would be massive sales in West Africa.

Port Harcourt is a remarkably dangerous place. Once considered a jewel in the dark continent, war and corruption has destroyed it. And while 2.3 million barrels a day come from its belly, none of that is put into the most basic of human needs. All the oil service company personnel operate from bases surrounded by high walls with razor wire on top and armed guards on duty twenty-four hours. The sensible people only leave the confines of the base to go to a rig or to the accommodation, that's within another secure base. If you must go out it's best done in a large group. All the transportation between these places is done with an armed driver and a guard who usually carries an automatic weapon and 130 rounds—hope that's enough.

We drove into town, past filthy ramshackle neighbourhoods and the kind of abject poverty that puts every creature comfort you have at home clearly in perspective. I was immediately thankful that I was born on the right continent. After a few miles I asked Oscar what 'No wahalla' means. He explained—it's basically 'No problem'—and for the next six months it was 'No wahalla this', 'No wahalla that'.

When we arrived at the base, Oscar beeped the horn and the two heavy steel doors swung open. The compound was 500 square metres of concrete with three large hangars on one side and three single-storey office buildings on the other. In the centre of the compound an ancient truck was parked and two security guards were pointing their rifles at a local man who was on the ground, cowering, his arms doing a frantic explanatory pantomime, he was talking so fast it came out in one long syllable.

Oscar ignored all this and pulled up in front of the largest of the administration buildings. I jumped out and ran over to the guards. 'Stop pointing those weapons at that man.'

They turned and smiled. 'Dis man was stealing diesel boss.'

I looked at the accused man more closely; he was badly beaten, obviously suffering broken ribs, possibly haemorrhaging, going from his difficulty in breathing and the profuse amount of blood running out of his mouth. 'Who told you to do this?' I asked the guards.

The bigger one stepped forward. He had a cold look; he was enjoying his job and I wondered how many people he had killed. He pointed over my right shoulder but nothing was said.

I turned and saw the angry base supervisor marching towards us. He looked straight through me and barked at the guards in a thick German accent, 'I told you to flog him well.'

The local man started crawling away slowly, under the truck.

The heavyset German had a round head and fair complexion, which in the African heat made him look like a Bulldog that just swallowed a bee. He extended a sweaty hand. 'Hello, I'm Carl.'

'What the fuck's going on Carl?'

'Ya ya come, you don't know how we do things here yet.'

By the end of my first day in Nigeria I was disgusted to a point that made me feel ill.

After meeting all the expat crew stationed there, it was apparent that this base was a kind of Betty Ford clinic, as most of them were disgruntled middle-aged habitual alcoholics, who regularly entertained each other with a fist-fight. I celebrated Christmas and then the New Year in the company of what's best described as lobotomised monkeys. They started out well, lots of handshakes and backslapping, but quickly degenerated into the kind of malevolent lunacy I thought was only a myth in today's oilfield. Right down to throwing full cans of beer skyward and unloading 12-gauge shotguns at them. This was followed by a rousing game of hurl-fireworks-at-each-other, the indoors version of course. I did get on well with a couple of them, but on the whole the crew was burnt out; for them the prospect of working on new projects with new equipment presented all the excitement of a blocked toilet to a plumber.

Luckily I spent more time offshore working on the rig than on the base. During one spell in town, the mechanic announced his new house was finished and he wanted to show me.

'I have been building it for almost one year,' he said proudly.

It was just around the corner from the base so I said we would go and have a look at lunch time. When we got there I couldn't believe what I saw. There in amongst the rusty tin and mud bricks of a foul shanty town stood the mechanic's new house, constructed entirely of blue plastic milk crates bound together with baling wire. There were hundreds of them, with tin pop-riveted to the outside, forming the house. The whole thing stood about one foot off the ground on another series of milk crates. The floor was made of plywood from the packing crates used to ship our equipment. The toilet was a hole cut in the plywood floor in the back corner.

The mechanic's wife came out followed by a procession of children. They lined up around the outside and with some help from the neighbours demonstrated how the house could easily be picked up and moved once the crap piled up underneath the toilet. He was already accumulating more milk crates to build an extension, possibly a nice porch or gazebo. Apparently the highest cost involved was the gun his wife was brandishing, because milk crates are highly soughtafter in the Nigerian building trade.

The crew's accommodation, a simple house which seemed palatial in comparison, came with its own set of problems. Getting home was one. For example, once, I was on my way back from a job, the chopper touched down just as the sun was starting to set, its rotor wash sending up a cloud of dust that smothered the small heliport. The driver and guard were waiting for me. That was a relief because on the last occasion I sat at the heliport for two hours, waiting, too afraid to take a taxi, because shooting me would be more lucrative than driving me to town.

As we drove through Port Harcourt I was told there had been a lot of rioting that week because of the elections. It was all very tribal, the Muslim 'Felani' in the north clashing with the 'Ebu' Christians in the south. When they get really pissed off with each other they wave limbs from banana trees over their heads, and if you see them throw the limbs then it's going to the next level. That's when everyone runs home and comes straight back with a gun, or a petrol bomb, or a machete.

The car was all over the place and it became apparent once he started talking that the driver was shitfaced. He took us on a brief but exciting detour into a lane of oncoming traffic, turning sharply down an alley and into the middle of a pre-riot banana branch waving session. As soon as the crowd pinged my shiny bald white head they rushed the car.

Within minutes the driver was panicking; he stalled and flooded the engine and frantically tried to restart it. The crowd began to produce weapons and beat their fists on the windows. The Pajero rocked under the surge. I remember screaming at the guard to do something. He racked the cocking lever on the side of his AK, cranked down the window, stuck out the barrel, roughly pointing at the sky, and emptied the magazine.

Everyone shat their pants. The weapon kicked in the guard's hands, as empty brass casings spat across the inside of the car, hit the windscreen and glanced off directly into the crotch of the driver, who was still keying the ignition and pumping the throttle like the drummer of a speed-metal band.

Empty shell casings are extremely hot, and the driver was wearing shorts.

He suddenly shot up, banging his head into the roof, but at the same time he somehow held the ignition on and bunny-hopped the car straight over a man who was trying to clamber onto the hood over the crash bar. We rocked over to the right as the car went over the man; I scrambled over my offshore bag just in time to see him emerge from under the car, one big Desert Dueler tread mark running across his flat body.

The guard had changed magazines and was hanging out of the window now pointing his rifle directly at the crowd, over his trigger freeze problem; he looked like he was enjoying the whole thing. We bolted flat out back to the base, and I made the journey laying flat on my face on the car floor.

Arriving back at the staff house, I relayed my story to the crew who just shrugged their shoulders as they had all been through similar things before; it's just part of working in Nigeria.

A few days later I found myself returning to the staff house alone, everyone was on jobs, so I sat down to enjoy a quiet night in front of the TV. We had a satellite dish on the roof and could get half a dozen decent channels, the house favourite being the cartoon channel. The boys would sit and watch cartoons through the night. The fact that they did that was disturbing enough, but what I found truly remarkable was that this channel carried commercials. What could you possibly sell to someone who voluntarily watches *Deputy Dawg* at three in the morning?

On this night I tuned it to HBO Movies: *Fight Club* was just starting, I hadn't seen it and was looking forward to it. Then halfway through the movie the wall socket behind me started making more noise than usual. Our electricity was supplied by a massive generator in the backyard that had come from some rig and was far too big for the house. The lights would regularly jump from sixty watts of glow to 100 and back down to ten, and the wall sockets would crackle and spark, giving the impression that someone was being electrocuted in the basement every half hour. But I was so used to it I just ignored it. Only moments later I could smell something other than Africa. Turning, I saw the wall socket, the airconditioner, and a good deal of wallpaper on fire.

The fire extinguisher in the kitchen was empty; it had been used up during the New Year's Eve indoor fireworks display. I grabbed the small one from the car and put it out, but was worried the fire could reignite in the roof or wall space so I checked all the rooms and found one of the guys asleep. He was most upset with me; not for waking him, but for putting out the fire.

'Let's re-light it bro and we'll get a new staff house.'

I talked him out of it.

Incidentally, the same guy would go jogging every morning; he was making a brave effort to do something about all the years of smoking and drinking. One morning I was standing at the main gate to the compound when he came jogging by. I was amazed that he was outside alone; he was taking an awful risk. But when I saw the reaction of the locals I understood why he had remained unharmed for so long. They would stop what they were doing and watch him jog by, then immediately look up the road at where he had come from: Who was chasing him? Why else would a man run down the road? He must be crazy, look at his red face, stupid white man.

Local kids would always loiter outside any place the expats went, especially bars. At ten years of age, they were already professional tiny hitmen. They would single out the weakest man, usually the drunkest, and handi-vac the contents of his pockets. In Nigeria, don't turn your back on anyone, ever, even if your pockets are empty . . . think of the worst crimes, and they've done it, enjoyed it and improved on it. The security staff would kick the kids and chase them away. I found the best system was to throw a handful of change in the opposite direction of where you were going.

I was to discover later that adult thieves are dealt with more vigorously. The crew and I were in a mini-bus, driving across town on our way back from a job, when the driver asked if we'd like to see the public hanging at 2 p.m. It was 1.55 p.m. and we were a block away from the police station, how convenient. Outvoted, I found myself sitting in the bus watching three shirtless, handcuffed men standing behind roughly constructed gallows—I was kind of surprised it wasn't made of milk crates. Two police officers stood to the side, one wearing pyjama pants and a combat jacket, the other in combat pants and a pyjama top. The first two men died quickly, the rope snapping their heads back, breaking their necks instantly. The third man was at least 300 pounds and built like an ox; his neck did not break. We watched him thrashing about on the end of the rope and started yelling at the two cops to do something. They looked at each other and in a well-rehearsed manoeuvre laid down their guns, grabbed a leg each and pulled down, throttling the man to death.

But for all the public executions and floggings designed to create fear of authority, violent crime is an everyday part of life in Nigeria, the most corrupt country in the world. If there was something nice to say about the place, believe me I would say it.

The most outstanding event during my time there was to give me nightmares for months.

Late one night I woke to the sound of screaming, coming from the TV room. I thought I was alone in the house but when I went to investigate I discovered one of our crew standing butt naked and holding a chair out in front of him rather like a lion tamer does. In front of him stood a Nigerian woman, obviously a prostitute, fully dressed and wearing a platinum-blonde wig. She was waving a knife and trying to rob him, having waited until he was naked before making her move. My appearance only made her more determined; now she wanted my money too.

'Pauli, help me man, this fuckin' bitch is mad.'

I turned on my heel and ran out the back, around the house to the front gate, where my highly trained, super-alert security guard was on duty, fast asleep against the wall. I woke him gently, tapping his shoulder and keeping my voice even and soft, not wanting to startle him in case he shot me. He looked up at my smiling face.

'Hi Daniel, would you like a nice cup of tea?' He knew I had done that for the other security guys as they were not allowed in the house.

'Oh yes please sa.'

'WELL TOUGH FUCKIN' SHIT . . . BIG WAHALLA IN THE HOUSE, YOU GET HER OUT NOW.'

Up he jumped. I followed him through the front door; blondie had our naked lion tamer cornered now. She was big, much bigger than me—imagine Mike Tyson in drag. As soon as she saw the guard, she dropped the knife and started babbling at him, but he didn't break his stride. He just stepped up and with his whole upper body swung the butt of his rifle into her jaw.

Both her feet left the ground, she slammed down hard on the tiled floor, her wig flew off followed by a long arc of blood. I knew he had killed her, but my legs were frozen to the floor. We watched him drag her out, feet first, through the front door. A few moments later he drove off with her body in the back of the truck. The room boy casually walked in and started mopping up the blood.

I should have left Africa right then, but I had one more job to do.

Two weeks later everything was going just fine until all the roughnecks and rouseabouts, and everyone who wasn't white, walked off and came back five minutes later with weapons. Mutiny is the best way to put it.

There were sixteen expats on the rig at the time, the other eighty personnel didn't want to do any more work until they got more money. All the offshore workers are supplied by a government body called 'The Labour Mass' and they had decided to strike, with weapons, in an effort to force more money out of the oil companies. There were five rigs involved in this, the Labour Mass just picked a day and time, gave the men enough notice to smuggle weapons out to the rig and stash them, and on a predetermined day they made their move. They had control of the rig, ballast control, the radio room, well control, everything. They boomed the cranes over the heli-deck so choppers couldn't land or resupply the rig.

This went on for the next three weeks, one enraged man after another speaking on the radio, occasionally breaking for a barbecue and an impromptu chanting session on the heli-deck. The news networks were saying all kinds of outlandish crap, like herds of rig personnel were being locked into freight containers and dangled over the sea, sometimes even dunked into the sea so everyone inside was waist-deep in water and in total darkness. No-one was hurt, we just watched TV a lot. Eventually we ran out of food . . . that sped up negotiations.

Finally the US navy got involved. As soon as the words 'SEAL' and 'take the rig back by force' were mentioned, the mutineers dropped their weapons, saying, 'Okay we give up . . . can we keep our jobs?'

I got back to Port Harcourt and quit, jumping on the first flight home, never to return.

11 GOBBING, 2002

I was back at Louise's agency two weeks later; she had me working on a campaign for hair products for young women.

'But I'm a thirty-five-year-old bald man . . . I don't know anything about hair . . . it's been ten years since I last used shampoo!'

'That's why it's your project Pauli,' Louise said, and as luck would have it we aced it.

She helped me get organised and I enrolled in some courses in advertising at the University of Technology Sydney and I studied hard for the next five months. For the first time I had a sense of choice: I could do something with my life other than oil. I liked the study, I enjoyed the classes and exercises. I was happy to learn but not to compromise my lifestyle and inevitably I ran out of money. So I soon found myself in China.

The last part of the journey to China was the best. I got on the wrong ferry at Hong Kong International Airport: you're supposed to arrive at the airport and go straight to a ferry which will take you to any one of twenty ports in mainland China where you get off the boat and finally get processed through immigration. Provided of course you get on the right boat to start with. What can I say, it's a rabbit warren in Hong Kong, so I ended up in a remote port.

I was already destined for an isolated province, but I arrived at a *really* isolated province. Even the immigration guy looked surprised. There were no phones, no taxis, or buildings, or other Westerners. And it was getting dark, although that's never bothered me. Darkness is your friend in dodgy remote Chinese ports where a tall bald white man in a Mambo T-shirt tends to stick out like chairman Mao at the MTV music awards.

So I had to fly via a local domestic carrier to the right town—not good.

China's answer to the global terrorist threat on airliners is simple. First they search you, then they search you again, then they give you the proper search, then in case they missed something during the proper search, they search you again, that's the search when they squeeze out your toothpaste, saw the heels off your shoes and X-ray your underpants.

Coupled with all the searching, you're bombarded with a kind of video-movie of what would happen if some terrorists decided to hijack a plane. Like a tribute to 'the golden years of terrorism', it features a man in black coveralls and a black ski mask in the middle of an aircraft fuselage who is brandishing an automatic weapon then gets shot a couple of hundred times by a small group of other men in black coveralls and black ski masks . . . which begs the question, did the right guy in black get shot here? Perhaps some sort of name tag is in order, or even a good pair of Kevlar comedy breasts.

So there I was on the plane, waiting for the all-singing, all-dancing black coverall-wearing ski mask appreciation society gala performance. Instead I ended up in an aisle seat next to an elderly Chinese gentleman, who must have been ninety and looked like he had built the whole wall himself. He had no teeth, which proved to be a bit of a problem when the in-flight mini-gruel was served. I did feel sorry for him because he had to deal with the joy of scoring my meal, combined with his meal, but he shook so much he dropped half his food in my lap. I would have been better off just up-ending my tray in my own lap and calling it a day.

After dinner I tried not to think about the boiled-gruel stains on my pants and my new friend decided to spit on the floor every five minutes, then he had to go to the toilet every ten minutes for the rest of the flight. Either the old man hadn't had a meal in a few days or he had a prostrate the size of a nuclear submarine.

The town is called Shekou and feels palpably weird, like I wouldn't be altogether surprised to pull into a local bar and find my drink being poured by a Cyclops. And there's a real problem with counterfeit money, so every time I got change I scrutinised my bills like a diamond merchant.

I soon became quite used to people staring at me. Westerners are rarely seen in this part of China so it's expected that locals will have a good look. I should have been happy, all things considered: I wasn't getting shot at, not everyone in this country was carrying a machete, they don't hate white people and you can eat the food without that niggling feeling that there's a human hand in the stew.

The only thing I couldn't get used to in China was the gobbing. Everyone, and I mean everyone, hacks up a big ball of phlegm and spits it out on the street, every five minutes. Women, children, babies, monks, doddery old people who look like the next big gob could kill them—everyone has a good gob, all the time.

Perhaps the answer to China's economic problems lies not in oil and gas exploration, but in utilising its other natural resource: spit. It's a lot cheaper to find than hydrocarbons, all you have to do is set up millions of giant spittoons and find a way to convert the spit into some sort of industrial lubricant. They could spend the money on driving lessons for everyone, because when the locals aren't gobbing all over the place they are driving around like Stevie Wonder. (In China I came frighteningly close to getting flattened by anything from kids on rollerskates to rickshaws and semitrailers, but that's possibly because I was too busy trying not to step in all the gobs.)

My boss was a big gobber too . . . I think in his youth he gobbed for China. No problem, mid conversation . . . Whap! Right there on the floor, watch your step. Even the Chinese President has a sly gob in parliament; I saw him do it on local TV one night, God love him.

I try to enjoy local traditions and customs wherever I go in the world, so I decided to perfect my own gobbing technique and really impress the guys at the next drilling meeting.

Food is always another wonderful experience in a new country. China is crowded, all knees and elbows and gobbing, but apart from that the food is pretty good. Compared to Nigeria, it's the Ritz Carlton.

One morning's drilling meeting was especially fun. On this particular day, I met the tool pusher and driller who would be working with me offshore. They are with a Houston-based company and were on their first venture in this part of the world, real genuine redneck Gawd-damn American good-ol'-boys, with giant belt buckles and their bottom lips packed with two pounds of chewing tobacco. Coincidentally, these Texan boys enjoy a good gob too.

Watching their first meeting with the Chinese roughnecks was a treat; it could have been a MasterCard ad . . . 'Price of one round-trip ticket to China, . . . $3000. Price of enough beer and cheeseburgers to keep you fat-n-stupid while in China, $5000. Finding out your entire Chinese drill crew also enjoy a good gob with absolutely no social graces . . . Priceless'.

Really good drilling people are allowed to be surly and indifferent about personal hygiene. But these guys were shocking.

We went out for breakfast after the morning meeting broke up. Redneck 1 says: 'I wanna eat what you boys eat.'

The Chinese guys exchanged blank looks and then all looked at me. I've seen this happen before, in other parts of the world, when expat oil workers try to experience the local culture with the best of intentions. I've ended up sitting down to eat in a backstreet dump with rats running along the rafters; I had to step over a goat to get to the toilet which was just a hole in the ground anyway. I shrugged at the Chinese guys and they shrugged back at me, but the rednecks insisted so off we went to a local food stall.

Redneck 2 takes one look at his traditional Chinese breakfast and says, 'Jesus Christ, I'm not eating this shit.'

Redneck 1 meanwhile has pulled off his genuine imitation crocodile Tony Lama cowboy boot and sock to investigate the galloping jungle foot rot that appeared to be eating his right foot off, displaying his exemplary table manners . . . and then the gobbing started.

To the Chinese, the Texans must have looked like something from a *National Geographic* special: Two huge hairy white men, with chrome hubcaps holding up their pants, and the blackest gobs they'd ever seen. Their street cred went up instantly. If I had a flip-top head and managed to hack up an entire lung, I could not have topped those guys.

For the rest of that day we had a good look around the rig before it got towed out to location. While the rig had been in a dry dock getting painted and fitted out with a new drilling package, a stray dog came on board. I made friends with him and named him Colin; he liked me a lot and followed me everywhere, probably because Colin knew I was not likely to eat him. Besides I was nice to him and gave him lots of human food and for a dog in China that's a rare treat. I also made sure after seeing a couple of the boys eyeballing him that under no circumstances were they to eat Colin. I had the welder make Colin a little house that we put on the drill floor right next to the control station that the driller stands in, coincidentally called a 'dog house'. Colin was the only one allowed to shit in his.

Colin was a Chow, an interesting Chinese breed that looks a bit like a Pomeranian on steroids; powerful, but in a short compressed way. He was very dirty at first, covered in oil and all kinds of crap, but after a good wash with the steam cleaner and a proper blow dry with the high pressure air line, he came out clean, with really big reddish-blond hair. He looked like an Asian David Lee Roth, except he really could lick his own balls.

Colin became the rig mascot and soon was embarking (no pun intended) on a cruise out to a quiet part of the South China Sea, hundreds of nautical miles from any major shipping lanes, where he was going to listen to his Van Halen CDs, drink out of the toilet, hump the furniture and not get eaten by the welder.

While I was hanging around Shekou I met Cameron, an aircraft engineer. Cameron was funny, in a slap-happy trigger-finger kind of way. A big heavyset character, ex-US Ranger, he was majorly into motorcycles and having sex with women he hardly knew. Every time I was in town I called Cameron and the games would begin.

Sitting in a downtown bar one night he told me about a mad driller who had been there only a month before. 'That Kiwi bastard belted the biggest guy in the room, kicked off the worst bar brawl in Shekou's history.'

'What started it?' I asked.

'Oh man, I think someone called the All Blacks a bunch of pussies and Maurice went bananas.'

'Did you say Maurice?'

'Yeah . . . a drilling guy, five ten, grey hair, maniac, from somewhere in the south . . . he's got these dogs man . . .'

I explained that Maurice and I were good mates and Cameron rocked back laughing. According to Cameron, the incident occurred in a biker bar and all Cameron's mates got into it with the giant Maurice punched out, who was the boss of a rival bikie chapter. It escalated from there to war. Cameron was thrown through a thin wooden wall into the bar next door. That started another fight, as people from both bars flooded through the hole, over the top of Cameron. The whole block erupted. Local Chinese police, too scared to come near the place, left them alone to murder each other. Maurice somehow got away. 'Next time you see that bastard, tell him the whole bar was destroyed.'

We had a good laugh, then Cameron suggested we go for a spin around town on his old Ural bike. The Ural is a Russian-made flat-twin thumper with a sidecar. Cameron took off with me in the sidecar, and we tooled around Shekou's dark streets.

After a while we bumped into Dave, a mate of Cameron's. Dave was also drunk and decided to join us—he was so big he only just fitted into the sidecar—so I rode pillion. We had just taken off when we bumped into another of Cameron's drunk mates, John, who was in a wheelchair.

'There's no room ol' buddy,' Cameron said.

But John just grabbed onto the sidecar and we took off again.

Rounding a corner into the main drag through town, we passed a police car going the other way. He hit the siren and U-turned at some traffic lights. Cameron stopped but John was demanding we keep going.

'The chair can take it man.'

As soon as John let go of the bike, Cameron bolted, leaving an angry John curbside.

'We're in a police chase now . . . and my visa expired a week ago,' I yelled at him.

'It's okay Pauli, we do this all the time . . . The cops here can't drive for shit.'

He took the corners so fast that Dave's bulk was raised off the road. Finally we darted down a tiny alley that was barely wide enough for us to fit, the police car stopped, unable to continue. Cameron dropped me off outside my hotel. I sat on the front step and had a smoke. As I was butting it out, Cameron and Dave shot past on the Ural being chased by another police car.

12 RIG UP, RIG DOWN, 2002

I had finished all my advertising courses while at home in Sydney, passing some well and others by the skin of my teeth. The day I received my final results there was an agency party for one of their larger clients that I attended. Happy in the knowledge that I didn't have to spend any more evenings at lectures or studying, I was in a great mood, but everyone at the function was even happier than me. Strangers were hugging me and talking the kind of bullshit that makes you want to move deepest rural Australia and build a mudbrick house. After a few hours I excused myself, later realising that I was probably the only person at the party who was not on drugs.

In some respects the advertising world is just as bizarre as the oilfield, but there was no time to find out if I was right about the party. The phone rang very early: there was a job in Japan, starting immediately. I jumped at the opportunity to go, as Japan is safe, clean and mostly bullshit-free. I had been to Tokyo briefly a few years earlier, and the people were as polite and as efficient as you would expect.

I had a two-day layover in Singapore then departed for Osaka, Japan, on a stormy Friday night. The job was twofold. First I had to go to a factory where some pipe was being fabricated, then to a rig up in the Japanese mountains. Osaka was much the same as Tokyo. They have the cleanest taxis in the world and the drivers wear smart uniforms with black hats and white gloves. They pull a lever to open and close the door for you.

There was a representative of the pipe company waiting for me at the airport. He chatted politely all the way to the hotel, organised everything, even what I wanted for breakfast the next day. I'm not used to that treatment; usually, once you walk out of the workshop in Singapore, you're on your own. His name was Shouji, but I called him 'Turbo San' as everything the man did was at top speed. He would run to accomplish a task with the kind of urgency that left you wondering if he would get severely beaten or have a finger cut off if he was too slow. He had a complete itinerary that included, much to my amazement, cigarette breaks. He was so organised that I went to bed exhausted . . . and a little freaked out at having so much unexpected attention. I half expected him to spring from the wardrobe and tuck me in.

The next morning my breakfast arrived just how I like it. Turbo San was waiting in the lobby with another man who looked a bit like Eddie Munster with a bowl haircut. Turbo introduced us, Eddie was quiet, staying in the background, never joining the conversation. He wore a basic black suit, with a tie that looked like it had been made from my grandmother's curtains. I stopped giving him shit not too long after meeting him as I discovered that Eddie was a 'kendo' champion and could kill me with his big toe.

I asked if we could take the subway to the factory—a bizarre experience. Nothing in the station is in English and every level is a carbon copy of the last. We went down crystal-clean corridors past tiny neon caves where Japanese hawkers sold tiny perfect meals to tiny perfect clones. Everyone is basically dressed the same, though occasionally, however, you see the odd punk, straight from a Sid Vicious production line, complete with 'Never mind the bollocks' T-shirt and safety pin through the nose.

As we waited for our train, Eddie walked over to a huge bank of vending machines and got himself a paper. I noticed one of the machines was getting more attention than the others. So I had a look. The other vending machines sold every kind of drink, snack, cigarette or consumable imaginable, but this one sold something only the Japanese would want. The machine itself was cool; very retro with big chrome knobs and dials. It had a large glass window which displayed Polaroid photographs of schoolgirls in pig tails, with their name and age underneath.

When fed money the machine spat out a 'soiled' pair of knickers with bunny rabbits printed on them in a zip-lock clear bag, with a dirty letter to you from said child, complete with a lipstick kiss at the bottom. Turbo looked embarrassed, and laughed out loud as the Japanese do when embarrassed.

'Pretty girls,' he said, beaming.

We left the porno Wurlitzer and got on the train, which was so clean it was like riding in a long thin hospital. It stopped, lining up perfectly with markings on the platform floor. Everyone got off without any of the shoving and pickpocketing I was used to.

After our 'immensely serious' working day had ended, at five o'clock exactly, the senior man in the room and director of the pipe company stood up and announced to a packed boardroom that we would meet in an hour for drinks and dinner. Everyone then bowed to each other in a polite headbanging session for half an hour.

For the Japanese, work and play is like flipping a big switch. We had only been in the bar for ten minutes when the director jumped up onto a coffee table and with microphone in hand belted out a Sinatra number, much to the delight of everyone.

I was asked what I would like to drink; given this crowd's expense account, I requested my favourite single malt and was assigned a small woman who had a whole bottle of thirty-year-old Macallan. She didn't speak, just poured and went for ice. Ten minutes later I was on the coffee table, with my seat cushion up my shirt, doing my best bloated near-death Elvis version of 'My Way', complete with the belching and sweating. They clapped like lottery winners; Turbo hugged me with arms as broad as the *Enola Gay*.

We all got ratted and then went for dinner. I had Kobe beef, easily the best steak I've ever tasted. When I heard how much it cost I asked if they got a free TV set with that. The cattle which provide the heavenly steak are called Wagyu and come from Kobe just down the road. They are raised on a diet of grain and beer, and they get massaged daily. It's hard to imagine such a profitable commodity based on a grain-munching, beer-swilling animal, unless you've had experience with large multinational oil companies.

The next morning I took the Bullet train to Tokyo and spent the day drooling in as many custom-motorcycle shops as I could visit, then continued up to the town of Nagaoka, 260 kilometres north, which was near the rig. Supersonic concrete gave way to a blur of beech trees through my squeaky-clean train window, as we left the high-rise metropolis which sprawled along the south coast.

Nagaoka was a world away from the industrial epicentre I left behind. It resides in quiet tradition that's guarded closely. Its rolling green hills open up to snow-capped mountains. The town is split in two by the Shinano River that flows from the nearby Higashiyama mountain range. A vast patchwork of rice terraces were peppered with stooped old farmers, who would always smile happily, unfazed by an inquisitive *gaijin*, or 'outside person', wandering about in the middle of nowhere.

Nagaoka is the birthplace of Admiral Isoroku Yamamoto, the Harvard-educated naval strategist who planned the Pearl Harbor attack. Apparently he never wanted to go to war with the US. By intercepting and decoding a secret Japanese transmission containing Yamamoto's itinerary, the Americans were able to shoot down his transport aircraft over the South Pacific in 1943, two years after Pearl Harbor. It was the first time the US succeeded in eliminating a major enemy leader by direct attack.

The rig was a thirty-minute drive from Nagaoka, at the foot of a majestic valley. It looked like a wart on the face of a centrefold, but it was the most organised land rig I've ever seen. Everything was done just so, and the crew started their shifts in company colour-coordinated starched tracksuits doing sit-ups and exercising in perfect unison. They have a work ethic that puts the rest of us to shame. The job went perfectly, they even cleaned our equipment for us when we rigged down.

I had two more days of exploring in Nagaoka before my train departed for Tokyo and home. On my last morning there was an earthquake, another one, I'm just lucky I guess. We were standing outside the train station eating rice cakes when everything started shaking. People exploded out of the station like shrapnel from a grenade. Like Californians, the Japanese are used to earth tremors except that they can run in terror and still make it look civilised, you know, without the looting and trampling of children. Nagaoka's 200 000-strong population lost thirty-one that day with 3400 injured. It was a 6.8 quake, the deadliest since the 1995 quake in Kobe, when all those expensive overweight drunk Wagyu cattle must have made a mess. I went home to quake-free Sydney for a week of cheap steak and looting.

That week in Sydney passed so fast that when I got back to Singapore I thought I'd dreamt the trip home. Sometimes I move around so much I wake up in a hotel somewhere and it takes a few moments to remember where the hell I am. I've caught myself about to pee in the closet more than once in a dark hotel room.

13 LEGLESS IN RUSSIA, 2003

Singapore is where most oil service companies base their Asian operations. There is a massive industrial complex on the island's south-east coast called 'Loyang Offshore Supply Base'. It's from there that everything starts. I had been freelancing on a day-rate basis for the last four years, so wherever I went in the world, it began and ended in Loyang.

Singapore itself is basically one giant island shopping mall; all the crews who constantly pass through the place tend to congregate in the same places. Namely Orchard Towers, a four-storey building downtown that houses seedy bars from top to basement, affectionately called 'Four Floors of Whores', with some of the most unimaginative names in public house history such as 'The Bar', 'The Pub', 'The Beer House', and full of drunk rig hands and Filipino prostitutes looking for a meal ticket.

The word from Loyang was that there was enough work kicking off in Russia to keep me going for two years. The first job was on a mono-hull rig offshore for Shell, and later BP were planning on drilling a wildcat well, or exploration well, in the same region probably with a semi-submersible rig. All this drilling was to take place off the coast of Sakhalin, an island peninsula running some 300 kilometres up Russia's north-eastern seaboard and ending in the Sea of Okhotsk. Sakhalin is predominantly a flat tundra with only a few hills dotting an otherwise harsh landscape, and winter temperatures that plummeted to minus 60.

We would be flying via Seoul, Korea, to Yuzhno, the biggest town on Sakhalin and located on the southernmost point of the peninsula. From there we would take a train all the way to the top and a town called Nogliki where a camp was in the final stages of construction. Choppers would ferry men to the rig from there, especially in winter when the sea froze fifteen feet thick around the rig.

Hearing about all this in an airconditioned office in Singapore was surreal, as usual, I had no idea what I was in for. I went through the normal preparation for a new location but I couldn't imagine what minus 60 would feel like. The rest of my crew arrived in Singapore over the next few days; only one had been to Russia before and he said in winter you could go outside with a hot cup of tea, throw the tea up in the air and it would land frozen solid on the ground.

It's a constant battle trying to get your gear and logistics sorted out, always the cheapest option. Unfortunately most of this is organised through a management system run by personnel who either have never worked in the field or haven't been offshore in twenty years. But they regularly stand around crowded oilfield bars telling stories about the time they put out the fire, drilled the well with one hand tied behind their back, got the chopper just in time, and fucked Playmate of the Month in the back seat of the car on the way home.

A few days later we were on a plane and picturing attractive buxom Russian girls mincing about in the snow in furry bikinis. Collective daydreaming shut down when we boarded the Soviet-made airliner in Korea. Next stop Mother Russia.

The flight attendant looked like the offspring of Boris Yeltsin and Eva Braun, and the seats had not been reupholstered since the mid-1970s. The whole aircraft looked like Ken Done had thrown up all over it. Instead of having individual seat pockets containing the emergency card, sick bag and in-flight magazine, there was just one great big photocopy of the emergency card nailed to the wall next to the toilet. Someone had written something in ballpoint pen under the picture of a man demonstrating the crash position: 'In the event of an emergency landing do not attempt to suck your own penis.'

After a while the captain crackled to life over the PA system. He sounded British and was definitely in a bad mood. 'Yeah this is the captain. I'm up here on the flight deck with first officer . . .' SNAP . . . SNAP . . . We could hear him clicking his fingers at the co-pilot, who fired off his surname loud enough for everyone to hear. 'Right . . . We've levelled off at our cruising altitude of . . . SNAP . . . thirty-odd thousand feet and ah . . . if you look out the window on the right side of the aircraft, you'll see a big wing.'

Nice one, I thought.

Yuzhno is rough. There were thirty-seven murders, not to mention eight bear attacks, in the month when we arrived. It has the highest crime rate in the entire Russian federation. It helps to be an alcoholic just to live there. Our contact was nice, but he looked like he was on the local wife-beating team. Eighty years of communism doesn't just disappear and in this part of Russia you could be forgiven for assuming Perestroika had just happened.

Getting processed into Russia is quite an ordeal; there's a lot of queuing with people who look like they're auditioning for *Schindler's List*, as well as some very novel baggage-handling techniques. We waited two hours for our bags to travel fifty metres on a trolley being pulled by a tractor that looked like it had just finished ploughing a field. Then the bags, smeared in mud and cow shit, were hurled through a hole in the wall. It was like going back forty years, with bad fashion and lots of vodka.

We piled into a big 4WD and drove to our agent's office where he gave us border passes and train tickets. The train was like something out of an old war movie, with wooden carriages, lots of smoke and billowing steam. The journey up to Nogliki was going to take sixteen hours; we had fairly nice compartments with a heater and comfy beds. I shared my compartment with an American driller named Bobby; it was his first time in Russia too, and so far he was loving it.

Just as we pulled out of the station a guard came into our compartment. He was wearing a big furry coat, a huge hat with ten pounds of brass macaroni on the brim and a shiny AK-47 rifle. It doesn't matter where you go in the world, the two things you're guaranteed to see are Coca Cola and the AK-47. The guard explained that the whole train belonged to the company we were working for, and we were not to leave this carriage under any circumstances. We even had to sign a form to this effect, and on departing he turned and said, 'No vodka da'. We both grinned and nodded.

Two hours later Bobby was getting bored. The window was steamed over with condensation, and I had my nose buried in a book, so he got up and announced he was off to find some Russian dudes to talk to.

'You can't go into any other carriages Bobby.'

'Fuck all that. C'mon.'

We carefully opened the sliding door and stepped into the long narrow corridor. The motion of the train rocked us to and fro and every now and again we had to hold on tight to stay on our feet. Bobby opened the outer door of the carriage; the wind slammed it back against the wall. Ice covered the hand rails and the wind bit into my face. We were standing on a small grated platform, the frozen track whistling past below us.

'Jesus, Bobby, fuck this,' I said. We had to jump over the train's carriage coupling in order to get to the other carriage.

'Come on man, it's just like a Western' and with that he was over, on the opposite grating, thumbing at the door lock.

I jumped over and huddled next to the door, the cold was starting to freeze me. Bobby got the door open and we stepped inside the carriage. I slammed the door shut and turned around to see about twenty Russians, all motionless, mid-conversation, staring at us. Everyone was smoking; the air was thick with the stench of foul Russian cigarettes, BO and vodka.

Bobby raised a hand and beamed. 'Hey fellas.'

'Just like a Western mate,' I said and elbowed him in the ribs. All I could hear was the track's rhythm and the awkward silence. My brain was frantically searching for the Russian 'Hello' but I was blank.

Someone yelled out from the back of the carriage, but the smoke was so thick you could not see that far. We could hear a weird squeaking sound near the floor coming closer. Then out of the blue smoke a man on a small wooden trolley emerged; he had lost his legs well above the knee, and was propelling himself along with his gloved hands. The trolley looked homemade, using furniture castors. There was a huge bottle of vodka wedged in the man's crotch between his stumps, and a small silver cup dangled from a chain around his neck.

He pulled up at Bobby's feet, pointed at the two of us, yelled some more abuse and punched hard up into Bobby's crotch.

There was that weird two-second pause which happens when something hits your balls. Bobby's hands shot down grabbing at his crotch, he spun around, his face distended as if about to sneeze and then the pain hit him. It was like watching a big tree fall over. The legless Russian bobbed up and down on his trolley with excitement. Two men next to me burst to life, so I backed up, fumbling to open the door, but they grabbed the legless man, barked at two guys near the window, who opened it, and threw him out of the train . . . trolley, vodka, the lot.

'Fuckin' hell, Bobby, get up, get up.' I was back at the door, my right leg vibrating at the knee with adrenalin: it's a condition called St Vitus's Dance, and I get it when there's going to be a fight, or if I have to speak publicly.

To my surprise the two Russians helped Bobby to get up and walked over to me, showing the palms of their hands as if demonstrating there was no threat. Then the train stopped suddenly and the guard from earlier came storming in. It appeared everyone on the train was blind drunk, except us. The guard yelled at everyone in high-speed Russian, but after a few minutes he put on his big furry coat and went outside with two others to retrieve the legless man. The Russians told us that this happened every time there's a crew change: Trolley Man makes a prick of himself . . . and they throw him out the window.

The train's path through the flat landscape is on raised tracks, and it never goes faster than about twenty kilometres per hour. In winter the snow drifts on either side are deep enough to cushion Trolley Man's plunge. He just sits in the snow drift freezing his stumps off while the boys stop the train and carry him back inside. He spends the next few days building a new trolley; he even steals the little wheels off the furniture from rigs in preparation for another window exit.

I thought it a bit much, treating Trolley Man like a crash-test dummy. But the Russians explained, 'He was in war in Chechnya, many here from war . . . he likes go out window.'

Apparently, almost the whole crew had come from the Ministry of War. Trolley Man had stepped on a mine, and the government had rewarded him with a new job as a radio operator on the rig.

Bobby and I sat in the Russian crew's carriage and drank vodka. They had to make the journey on wooden benches and we felt quite ashamed to have our own private cabin with heating and beds. But that's the way it is, the Russians didn't care, most of them lived in tiny one-bedroom flats without hot water or a phone. For them a rig is virtual luxury, with hot showers, good food, they don't have to worry about getting their brains blown out for Russia and it's all free. They are hard men, good workers, I even took a shine to Trolley Man—he may have been an abusive violent alcoholic, but any double amputee who enjoys taking a dive out of the window of a moving train is okay in my book.

By the time the train pulled into Nogliki Station, Bobby and I had sobered up but had massive hangovers. An army truck was our transport to the camp, which was basically just a series of port-a-cabins all joined up, with a high fence surrounding them and twenty-four-hour guards patrolling the perimeter. I think the security was more to keep us in than anything else.

My cabin was comfortable, I shared it with Peter: he had been with the company for a long time, and he has pissed more blood, drunk more beer and fucked more bimbos than anyone, and, oh yes, he's never been sick at sea. (A week later we were on a six-hour crewboat ride to the rig and Peter spent the whole trip on all fours vomiting.) Peter's a real character and always has a story that leaves you feeling like you just got all the enamel peeled off your teeth. But he's good at the job and I never had a problem with him.

We were on board the rig for a month, the job went well and my crew change came around. After a month offshore you're really looking forward to going home. I had done back-to-back jobs, so all I could think about was getting home to Sydney.

I spent a day back at the camp, waiting for the train. The sixteen-hour trip was a quiet one as there were no Russians this time. The camp had given me a packed lunch and a bottle of water, so after a few hours I decided to eat. The first bite was the last—as pain shot up my jaw. I spat out the contents of my mouth on the floor and jumped up to look at my teeth in the mirror. One of my back teeth had an abscess, I thought, it really hurt. By the time the train arrived in Yuzhno thirteen hours later, I looked like I'd jammed a cricket ball in my mouth and the pain was excruciating.

My agent was waiting there to drive me to the hotel because my flight to Korea didn't depart until the following afternoon. Running up to him, I saw his expression change. He asked if I'd been fighting.

'Get me to a dentist . . . dentist . . . dentista . . . tooth doctor, understand?' But he looked confused. 'It's my fuckin' teeth man.'

He nodded finally, pointing at his front teeth, 'Da, da, dentist.' He smiled, put a hand on my shoulder and announced, 'Today is Russian public holiday.'

'Oh fuck off . . . I need drugs then . . . pharmacy . . . pharmacy . . . chemist . . . drugs.' I couldn't see straight I was in so much pain.

'Okay we go.'

He took me to the local hospital then he did some fast talking to the girl at the counter, who looked over her shoulder at me. I was sitting on the floor, twitching.

Then the dentist appeared in front of me. I couldn't believe it. Russia's supposed to have good dentists. His white coat had blood splattered all the way up his right lapel and there were Cyrillic tattoos on his knuckles. This is bullshit, I thought, as he walked me into a barren room. I took one look at the selection of tools decorating a small table and walked out.

My agent then took me to a chemist, and I immediately started munching on painkillers until I passed out. I woke up in the hotel the next day, and just for a second I thought I was okay, but it was a fleeting second—oh this is bullshit! The phone rang; the agent had managed to book me on the early morning flight to Korea.

I had a brief, painful layover in Seoul where I threw down more painkillers. I checked the bottle, the Russian chemist had written in English on the label 'Only four a day'—fuck, I'd had double that already, but at least the pain was starting to ease off. I couldn't stand the thought of an eight-hour flight to Singapore, but it was the fastest way to get to a dentist that would do an extraction without using a chisel.

The pills began to really kick in as I was boarding the plane. I was fast approaching a vegetative state, but I stayed just conscious enough to make it to my seat. The elderly Russian man sitting next to me thought I was handicapped and I discovered that I'd been drooling all over myself. He offered to help me get to the toilet; unable to talk I shot him a filthy look but it must have seemed more like a cry for help because he called the flight attendant and told her that I was a handicapped gentleman who needed some assistance. I was just trying to focus on my seatbelt, when the attendant came.

She was your typical Singapore Airlines girl, very pretty, very small, so off she went to get help. Two more small pretty girls showed up and they talked about how come they didn't know there was a handicapped man on the flight who had special needs. All I could do was grunt; I was so trashed, my head was so swollen, everything just came out in one big syllable.

'Iim-nut-handicapped-is-my-tooof.'

She smiled. 'Yes, okay, Mr Carter, this way.'

I could barely walk, and I practically fell into the toilet cubicle. I tried to smile, she smiled back and slammed the door shut. I looked at myself in the mirror. A long string of drool was making its way down my shirt, my head looked disfigured . . . freaky. 'Wow you look really bad,' I told myself. 'I think you have an abscessed tooth, you can die from an abscessed tooth.' And that was really funny, so I sat there and had a good laugh, then attempted to urinate.

Once I'd lined myself up with the bowl, I let fly, but the aircraft hit some turbulence and I pretty much just peed all over the place. That was really funny too, and I laughed out loud, because there wasn't any turbulence at all, I was just fucked. I have never experimented with drugs, other than grass and that was ten years ago. Not because I didn't want to but because we are randomly drug-tested at work. This was different from any drunken state I had ever been in, I was lucid but totally spazzed out when it came to hand–eye coordination or talking. At least there was no pain; I'll take hallucinations and peeing on myself over that pain anytime.

As happy as I was to amuse myself in the toilet all day, the flight attendant came back.

'Mr Carter, everything alright sir?'

I tried to open the door and talk, but it just wasn't going to happen. This is when I discovered flight attendants can open the toilet door from the outside. She looked at me with a mixture of pity and contempt.

'I-doynt-evn-like-taaaking-aspeerin,' I said.

She explained that I had been in there for more than an hour, and I should go with her now to a special seat. I wanted to tell her I was not handicapped, and that I reserve the right to pee on myself for special occasions only. But she was talking to me like I was a child.

'Thish-is-sush-bullshit,' I said.

She sat me down at the back, I had a whole row to myself. Then she appeared next to me with my painkillers in her hand; I must have dropped them. She asked if I needed to take one.

'Nooooo-ooo,' I said and so she gave me my mini-meal. Embarrassed enough, I shifted over to the window seat and tried to negotiate the mini-food onto the mini-fork and eventually into my mouth. I had not eaten since I left the camp, and that was two days ago. It's okay, I thought, I'll just chew on the left side, but getting the fork lined up with my mouth was more difficult than I had expected. I was dangerously close to taking out my eye. Finally, the angle looked right, and I jabbed the fork directly into my abscessed tooth.

'AAAAAAAAH!'

So then I used my fingers instead . . .

The flight attendant appeared next to me again. She tried not to frown at the grown man who just pissed all over the plane and was now playing with his food. She asked again if I needed a pill.

Our descent into Singapore airspace was like having my toenails pulled out with a pair of pliers, and I was in tears by the time we got to the gate. The pills had worn off in lieu of being handicapped; I had regained the power of speech and explained what had happened to the cabin crew, who kindly let me get off first and arranged for my bags to go first as well.

Every step from the airport to the dentist hurt. Our workshop manager, Joe, is an ex-offshore man and thoroughly reliable and he had arranged everything for me. A car was waiting and I went straight to an excellent dentist.

The dentist looked excited to see me. He took X-rays, rubbed his chin a lot while he studied them, then looked at the pills I had taken. 'How many did you take?'

'Eight, I think.'

'Eight! Mr Carter that was extremely dangerous.'

The dentist then explained that I had two options: I could book in for surgery, which he recommended or he could do the extraction now, however, there was a chance I would lose the sense of touch in my lower lip permanently.

'Just fuckin' take it out now.'

Twenty minutes later the tooth was out, I had a mouth full of stitches, more pills, and a quiet hotel room waiting for me where I could sit and drool in peace. The dentist said that when I woke up the next day I should hopefully have regained my sense of touch in my lower lip, and thankfully, I did.

I spent the next five months in Sydney, with one trip to France to visit Mum and John for two weeks. While I was there I rented a car to go exploring. Mum and John lived in the Dordogne region, which is predominantly rural and full of picture-postcard villages that made me want to wear collarless shirts and baggy pants with braces.

One day I was driving through the rolling hills going nowhere in particular when I saw a well-dressed man strolling through a grassy field with a big bird on his arm. I stopped the car and hopped over the fence; he saw me coming and smiled, motioning for me to come over. We had a polite greeting, almost formal. He had a beautiful hawk perched on his gloved hand, a basket over his shoulder and a white ferret in the pocket of his tweed jacket. He was hunting rabbits.

'Please have a seat,' he pointed at a blanket near the fence.

I watched him pull out the ferret, whose name was Claude, from his pocket. As soon as Claude hit the deck he was off down a rabbit burrow. A few moments passed and then panicked bunnies took off across the field, their bums streaking a white fluffy blur in three different directions.

The hood was pulled from the hawk's head; it lined up the nearest target and was airborne in seconds. The bunny didn't stand a chance. I had no idea that rabbits scream when they die; it sounded like a child. The hawk held the rabbit in its talons until the Frenchman strolled up, then it returned to its perch atop the gloved hand. Claude came lolloping up and sat next to the man's leg, patiently waiting to be picked up and returned to the tweed pocket.

I can't remember the hawk's name, but going from its ability it should have been 'Death from Above'. What is it about birds of prey? They know they look cool. Anyway, at least it was more civilised than blowing the bunny's head off with a shotgun.

14 THE GHOST OF A FLEA, 2004

I have a friend in Sydney who has a pet ferret named Freddy. We go out riding our motorcycles together, and Freddy comes along too. He's an experienced passenger and just curls up inside Andy's backpack and falls asleep. Andy could strap Freddy to the handlebars if he wanted, and he wouldn't wake up. When I first discovered Andy was riding about with a ferret in his bag, or sometimes stuffed in his jacket, I was worried the ferret might jump out or bite Andy. But over time I learned that ferrets have a defined lifestyle. They sleep for an hour, then go nuts for half an hour, back to sleep for an hour and so on all day. So if you go for a ride with a ferret in your pocket, make sure it's after they've had the half-hour of going nuts.

Naturally curious and interested in anything they can climb into, a ferret in a new room is very entertaining. We would pull up outside a pub, go in, order a few beers and rack up the pool table. Andy would pull a totally limp Freddy out of his jacket. Freddy would wake up just in time for the cue ball's crack into the pack. Andy calls it Freddy Pool: the balls spin across the table, and soon Freddy is into it. He loves pool, and quicker than you can say 'No ferrets on the pool table' he is off down the nearest pocket.

After a couple of minutes, Freddy would spring from a random pocket, scarper across the table and down an opposite pocket. This went on throughout the game, but you had to be careful not to play for more than half an hour, as the little shit would just fall asleep somewhere inside the pool table and then you had to wait for an hour until he woke up. This happened on one occasion.

We were in Wollongong playing 'Freddy Pool' when he fell asleep in the table. No problem, it was early afternoon, in the middle of the week . . . then four bikers came in and started playing doubles for money.

Andy and I sat there, waiting, middle of the fifth game, when suddenly Freddy took off over the tabletop.

'Fuck . . . hey, did you see that fuckin' thing?' said one of the bikers.

'See one what?' said his mate.

'There's a fuckin' rat in the table.'

'Don't be fuckin' stupid Macca.'

'I'm fuckin' telling ya, there's a fuckin' huge fuckin' rat, inside that fuckin' table.'

'You cunt . . . anything to cop out of twenty fuckin' bucks a game.'

'You sayin' I'm a fuckin' liar Davo?'

'Next it'll be . . . Sorry boys, can't finish the game cause a fuckin' emu flew in and stole the fuckin' cue ball.'

The two men began to shape up to one another when Freddy stuck his head out of the corner pocket, wondering what the hold up was.

'There's the fucker, get it Davo!'

Davo was amazed, he just stood there, his mouth slightly ajar, while the other three bikers started laughing. Macca was intent on bloody murder; he hovered over the corner pocket brandishing the cue over his head.

Freddy popped out of the opposite corner pocket, ran into the middle of the table, did a nice little figure of eight and disappeared back down the same pocket. The cue came down hard, completely missing Freddy and splintering on the table's edge, sending fractured wood in all directions. Now all three of Macca's mates were folded up laughing. The bar manager came over with a security guard to calm him down. Macca threw twenty dollars on the table for the broken cue and stormed off, followed by his mates who were still laughing.

'There really was a rat in the table mate,' they said to us as they picked up their helmets and gloves. A few moments later we heard the big 'V' twins fire up and roar away.

'Can we go now, I don't want to get my head kicked in over your ferret,' I said.

'Oh shit,' Andy said, looking at his watch. 'He's gone to sleep again.'

'Jesus, Andy, is the fuckin' thing narcoleptic? Wake him up!'

Andy got the keys to the table from the bar man who told us that it was the best laugh he'd had in ages. We opened the table, retrieved the sleeping Freddy and made for home.

During that trip home I decided to change laundromats. The previous couple I had been going to changed the colour of one too many shirts, so I wandered into a slick-looking new one down the street. All I could see behind the counter were legs and the best-looking bum in history. Her back was turned, giving me a chance to take in her figure. She turned, and I was caught. Dazzling smile . . . stunning. I felt like a twat, she was so sexy, her cheeky enthusiasm toyed with my embarrassment, boggling my loins to a point that left me instantly unable to talk.

I went back the following Wednesday, at the same time, and there she was.

I found myself feeling butterflies every time I went to get my laundry done. I tried to look cool; I'd park my bike in front of the door, toe out the kick-stand and walk in grinning like a lottery winner. 'Hi, how are you today Paul?' Wow she remembered my name. But I mostly fumbled with my backpack and came out with hopelessly inane conversation. But she always flashed me that smile and said, 'Have a good day.'

That went on for months. Her name was Clare. I would look forward to laundry day and another chance to fuck up my thirty-second window to ask her out. Then one Wednesday she said she would rather be with her family as it was her birthday.

'Oh, many happy returns.'

I would have been better off saying 'Sucked in'! Many happy returns! Jesus Pauli, that's hip and youthful. So I walked down the road and bought a big bunch of flowers. She was happy to get them, and as no-one was in the shop we chatted for a while.

'What is it that you do for a living?' she asked. 'I'm curious because you can tell a lot about a person from doing their laundry.'

'Really?' I said.

'Oh yes, for example, you're single, you only wear something once, your clothing labels are from other countries, so you travel a lot right?'

'I'm impressed.' I was, of course.

'You disappear regularly, and your clothes have numbers written on the tags when you get back, so it's got to be something like the merchant navy or mining. Am I close?'

I explained that the numbers are room numbers, that I work on the rigs and the laundry guy always writes your room number on your gear. 'You're right about everything else too.'

She smiled. 'So where was your last job, somewhere interesting?'

'Russia, Japan, and before that Africa.'

She thought I was lucky, travelling so much, she had just returned from a trip to South Africa. 'Whereabouts in Africa were you?'

'Nigeria.'

'What's it like?'

'Oh, it was definitely interesting.' I had to ask her out, but she'd seen my undies. What if she was an environmentalist and decided that I was nothing but a meat-eating eco-vandal who raped the Earth for a living?

'Would you like to have a coffee with me?'

We had coffee the next day. I was happy; it had been a few years since I had felt that way. Clare was wonderfully easy to talk to. It felt different, she was different, strength of character hovered under her features. All my previous relationships had ended because I was away too much. Perhaps this would be different. These emotions are hard to fathom, especially after years of listening to hundreds of men sit in the locker room offshore going on and on about their divorces. Here are a few quick snippets of oilfield marriage advice:

'Don't do it.'

'Cheating bitches.'

'She took the kids and the fuckin' dog.'

'Hide your money man.'
'Fucked the whole team while I was offshore.'
'Got home to an empty house.'
'I'm gonna have her knee-capped next month.'
'So I fucked her sister.'
Etc., etc.

It's simply fear, I think. I always had this notion that I could just roam the planet and run pipe, get into adventures, continue fucking about like I had since I was in my early twenties. Meeting Clare made me think about the next ten years—shit. Basically, I'd have to pull my head from my arse and take stock. What had I done over the last fifteen years? All my friends are genuine grown-ups; they have mortgages, kids, and jobs that don't involve making conversation with 'Billy-Ray' during a typhoon about fuckin' turkey season back home Gawd-damn.

There was one person I could talk to about this: Ruby. The constant in my life, my oldest friend, we go way back, nothing was real until I told Ruby. She always threw new light on everything. I had been threatening myself for the last few years with the idea that I could do something else with my life; Ruby had been telling me that for a lot longer. She laid down the rules of life, she never minced words or dressed up a situation. Ruby had saved me from bad decisions many times over the years, so with her I would always listen.

Luckily Ruby liked Clare and told me to go for it. 'You're thirty-five, bald, and you've been sleeping on my couch for the last ten years . . . what, do you think you're Brad Pitt or something?'

With that she had a laugh—her laugh is priceless, like watching someone yawn. You find yourself laughing with her; throw in a few drinks and I'm on the floor, crocodile tears streaming down both cheeks.

'I'm going to get out of the oilfield soon,' I announced.

'Keep polishing that turd Pauli.'

I spent more and more time with Clare. Her company was relaxing in a matter-of-fact way, I liked that. With nothing but time on my hands I occupied myself working for Louise in her advertising agency. I loved it, the people were fun and civilised, and the most danger I faced was a wayward paperclip or perhaps an overly hot cup of coffee.

After one particularly long stint offshore in the Philippines I returned home to a message on the answering machine, from Louise . . . Could I come straight over and have a superb dinner with lots of great wine and Barry stories. As usual it was a blast. The next day she sent me off to a photo shoot, my first. It was a studio shoot in town. I arrived, found the right studio and walked into a large white room filled with semi-naked girls, the photographer, the hair stylist, the make-up guy, who winked at me, and the client, who spent most of the time chain-smoking with his head out the window. Two days earlier I was on the drill floor on a shitty rig in the southern Philippines, and now I was getting paid to stand here and find inspiration.

In the three years that I have worked as a freelance copywriter in advertising, albeit in a random staggered way, I have had more drinks, dinners and parties thrown at me than in the fifteen years in the oilfield. But without fail after a few months I would get what my old boss called 'a rabbit up my arse' and I would start looking for a rig again. The characters you meet in the oilfield are unbelievable—from full-on rocket scientists with multiple Ivy League degrees and a keen interest in painting to-scale miniature sixteenth-century military figurines on their bunks, to Billy-Bob the brain-dead redneck ex-con whose misspelt jailhouse tatts, fart jokes and new truck back home are all he can talk about. Put a combination of twenty guys like that in a rundown backwater bar in some Godforsaken corner of the world miles from anywhere remotely 'civilised', throw in a civil war, a donkey, some festering prostitutes, and anything can happen. And I think that's why it's so addictive—not the drilling, not the job, definitely not the food, but the people and the situations you meet them in.

In the Philippines a few years ago I was in a bar with the boys when a gun-fight started, yes, a gun-fight. Everyone had a gun in that part of Manila. The time passed in super-slow mode, like recalling a car accident. But the part of that night that most sticks with me is when one of the guys went from drunk to sober in a second. We were hiding under the table together when I saw the first flash of panic on his face. Panic is a black leopard that sinks its claws deep into your skull; it makes your body burn and shake. Some people ball up, some freeze, some focus, I tend to poop my pants.

He focused, grabbed my collar and in a clear white moment said, 'If I get shot, you have to call my brother and tell him there's ten grand buried in a coffee can in his front lawn.'

I was blank . . . the guns were still going off, rounds were breaking windows and slapping into the wall somewhere above us. The fight lasted less than a minute, and spilled out into the street, where the two men exchanging fire were joined by two security men from the bar.

I took a quick look out the broken window; down in the street I could see one of the bar's armed bouncers crouched behind a car, his head almost in the wheel arch, one arm laying across the hood blindly firing in the general direction of the other men. I sat down on my unfinished cheeseburger and laughed a nervous relieved laugh. Mike was still under the table, lighting a cigarette. The others were scrambling to get out the back door.

'You buried ten grand in your brother's front lawn?'

'Fuck no, but he's a prick and it would have served him right.'

Towards the end of my fifth month at home I got a call to go back to Russia. I only had three days to get ready, and a bunch of copy to finish for Louise. It was a Sunday, my flight was on Monday morning, I was racing across town on the bike to get to a meeting. Just as I passed a set of traffic lights I sensed a car, way too close, and doing well over the speed limit. It came up behind me fast, hitting my bike's rear wheel as it was changing lanes.

The bike bucked, kicking me up on the tank. I held on but was overshooting a right-hand corner. I grabbed a handful of brakes but locked up the rear wheel . . . that was it . . . I laid it down. BANG . . . the impact was remarkably soft. I knew I was okay. I looked over my right shoulder as the bike and I slid down the road, the car that hit me was speeding off through the entrance to the Eastern Distributor Tunnel—bastard.

The corner . . . my head snapped back. The bike and I had parted company and I watched my beautiful 650 Twin slam into a metal fence. This can't be happening! I just had it resprayed.

Passing my demolished bike I bounced off a curb, somehow made the corner and slid through another set of traffic lights that were conveniently green. People sat behind their steering wheels watching me, mouths open, as I passed by them on my arse. I stopped just as my feet touched the curb of a cross-street.

I got to my feet, but my right leg was shaking too much to stand.

My phone disintegrated in my hand when I opened it. A man came running up.

'Are you okay? Don't move, don't take your helmet off . . . your brains could fall out.'

I looked at the man and pondered that. 'Can I use your phone please?'

'I saw the whole thing, you're really fucking lucky mate.'

I called Ruby; she was on the way. An ambulance came roaring up, the medic sprang out. 'I'm okay . . . well, he thought the helmet was holding my brain in.' The medic shot a fuck-off look at the man who nodded in that knowing way.

'You'll live,' he said and smiled then gave me some dressing for my right hand and soon they departed.

'Hope I never see you again,' I said.

Ruby arrived and took me to hospital, just to be sure. I'd cracked a rib.

'You can't go offshore now . . . shame, just gonna have to stay and be an ad man.'

Bollocks, I've never missed a job. The next day I was on the flight trying to work out how I was going to get into a survival suit, life jacket and four-point harness for the flight to the rig, let alone work.

15 AH MENG, 2004

I was back in Singapore again, begging for used thermal coveralls, but this time it was a different rig. BP had decided to drill that wildcat well offshore in Sakhalin. Erwin Herczeg was in charge of this job—the godfather. What a relief. No matter what blew up, broke down, fell over or just stopped on the rig, he could fix it, get the job done, do it in record time and have all the boys back on the beach in one piece and wearing the obligatory give away client baseball caps. It had been a few years since we had worked on a job together; I was looking forward to it.

After ten days in the workshop standing-by we finally got the call. This time we would go from Yuzhno by charter flight to a small jetty on the northernmost tip of the peninsula near the small town of Okha. From there we would take a supply vessel to a supply barge which was moored a few kilometres offshore in international waters. And finally a chopper to the rig.

By the time we arrived in Yuzhno the weather had turned. It was the middle of their summer but to us still cold enough to warrant thick jackets and beanies. The small charter aircraft was waiting on the tarmac, its strobes flashing and the door ajar. One prop was spinning, sending waves of invisible rollers over the grass behind us. We simply transferred from the jet to the charter. All the passengers were involved in the rig operation: one big Dutch guy who was with the company supplying the drill bits for the job was not happy with the look of the aircraft.

It did look as ancient as everything else on Sakhalin, like a flying version of the Nogliki train. The Dutch man walked around it kicking the tyres and swearing over the noise as the flight crew looked on. Eventually we all got on board, the bags were stowed by throwing them in the back; it was loud, cramped and very uncomfortable.

The weather had worsened by the time we arrived on the tiny Okha airstrip so the supply vessel was going to have to wait until the next day. Our accommodation for the night was a forty-minute truck ride inland, into the woods. It was very weird, we drove down a small dirt track ever deeper into an ominously black pine forest.

'Where the fuck are we going, there's nothing out here.' The only place I knew of for hundreds of miles was Okha, and we were heading away from there.

One of the BP guys leaned over. 'There are beds at this place, don't worry, it's not flash but it's all we could get at short notice.'

'What is it?'

'Oh it's an old asylum.'

I looked at Erwin. 'Isn't that like a nuthouse?'

'Well it is now buddy,' he replied, laughing.

Darkness fell quickly, adding a sense of urgency that silently crept up everyone's spines. Then, towering above the woods, black against the sky, stood our lodgings. The building was another award-winning design from the Russian 'Fear Works' school of architecture. The only thing missing was a few well-placed gargoyles. It was a nuthouse. I pictured a Soviet version of *The Shining* with some crazed Boris hobbling about in the snow with a big fuck-off axe.

Random lights shone weakly in the upstairs windows, but when the truck circled and backed up to the main door, only its red tail lights illuminated the entrance. It started raining hard as we unloaded the bags, a dark figure opened the heavy iron door and right on cue a bolt of lightning cracked down over our heads. I wondered what this place must have been like during the Cold War, I thought about the possibility of salty-looking KGB film noir spies torturing people in the basement.

The woman in charge was perfectly suited to the spooky scene; Hollywood could not have cast this any better. She had a pronounced limp and actually said 'Walk this way' when she led us to our rooms on the second floor. I sniggered all the way up the stairs, along the barren corridors which were like huge dark tunnels.

I was sharing a room with Erwin; it smelled of disinfectant and looked like a cross between Hannibal Lecter's cell and your average public toilet. It was fairly empty, furnished only with two iron beds, each with one inch of antique foam, and a small table. I wished I had a crayon so I could write 'Redrum' on the door. Every time lightning flashed through the curtain-less window glass, thunder shaking the building, one of the guys down the hall would scream, 'IT'S ALIVE'.

Erwin sat on his bed, smiling. 'All work and no play makes Pauli a dull boy.'

'Very funny . . . I hope they feed us.'

Dinner was boiled mystery meat and boiled something else, yummy. We sat up late, swapping stories, catching up on the last few years while the wind beat a distinct rhythm through the rain on the cracked windows. We woke early to cold showers, clear skies and no breakfast. Then it was back on the truck to the jetty and the waiting supply ship.

Our voyage was brief, three hours and we were alongside the supply barge, our home until the rig was ready for us. The POB (Personnel On Board) situation on many rigs is a constant problem—no bed space. Sometimes I have had to 'hot bed' it, jumping straight into the night-shift guy's smelly sheets too tired to care. To avoid this we would stand-by on the supply barge until the last moment, then make the trip to the rig.

Inevitably there were problems with the drilling and we ended up standing-by for a week. I was glad as it gave my rib a chance to heal. The vessel was comfortable, the people on board were really nice. Most of the crew were Indonesian, the rest Australian. But on the third day a massive typhoon started looming closer to our location. Tracking up the coast from Japan, it hit hard early in the morning. I knew this because I woke up on the floor with all my gear on top of me.

Remember those old *Star Trek* moments when the ship was being attacked and everyone would grab a handrail then collectively let go and do a high-speed dressage manoeuvre over to the opposite handrail while the director shook the camera? Well a typhoon is nothing like that. If it's bad enough, it will pick you up and hurl you into the nearest wall. I could hear one of the boys throwing up with all his heart in the toilet.

'Don't open that fuckin' door.' I'm usually okay as long as I don't smell it.

Erwin was starting to turn green. 'I need to go on deck . . . see the horizon,' he moaned.

We pulled on raincoats and carefully made our way outside. The main deck was big, fifty square metres, and covered in equipment. Drums of drilling chemicals were scattered about and rolling all over the place. Containers had broken loose and skidded across the deck; the forklift lay on its roof. Every alternate wave broke over the side of the barge; crashing down hard on the cold steel floor. The hull vibrated as tonnes of sea water slammed like the wall of a liquid building into the bulkhead.

I tried to elevate Erwin's mind from that horrible inner focusing you do with seasickness. Waiting . . . swallowing . . . sweating on your elementary canal to go into spasm. With one eye closed and my right leg tucked behind my coat, I hopped up to him. Horizontal rain stung my face, I had to yell as loud as I could over the wind. 'Arrrr me laddy, there we were, hard aground on the mahogany reef.' . . . Nothing . . . 'We was pickin' the weavels out the biscuits-n-drinkin' our urine all day I tells ya.'

In the middle of my performance, a huge wave deposited a fully grown seal bang in the middle of the main deck. Equally surprised to see each other, all three of us exchanged looks and shared a 'What the fuck are you doing here?' moment. The seal remained firmly planted on the spot . . . ten feet from us, unexpectedly caught in the spotlight of the human world, his eyes wide as saucers darting left to right. I'd never seen a seal go from sheer terror to relaxed indifference . . . he almost smiled.

As if realising the most he had to fear was putting a flipper in some wayward vomit, he opened his pink mouth and belched. Erwin and I watched him casually make his way over to the only shelter available, in the welding shop. Within an hour the boys were throwing him toasted sandwiches. I was waiting for him to come out and ask where we keep the good brandy.

The typhoon moved on, leaving days of cleaning up to be done. We made repairs and double-checked our equipment. No choppers were flying when our turn on the drill floor arrived, so we boarded the supply boat again. The rig, when we got there, loomed out of the fog, a decaying hulk, its structure forming an alien-fabricated atoll that reminds you of your fragility.

The crew stood on the deck of the supply boat, waiting in silence for the crane to lower the 'Billy Pugh'. 'Billy Pugh' is a manufacturer's name, commonly used for a personnel basket. It looks like a giant upside-down ice cream cone, with a flat ring about two metres wide and a cone of rope netting attached to the ring and fixed at the top to the crane's hook. Each man was running over the what ifs in his mind. The first thing most of us usually do is take a good look at the derrick: Are there any stands racked back? Are they tripping in or out of the hole? What's my bunk going to be like? You just throw your bag inside the rope netting, step on to the ring with the other guys, grab the rope and hold on. The crane lifts you the 200-odd feet straight up and onto the heli-deck.

The concept is simple; up to four men at a time are hoisted to the rig. I felt sorry for one of the guys; he was pacing about, biting his nails, double-checking his survival suit, flashing occasional worried looks at the sky. If you do fall from the Billy Pugh you're stuffed; the water is so cold, survival suit or not, if the impact doesn't kill you the water temperature will. This guy was a young Russian wire line operator; I wandered over to him, smiling. He smiled back, rather like someone would with a gun to their head. Not only had the poor bastard been throwing up for the last nine hours in his cabin, he was now explaining in superfast broken English that he was scared of heights.

'You can ride with me if you like, you'll be fine,' I said in my best adult BBC serious English.

He nodded up and down quickly.

Our turn came, the bags were thrown inside the net, we stepped up, and grabbed on, the crane was taking up the slack fast as the boat was starting to heave.

'Look at me,' I said to the young Russian. He fixed his eyes level at mine. I smiled as we rose fast into the foggy airspace of salt spray and high anxiety.

Touching down he instantly lifted, resilient in his relief. I congratulated him.

'Not so bad,' he said, beaming.

The rig was a 600 Series semi-submersible; it had been sold just before this project kicked off so no-one was interested in its shitty state. The whole thing was a mess; from the top of the derrick to the Blow Out Preventer (BOP) deck it was a rusty eyesore that belonged in a graveyard, not hovering over a wildcat well.

Two weeks later we were all back on the supply barge, waiting for the next well section to come up. The barge, *Ismaya*, was built in Ireland in the 1950s and had gone through many roles in her long life. Converted into a drill ship in the early 1970s, *Ismaya* spent many years working in South-East Asia. Erwin had been on board when she was drilling in Indonesia.

One morning Erwin and I were having coffee when Garry the engineer joined us. He had worked with Erwin on the *Ismaya* so I learnt about some of the best years of her drilling past. According to them the rig's best crew member was 'Ah Meng', a young orphaned orangutan who the barge captain found in some harbourside market. He brought her back to the rig and there she stayed for many years.

One of the Indonesian crew members was a cabinetmaker. He built a bar room below decks, fashioned from beautiful teak, impossible to get now. When finished, it was the best rig bar in Asia; and it became Ah Meng's domain. She ran the bar on the rig for the next fifteen years. It was always clean and organised; she made cocktails. There was never any fighting because everyone had too much respect for Ah Meng . . . and if she wanted to she could pull your head off and throw it over the side. She had her stool, no-one sat on her stool, ever. A favourite crew pastime was waiting for new people to come on board and unknowingly sit on Ah Meng's stool. Only to be launched through the air into a large couch against the far wall. Even funnier if you could get a new guy to sit on the couch/landing area and another to plant himself on Ah Meng's stool.

Whenever the rig was in Singapore getting work done in dock, the boys would take Ah Meng out on the town. Erwin lived there for twenty years and remembered seeing her around now and again. Even the odd older taxi driver can recall having her in the cab. Since hearing the story I have asked every cab driver I met in Singapore and had three tell me she was just like any other tourist.

When the *Ismaya* was sold to a new drilling contractor, the company said Ah Meng had to go. The crew was in Singapore at the time, and decided to phone the Singapore Zoo for advice. The zoo had heard of Ah Meng, and immediately asked if they could have her. Apparently they said they would send a van over to the harbour but were told that Ah Meng was on her way in a cab with the barge captain. The crew were in tears waving her off.

Barely in her twenties, she started a new life at the zoo. But Ah Meng was not to be paraded in an ordinary enclosure. Because of her bizarre circumstances and gentle nature, she became a kind of 'meet 'n greet' ambassador for the zoo. And as so many people have since told me, she is still there today and will probably continue to delight thousands of people for a long time. You can have your photo taken with her every day at lunch time. I made a date with her, hoping she would give me some tips on bar brawls and cocktails. She had a level gaze, summing me up in a second; I put my arm around her and wished she could talk.

EPILOGUE

No matter what happens in my lifetime and yours, we will always be involved in the oil business. Every time we start the car, heat the house, cook a meal, watch a war on the news, it reminds me that everything relies on fossil fuels to exist. Try not to think of the human cost, or the environmental cost. By 2080 we need a viable alternative to oil and gas, because by then one-third of our energy needs will have to come from somewhere else. Like solar power, wind power, geothermal power, hydrogen fuel cells, a genetically engineered three-storey hampster in a fuckin' huge wheel—I don't know.

In the meantime I'll keep drilling and writing bad copy. Who knows, I may even find normality . . . even marriage, children, a dog . . . who I will name Colin.

Get back to you in fifteen years.

ACKNOWLEDGEMENTS

First and foremost, I'd like to thank Erwin Herczeg, for watching my back on more occasions than I care to mention and proving to be the perfect role model. Thanks also to Drew Gardenier for getting me started in the first place, and letting me get away with a damn sight more than I deserved to. Special thanks to Sally and Simon Dominguez and Lou and Doug Frost, and Susan Coghill, without whom this book would never have happened. My thanks to all the boys who backed me up, covered my arse and listened to my bullshit over the years; you know who you are. To the team at Allen & Unwin, especially Jo Paul, Lou Johnson, Alexandra Nahlous and Catherine Milne—thank you and sorry I can't spell. Last, but certainly not least, all my love to Clare, Elinor, Johannes, Allan and France. God bless.

THIS IS NOT A DRILL

ANOTHER GLORIOUS DAY IN THE OILFIELD

CONTENTS

1 SILENT ALARM 179
2 GET BEHIND ME SATAN 196
3 JUST ADD WATER 209
4 ENDURING THE RIGGERS 217
5 THE OLD MAN 228
6 THE TENDER TRAP 240
7 KABUL ON THIRTY ROUNDS A DAY 259
8 LEARN OR BURN 282
9 TURNING MARGARITAS INTO SWEAT 292
10 HURRY UP AND WAIT 307
11 THIS LITTLE PIGGY 322
12 THE LAST STAND 337
13 THE WHOLE OIL THING 347
ACKNOWLEDGEMENTS 350

And the sea will grant each man new hope,
As sleep brings dreams of home.
                                            Christopher Colombus

1 SILENT ALARM

'Just another glorious day in the oilfield,' said Erwin.

I could only look at him. I had stopped feeling my feet ten minutes ago; my hands were so cold that I wasn't sure they would stay whole if I tried to move them.

In front of me was an assortment of 120 men in various stages of undress, all moving in super-fast time, all with the same strained, panic-stricken expression on their face. The sort of face you pull when the hotel door slams shut just as you are putting the room service tray out in the hall and you realise you're locked out and naked. Except this was no hotel corridor, this was a semi-submersible drilling rig . . . in imminent danger of becoming a submersible-we're-all-fucked-and-half-of-us-can't-swim rig.

It's 2 a.m., minus thirty-six degrees celcius, we're miles from land and the rig is capsizing. In the middle of the insanity and chaos stood Erwin, that familiar lazy grin seesawing across his face.

The abandon-rig alarm went off some ten minutes ago. 'THIS IS NOT A DRILL' is all I remember hearing. As soon as I got out of bed I knew it was serious. The rig was listing five degrees to port. We've got fifteen minutes to get to our lifeboat. The fluorescent lights blinked on 'This is not a drill'. Again the recorded voice. The continous ringing of the alarm made a fist in my gut. As I scrambled to rip my survival suit out of its bag I could feel the rig slowly continue to tip. This is really happening, I thought, this is not a drill.

The abandon-rig alarm is the one sound you never ever want to hear on an offshore drilling rig, especially when the water temperature kills after just three minutes. Its sound bores right through you, getting through to your brain faster than anything you could imagine. It's all the motive you need to get to a lifeboat no matter what gets in your way. It's a licence to survive with an international adaptor on it, everyone instantly knows the score and it sorts out the men from the boys quicker than anything I've seen. Adrenaline burned in my joints. In fifteen years, this was my first abandon-rig alarm.

My survival immersion suit, I must have it ready, get out, get out now.

Dave, my room-mate, tore open his locker and started throwing stuff all over the place. I opened the door and shot a glance down the corridor; rubbish was scattered everywhere, in every room gear was flying out the door. What is it about abandoning a rig and the threat of dying through the most excruciating freezing process imaginable that brings out the litterbug in people? Men ran in all directions. Some, ripped from their sleep, stood dumbfounded in their jocks, unable to focus. No-one yelled or tried to communicate, everyone was concentrating on getting to their lifeboat in time with the right gear.

Slow down, get it right, I screamed silently and forced myself to check. Survival suit on, seals intact, life jacket on, passport, wallet. I went for the door.

'Smokes!' yelled Dave. 'You'll need them.' He was shoving a whole carton of Camels down the front of his survival suit.

We exploded out of our room and sprinted down the corridor. Red lights flashed, the alarm had turned into a hum . . . I had blanked it out, wasn't listening now. How much time have I wasted? Are we at eight or nine degrees now?

Both of us were only too aware that if the listing got to ten degrees then they couldn't launch the lifeboats. We passed the galley, unwittingly smashing plates and glasses that littered the floor. A young kitchenhand stood in the middle of the debris, wearing only the bottom half of his thermal underwear, his bare feet bleeding onto the floor and a yellow streak running down his right leg. Dave went straight through him. If this guy couldn't get himself to his lifeboat, we weren't going to stop and give him directions.

We took the stairs three at a time. Lifeboat number 1 was on the starboard side, right under the heli-deck, but it may as well have been in Cleveland. Something inside the room we needed to cross had slid across the floor and blocked our escape; the door was stuck.

'OUTER STAIRWELL, GO GO!' I turned around and ran back the way we had come, precious minutes wasted. There was real fear in Dave's voice, it made me move faster.

We went back through the galley, the kitchenhand had disappeared. At the far end of the corridor was a hatch to the outer stairwell; I hit it so hard I felt my shoulder crack as it flew open. We descended the stairs without really touching them. The freezing air bit into the sweat on my face, and everything lay at a bizarre angle as the rig slowly continued to tip. Dave lost his footing at the bottom of the stairs and went down hard into a container that lay across the walkway. We were fifty yards from our secondary lifeboat. I pulled him up and turned to run.

The crew were mustering and preparing to launch what looked more like an orange submarine than a boat. Someone was there in the flashing light. It was Erwin, standing on the ramp in front of the open hatch. 'COME ON, RUN AS FAST AS YOU FUCKING CAN!' He was pulling us forward with his mind and giant hand gestures.

Dave passed me like an orange Carl Lewis and boarded in standard 'I'm not going to die out here' fashion, diving into the open hatch head first, having just ran a quarter mile of corridors in record time wearing a survival suit. I was happy he went through the hatch first as he cushioned my fall. My shoulder, his badly sprained ankle and our respective head injuries didn't stop the wonderful sense of elation that swept over us as Erwin slammed the hatch door and locked it down.

Andy the skipper was, as he liked to put it, 'well hard', and took every opportunity to give me his opinion on my new work boots. My feet were sticking straight up in front of him as I had landed upside down between two seats. 'They're so gay,' he said and grinned, pointing at my boots, on his way to the pilot's seat.

His left hand started the deluge pump then opened the air system, pressurising the vessel, while his right primed and started the motor in well-rehearsed synchronicity. We all sat there strapped into four-point harnesses, collectively focused on Andy's left hand hovering over the launch handle.

Dave pulled out the carton of Camels and passed it around. One by one each man nervously did that self pat-down thing you do when you need a light. Dave looked around at forty guys, each with a cigarette hanging from their bottom lip, looking blankly back. 'Not one of you dickheads brought a lighter, did you?'

Andy had an emergency radio pressed to his ear, waiting for the word. 'Stand by' was all we heard. Another ten minutes, a lifetime. 'Okay guys, it's a ballast control fuck-up. We have to wait,' he said. I strapped myself into a seat.

An hour went slowly by, my bum was going numb. Finally Andy put down the radio. 'It's under control. They lost a valve and the port-side pontoon started filling up with sea water, and then the emergency pump failed to start,' he explained. 'So now they have re-ballasted down on the starboard side to level out the rig while they try to fix the valve and pump. We have to wait in case they can't do it and we sink.'

'I'm glad I'm not the poor bastard trying to fix that pump,' said Dave.

Another hour and the situation was under control.

It took just fifteen minutes to get 120 men into the right gear and in a lifeboat. Not bad. The door that Dave and I couldn't open was blocked by a desk that slid across the room at just the right angle to stop us from getting it open. My shoulder was okay, but it was going to hurt for a couple of weeks. Dave got a nail gun from the warehouse and the desk was soon permanently fastened to the floor.

My first encounter with the oil world was early on in my life.

I was around ten when my mother started working at Tri-State Oil Tools; it was during the boom years in the early eighties when increasingly more offshore activity was turning Aberdeen, where we lived at the time, into the new centre of the oil industry in Europe. It had the largest heliport in Britain, ferrying men from all over the world offshore. The workshop next to my mother's office pulled at me like a giant magnet.

There was a perpetual stream of oil men passing through and every last one of them had a story or a dirty joke to tell. I started skipping school to hang around and listen to them on crew change, swapping stories and talking shop. They gave me the odd glass of beer, shoved American money in my pockets, gave me knives, ball caps and dirty magazines. I loved them.

It didn't take long really. As soon as I was old enough I started roughnecking on a land rig and that was it.

The oilfield is a strange beast. It can quite unexpectedly creep under your skin and become as compulsive as your favourite legal addictive stimulant. I was hooked, and I still am. Although now the characters I wanted to be as a boy are getting harder to find. You have to really look for them as our brave new oilfield embraces shiny new Health, Safety and Environmental policies, Preventative Maintenance is of course paramount, and don't even think about stepping out on deck unless you can identify at least half a dozen hazards to correct. All this does help save lives and avoid accidents. Whole fleets of brand new sixth generation, fly by wire cyber rigs are getting spat out of shipyards all over the world at the moment, with new improved crews.

The guys at the top—the big players and the politicians they grease—will go on exploiting natural resources for generations. The rigs will still be drilling long after our current power brokers are gone and the next wave of bureaucrats have grown up ripping off a few Third World nations, backslapped their way into a massive retirement package and wobbled their massive bottoms up and down some Iberian beach playing crazy golf until they drop dead, unloved, in their mock Tudor retirement McMansions.

The guys at the coalface I looked up to are still around, mind you, but not for much longer. They're all hitting their sixties, leaving the rigs and taking with them that wonderful old-school oilfield headspace. The one I listened to so carefully as a boy. But still, I find myself in the oilfield . . .

The Russian rig was always going to be fun. It was real frontier bullshit, with genuine old-school oilfield bad boys and guys who are so far gone all they know is drilling and that's it. They don't give a shit about anything but the rig and God help anyone who can't fit in.

I was thankful Erwin was there. He's our most senior offshore operator, a big man with broad shoulders and a hard, level gaze. Now in his mid-fifties, he is the most experienced and easily the best operator I have seen. Erwin has done it all; run every kind of pipe, on every kind of rig, on three continents, in more than a dozen countries. The first time I went offshore, wet behind the ears and totally ignorant of rig life, I met Erwin and instantly liked him. A few years later, after rig-hopping around South-east Asia, I landed a spot on his crew. I was lucky—his reputation is well-deserved, though he never brags about it. He taught me with a combination of patience and good humour, and guided me through my first five years in the oilfield.

Without trying, Erwin always retains a presence of authority and calm even when the worst is happening all around him. He's the guy with the light around him, the one that looks like he's got a weapons-grade temper but in fact doesn't.

Erwin's presence instantly lifted my mood, and within a few days of his arrival we were all joking and laughing about the operation. You know, 'Gee whiz, we all nearly drowned yesterday', that kind of thing.

My crew on this gig were all from Azerbaijan and finished every sentence with 'fargin'. They'd walk up to me and say, 'Paul, when we go to town drink vodka fargin?', 'I don't like Russia rig . . . food no good fargin'. And so on.

On the rig, I was sharing a room with three blokes: 'Sick Boy', who didn't talk much and snored like a pit bull being hot-waxed; a very nice Canadian named Dave Nordli who everyone called 'The Seal Basher'; and a habitual alcoholic called 'Vodka Bob', who had the DTs—the shakes—so bad he couldn't fill out his daily report.

Vodka Bob drinks Guinness for breakfast when he's not on the rig. Sometimes he chases it with Smirnoff neat. His prefabricated concrete flat is cheaply furnished and sits in a run-down housing estate in Moscow, but it's better stocked with liquor than your average supermarket. He's been working offshore for fifteen years—the same as me, only Bob has not been as lucky.

Bob got up around six. I watched his ritual every morning. As he took long drags on a Texas Five, he'd put on his gear, slipping his fingers into leather gloves creased and moulded from the cast of his hard, thick hands. He's thirty-six, the same age as me, his body strong—not toned like you see reflected in overpriced gym mirrors in Sydney, but powerful from years of heavy work. It's work that's kept Bob alive, because if it were not for his regular abstinence enforced by the no-alcohol rule offshore, Bob would have drank himself to death years ago. Vodka Bob performed this routine each morning in meditative silence, under the watchful eyes of 1998's Playmate of the Month, who was taped to the wall by the shelf above his bunk. She was vaguely reflected in the tattoo descending Vodka Bob's back. He'd pull a comb through his long hair and have a last drag on his smoke. He was ready for work.

I think Bob had a better sense of himself by the end of his hitch offshore, his body winning a war of attrition against his will to drink. If only he could find the strength to avoid the bottles lining his flat.

Sick Boy was one of the assistant drillers. He's big, covered in tattoos, lives in Thailand and roars around the rig with a broad Scottish accent and a never-ending ability to make you laugh. He was fun to be around, and the drill floor was always organised when Sick Boy and the other AD, Scott, were around. Sick Boy got his name for all sorts of reasons. Besides knowing how to bleed and butcher a human, he is a skilled storyteller and exponent of the cling-wrapped toilet bowl. If it's done right, you just don't see the plastic stretched across the bowl until you stand up and wonder why your poo is levitating.

Kamran was one of my guys. He's a monster really, six foot eight inches tall, three hundred pounds, with a neck the same circumference as my thigh. His hands are so big I can't shake them properly. And he's a true walking penis; all he talks about is chasing women. I think he's been on the rig for far too long; he should be sent home next week.

The Americans on board got on very well with the Russians, there was a sense of mutual respect that hovered around their interactions. And modern Russia was alive and well, you could tell from all the vodka that somehow found its way on board one day. Its presence instantly lifted our comrades' moods, smoothed out any dramas and turned them into toilet humour, in a Boris Yeltsin kind of way.

Most of the American guys on the rig were from Louisiana; they're all Coonasses (Cajuns), you know. Considering they had just lost twenty-two rigs in one hit and most of New Orleans to Hurricane Katrina, they were in relatively good spirits. It was us guys out there manning dodgy rigs in the Russian sea who were taking a chance. The seas there are notoriously wild. The choppers were older than me and could only fly by line of sight; they regularly had to turn back because of the weather. That got interesting when they were past their PNR (point of no return). With half their fuel gone, they were committed to finding the rig in fog thicker than a 'Big Brother' housemate. So if anyone was going to get hurt, it was meant to be us. Not the boys drilling a couple of miles offshore from Bourbon Street.

Only a few days after the abandon-rig alarm, the weather turned nasty. We had a fire and H_2S drill on the same morning, with wild seas, a listing rig and the wind blowing at sixty-five knots. Hard-hats were flying all over the place and the drill was a complete shambles. The tool pusher—the rig name for the drilling manager—was so angry he wanted to keep doing the drill until we got it right, but the weather was too bad to do it safely. He wouldn't give the muster list and radio to the company man so he could shut it down, and I eventually had to talk the radio out of his hand; he was like a retired greyhound with a stuffed rabbit. There was a massive hurricane tracking up towards us and all reports suggested it was bad. We were thinking we might have to evacuate to the 'Asylum', a former Soviet mental institution that now houses offshore personnel en route to the rig and the closest thing to a hotel for hundreds of miles. I'd stayed there before. It was creepy and still a dump, but with vodka now . . . super.

The H_2S is a bastard drill to do in bad weather, but you've got to do it. It's called a 'sour well' when we encounter H_2S, or hydrogen sulphide gas. H_2S can hide in the formation and slowly migrate to the surface; it's heavier than air, completely odourless and deadly. Just one hundred parts per million will kill a man in a few seconds. It's very similar to potassium sulphide, the gas once used to put criminals to death in America's judicial gas chambers.

The worst case of H_2S happened a few years ago on an offshore rig. Everyone except the derrickman was killed. He was working at the top of the derrick and was therefore well above the deadly invisible cloud that engulfed the rig. All he could do was watch as one after another the crew just dropped to their death.

With no warning because the gas has no smell, you don't even know that you've breathed it in, you just suddenly asphyxiate. On a brighter note, we have gas detectors that go off like a howitzer if someone so much as farts, so no-one was going to drop dead on my watch!

There was a Spanish 'mud logger' on the rig called Miguel. Miguel made the drilling fluid we pump down the well. He spent his days in the mud pits, basically a big dark steamy room located deep in the bowels of the rig with huge vats of thick, slimy drilling mud. He wore what looked like a badly made 1960s sci-fi spacesuit, which in turn made him walk like the monster from *Young Frankenstein* and sound like a Spanish Darth Vader. He had to wear it because he was mixing the kind of nasty chemicals that would rot your head off, disfigure the next five generations of your offspring and make you internally combust if you got too close. It's a lonely job but Miguel seemed to enjoy it. I think on some level the suit gave him power, like when grown men think, just for a second, that their power drill is actually a machine gun.

When we were out here last year Miguel was very upset that we didn't have any movies to watch. 'Dis eez fakin sheet,' he protested, his accent so thick he would have a UN interpreter squinting in desperate concentration. But this year Miguel came prepared with more than two hundred DVDs, and was soon the most popular mud logger in history. For a while there everyone was banging on his cabin door twenty-four hours a day as they all have laptops and very short attention spans.

After a couple of days Miguel got pissed off with this and said he would ration the movies to one per day, of his choosing, to be screened at 7 p.m. So one night all the guys on day shift settled down in the big TV room to wait for Miguel. He walked in, striding confidently down the centre aisle. 'I hab a super mobie por cho guys,' he said, smiling. When Miguel smiled, you smiled back, not out of politeness, but because he's so scary. Apart from being a big man, Miguel has a face that looks like it's been set on fire a couple of times and put out with a cricket bat.

Miguel held out the disc in his big, weird hand—years of chemical burns had turned it into leather from a mad cow—pressed the open button on the player and dropped the disc into its cradle. Little lights flickered to life on the display. Miguel turned back to face the packed TV room and proudly announced, 'Di Cunt of Monte Christo.'

After that, he didn't share with anyone. People were paging him on the rig's PA system, 'Can the Cunt of Monte Christo pick up line one please?' The 'Monte Christo mud pits', as the sign read, was not a place to venture alone, as the 'Cunt' himself was a force to be feared and in that spacesuit he cut a fearsome profile.

I went down one day and found Miguel skulking about with a sack of caustic soda that weighs more than I do casually balanced over his huge right arm. 'Hi Miguel,' I said, looking him directly in the eye—literally, as he only has one—and smiled. 'Brought you a coffee, mate.' I handed the mug over.

He knew we were shut down waiting for a chopper to arrive. Work has to stop for half an hour as the crane cannot operate if a helicopter is on final approach. We sat down on some big sacks of Christ-knows-what and had a good bullshit; he was laughing by the time I pulled on my gloves and stepped out through the hatch.

Later that afternoon Miguel brushed past me in the hall and shoved something in my top pocket. I looked down, a little confused, and pulled out a Vequeros Colorado Maduro cigar. These are easily one of the best Cuban cigars, but also one of the hardest to find because they don't have propylene glycol in them, an additive used in the humidification process. Without it, export outside Cuba is 'impossible' unless you happen to find yourself in a Russian mud pit talking to a Spanish one-eyed mud logger.

I'm not kidding about Miguel's eye—he got some acid in it years ago on some God-awful rig in Brazil and lost it. His favourite party trick is to pop out his false eye and quietly drop it in your beer. Then just as you're finishing off your pint you pull focus on an eyeball rolling through the foam towards your open mouth. Without his prosthetic eye, which at best resembles an old marble because of too many drunken episodes that ended with it rolling about on some bar room floor, Miguel looks like he should be put down—or perhaps just left in his spacesuit to creep around in the mud pits.

Miguel rides a Harley Dyna Wide Glide and is a card-carrying member of the 'Sons of Bitches', a motorcycle club of which Erwin and I are also members, although by law in his country you can't ride a bike with only one eye. Miguel dropped it a few years back when some housewife pulled out in front of his bike on a suburban road. The impact was minimal but contained just enough force to pop out his eye. He picked himself up to confront a tearful middle-aged lady, who fainted when Miguel casually retrieved the eye that was rattling about in his helmet and stuck it back in his head.

Weeks slowly rolled by as temperatures plummeted. The weather regularly pummelled us with blizzards, and on the drill floor the work was hard. The rig was not winterised; there was very little protection from the constant wind and snow. Every few hours the rig's vibration would shake free giant clumps of ice from the cross members of the derrick above us, sending frozen missiles down to shatter on the cold steel floor. Choppers were few and far between, and guys started to miss their crew-change dates, unable to get off the rig. Even the supply boats could not get in for days on end. It all took its toll on the crew, and eventually we started to run out of food, with the offerings up in the galley starting to look less like a decent meal and more like something you'd throw in the dog's bowl. Tempers frayed. I tried to keep my boys in good humour, but sometimes jokes aren't enough, and sometimes morale degenerates to the point where a fight kicks off. Usually explosive and short, fights on a rig tend to be vicious as no-one is prepared to back down, so they fight harder. The resulting 'What happened?' questions are almost unanimously answered in the same way, with the standard 'He fell'. Or the most popular and timeless 'I walked into a door'.

It happened so much that the company put up signs in a vain attempt to stop the boys from scrapping—or maybe it was to encourage a more creative line of excuses. It was a little hard to believe that anyone could reasonably walk into a door on the rig when every single door had a huge yellow triangular sign on it depicting the universal black toilet man walking straight into one.

During this time of domestic unrest, we had a very special visitor on board. It was only a brief visit as he was on his way to Africa via Asia where he would find another rig to rest on. He likes rigs because it's in his nature to claim the highest point on the horizon. And once claimed he will defend it with his life. He is a falcon, a fearsome predator.

In his first week, he killed an owl who dropped in—I presume because it got lost, having been blown offshore in a storm that came through one night—as well as a crow and half a dozen sparrows. The owl was minding its own business on the heli-deck, probably wondering what the big 'H' stands for, when our guest just leaned forward off the railing of the crown block at the top of the derrick and plummeted straight down two hundred feet, whistling past our derrickman's head, wings swept back to reduce drag and increase speed—speed he needed as the owl was much bigger than him. At what seemed like inches from impact into the drill floor, he shot horizontally straight out of our level 'V' door, just a blur, a weightless arrow, down the catwalk and across the heli-deck in seconds. The noise of the rig covered his lightning approach. In the last few feet he threw his legs forward, extended his wings and buried his talons deep into the unsuspecting owl's back. An explosion of feathers erupted as the owl fought back but to no avail, he was already too seriously wounded from the first strike. Our assassin made a meal of the owl and returned to his throne on the crown block. What remained of the owl was given a burial at sea; he never knew what hit him.

At 3 a.m. one morning I was talking to the tool pusher in the 'dog house', the room where the driller stands on the drill floor, when our guest came down from the derrick, flew straight in, and perched himself on a cable in the corner not three feet from my head and went to sleep. Not afraid or even curious, he just got too cold up there, as the wind and rain had been lashing the derrick for several hours now. All week we had been steadily sliding past freezing point, and the temperature would continue to fall past minus fifty as we headed into winter. And after all, it's his rig isn't it? So get the fuck out of the way, I'm coming in.

The tool pusher ran off to the galley to get him some bacon. I ran off to get my camera. I was impressed and named him 'Blitzkrieg'. He was equally impressed with me, and shat on my hard-hat twice that morning.

In the migratory season all kinds of birds come through. When the weather suddenly turned foul a huge swarm of tiny finches, too many to count, diverted to our heli-deck and huddled together against the wind, the horizontal rain buffeting them into one big circle of tiny feathers. Then the sun came out for ten minutes and they started to hop up and down and chirp. But, as if God himself was fucking with them in much the same way we did when trying to run cockroaches to death in the galley at two in the morning by flicking the light switch on and off, it started raining again. The third time the rain and wind disappeared and the sun popped out the finches all went apeshit, hopping about on the heli-deck until one of them lifted off above the rest, his tiny wings flapping like fuck. 'DO WE STAY, DO WE GO . . . OR WHAT?!' he chirped to the others. They launched themselves in complete unison back into the sky and in a few seconds they were just a brown cloud trailing the horizon.

Little sparrows buzzed about down on the main deck, jostling for space around the garbage bins. They regularly got bullied by a crow that arrived from nowhere. His reign over the bins was short-lived, though, as one day he strayed too close to the derrick—that's Blitzkrieg's turf. Once again death from above came hurtling down silent and fast. All that remained were a few black feathers and some blood on the floor by the bins.

Blitzkrieg picked off the odd sparrow, snatching it straight out of the air and devouring it mid-flight. He made endless circles around the derrick, occasionally shouting out a warning to everyone above the blaring rig's white noise. 'Come too close and you're a dead motherfucker,' as the tool pusher translated for me.

I liked Blitzkrieg, he kept it simple. When he's rested up and there's a break in the weather he moves on, making the next leg of his long journey, rig-hopping down the coast past Japan and Korea all the way to Africa. He makes the trip every year, playing 'beat the clock' with the elements, returning to the same rigs again and again. He's warmly received on every drilling derrick from Russia to Sudan. Accepting whatever name they give him, he knows every local custom, speaks a dozen languages. He blends in, disappears into the steel and kills anything that comes too close to his rig. If there was a symbol for our industry, it's him.

2 GET BEHIND ME SATAN

We were more than two months into the job and the well was doing all kinds of shit. We were taking losses. That means all the drilling fluid inside the well was overcoming the formation pressure. With this type of exploration or 'wildcat' drilling, it's always a gamble—over-pressurised formations become really dangerous in these situations.

We kept pumping mud to maintain hydrostatic pressure, but it's sustainable only if crews can keep up the pace of mixing new mud at the same pace that losses occur. We can only produce mud so fast, and 'The Cunt of Monte Christo' could only mix new mud as fast as his spacesuit and bad vision would allow.

The well was taking thirty barrels an hour in losses and it was increasing. If it got above one hundred it was all over. So we drilled ahead, mixed and pumped mud, keeping a furry eyeball fixed on the digital mud fluid-level gauge like a degenerate gambling junky stares at a roulette wheel in a windowless casino. Just like us he's overtired, jumpy from all the coffee and worried about the loan shark who's going to take his thumbs if he loses.

Our loan shark was the oil company; they had a pretty new logo but would happily drill all the way, indeed into Satan's special 'Beelzebub Reserve', looking for what we call 'shows'—traces of hydrocarbons. The next time we tested the well we were going to knock on Satan's door again; if we got a hit then the dealmakers would keep us in war and V8 supercars for another five years.

The only problem was, we had just hit compressed chert at 2470 metres, one of the hardest rocks to drill through. So the stakes had been raised. If the bit wore out before we were through the chert then we wouldn't have enough chemicals to mix more mud and keep pumping above the losses. And the dealmakers would have to go home and trade in their V8s for public transport.

But after two months of relentless drilling we finally got what we came for. The money men found their hydrocarbons, the chert gave way to soft limestone, we drilled into this formation and started preparing to run casing. After that the well testing would start, and that involved 'flaring' the well.

It's wild when a well flows. A live gas well is a remarkable thing and you're playing a dangerous game with Mother Nature. The gas is very carefully flowed up to the rig, with the aid of enough German uber-engineering to relaunch the space program, and diverted through a long high-pressure armoured hose to a giant arm that hangs over the side of the rig. At the end of the arm lies a directional head with jets jutting out forming a circle around it. The liquid gas flies up the well expanding at an unbelievable rate, the rumble turning into a roar and sending nervous looks in all directions. By the time it has reached the drill floor it's breaking the sound barrier.

In a second it slams into the head, the ports open, the burners ignite, and everyone snatches their whole body back like a collective hand caught over a Bunsen burner as millions of cubic feet of highly volatile liquid gas vaporise and explode, lighting up the night sky in a fireball that sends an invisible shockwave over the rig and makes every living thing in the sea for miles stop and look.

The sound alone is like ten jumbo jets taking off at the same time. The crew run about madly checking and rechecking the heat levels, as a flare boom will peel the paint off the walls and melt your boots to the deck. But all this power flying through the rig is a mere sneeze for Mother Nature—if she wanted to she could spit us into orbit.

'We got a real barn burner here,' said Gerry, the night tool pusher. Gerry knew the rig inside out, back to front and upside down. He's got the power to pull the dragon from the ground, as he liked to put it. He looked down on the rig from the heli-deck, surveying the crew who scurried about trying not to let the rig turn into one giant floating charcoal brick. He smoked his well-chewed cigar through clenched yellow teeth, bending his head down to his hand to do so as forty years of lifting badly has left Gerry with the elbow dexterity of an arthritic ex-tennis pro.

Gerry's old, but he intensely dislikes being told he's an older man. I was in his office one day when the mail bag arrived. He was sitting there thumbing through his correspondence when suddenly he spat his cigar across the desk and started ripping up an envelope. In some insurance form he had been referred to as an 'old age pensioner'. 'I hate that shit, it's like telling you the same Gawd-damn thing three times,' he protested while retrieving his cigar from the small fire it had started in the corner.

'Motherfuckers, I'm still a workin' man,' he mumbled while pouring his coffee over the fire.

The logistics coordinator, Blane, lives in the same state back in the United States as Gerry. I was telling him about Gerry's cigar-spitting tantrum. He laughed and told me about the time he went over to Gerry's cabin in the mountains. Gerry looks like Grizzly Adams would if he'd become really surly and indifferent about his personal hygiene.

It was the middle of winter in Washington State. As Blane walked up to the front door he saw that an entire felled tree was poking through the open doorway and extending some twenty feet into the snow. A tractor was parked with its front end flush up against the end of the tree. Apparently Gerry's chainsaw had broken down so he just pushed the whole fucking tree into the house so the top was jammed into his fireplace, which was directly opposite the front door. As the night wore on Gerry would periodically put down his beer, jump in the tractor and push the tree in another foot as the fire burned down.

It was getting very close to three months since we arrived on the rig. My brain had turned into soup, I was now past it, part of the substructure, the rig had slowly eaten its way into my head like rust on a gangway. I was in the company man's office—he's the one in charge of everything—and he was halfway through the morning meeting. It felt like the millionth morning meeting, and I'd stopped paying attention weeks ago, opting instead to perfect my cow-like ability to sleep while standing up.

All the service company supervisors were packed in, the tool pusher, the petroleum engineer, the mud engineer, the deck pusher, the logistics guy, the directional driller, the sub-sea engineer, the well test supervisor, and the galley boy who had decided to attempt to empty the bin located under the company man's desk was there too—all in a room the size of your average broom cupboard. Everyone else was crammed into the corridor, craning their heads into the office to hear what was going on. Half of the guys looked and smelled like they did most mornings, coming straight to the meeting directly from drool-filled sleep. The rest had coffee and smokes.

Erwin was up on the drill floor running the last well section with the Azerbaijani boys. I knew the end was in sight but after three months I was hopelessly institutionalised; I had to look at the 'ten day operational forecast' printout in my hand just to figure out what day of the week it was.

I wasn't listening; I was having a perverse fantasy involving my girlfriend Clare and a giant beach ball. 'Pauli, how long is it going to take to rig down all your tools, get your manifest sorted, and be ready to go?' asked Colin the company man.

What the fuck? We're still running pipe, I thought.

'Pardon?' I looked back blankly.

'Wake up, mate. All the control lines are installed in the SSSV, tested, the hanger's done and landed, we're going to be laying down your gear soon, so you can hopefully get squared away and be on the chopper at midday. It's the last flight so you either get on it or stay on the rig for the tow down to Korea. So how long to rig down?'

Shit. We had eighteen containers scattered all over the fucking rig, and there were tools, and spare parts, and all kinds of gear from the drill floor to the sack room. And it all had to go back in the right order, in the right container, with the right paperwork. I glanced at my watch. Fuck. It was 7 a.m., and every man and his buddy were going to want to use the crane all day, and there was some very bad weather inbound.

'Three hours,' I said. Fat chance.

I left the meeting, stepped out on deck, pulled up my collar as it was snowing heavily and made for the drill floor. I explained to Erwin that we had to get the square peg in the round hole and do it blindfolded with one hand tied behind our backs. But that didn't matter, I could have said that John Howard was going to be eaten by aliens and Erwin was the only guy who could stop them, and he would have. Because Erwin saw the chopper in his mind, he imagined himself climbing into it, he could see a cooler full of chilled beer being fondled by a big-breasted slightly tacky female co-pilot. It was there within his grasp, the end of the oilfield rainbow, the elusive chopper, the Holy Grail, and the only way to preserve your sanity and get the fuck off the rig.

What happened next is still a mystery to me, but I can say that it was like being part of a massive, synchronised ballet. Every guy could see the end and performed at his best, anticipating his crew member's next move so well it was simply fluid, harmonised, perfect.

Twelve noon rolled around. And we were ready. Somehow everything came together, the oilfield equivalent of a hole-in-one. We even had time to shower and eat something. Had Erwin not been there, though, I'm pretty sure I would have been sitting on that rig all the way down to Korea.

The chopper finally arrived and we all lifted off in rubber survival suits, exhausted and euphoric at the thought of going home. Watching the rig get smaller through the window until it was eventually swallowed by the sea, I felt fantastic. I could have swum back to Australia.

Our chartered fixed-wing flight was on time—another surprise—and by 7 p.m. that night we were all sitting in a bar in Yuzhno-Sakhalinsk. Yuzhno is the biggest town in Sakhalin, an island peninsula running some three hundred kilometres up Russia's north-eastern seaboard, and it's rough, with the highest crime rate in the entire Russian federation, not to mention frequent bear attacks.

Most of the men in the bar sat on stools, nursing beers and ignoring one another, but my Azerbaijani boys from the rig were already getting out of control. Kamran in civilian clothing looks like a giant silverback gorilla would if someone had snatched it from the zoo, shaved it, taught it basic sign language, dressed it in a bad Hawaiian shirt, stuck a Charlie Chaplin moustache on it and let it loose in a bar full of lumberjacks. Erwin was in the corner watching motorcycle speedway racing with a glass of wine, which tends to put him in a catatonic state. The others were ordering vodka, lots of vodka. Russians are generally traditionalists and with any social interaction old-school rules apply: men pull out chairs for the ladies, hold open doors to let others pass and maintain eye contact when they shake your hand. After the first bottle of vodka is consumed, however, all this degenerates into a kind of giant footy brawl with shooters and lots of incredibly loud, cacophonous singing.

The Russia that ran on fear and secrets ran on vodka too, mind you. Why do you think all the spies in those old 'film noir' movies were always leaning against lampposts in dank Moscow back streets trying to light endless cigarettes with damp book matches? That's right . . . they were hammered on vodka, just like Boris Yeltsin.

Russia is still getting hammered on vodka to the tune of 15 litres a year per person. Except it's a federation now, a federation of quarrelling nationalities forming a big black space in the world map that's entirely full of places ending in 'stan'. In fact, the only consistency left that transcends all former Soviet borders, other than oil, is vodka. Generations of hardened piss-heads survived Stalin, the Nazis, perestroika and, of course, communism on vodka.

The space race ran on vodka. In Star City circa 1965 gallons of the stuff were consumed daily. Launching rockets must be a bit like playing pool: you get better at it after the first drink. The humble potato has been fuelling a powerful toxin since the twelfth century.

From the time we started keeping track of things in Russia, it's been slowly improving. Things are better now than they were only a decade ago. Things are better, actually, than they were at 7 a.m. that morning. As our Western influence—with its drugs, crime, Diet Coke and Levis—creeps from one end of Russia to the next so does the need for the Russian people to see it and live it first-hand. Russia is a place in flux. Go to any of its major cities and you will find all the same distractions you have at home, only they're more expensive, ergo there is a never-ending stream of people waiting to get out. Any random Russian would gladly trade a two-bedroom flat in Moscow for a sleeping-bag in Sydney. And for a great many Russians, having just about anything you ever wanted at your doorstep but knowing you can never afford it is just a bit frustrating. I'm talking about Levis here, not Ferraris. Would the last person to leave please remember to turn off the lights and close the iron curtains?

No matter where you go in Russia you are guaranteed to see three things: the AK-47 assault rifle, too much pre-fabricated concrete, and a shitload of vodka. Much like the concrete, there is a massive array of different Russian vodkas to try—around sixty-nine brands in total, ranging from the nasty paint-stripper-peel-the-enamel-off-your-teeth vodka to the two-hundred-dollar-a-bottle premium vodka.

According to the Bureau of Alcohol, Tobacco, Firearms and Explosives—which sets the rules for spirits sold in the United States—vodka is defined as a neutral spirit 'without distinctive character, aroma, taste or colour'. Therefore you'd think all vodkas would just taste the same, leaving your 'premium' vodka as a bit of an oxymoron. To me they were all very similar, but hey, I was just happy to be there. You can mix vodka with just about anything or pour it in your lawnmower if you run out of two-stroke. Vodka suits any occasion, goes with any food, and is enjoyed by silverbacks. And is the only alcohol you can store in the freezer because it contains absolutely no water—perfect for rigs in minus-fifty-degree climates and any other frozen place on the planet.

In this particular bar, vodka came in bottles, pots, aluminium canisters—you name it. One was a glass rendition of an AK-47, complete with polished rosewood and red satin-lined presentation box, the muzzle being the pouring end. There were even porcelain nuclear submarines and babushka dolls with disturbing faces (you have to pull their heads off to drink out of them—just what you want to do with a babushka doll). And that night we sampled them all. The best one by far was the black glass missile with a bright red warhead lid appropriately named 'Red Army Vodka'.

On that night, we were drinking vodka from a bottle that after each pour said 'cheers' in Russian by way of a tiny device in the base. As we drank our way down, the electronic voice kept saying cheers in ever-increasing degrees of drunken slur—*Yura, Yura, Yura*—so that by the time we were on the last drop it was just a mono-syllabic grunt. This proved to be Kamran's favourite. He danced about to an Elvis song and answered the bottle—all he needed was a banana in his free hand and the picture would have been complete. People didn't know how to react to him; some looked nervously over his huge shoulder as if searching for his handler, others just ran.

Over the years spent on the rigs and in Russian pubs in between I've seen vodka drunk in all manner of interesting ways. There's the 'paper bag full swig from the bottle while urinating on a dumpster' method, a popular one. There's the 'neck a shot immediately followed by a chunk of black bread smeared with caviar' technique, or the 'shot with a whole poached egg'. After a few of those your average hairy Russian man looks like a giant alcoholic hamster who forgot to hibernate. Some vodkas are followed with raw pickled herring on a stick, some are accompanied by chillies or gherkins or both. Some are combinations of all the above . . . and then they set it on fire. That's my favourite. The gentle waft of burned hair mixed with those harsh Russian cigarettes evokes thoughts of the heady days of revolution and cheap rockets.

My crew had just got to the 'setting it on fire and drinking it' stage of the evening. Huge cheers erupted after each shot when the mini inferno was downed by a crew member feeling no pain and the subsequent fire was put out.

'No more setting the drinks on fire,' I eventually protested. It was getting late and at this point we would have been better off just up-ending our shots on our heads and chasing each other about with cigarette lighters. Everyone in the crew was hammered, they could all speak fluent Russian and they were dancing with the locals who, for some reason, were all dressed very similarly; indeed, practically every male was wearing the unofficial uniform of black leather coat, blue jeans and weird pointy black leather 'brothel creeper' shoes. The only colour in the room was worn by the women, who minced about giving everyone their best 'in your dreams' look. Ultra-bright genuine imitation rayon and sequins gave way to turquoise blue combined with scarlet red, the kind of combinations you see when hippy activists try to dress up. And the gear in Russia is badly made, with uneven stitching and heavy coarse materials, and everything bulges in all the wrong places. Think doll's clothes blown up to life-size. Not that this made any difference to the guys after three months offshore.

Erwin appeared through the smoke, talking about motorcycles and drinking on an empty stomach and how he's got me a 'nose bag'. Then he dragged me into a back room, sat me down in front of a wonderful, piping-hot bowl of borsch and disappeared. It's a traditional dish, basically beetroot soup and meatballs sealed with a lid of pastry on top. It's definitely of the poor-man's food variety, the kind found in every Russian household. Winter food, warming, filling and incredibly appropriate, as outside the temperature was sliding past minus thirty-six degrees. And after the crap we'd been getting on the rig, this was manna. I loved it. Slurped and chewed it with all the gusto my inebriated state allowed.

Another member of my Russian crew, Avas, staggered in singing, fell into a chair and slammed a bottle of Absolut onto the table. He ordered a nose bag of borsch from a Russian waitress who looked like a drag queen who had stapled a dead tarantula to each eyelid. The vodka was finished off like an aperitif upon which Avas belched 'AAABSOLUT', banging down the empty bottle and laughing. If only the New York advertising punters could have seen that.

Kamran walloped around the corner, barking something in Russian and pointing a hairy finger at the even hairier waitress. She came over, he sat down and ordered, then looked at me and said 'Ugly girl' loud enough for everyone to hear. I looked around but no-one was listening. Kamran's ability to simply state the obvious was bizarre. He would wander up to me on the rig while I was writing, sit down opposite me and say, 'So you like writing then,' like he had been hypnotised by someone waving a turd to and fro in his face. The waitress was in fact truly horrendous. She looked about as female as Mike Tyson would if he went through his girlfriend's handbag and ate her lipstick.

Avas was trying to negotiate a meatball into his mouth but ended up chasing it across the floor and under a table occupied by two rough, salty-looking Russians. Meanwhile, I was also having some difficulty with a meatball that had landed in my crotch. The two men next to us were not happy with Avas under their table and Russian eyeballs were turning red. Avas banged his head and let fly with a high-speed abusive torrent, and the two Russians stood up, gold teeth gleaming, veins bulging in their leathery necks.

'Oh fuck,' I said and jumped up, sending my meatball flying across the floor. I faked a smile, showing them the palms of my hands. Why didn't I learn all thirty-three letters of the Russian alphabet when I had the chance? One of the boys on the rig had the sort of phrase book you get at school and had tried to teach me some basic sentences. But I never really thought I'd need them so could never be bothered trying.

My brain frantically searched for something and came up with '*Da*'. They glared at me. '*Dobrae utro*,' I added, which means good morning and explains why Boris Yeltsin always went for the hug instead of the talking thing. The two Russians walked over, their gaze fixed and powerful. Then, as if a blockage somewhere deep in my brain burst, I let go with one. 'The dog chased the cat,' I spluttered in Russian.

Kamran defused the fight that was imminent, simply by standing up. Avas emerged from under the table, having retrieved his meatball—and indeed he was eating it—and apologised to the two men, who, having looked long and hard at all three hundred pounds of Kamran, decided that the fight wasn't worth it and left.

Kamran sat down, looking like a disturbed silverback. He wrapped a massive arm around my neck, tapped his finger against his temple, pulled focus on a space three inches above my eyes and told me what the Cyrillic tattoos on his arms meant, then ordered another bottle. This was one of the few times that I felt grateful for his jailhouse tattoos and size—they definitely saved us. I went back to scanning the floor for my meatball, but Avas had already finished it off, greedy bastard.

3 JUST ADD WATER

My work takes me to some strange places, usually Third World, and often during a coup, jihad, civil war, uprising, or riot of some description. If all that fails to happen then, with my track record, there will be a natural disaster. Only in the oil industry, the messy try-not-to-cut-a-limb-off side of the oil industry, does one realise first-hand that no matter what's going on in the world, the drilling goes on regardless—mind that landmine.

After enduring the sheer madness of Nigeria, getting shot at in the Philippines, being locked up in Vietnam, getting dysentery in Papua New Guinea, suffering the worst toothache of my life in a Russian tundra hundreds of miles from the nearest dentist—oh yes, and there was that whole rig-sinking thing on that last three-month long job—I thought a nice holiday was in order. Europe with its safe civilised streets, what could possibly happen there?

But before my long-awaited holiday could start I had to get some training courses out of the way. I was looking at a very hectic week. Erwin and I arrived back in Singapore looking and feeling like a couple of parolees. After three months on that rig, I realised I had been out there too long; it was definitely fiddling with my sanity. It's the little things that make a difference—after a normal, relatively lucid man has been effectively institutionalised on the rig by the rig system, just walking about in regular clothing feels special and everything your senses experience is welcome. People, traffic, toilet paper that doesn't feel like a lump of coal, toilets that flush instead of trying to suck your guts out of your backside, warm showers, real food, walking more than ten feet in a straight line, lawn—everything.

The following morning was day one of the next job's DWOP—Drill the Well on Paper—meeting. During these meetings everyone involved in the operation, from the brightest minds in the oil world to a third-generation driller with the attention span of a nine-year-old and obvious anger-management problems, sits around in a nice hotel conference room packed with three-dimensional well bore schematics and more laptops than a Tokyo subway and gets blind drunk for three days. If drinking was an Olympic sport these guys would be the best in the world. I'm not quite sure how I survived it, but I did. Just.

Then we headed off for our training courses, one of which required the crew to simulate doing their job on the drill floor while the training staff introduced various problems, up to and including emergency situations, all designed to closely monitor what each individual does under varying degrees of stress. This is done every few years and, since my last visit, the facility had introduced a new safety protocol: heart monitors. This seemed unusual but necessary given that in the previous year some poor sod had too much excitement and dropped dead of a heart attack.

We all lined up while an extremely attractive nurse shaved our chests, taped a small transmitter to the small of our backs and stuck little round suction cups all over us. Two of the other guys had also just come from long jobs offshore. One of them, an American named John, had spent more than two months on a particularly rough rig in Africa and the poor bugger now had to go through all this shit on his own time before he could go home to his wife. I felt sorry for him. He was young and I could see his mind was already home in bed.

The nurse wasn't helping much. John lit up like a Christmas tree when she walked in and started preparing to shave us. 'Gawd-damn,' he said as she bent over to pick up her bag. Her nurse's uniform looked like it had been borrowed from a B-grade porno, and in the right light you could see straight through it. Her serious bedside manner and ample bosom just made it worse. From the look on John's face you'd think she was getting him ready for a lap dance, not an extremely expensive exercise that we all had to pass if we had any chance of working on the rigs again, regardless of how hot the nurse was.

The nurse turned to talk to a doctor who had stuck his head round the corner, allowing all of us to take in her profile. My young friend piped up again, 'Gawd-damn.' I looked at him but he just gave me an ambiguous grin and said, 'She looks like a dead heat in a zeppelin race, man.'

Ten hours later we had finally finished the exercises when a middle-aged man in a white lab coat came tearing up the metal staircase onto the fake drill floor.

'Number five is having a seizure!' he shouted. Somewhere an alarm sounded. 'Where is your number five?!'

Oh shit, who's number five? We all exchanged blank looks. Everyone was on the drill floor. Everyone except John.

The whole crew took off looking for him. I ran into the change room—empty. I looked frantically at the toilet doors and noticed that one of them was closed. I kicked it in and found John with his dick in his hand, no doubt engrossed in some lurid fantasy involving the nurse. 'Nice one, you fuckhead!' I yelled while he tried to shove his boner back in his pants. 'Next time take off the heart monitor first.'

John fumbled to deactivate the black box and promptly dropped it in the toilet.

The next day I was sitting in a departure lounge in Singapore's Changi Airport about to board a flight to London; finally, my happy, quiet, safe holiday could begin. As luck would have it, my arrival in the UK coincided with a wave of terrorist bombings. Only a few hours before we landed, the aircrew had announced that London had succeeded in winning the much-coveted host city campaign for the 2012 Olympics. Now elation had dissolved into horror. The sun was shining as I wandered the streets, but the air was thick with uncertainty and people hurried past me with pained, worried faces. Literally millions were stranded in the city, unable to go home because of the gridlock created by the closure of the underground train system and all the major bus routes.

Within a few hours the streets went from crowded to bizarrely empty. London had been brought to a standstill. I could feel the panic leaching up my spine, and soon I found myself no longer admiring the grand old city buildings but visualising them going from sturdy symbols of culture steeped in rich history to shattered rubble. Britain's backbone could be brought down like New York's by our generation's Achilles heel. Namely some shithead with high explosives strapped to his back. I should have stayed on that crappy rig; I'd be halfway to Korea by now.

I hired a car and waited for the traffic to ever so slowly start moving again. I found the A1 and headed for bonny Scotland; perhaps I would spend the next three weeks in the highlands drinking my favourite single malt. Pitching a tent in the heather and drinking the Macallan all day sounded pretty good . . . Unless someone decided to blow up the entire Spey Valley, I felt confident I would be pretty safe.

Instead I was pulled over for speeding before I'd even reached the city limits. It was nice to see the police officer approaching my car with only a stern expression. Gone are the days when your local 'bobby' carried a truncheon and a whistle in his pocket. Gone forever are the days when a criminal would hear the words 'STOP . . . OR I'LL SAY STOP AGAIN!' as he was pursued down the street by said bobby blowing his whistle while brandishing his truncheon that's about as threatening as your average dildo. Now they carry automatic weapons and only say 'STOP' once. And you'd better stop.

Luckily, in this case, no shots were fired and I ended up having a perfectly excellent conversation with my terribly polite and completely informative constable—yes, strange, even for me. He let me off with a warning, then told me a story about two of his fellow officers that's worth retelling.

One dark and stormy night they were sitting in their police car, close to the Scottish border in Cumbria, patiently waiting for someone like me to drive by a little too fast. It was the dead of night, black as pitch and so overcast there was no moonlight, no ambient light, just the black hills and these two cops sitting in their car with a thermos of hot soup.

Then from the south they heard a screaming high-performance engine. The sergeant got out, grabbed the hand-held speed gun and pointed it into the darkness. The vehicle they both heard shot by them at an unbelievable rate, straight out of the night, doing 190 miles per hour with no lights on at all. Both men stood stumped on what to do next. While they were discussing the matter, the car screamed past them going back the other way at an even faster pace. This went on until a road block was finally set up, to reveal two Tornado pilots in a black Lamborghini with full night-vision helmets on.

I drove on. The A1 had gone from being the biggest carpark in Europe to a fast-flowing motorway, and before long I was in the Cotswolds heading for my sister's place. The last time I dropped in on my sister seven years ago she lived in Dorset, famous for its cider. We spent the day in her local pub, called 'The Headless Woman'. I sat at the bar next to a farmer who looked like he'd just come from Middle Earth and heard all about how, back in 16-something just after the pub opened, the local witch was beheaded on the bar for possessing a cow. He gave me a pint of 'Scrumpy', the local brew, a dark cider that tasted great even though it had toenails floating in it and got me so drunk I passed out tongue-kissing his border collie.

This time we stayed away from the local pub and instead enjoyed a walk in the rolling green hills with my sister's dogs. She has two, both Northern Inuits; basically they're wolves, only they howl more and eat more. At one point I got a stick and instantly became the target. I took off running through a wheat field feeling a bit like Kevin Costner, until they bailed me up and ate my new denim jacket.

In Britain everyone appears to have a dog. The last time I was there almost every street I walked down, from central London to Aberdeen, had a dog turd with my name on it;

I spent more time looking at the ground directly in front of me than at the sights. However, this has changed. Britain is poo-free thanks to heavy council fines, and wandering tourists are no longer head-down but are able to zigzag about willy-nilly with a camera permanently pressed to their preferred eye. As a result I had stupidly developed a false sense of security about all things poo-related.

Consequently, I was a little taken aback a week later while wandering down a crowded Paris street. I was there for only a few days, trying to drum up new business. I left the meeting feeling positive and decided to kill my last few hours watching the fourteenth of July Bastille Day parade.

I stopped, turned to cross the street, and there directly opposite me was a huge Chanel store. Standing in the entrance was an immaculately dressed middle-aged woman holding a delicate silver lead in her gloved hand, attached to which was a spotless white poodle puckering up and attempting to squat, and no doubt eventually shit, right in the middle of the signature black-and-white doormat that probably cost more than my car.

But people wandered past looking relaxed and there was an air of celebration in the city. The French lady politely ignored her poodle, which was punching out the poo of its life. Well-dressed young people stepped over it as they made their way up the expansive marble steps into the Chanel building.

Finally it was over, the little dog bounced up and down with joy next to what looked like its own bodyweight in shit. Then, to my surprise, the lady opened her Louis Vuitton handbag and produced a dainty pink tissue. Oh, I thought, she's actually going to make some sort of effort to get rid of it. I was curious about what technique she would adopt for such a delicate manoeuvre, short of retrieving a shovel from her bag. But, no, she simply bent over and wiped the dog's bum, stuck the tissue on top of the turd and minced off down the street.

I enjoyed the parade. All of France's military might have marched by, gleaming in bright colourful splendour. I left central Paris looking like Ken Done just threw up all over it. Here's a hint: wear your old shoes if you go, and if you visit the Chanel store remember to check the mat before you wipe your feet.

4 ENDURING THE RIGGERS

There was a time when I didn't know my father. There was a time when he didn't know me. Now, there's rarely time enough to take a breath between conversations.

He is very happily retired these days, but in his past he was a Royal Air Force squadron leader, and after leaving the service he embarked on an oilfield career that he excelled in, reinventing himself as a directional driller and, by all accounts, a very good one. In his mid-thirties at the time, with my mother and two young children to support, a complete change of career and environment must have been hard to deal with, let alone working on the rigs. I never made the effort to spend any time with him following my parents' divorce when I was nine. And it didn't help when my mother, my sister and I moved from England to Perth when I was fifteen. It is only now, at thirty-six, that I've started to realise what I have missed. He is, after all, my father, and as I discovered on my last visit he has the same interests as I do, indeed he has the same walk when he's pissed, the same laugh and the same ability to fall on his feet no matter how badly he's fucked up. Every now and again I run into an old drilling hand on some rig in the middle of nowhere who knew my father; it's a big industry, global, but within the drilling side it's very small. You can have a bad job one week in the Middle East, and a week later they're discussing it on a rig in Australia.

Dad looked relaxed. A few years had gone by so we had a lot to talk about. I told him about Clare, my girlfriend, and how, despite all the years of listening to horrific divorce stories in locker rooms offshore from here to North Africa, I was ready to ask her to marry me. His response was perfect: 'Marry for love, son, but if she's rich, don't forget your dear old dad,' and with that he burst out laughing. We cracked a bottle of Macallan and talked through the night.

I told him about a motorcycle accident I'd had a few years earlier. The recently restored bike was pristine until I had a classic 'Get Off', sending my bike that had taken two years to complete into a wall, then I went offshore the next day with a cracked rib and large chunks missing from various parts of my body. I nearly lost my job at the time as I had trouble strapping myself into the four-point harness on the chopper in Russia. Dad gave me a hard look, had a sip on his whisky, delivered a brief lecture on late braking and wearing leathers, then launched into a story about the time he decided to ride his Vincent 'Black Shadow' down the hall and through the bar of an Officers' Mess on an air base forty-odd years ago.

He was drunk, but that goes without saying, got as far as the entrance, hammered the throttle, dropped the clutch and just held on, but didn't actually go anywhere. After a couple of seconds he realised that the thirty feet of red hall carpet the bike was sitting on was being hurled out the door and into the carpark by the Vincent's spinning back wheel. Then he ran out of carpet, and the bike shot out from under him and landed in a trophy cabinet halfway down the hall. He was in serious trouble, but landed on his feet.

'Wasn't too long after that when I met your mother in Germany,' he said and smiled, then mysteriously left the room. When he came back he handed me a small velvet box. Inside, twinkling at me, was a beautiful antique engagement ring. 'This is the only engagement ring in the family, son. It's very old, I've been holding onto it for you.'

I told him I was going to Afghanistan to write about the use of private military contractors and oil. He gave me his take on working in that part of the world, as many years ago he had been tasked with finding a flight crew who went down in the desert, and during his time drilling he had worked predominantly in the Middle East. So between his four years running the desert survival school in El Adem for the Air Force and fifteen years on rigs directional drilling in the desert, he had some good advice to give me and a few great stories as well. It wasn't the first time he had suddenly opened up with insights into his past. The last time I was here I had a blast with him and a couple of his mates in London. I was only there for less than a day before the office phoned and told me to go back to the rig, but that short day was one of the best I'd spent with my dad.

Einstein once said: 'Imagination is more important than knowledge. Knowledge is limited. Imagination encircles the world.' My imagination has saved me, and tortured me, but only once did it run away and leave me sitting alone at a table with the only two men who really scared me. It was some ten years ago, and it started on a flight.

'You don't look nervous,' she said with a smile, as we dropped out of the sun and into a typically British winter. I had been calming my nerves by chatting to the woman sitting next to me on the flight. Since we departed Singapore she had regaled me with everything from her messy divorce to her daughter's academic prowess, and even better her ex-husband was paying for her daughter's education. I was starting to appreciate her ex-husband's side of the story after being married to this woman for twelve years. The in-flight movie was *Silence of the Lambs*, and I have to say it had me on edge because there I was trapped in a conversation about how scared she was after watching it. 'It's about time they made a film with a strong female lead who saves the day. I'd like to see my ex-husband in a cell like that one.' The woman was opinionated and annoying in a way that just made you angry enough to fantasise about getting out of your economy-class seat and gaining instant access to first class, pausing on your way through the curtain to blow a raspberry at her.

But she was distracting me from the uneasy nerves that pulled at my gut. Yes, I suppose I didn't look nervous, but nerves turn some people green and others into stand-up comedians. I was doing the latter. She was laughing so much that little bits of spittle would occasionally land on my face, only fuelling my desire to walk off. 'God, that's so funny,' she spluttered, only just managing to stop her false teeth from landing on her tray table.

I gave her a convincing grin and thought about Dad. It was 1997, I was twenty-seven years old, and in a fit of impulse I was about to arrive unannounced in London where I planned to surprise him. We didn't really know each other, but I'd slipped into the past and had forgotten that I was considered a 'grown-up' now. So the nerves that shook me as a boy in the presence of my father seemed to have manifested and turned me into a comedian at the thought of just turning up at his place.

Dad answered the phone in a strong voice, and sounded overjoyed when he heard I would be on the train within the hour. 'I'll be there to pick you up,' he said.

The arrival hall in Heathrow spread out in front of me. All I had was a small grip bag, no check-in luggage, so I was one of the first people to pass through the big automatic doors and get the full onslaught of faces all registering blankly past me. There towards the back was Dad. He had surprised me in return by driving to the airport. He had grown a full beard and turned a little greyer, but otherwise looked happy and relaxed.

The drive to his London flat was filled with long tortured moments of awkward silence. He dropped me off, gave me the once-around his place and was out the door before I could string two words together. I wandered about the flat for a while, a bit baffled, and decided to make a cup of tea. And that's when I saw the half-empty bottle of Macallan on the shelf. I had two big drinks and flopped down on the couch, feeling light-headed. The phone rang. It was Dad. He said he was at his club with some mates and that I should join them. He told me to go into his closet and find a shirt and tie. Seeing nothing for it, I grabbed a cab and was soon standing at the entrance to what looked just like a regular Victorian terrace house. I rang the doorbell and a man in a suit answered, gave me a wormy dyspeptic smile and asked if he could 'help' me. So it would seem that I had just arrived at a gentleman's club in a Billabong T-shirt and jeans, and that's not acceptable attire at a men's club, so he gave me the pleb's one-size-fits-all shirt, clip-on tie and sports jacket combo.

In I went. The building was old and smelled like a church would if the congregation smoked cigars. It was full of middle-aged men sipping brandy who looked over their glasses at me while folding copies of the *Financial Times*. Dad was at the back in the corner with another man. They were just sitting there, looking at a bottle of wine lying over to one side in a silver cradle.

'Nice outfit,' Dad said and shook his head at me. I was introduced to his mate, Mick. He was heavy-set, his nose had been broken a few times, his voice carried a gravely tone, and he looked me in the eye when I shook his hand. I liked that. He had an Irish accent and could, I was to discover, drink his own bodyweight in alcohol.

Eventually I had to ask about the wine. They had just purchased it at auction. I reached out towards it. 'Please don't do that,' said a sharp pronounced voice from behind me. I can't remember his name, but I nearly jumped when I turned and saw him; he looked just like Hannibal Lecter from the in-flight movie. He gave me a look that ever so discreetly suggested that if I did touch the bottle he would wait until the wine had breathed, then eat my liver. So I just sat there and sipped on my beer.

I had another two beers and, after being offshore on the rig for more than a month prior to this, combined with Dad's whisky, I was suddenly quite pissed. Nevertheless, for all the jokes and stories I could feel something else going on, like I wasn't supposed to be there. I'd been around some heavy guys on the rigs by that time, older men who included me in the conversation in the bar after the job but not yet to the point of telling me who they were plotting against. I could smell the same guarded undertone here; there was a slightly sinister edge to the table, and I felt like I'd just interrupted their plot to do a bank job or something. We continued with polite conversation that passed the wait, the wait for the 'Corker'.

'He's a specialist, and besides I want to see his technique.' Dad was making no sense to me as he chatted with the others. What the fuck is a 'Corker'? I was thinking.

Dr Lecter picked up on the giant question mark above my head as he puffed occasionally on the end of his cigar. He leaned in towards my right ear and said, 'The Corker will be here soon. He will open the bottle using his own method . . . that will be as entertaining as it is rewarding. Clarice, would you like to try the brandy?'

Fuck, he sounds just like him too. I was having deja vu. And did the motherfucker just call me Clarice? I nodded at him.

'This really is a special day, young Paul.' The Doctor had a thin smile and a bright gold pin buried in the middle of a dark red neck tie. I felt like the prey before the giant angler fish, caught in the twinkle of bio-luminescence before death. 'Do you have your father's passion for single malts?' He poured me a glass of brandy and pushed it across the table.

'Thank you, yes, I love it. I always pick up a bottle duty-free when I crew-change back home,' I said. The brandy tasted like money. I don't belong in here, I thought.

'I've known your father for many years. You're a lot like he was at your age. I suspect working on the rigs agrees with you. He was also an adventurous soul in his past, although now, I dare say, he's slowed down a bit.'

'I'm not running the London marathon, but I'll kick your arse any time,' Dad said and grinned over the table at Dr Lecter, who smiled and shucked the end off a thin cigar. He replaced the silver cutter back in his black waistcoat pocket and struck a match.

'He still figures largely in your value system, even though you have not spent much quality time together.' The cigar spat flames from its end as the Doctor puffed and rolled it around between pursed lips. I was mesmerised.

'What line of work are you in?' I changed the subject and finished another brandy, banging the glass down on the table by accident.

'I was in the service with your father, and now I practise medicine.'

'Oh really, what kind?' I tried to sound sober.

'Psychiatry,' he said.

Oh Christ. Do you eat people? I wanted to say. And why aren't you locked up in a perspex-walled dungeon? This was entirely too weird.

'This is a celebratory drink, a one of a kind, for a one-of-a-kind criminal. It's good you arrived like this. Why don't you tell him now, Allan?' he eyeballed Dad.

Dad stopped talking and suddenly became serious. He looked across the room. 'The Corker's here,' he said.

My jaw slightly agape, I swivelled my head in the direction of the door. There stood a middle-aged short, balding man in a blue suit. He saw us and smartly walked over. In his right hand he held an old-fashioned black leather doctor's bag.

'Good afternoon, gentlemen,' he quipped as the bag's catch sprang open. His hands, manicured and soft, laid out a series of objects in a well-rehearsed method.

'We're so glad you could come. Can we offer you a drink?' asked Dr Lecter.

'Thank you, no,' replied the Corker.

'This is something you won't see very often, Paul.' Dad leaned back in his tub chair is if he was about to get a lap dance.

The table was cleared of empty glasses, and on it sat a Bunsen burner connected to a small silver gas canister, a French garrotte of platinum wire, and a high ball of ice water, into which the Corker coiled up a pheasant feather.

His tools ready, the Corker carefully slid the bottle in its cradle so it sat directly in front of him. The wine was French, if memory serves, a 1945 Château Pêtrus—not that it meant anything to me at the time. I just wanted to see how this little fat man was going to open the bottle with the assorted kit on the table in front of him. Especially the feather, couldn't wait to see what he did with that feather.

What did Dr Lecter mean by criminal? Who's the criminal? I didn't know it, but I was about to have the best time I'd had in years, with these characters. I later learned that the celebration was due to the three of them successfully tracking down a particularly nasty con artist who had taken an elderly friend of theirs, Bill, to the cleaners. Once a mountain of a man, Bill had become frail and his wife had passed away. Susceptible and in bad health, he had been duped in the worst possible way. The poor old boy had bought into the con, and as a result he had lost his life savings, his home, even the car. The con was clever, but this time it was played out on the wrong man. Dad, Mick and Dr Lecter, all ex-military, financially independent and bored silly, decided to go after the bastard. They had a real soft spot for Bill, himself a decorated veteran of the worst parts of World War II. The con man was systematically tracked from Dorset in England's south all the way to the north of Scotland, where they eventually caught up with him, in disguise, his features changed and posing as a priest in a small town. They recouped Bill's savings, his house was saved, even the car was returned. The con man had an epiphany, no doubt at the thought of Dr Lecter making soup out of his brain, and turned himself in,

God bless him, and as I understand it he's still languishing in prison. Bill has since departed our world, but I know he went with his affairs in good stead and a smile on his face.

The cigar Dr Lecter gave me was making my head feel five pounds lighter, and I forgot the whole 'don't inhale' thing. Nimble fat little fingers adjusted the flame jetting from the tip of the Bunsen burner, heat sending invisible waves into the air that distorted Dad's face across the table. I laughed, but it turned into a cough. 'He's turning green,' Mick said and looked at the Doctor, but he was fixed on the Corker's hands slowly winding his fingers around the polished wooden ends of his wire garrotte. He pulled the wire taut with a 'twang', looked at me briefly and started to heat the wire in the flame until it glowed white hot.

'How's that cigar, Paul?' I heard the Doctor ask me through the brown cloud around my head.

'It's great,' I replied, my head swimming in cotton wool. 'Cheers.' My glass bounced off his with an unmistakable crystal 'ping'. The brandy was like slipping into a warm bath.

'Was it rolled on the thigh of a pretty girl?' I asked. I'm used to Marlboros and Mekong whisky in the back room of some oilfield bar while semi-naked dancing girls gyrate up and down on a pole. Instead, I was sitting there in London in the middle of the old-boy network, drinking vintage brandy and puffing on Cuban cigars while a little bald man opened a bottle of wine with a feather . . . oh yes, the feather.

Once the platinum wire was ready, the Corker wrapped it once around the glass neck, pulling it taut, then in one fluid move he dropped the garrotte and pulled the feather from the glass. It sprang into a metre-long rainbow of wet icy colour that he gently stroked across the hot neck of the bottle. It literally jumped apart, the little man catching the severed top in his free hand. I picked up the top of the bottle; the glass was perfectly cut. The top had been dipped in wax, but I could see the cork inside and it looked intact. The Corker packed up his tools, bid us good day, turned on his heel and was gone. His job was, evidently, done.

I was on a rig a week later telling the story to some mates, who grabbed a blow torch and some baling wire and set off to try it out. It didn't work.

The wine was savoured and sniffed, held up to the light and rolled about on tongues. I stuck to the brandy, the wine would have been wasted on me anyway.

Dad was enjoying himself. He came back from the bar with a bottle of Macallan and before long I was hearing stories.

There were three that I have never forgotten.

5 THE OLD MAN

It was 1960, my father was a navigator in the RAF, flying on B Flight of 3 Squadron based at RAF Gelsenkirchen in West Germany. It was there that he met my mother, but that's another story. At the time, he was flying the Javelin Mk 5 all-weather night fighter, a delta wing two-seat interceptor which flew in the 1950s and 1960s. It was B Flight's turn for night flying, and Dad and his pilot, Lieutenant Bill Swettenham, flew a routine sortie of practice interceptions through the early evening of a cool clear April dusk. Later in the night they were briefed for a second mission, where they would go up with another Javelin and practise interceptions, taking alternate turns at being the target. The flight commander, Squadron Leader Peter Stark, was the leader in the other Javelin, with Flight Lieutenant John Lomas in the back cockpit.

Dad was young and full of beans, this was his first operational flying tour, he loved his job and really enjoyed the challenge of chasing unseen targets on airborne interception radar. His face lit up with recall as the ashtray became Stark's Javelin in his right hand with Dr Lecter's silver Dunhill lighter in pursuit between his thumb and index finger. This night was good, Dad said, the weather was excellent, visibility eight miles with minimal cloud cover, and the two jets played cat and mouse for almost an hour. It was during their return or 'recovery' to base that problems for the leader began to show. Interceptions were completed at height in those days, as the potential threat came from high-level Russian bombers. The procedure for recovery was to return overhead to base at height, in this case about forty thousand feet, go into a dive circle, then the first aircraft would dive more steeply in the direction opposite the active runway to about ten thousand feet while the second aircraft would complete one orbit in the dive circle and follow the leader down two minutes later. This separation was made so that the aircraft would land separately two minutes apart, giving the controllers maximum practice.

Dad and Bill were halfway down the dive descent behind the leader when he transmitted a short, garbled radio call to the tower saying that he had serious hydraulic problems and that two of his three hydraulic pumps had failed.

'Pumps one and three,' said Mick and winked at Dad.

'That's right.' Dad looked back at me. I was keeping up with the story so far but it had suddenly got a bit technical, as these stories sometimes do.

Dr Lecter's gold pin drew closer. 'If Squadron Leader Stark had lost his number two and three pumps, then he would have lost all his flying controls and immediately ejected.'

'Right again.' Dad was back on the ashtray with the Dunhill closing fast. So John and Peter were now hurtling towards Earth with only half their flying control, making the aircraft soft to handle and very slow to react. Peter no longer had airbrakes, flaps, undercarriage lowering or wheel brakes for landing.

Peter Stark was a big man. South African by birth, he had joined the SAAF in World War II and had extensive flying experience. 'He was imperturbable and only spoke when he had something to say,' the Doctor said as he put his feet up, leaned back in his chair and disappeared into a cloud of cigar smoke.

'Indeed,' Dad agreed, 'and right now he was busy. We used our airbrakes to control speed on the descent, but Peter was going in hot. Although he got a good radar pick-up and clear directions to the airfield, he had no flaps to limit his approach speed.

'Without hydraulics to lower his undercarriage, he had used the emergency air bottle provided for this eventuality to get his wheels down, but once they are down the wheels cannot be raised again, even on the ground.'

The lead Javelin's radio contacts were infrequent and broken, but Peter managed to touch down just after midnight on runway 27 heading west. 'Just how fast Peter was going must be left to conjecture but he landed bloody fast,' Dad said. 'Our normal touchdown would be around 145 knots. I reckon he was at more than twice that speed. He literally had no means of slowing down and must have been worried that pump two might also fail at any time. If that happened he would have been too low to eject. The relief must have been massive when he knew he was on the ground.'

'At least he was on the deck, but how do you stop a seventeen-ton fully armed jet that's running out of runway?' asked Mick.

'You don't,' said the Doctor. 'You get out of the fucking way.' He was laughing.

'There's an emergency braking lever back on the left side of the cockpit,' said Mick.

Dad nodded sagely and said, 'Yeah, Bill and I were flying alongside Peter at two hundred feet, we were right next to him as he touched down and hurtled down Gelsenkirchen's main runway in the dark, heading for Holland. Bill and I knew Peter would be reaching back frantically pulling on the emergency brake lever. In the event, when he pulled the lever the remaining pressure just bled through the leak that happened during the flight when a union failed. So there were Peter and John, they hadn't slowed down at all, completely out of control doing three hundred knots down the runway with no way of stopping and literally going west.

'We watched him shoot off the end of the runway at flying speed. Bill said, "I guess the emergency brake didn't work." Then Bill broke off and banked hard, executing a remarkable landing on a parallel peri-track.'

Dad and Bill landed without incident, climbed out of their aircraft and ran over to the squadron hanger, only to discover that nobody had realised Peter and John had just started an off-road trip through the German countryside. They had made no further radio calls and the tower personnel didn't notice that they never taxied past.

'I called the ops desk to alert fire and ambulance crews and the CO,' Dad went on. 'Then Bill and I grabbed a Land Rover and took off after the boys. We soon found a bloody huge hole in the boundary fence, and all the approach lights for runway 9 were smashed to bits.

'Peter and John would have just sat there in the cockpit as one of Her Majesty's very expensive brand new aircrafts ran on and on through the German countryside. Peter could not raise the undercarriage as the emergency air system he used to blow down the wheels prevented this, so they went on like that for more than two kilometres.'

Following the Javelin's path, Dad and Bill drove on in the dark, through several large fields, finding large stone walls demolished and the occasional, surprised, slightly scorched sheep, through an orchard, through someone's garden. Peter and John had passed through the greenhouse, through the garage, collected the washing and the washing line, then through another wall into the carpark at the rear of a pub. By chance the port wingtip had taken a few bricks out of the corner of the pub, sending the jet into two parked cars and turning it around towards the building across the street where it lurched over a ditch, losing its wheels, and finally came to rest in a wood directly opposite the pub.

Miraculously, no-one was hurt.

I fell back laughing. 'Go on, then what happened?' I leaned in.

'Peter and John didn't realise it but they were now in Holland,' Dad continued. 'Peter, disoriented after his cross-country rampage, jumped out leaving John to stay with the jet, then he took off heading east to get help.

'All the locals came staggering out of the pub—they had been in there all night drinking and had just heard seventeen tons of aircraft thunder pass, still at some speed. One of them pointed out that his car was missing, then noticed the missing bricks. Of course, they all assumed that John, who was sitting on the ground near the road, was the pilot and had shown great skill in avoiding the pub in the dark. They ran over and the publican gave John a bottle of Dutch gin to steady him and to thank him for his heroism. John knocks off the whole bottle—he doesn't speak a word of Dutch, he's just happy to be alive—and lets them pick him up on their shoulders and dance about on the road.'

That's when Dad and Bill reached the back of the pub, nearly knocking over Peter who was running back down his trail of destruction. Peter got in the car, and when they drove round the corner they saw John enjoying an impromptu street party.

The fire engines, ambulances, and everyone else including the station commander—in full dress uniform—arrived shortly afterwards. 'The station commander at that time was Group Captain Desmond Hughes DSO DFC AFC,' Dad explained, 'a most impressive officer who was generally admired by all under his command. He had been a pilot in the Battle of Britain, his wartime record was superb and he went on to command RAF College at Cranwell.

'A huge crowd had gathered around John and us. The commander stepped forward. He had seen the downed aircraft in the wood on its belly, obviously a write-off. Even then the loss of our latest warplane would have been considerable to the RAF and the United Kingdom at large.

'In his deep, powerful voice, the commander asked John, "My boy, what have you done?"

'Standing there in his flying suit, helmet in one hand, empty bottle of gin in the other, John saluted and said, "I'm sorry, sir, but I've drunk the whole bottle."'

With half the bottle of Macallan gone, we were all laughing loudly, and some of the other men in the club had joined us to listen to Dad's stories.

The next yarn followed soon after. It was less than a year after Peter Stark's crash, and all the same guys were still flying at RAF Gelsenkirchen in the same Javelins. There were two marks of aircraft, the Mk 4 and Mk 5, but the main difference was the size of the fuel tanks and therefore the range. As they routinely flew in pairs, the ops desk tried to give each pair the same mark so they flew together for the whole mission, and on those occasions when different marks came up at the same time, the longer range Javelin 5 would go up first, followed ten minutes later by the Javelin 4, which would join up for the main sortie.

One Monday morning in May, Dad and his pilot were briefed to fly with Brian Mason and Bish Siviter. Brian and Bish were among the squadron's most experienced crews, and they had already completed four night-fighter tours when they joined 11 Squadron. And they were brothers-in-law. Ten years earlier Bish had married Brian's sister, and they had been flying together ever since. Brian was allocated a Mk 5 Javelin and Dad had the Mk 4. The plan was for Brian to take off first, then Dad would follow and join up ten minutes later. So Dad and his pilot were in the hanger checking the aircraft paperwork with two ground staff when Brian started up his port engine.

Cartridges were used to fire up the engines; a slow burning cordite charge would take about eight seconds to spin a small six-foot turbine up to fifty-five thousand rpm. This was geared down to the main engine rotor, and when that was running at two thousand rpm the fuel injectors would squirt fuel into burn chambers, and electronic igniters would fire the fuel and start the engine.

It had rained over the weekend and everything was really sodden. They heard Brian start his ignition sequence in the background as they poured over their paperwork in a small hut at one end of the hanger, then suddenly a massive bang.

'The first thing I remember was the sound of really fast-moving metal fragments ricocheting off the ground,' Dad said, 'and a moment later that horrible "Woooof" of a fuel fire.'

Trained to react in an emergency, all four men yelled 'Don't panic' and ran into each other. Then they all peered round the open door of the hut, and what they saw was frightening.

The starter turbine had disintegrated at maximum rpm, and the tiny blades had torn the collector fuel tank in half and set it ablaze, dumping burning jet fuel under the aircraft and starting a serious fire in the middle of a row of shiny, new, multimillion-dollar jets. The warrant officer grabbed the phone to call the fire section under the tower a few hundred yards away. The sergeant took a small trolley fire extinguisher and charged across the tarmac to help the ground crew. With great presence of mind Dad's pilot sprang into the aircraft next to the one on fire, quickly started it and moved it forward to safety, at the same time making room for the fire engines.

Meanwhile, the Javelin Mk 5 was completely covered in flames, and it was fully armed and very dangerous. Apart from the seven tons of fuel it carried, there were eight hundred rounds of 30-mm cannon shells and four live air-to-air missiles.

Dad ran to the edge of the fire. He could see Brian and Bish inside the cockpit, frantically trying to get out before they either burned alive or just went bang. Ejector seats weren't an option; they would just send them into the hanger roof at a rate that would have the ground crew hosing them into the nearest drain.

Normally in these situations the navigator would just jump off the back of the aircraft, leaving the pilot sole use of the ladder. But the flames, burning over the wings and all around the back of the jet, made this impossible. The only remaining escape route was forward. Suddenly, Bish the navigator was free of the perspex canopy covering the back cockpit, he shot a glance over his shoulder and saw only flames, so he clambered forward and dove off the nose of the jet. His old pal and brother-in-law Brian had shut down the engine, closed the fuel cocks and switched off the electrics. As the fire engines arrived he was sliding down the ladder to escape the flames.

'The next thing I remember was the post-mortem in the aircrew room in the hanger,' Dad said, finishing his whisky. 'Everybody who was anybody was gathered around the table, the room was packed. The fire had been put out by four fire tenders covering the aircraft in foam. A doctor was bandaging Bish's ankle, as he had sprained it leaping from the nose of the jet ten feet up.

'There was Group Captain Hughes again, asking questions. "What did you do after you climbed out of the rear cockpit?" he asked Bish.

'"Sir," replied Bish, "I climbed into the fixed combing between the two cockpits and helped my pilot out of his cockpit, then I jumped from the front of the aircraft, Sir."

'After a short silence, Brian turned to his navigator and asked, "What was it you did after climbing onto the fixed combing?"

'Bish looked his pilot and brother-in-law in the eye and said, "I helped you out of your cockpit."

'There was another short silence, then Brian lent down to reach under the table to pick up his flying helmet. He placed it in the middle of the table so that everyone in the room could see it. There was a size ten, half-melted rubber boot print right across the top of it.'

Dad was on a roll. I was captivated and happy that I was there to see all the boozing and storytelling, the benefits of a classical education displayed with real panache after drinking so much. It made me wish that I had gone to university, back when it was free. Now I suppose if you wanted to eat two-minute noodles and spend the rest of your life in debt, university could be a good idea. But while some of my friends were at uni, I was happy to work offshore. I was still interested in the life the rigs held up, the random adventure was fine with me.

'Let's eat,' said Mick as he stood up. 'What do you feel like?'

We all looked at the Doctor as if he would suggest the best place in London to enjoy a sautéed human hand.

We went through the city in a black cab; it was getting dark and people were starting the journey home. The taxi pulled up outside a French restaurant with long wooden tables outside and starched white tablecloths that clipped against the breeze. It was just opening.

'I love this place. Have the rabbit, it's the chef's specialty.' Dr Lecter looked excited and waited for us to enter through the old wooden doors.

After a while I got my second wind, like drinking yourself sober. 'What happened after Germany?' I asked my father.

'I was posted to Singapore, still on Javelins,' Dad replied.

Then over dinner I heard all about Gus, a young pilot who had befriended my father years earlier after Dad crashed in a paddock in the Welsh mountains—a paddock that belonged to Gus's father. Apparently on seeing a jet crash into his field, he went running up and pointed a shotgun at my father in case he was a German; though the war had ended some years prior to this, life in the Welsh mountains moved at a slower pace in the 1950s. Gus was amazed when he saw the downed jet. My father asked to use the phone to call for help, but it was going to take some time, so he sat down in the farmhouse and got talking to Gus and his dad. They stayed good friends from then on. Gus later went off to join the RAF and did very well, becoming a pilot and eventually flying Javelins in the same squadron as Dad.

Tragically, while they were based in Singapore, Gus was killed after ejecting from his aircraft at low level. As the squadron leader, Dad was tasked to fly Gus's remains back home to the Welsh mountains. Dad was driving down Bukit Timah Road in a Leyland Mini staff car—Gus had been cremated and was in an urn sitting on the back seat—when he hit a wooden cart being pulled by an ox. Dad broke his nose on the steering wheel and the urn slammed into the dashboard, knocking its lid off and turning Gus into one giant grey cloud that filled the Mini and sent my father coughing into the street. Blood pouring from a smashed nose, Dad did his best to scoop his old friend back into the urn, but after the wind had gone through the little car there wasn't much more than a finger or two left in the urn.

Dad made it to the airport, boarded the flight and chain-smoked a carton of Rothmans, ashing into the urn all the way to London. What ended up sitting on the family's mantle for years was mainly cigarette ash, most of Gus went down the road. It took Dad years to tell Gus's father what had happened, and the real reason why he arrived at the remote farmhouse in the middle of the night with blood all over his uniform.

We had dessert, the waiter taking good care of us, and one after another the stories came out.

'I was flying with your dad in the back seat once,' the Doctor said. He loosened his red tie and let a smile spread over his face. 'He had constructed this extendable arm from meccano, and on the end was the hand from a first-aid dummy with a flying glove on it. As a pilot, you'd be bombing along when your dad would stretch this thing out and say, "Excuse me," and tap you on the shoulder with this thing. It's impossible to reach that far forward in the cockpit, so when this hand reaches over and taps you on the shoulder mid-flight you fairly shit yourself.'

Meeting Mick and the good Doctor was superb fun. Seeing them bounce off my dad and being there for the resulting hilarity opened up my feelings towards my father and gave me a better idea of the kind of man he is. And after hearing him talk about his father and the way things were at that time in Britain, I had a new understanding. From that moment on I have had regular contact with Dad, even though it is usually just a phone call. That was enough for us to start again at being a son, and a father.

6 THE TENDER TRAP

Shortly after I returned from London, I was in Perth for a month, working in an oilfield workshop. Tasman Oil Tools had the contract to service a new Top Drive running tool that I was very interested in, partly because it's a new design that actually works and partly because, if it keeps working, it's going to replace me one day. So I wanted to 'know thine enemy', and after a phone call to Ross, the director, I found myself eye to eye with the thing. It was painfully simple, easy to rig up and I even liked the colour. Bad news.

'Not much to it really,' said Ross. He had done me a favour by putting me on his workshop crew as I was in need of a pay cheque, and he was happy to have someone on hand who knew their way around drilling tools. Ross is a great guy; he has that rare ability to work alongside his employees. He would pass the workshop, see something that didn't look right, and before you could say, 'Ross I can't get this fucking thing back together', he would have his shirt sleeves rolled up and be scanning the bench for the right tools.

I enjoyed working there—the crew were great and they got

along well with each other. The Russian rig aside, I'm more used to working for your classic, large, eco-friendly oil consortium. The ones who plant a tree for every well they drill and put an overpriced supermarket into every one of their petrol stations. They, along with car manufacturers, dump hundreds of millions of dollars into research towards new energy—hydrogen, nuclear, or mining Australia's vast uranium reserves—without making too much noise. But underneath all the environmentally friendly wallpaper and glossy corporate brochures, they're usually just another conglomeration of ruthless and aggressive bullies, located in a tall, imposing building down town. While I was at Tasman enjoying the workshop life, just such a giant oil consortium phoned, and predictably I said, 'Sure, I'd love the job,' and within twenty-four hours I was on hypocrite airlines bound for Japan.

The rig was just outside Iwamizawa, a small town one hour by train from Sapporo on Japan's northernmost island of Hokkaido. I love working in Japan, it's so clean and polite. When I arrived, it was the middle of winter. Coming from a Western Australian summer it was cold, really cold, the kind of cold that freezes your snot and makes your balls shrivel up and disappear in desperate search of some warmth. So I spent the first few days wrapped in layer upon layer of clothing, looking a bit like the Michelin man, until I slowly got used to the temperature.

The job started well. We had a new computer system on the drill floor that looked impressive, with just the right amount of lights, bells and whistles to attract every Japanese guy on location with even the slightest interest in computers to the drill floor like sociopaths to the 'Big Brother' house. But you can't trust computers. As if on cue, just as I had an assorted plethora of excited high-level Japanese oil company men in hard-hats and matching thermals crowded around our new computer, chatting, pointing and asking an unbelievable amount of questions, it turned itself off.

Fuck, aw fuck, I was shouting in my head, all the while smiling the idiotic way you do when something stops working at a critical moment and you have no idea how to fix it.

The Japanese consortium said 'Ohhhh' in unison and nodded.

Jake, my derrickman, walked over and pulled off his hard-hat and balaclava. 'What the fuck's wrong with it?' He knew as well as I did that after fifteen minutes we had to pay for the rig's time; if you can't fix the problem in that time and you don't have a spare unit then you get the bill for the down time. Time is money in drilling. If the rig stops, someone has to pay.

'I've no idea, it's the new system,' I hissed through my teeth. Through the freezing wind and snow I felt my cheeks burning and could see lots of Japanese eyes checking watches. Your time starts now.

'So can you fix it?' asked Jake.

'I know how to run the damn thing, but not how to troubleshoot it. Send two guys down, unpack the backup, you rig this one down, I'll get on the phone.' I could feel the panic rising in my throat like hot lava, but I knew that I had to keep on smiling and pretend like hell that I knew exactly how to get this thing going again.

Jake turned on his heel and waded through the crowd of snap-happy Japanese guys. The crane was already booming over our spares container. I checked my watch; I had ten minutes to fix this computer.

A big white phone sat in the middle of the tool pusher's desk. I pulled off my hard-hat, balaclava, gloves, goggles and unzipped the front of my jacket, then sat down, thumbed through my tally book, found the 'don't panic' number and dialled. Instantly someone answered. I had no idea what time it was in Houston, but it was like calling the White House situation room. I was asked my name and where I was calling from, what job I was on, what the problem was, and bang, I was transferred to some guy in R&D—reserve and development—in Louisiana.

With the manual in one hand and the phone in the other, I tried to stay calm as the R&D guy who invented the new computer suggested more and more unconventional solutions.

'We've never tried this before, okay, but just take the cover off the back, strip out the main power supply wires and plum it straight into the rig's power supply. Phone me back, let me know what happens, oh, and make sure you earth everything. Bye.' Click.

I looked up to a room full of curious Japanese men with cameras. It didn't take long but after a few minutes the computer was no longer an innovative, shiny thing symbolising all that is new in drill floor electronics. Instead, with all the cables and wires spilling out in every direction, it looked more like a scale model of the human intestinal tract.

I threw the switch and thank fuck it worked.

The Japanese consortium said 'Ahhhh' in unison, then it turned itself off again. 'Ohhhh,' they said.

I rigged up the backup unit, but it failed to start.

'Time,' said Jake as he followed me into the tool pusher's office, kicking the snow off his boots. 'You're supposed to be able to fix all our tools,' he added helpfully, lighting a cigarette.

'Well, I can't fix it this time,' I said, then picked up the phone and started dialling.

'Now we just look fucking stupid.' He glared at me across the small portacabin and sucked on his smoke.

'I'm going to sort this computer bullshit out,' I said firmly. I even convinced myself.

'So it didn't work Mr Carter?' the R&D guy asked, sounding as if he already knew it wouldn't and was waiting for my call.

'Oh hi, no it didn't work.' There was a pause, then he told me his last-ditch idea and said he hoped I would have 'a nice day'.

I slammed the phone down and walked back outside. When I got to the drill floor the boys were standing with the Japanese guys, all taking photos of each other. I did what the R&D guy suggested, and thank whoever it was that decided to give me a break, it worked.

'Ahhhh.'

I love working in Japan. Our clients didn't charge us for the down time, they helped us rig down after the job and offered us *sake* while we waited for the car. They organised all seven of our heavy containers to be returned to Singapore. They were polite, organised, and not one person said fuck, not even in Japanese.

The day after the computer incident, I left the 'bullet train' and the crew in Tokyo, and passed the wait for my flight to Australia via Singapore alone. I wanted to take time out to see a bit of Tokyo. I really love it. Love the graciousness of the old folk, the well-mannered way they welcome you and make you feel like you're all-important, and the complete wildness of the young kids with their crazy Americanese fads and fetishes. I went for a walk in the city's largest park, Mizumoto. It's huge, with long sprawling vistas making seamless transitions into boardwalks that hover over mirrored water from the Edo River. It was weirdly empty and completely peaceful. I spent the day covering as much of Tokyo as I could, unable to resist visiting my favourite places.

Since I was a kid I've collected knives. My dad gave me a pocket knife when I was about eight, and the first thing I did was cut myself, then I whittled down the leg of our coffee table. Some people accumulate stamps, coins or porcelain figurines. I'm into bikes and knives—go figure. Anyway Japan is the home of some of the most remarkable edged weapons. The deputy head of 'All Japan Swordsmiths Association', Shoji Yoshihara, makes possibly the finest blades in the world. He has been designated an important living cultural property of the Katsushika ward, which is the suburb of Tokyo where he lives. He made his first Katana sword at age twelve, studying the art at his grandfather's side. Making a sword the old-fashioned way, by hand, from scratch, from raw materials, takes time and supreme skill. Generations of craftsmen pass on their knowledge to the next generation, their entire lives devoted to the process. I find it fascinating. Yoshihara's blades bear his family's maker mark, 'Kuniie III'. Slipping one out of its *nebukuro* (sleeping-bag) reveals six months of solid work. Its graceful lines suggest only art; however, in the hands of a trained man this blade could easily pass through a human body. This is no letter opener, and at forty thousand dollars I handle it with extreme care.

Bikes and knives provide me with distraction. When I'm at home I'll spend hours tinkering on my bikes. It helps me think. And I've had a lot to think about. Putting the sword down I found myself retrieving the ring Dad gave me; I had been carrying it around for months inside the lining of my backpack. It was suddenly so clear to me what I needed to do. With that little velvet box in my hand, I was ready to go home and propose. No more custom bikes, or handmade knives. It was time to settle and make my move. I felt like the first prodigal monkey about to be shot into the grown-up space of kids, house payments and everything I'd tried to stay away from up until now.

Feeling euphoric, I wandered back towards the area where I had left the crew, down crowded streets, past tempura and grilled eel restaurants, until I found the boys. Ambu was sitting in front of the remains of one of his typical feeding frenzies—brown-sugar sweets, chilled cucumber skewers and *inago no tsukudani* (locusts preserved in soy sauce)—with sauce all over his chin.

Ambu is an Iban, a descendant of the headhunters who ran a major muck in their day, from possibly the darkest corner of the Malaysian jungle. Ambu is short, round and intensely funny. His frame disguises his power well. Ambu is strong and, given the right mindset, has no sense of fear. He wears the old-school bamboo tattoos of a 'headhunter' around his throat and speaks English like 'Tonto' from *The Lone Ranger*. 'Come we go,' he would say. I have known him for fifteen years, and he still surprises me. Sometimes I used to sit with Ambu and help him learn how to read and write English, and after a while he started reading everything aloud that he saw in English. 'Half-price specials,' he would suddenly stop and announce to the street. I told him I was going home to get married. 'OOOH, I come to your party,' he said, flashing me a huge grin and clapping.

Everyone had confirmed flights home except me, and the next day snow drifts and constant blizzard conditions made my exit difficult. I had made one of the most important decisions of my life while I was in Japan, only I couldn't get out of the country to do anything about it. I spent two nights in the transit hotel attached to the departure lounge at Narita International Airport waiting for a flight. Finally I was on my way to Singapore and then home, with no knives or bike parts this time, just a small box in my pocket that pressed against my thigh. It made me even more anxious to get home, back to Clare and the most life-changing exchange of words any couple can have. I kept checking the box in my pocket, just in case it had turned into a box of matches or a packet of mints—anything but an engagement ring. It was burning a hole through my leg. This is it, man, I'm going to get married. Christ, I hope she says yes. All kinds of elaborate plans for asking her the question were forming in my head, as romantic and surprising as I could muster without government backing and a helicopter.

I met Clare in a laundromat in Bondi. She was working there and I was going in with my offshore bag full of horrendously dirty rig gear every time I came home on crew change. This proved to be a little difficult when I realised that I only had that thirty-second window to ask her out. I mean, how do you do that? You're intensely attracted to the woman who's about to pull your manky, stained clothing out of an equally filthy rubber-lined giant grip bag that's been sealed tightly shut since you left the rig over twenty-four hours ago. Given all that's revolting about a working man's undies having time to develop a life of their own, I did struggle with how to attempt to ask her if she'd like to have a drink. Perhaps I should have gone out and bought a washing machine and done my own bloody laundry, waited a month so she had time to forget how repulsive it all was, then come back to ask her out. All that raced through my mind as she filled out the little receipt, hammered me with that fantastic smile and told me to come back at four. This went on for months. I ended up bringing in clean clothes, and then I asked her out.

'She's perfect,' I'd say to Erwin. We had been together for almost three years and I knew she was my future wife, but after years and years of listening to guys offshore talk about their upcoming divorces, and coming from an oilfield-broken home myself, I thought marriage was about as good an idea as Paris Hilton's hair extensions.

In Singapore, as I waited in line to enter the departure lounge, I checked the ring again. Then it was my turn to walk through the metal detector. It beeped. A pretty Singaporean girl with what looked like a TV remote on steroids motioned me over and waved her remote in ever-decreasing circles as the beep near my crotch got louder. I produced the box and she opened it, then shut it smartly and smiled at me in that knowing way.

I found myself grinning at strangers sitting opposite me in the departure lounge. They were filling out their arrival cards for Australian immigration. Occasionally, one would glance up the way you do when trying to remember your passport number without looking, and would accidentally make eye contact with me. I could see them thinking, 'Why is that man grinning? God, I hope he's not sitting next to me'.

As we boarded the plane, I was still checking my pocket. Yes, the ring's still there, not matches, ring. Every cliché ran through my head as I practised asking Clare to marry me. The flight was going to be a good one, it was only half full in economy and, being the 'red eye' departing at midnight, the aircraft was in darkness an hour after take-off, so I spread myself out over four seats and fell asleep easily under three blankets.

The main lights came on, burning through closed lids and waking everyone up. I sat up, the airline blanket crackling static electricity across my shoulders. They were serving breakfast, so I figured we must have been just a couple of hours from

Sydney. My hand reached down looking for the box, but there was no box, no matches, no mints, just air.

FUCK! A jolt of panic shot through me. I frantically shook out the blankets, dived my hands between the four seats I had to myself, then I was on the floor. It's on this aircraft, I'm going to find it, I thought, as I squashed my head under my seat and groped around under the life jacket. Nothing but empty blankets and headset bags. I crossed the aisle on all fours into the gap between the seats next to me. A little girl watched my progress as her parents slowly woke up and rubbed their eyes. A man asleep on his three seats woke up when I banged my head on his tray table, sending a glass of orange juice into his sleeping face. 'Sorry.' He looked back bemused at the sight of a stressed bald man four inches from his face who had somehow appeared from under his tray table.

I backed up into the aisle and into a waiting flight attendant. She handed me a paper towel. 'Have you lost something, sir?' she asked as I wiped orange juice off the back of my head.

'Yes, a small jewellery box with a ring inside.' I stood up to a dozen staring passengers, all stuffing their faces with omelette and coffee; I was obviously providing more entertainment than the TV in the seat in front of them.

'As soon as we have finished the breakfast service, we will help you find your box, sir. Would you like some breakfast?'

I shook my head and sat down feeling shattered. She pushed the trolley past me and down the aisle. I felt like there was a black cloud forming over my head, the sense of loss growing in my gut like a chemical spill.

After a while I noticed the little girl was standing there next to me. She had a stuffed toy kangaroo dangling from one hand, and in the other was my box. She held out her hand, and

I picked up the box and opened it—there was Clare's ring. A wave of relief crashed over me.

'Thank you, sweetheart,' I blubbered. I could have kissed her, but instead I got her a stuffed airplane from the in-flight duty-free magazine. Losing your engagement ring en route to a proposal is as naff as telling the teacher that the dog ate your homework, and I think that little girl knew it. All she did was look down and see a velvet box followed by a grown man on all fours.

Clare is, without question, the best part of getting home after a job. The look on her face when my key hits the lock keeps me smiling for days. It wasn't something I ever thought would be a permanent part of my life. Too often, the first victim of a life on the rigs is a relationship, but it was surprisingly easy to get used to the anticipation of seeing her after being away. This time I was bouncing off the walls with suppressed excitement and tension. I didn't sleep for three nights. I was so wired that one night at two in the morning I even got around to trying to assemble the Ikea furniture we'd stuffed in a cupboard months earlier, though it didn't take long before I realised that the multi-lingual instruction booklet alone would account for the entire Swedish suicide rate.

For me to ask Clare to be my wife involved getting into a mental state not unlike those karate guys before they headbutt a pile of bricks. Finally I abandoned my master plan and, just like everything else I've ever purposefully thought about in my life, I acted without the plan. I dumped the plan, fuck the plan, I can't wait, end of story.

It was early on a Friday morning. She had just stepped out of the shower and rounded the corner into our bedroom. I was waiting like a cartoon rabbit. You could have pumped my heart full of jet fuel and it wouldn't have beat any faster. You know those songs that stir up overwhelming feelings, there are one or two that without fail for a few seconds provoke your triggers to go off, and you're emotionally there, in that place, at that time, seeing that person, nostalgia like a tsunami covers your world, blanking out everything. And if you've had too much to drink when you hear it, especially if it's unplanned, you'll have to look away or leave the room, or smile like you're mental or cry. When Clare said 'yes' and I think about it, I get that feeling. Thank God she said yes.

When Clare said yes, in a sense it was like winning the spiritual and emotional lottery. It felt like it was a turning point in my future. For the first time in my life I had committed myself to something other than my own needs. I don't know if I deserve her love, but as the years go by I know Clare will always be there. Blind faith and complete trust works for me, life is just too bloody short.

We went to my favourite café in Sydney, Latteria. It's a great place, just a hole in the wall with wooden stools kerbside, and the best coffee and conversation of the day is had there. Our friends meet there in the mornings on their way to work, but on that particular morning I must have looked like I was sitting on the winning lotto numbers, I was bursting to tell them.

We started planning the wedding over the next six weeks, and everything was perfect. Then one morning I rolled over in bed, opened my eyes and there was Clare standing by the door with the kind of look that wakes you up in a second. Her hand was trembling as she held it up, a small white strip of card danced about in front of my face. 'Two stripes,' she said, her eyes wide open in shock. It took a full five seconds for the dustbin lid-sized penny to drop with a CLANG in my brain box.

I had a flashback. I remembered Drew, one of the first and best base managers I worked with. Not a big man, but in possession of a massive personality, Drew was the hinge pin into all the hilarity that threw fuel on the fire of creative pastimes in the Bruneian jungle. He was just fun to be around, and when there was nothing to do in the middle of monsoon season, and you were sitting in the staff house waiting for the weather to blow itself out, Drew was always able to think of something you actually wanted to do.

One of the guys had a massive one-hundred-and-fifty-pound Rottweiler called Summer who was playful, strong and dumb as a bag of hammers. At the far edge of the lagoon stood a cliff face, stretching up some fifty feet into the trees. During the monsoon it turned into a waterfall, transforming the lagoon into a river. Drew would wait until everyone was swimming about having a great time, then he'd climb around the back shallow side of the cliff to the top of the waterfall and sit in the hollowed-out rock at its edge. Summer would follow him because she was fixated on tennis balls and, of course, Drew would have made sure she saw him pop one in his pocket. Once settled in the curved rock right at the tip with a cold beer in his hand, the water cascading over him, he would show the soggy ball to Summer, sending her into a frenzy of excitement, then casually toss it over the edge.

The big dog would follow its flight path through the air, her tongue yo-yoing from the corner of her mouth, then with all she could muster she would jump into the abyss after it, treading air for a second then dropping. The guys swimming about below would get the plop of a tennis ball first, followed by the disturbing howl, before looking to see a one-hundred-and-fifty-pound out-of-control Rottweiler tumbling towards them. Summer loved it, but the plop of the tennis ball was to have the same effect on these guys as throwing a hand grenade into the pool.

Drew thought up another trip after that. Some of us had our dive tickets, so he rented a liveaboard dive boat and took us out into Malaysian waters to dive a wreck that was relatively new. We got to the right coordinates, set ourselves up and by mid-morning we were descending a rope towards the hulk of a cargo ship. It lay on the bottom in fairly shallow water at a peculiar angle, its bow pointing up towards the light. Drew entered first, through a missing window in the bridge. I followed. We secured a paracord line to a railing and descended a black corridor, our flashlights cutting through the water. Marine life had already taken hold of this vessel; instant reef followed by everything that lives off it had made this fallen beast their new home.

The odd fish twisted off, startled at our presence. I knew no-one lost their life when the ship went down so my fear was only based on getting lost or stuck somewhere and drowning. But the anticipation of exploring this wreck far overwhelmed my concern at the time. Curiosity would not get the better of me here, I thought. I started cracking glow sticks and dropping them like breadcrumbs to show us the way out.

This was only my second wreck dive, so I was still unused to diving within confined spaces. It's easy to become disoriented, which leads to the sort of confusion and panic that can kill a diver. The corridors we glided down gave way to more and more direction changes and stairwells cluttered with debris. I was fast approaching my bottom time limit, and we needed to turn back and start our assent with plenty of time and air for safety stops.

Drew pulled up near an open door. My torch lit up his face, and he pointed first at his gauges and then up. I checked my air gauge; it was time to go—now.

On the way back he pulled up again, spun around and gave me an excited wave, pointing off to his right through another open doorway. Why, I thought, am I risking my life here? Then Drew pulled his bag open. We were looking for the captain's cabin, so we could take photos of each other on the toilet.

Later that night, standing on deck, Drew finished his whisky, leaned over the railing and stared into the sea. He was in his early forties then, and still vehemently single. 'You ever going to settle down, mate? Have a couple of kids and live in the burbs?' I asked.

He laughed. 'Maybe.' He had another plan forming in his head and spat a wad of chewing tobacco into the sea. 'Pauli, there are two things every man should hear in his lifetime: "I'm pregnant" and "We have the building surrounded".'

With Clare standing there, test strip in hand, those words lit up in my mind like a giant neon tribute to my idiotic youth. Right, that's one down, I thought, as I watched the realisation of pregnancy and an up-coming wedding creeping across her face.

My immediate reaction was joy: firstly, because after years of hammering my body I wasn't firing blanks; and secondly, I knew that Clare loved the idea of being a mother. I did a little dance and hugged her, although I was shitting myself inside.

'I hope my wedding dress will fit.' She sat on the edge of the bed and smiled.

Huge plans were underfoot. I sold one of my bikes, thinking of all the baby kit we would need. I lay awake at night staring at the ceiling, making lists and worrying about money. Now and again the debate and conversation in my head would get so loud I thought I'd woken up Clare, but it was just the sleep kick she does sometimes. 'Myoclonic jerk' is the medical term. As you fall asleep your brain interprets it as your body shutting down, so it sends out a signal to wake it up. I wrestled with my ghosts of responsibility night after night; great changes to my work life and home life were forming, as our baby was forming. I thought about it constantly, our DNA combining in a split second, a future human genetically preprogrammed in a few nanograms of matter, defined on a cellular level instantaneously, the miracle of life. But what will our offspring be like? I peeled the onion late at night. I think I was dealing with it like I would a new offshore campaign—you know, logistics, consumables, equipment, paperwork—assuming all along, of course, that I'm infallible, and that naturally our child would be too. I'd look at Clare's sleeping face next to me, her peaceful breathing, in time with chance rolling invisible waves through our curtain. Only months later did I understand how fragile it all was.

Our identities are the sum of our life experiences, and each of us processes our world according to our individual mind and the neurons therein. At the time all I could do was think about making that world as safe and happy for us as I could. I guess what we are never changes, but who we are never stops changing.

I'd look back at Clare and start all over again. I should have relaxed, I should have gone to sleep, but I couldn't because somewhere deep inside me I had to have a plan. It's funny, but now I'm more prepared to accept things on faith.

Our wedding was going to be simple, straightforward and uncomplicated, and right up to the big day itself, it was. Clare had managed to dye her hair pink; her scalp had reacted to the chemicals in the hair dye and she was forced to rinse her hair early. She was already worried about a hundred and one things that breezed by me like a Hare Krishna at the airport, but this new pink hairdo was the last straw and the tears finally welled up.

Normally I'm a proponent of telling the truth in these circumstances—'Do you think this bag goes with these shoes?' etc.—but having gained experience in dealing with a pregnant stressed-out partner, I say lie, lie until your pants are on fire. 'You look great, baby,' I beamed back at her. She saw through me in a second.

Erwin and his wife Lucy arrived the day before. Clare was dealing with her pink hair while sorting everything else out at the same time, all our friends and family chipped in, and the next thing I knew my wedding day had arrived and I didn't have a hangover from the night before.

It was early on Saturday morning, I was standing on my balcony drinking coffee and Erwin came out. 'Big day, buddy,' he grinned at me. 'You nervous?' Of course I bloody was.

'Let's go for a ride,' he suggested. So we split, tearing off down my street and waking everyone up. The sun was rising over the harbour as we skirted round Double Bay. Not much traffic yet, I opened up the throttle just a little, this day could not start any better. I'm going to marry the love of my life, my best man, in all respects, was right there on the machine next to me, even the air smelled sweeter. We rode on through the city, enjoying the space before the traffic descended into the morning gridlock. Erwin got pulled over by a cop, but in the spirit of the day he turned out to be more interested in the bike than how fast Erwin was going. Magic.

We returned home to an empty flat, and two suits laid out complete with pressed shirts. I quietly shaved and dressed. The boys would be here soon to pick us up. We were getting married in a beautiful garden only a few kilometres away, and by the time I got there everyone was arriving. I took my place under a tree with Erwin next to me. Then I saw her, walking with Philip, her father. She looked amazing, I was speechless.

The ceremony itself was simple and short. I looked around and saw all the people who have been there for Clare and me. Ruby, my closest friend, winked at me. This is it. Clare looked at me through her veil, I had never felt so happy.

Recalling your wedding is a lot like trying to remember a car accident: you remember specific moments with astonishing clarity, in slow motion, but other parts are just a blur. The reception is just a blur, but I can remember dancing badly, drinking too much scotch, and running away from Steve, who in a kind of bizarre tradition puts me in a headlock at every wedding I go to.

It started some sixteen years ago, when Steve was just a scrawny kid. I was good friends with his older sisters and went to school with his cousins. Every now and again I would put him in a headlock and sometimes slam his head into the fridge door. Steve grew up, and now he's bigger than me and much much stronger, and he likes to get his own back. I know at some point he will get that look in his eye, and when he does there's nothing I can do about it. He's done it to me at five weddings including his own.

At one wedding in a very posh restaurant, everyone was in tuxedos and gowns, standing around an elaborate bar that slipped out into a wonderful courtyard garden, sipping cocktails and making polite conversation, when Steve's switch got flipped by that last drink. He turned from the charming, charismatic man he can be into what can only be described as Big Foot in a suit. He came at me in that half-run, his tongue slightly protruding, shoulders forward, with that low, deep laugh. I saw movement from the corner of my eye and turned to look. Steve was sending wedding guests out of the way in a hurried scurry, their mouths agape. I smiled at the nice people I was talking to and asked the lady standing next to me if she wouldn't mind holding my drink. Then I took off through the garden with Steve chasing me. We ended up on the grass outside a big window, where people who had paid hundreds of dollars for their meal got a breathtaking panoramic view of two grown men rolling around on the lawn in tuxedos, one screaming while the other laughed and made grunting noises.

So there was Steve at my wedding doing that half-run with that laugh, that look in his eye. I tried to run but it was too late. You can't stop him, I've tried that before—everything from punching to kicking to smashing things over his head. I even stabbed him with a fork once, but it just makes him more determined.

The next day I woke up next to my wife. Clare was so happy. She was looking forward to the baby's arrival and talking about painting the spare room. I was set to go offshore in a few days so I decided when I got back to start preparing our home for our new arrival.

Three months later, Clare was doing well, she had excellent test results and everything was on track. Then at the end of the third month we lost our chance to be parents. Sometimes life can only really begin with the knowledge of death, that it can all end, usually when you least want it to. Clare showed a strength of character that astounded me and made me proud beyond words. I had no idea how much power lies just beneath the surface of a woman's drive to motherhood. So for us, we will try again.

7 KABUL ON THIRTY ROUNDS A DAY

Everything in Afghanistan is the same shade of light brown, even the air.

Decades of war have left this once fertile jewel in central Asia with nothing . . . absolutely nothing. Bullets change governments faster than votes in Afghanistan, and that's why all the trees are gone, and along with them all the topsoil. Follow that up with seven years of drought and a population that dares not set foot in an open area for fear of stepping on a landmine, and you're left with air that's thick with dust and a frightening amount of faecal matter as open sewers run in all directions—I could feel 'Kabul belly' ready to leap out and strike me down at any moment.

My first glimpse of Afghanistan was through the dirty window of an old PIA A300. Impressive snow-capped mountains dropped fast into a giant dust-bowl shambles the size of Texas. The flight had been awful, though at least Pakistan International Airlines gave me a laugh when I picked up my ticket in Dubai. The airline's current advertising tag line, emblazoned on the front of my ticket read, 'PIA: We're better than you think we are'.

Tom was sitting nearby, asleep. He's made this trip so many times it would take a man with a bomb strapped to his waist screaming 'Jihad, jihad!' to wake him up. Tom's a polite, quiet man who looks like he could be your local GP or plumber, but he is far from it. He is a PMC or private military contractor.

There are basically four types of expat in Afghanistan: those who are there to help, those who want to make lots of money, those who do both, and the rest who are there to fight. After twenty-five years of perpetual war the country's infrastructure is shattered, and as for the economy—well, what economy? Afghanistan is on aid, billions of dollars of aid, but because it's just so dangerous the work that is starting to slowly change Afghanistan for the better needs protecting. All those engineers, aid workers, medical staff—all of the people in Afghanistan who are from somewhere else—are relying on good security. Enter the world of the PMC. It's a growth business. These guys are former professional soldiers, using their skill sets and trade craft in this new booming private sector. And believe me, there's plenty of work.

Although most big oil companies will never admit it, they use PMCs all the time. I had been around these guys before on rigs in nasty parts of the world, but they were always too busy doing their jobs, and I was too busy doing mine. I had always wanted to write about them. My chance to embed myself with one such organisation and to quietly take a look at Afghanistan came in the form of Chris and Tom one rainy Saturday in Sydney three years ago. They were with a firm who was moving from land-based operations into offshore security work, and not just in far-off war-torn parts of the world. Just look at the amount of piracy in the Strait of Malacca just off Singapore, where there's a gun-related incident every day. With 70 per cent of our planet covered in water, you'd think there would be more protection out there, but no, piracy is becoming a common occurrence. Forget the romantic gloss made popular in films—good-looking roguish but lovable buccaneers just having a romp through your cargo hold. Modern piracy is cold-blooded murder.

I was involved in a brainstorming session on the potential threat faced by offshore drilling rigs, and lots of specialists were there. That's how I first met Tom and Chris. They talked about Iraq and Afghanistan, and for me the seed was sown. I wanted to understand what's happening there, why it was so important to the oil business, why guys on rigs all over the world are talking about it. I had a chance to see it first-hand, not as a writer or oilman, but simply as the grey man in the corner; all I had to do was follow Tom—he had the access after three years in the country. And now, after a long wait and a lot of meetings, here I was retrieving my bag from the carousel in Kabul Airport.

We walked straight through customs into the mostly empty arrival hall. The sun made me squint as we hit the steps outside. I glanced over to my right where eight large four-wheel drives were parked alongside a dozen heavily armed Westerners standing around looking as menacing as their automatic weapons, shaved heads, wraparound shades and goatees would allow—almost every expat is a former military been-there-done-that-kill-you-as-soon-as-look-at-you kind of chap.

'It's all about posture and appearance,' said Tom as we walked towards the carpark where his driver was waiting. Not having a gun in your hand here is a bit like going out and forgetting your belt. 'Holding your weapon a certain way can make all the difference to how the locals react to you. That goes for how you dress, how you look, it sends a certain signal.' Tom has been in the country long enough to know. He has experienced the best and worst Afghanistan has to offer, and in credit to his character maintains a smile and a positive presence that instantly puts me at ease.

For me, arriving in Afghanistan was a lot like arriving in Sakhalin in Russia or Lagos in Nigeria, or a mixture of both; there were the same dodgy-looking heavy-set men loitering in corners with AKs slung across their chests, the same concrete meets fluorescent light strewn with bad plumbing, the same shitty roads. If you have a back problem, don't under any circumstances go on a driving holiday in Afghanistan; you'd be better off strapping yourself into a car seat and jumping off Everest.

We arrived at the Kabul InterContinental Hotel. It's not what you would think of normally when you hear the word 'Intercontinental'. This is not the sort of place with posh décor and uniformed bellboy waiting to take your bags to your plush room. However, it is one of the few buildings in this city that won't fall over if you piss on it. It sits on top of a hill with the Hindu Kush Mountains behind and a commanding view over the city spread out in front. My room was near the entrance on the second floor. It looked good for Kabul—that side of the building was obviously harder to hit with artillery. By the time I had relaxed and settled in, the first problem raised its ugly head. 'Oh no,' I wailed, and my hand shot to my belt as I scurried to the bathroom.

Twenty-four hours later I emerged ten pounds lighter and more dehydrated than a Kabul traffic cop. Just to be sure I would live, Chris and Tom drove me to the German Medical Diagnostic Center. The German doctor scrutinised my vaccination card, asked all the right questions, took blood, made me drink four litres of water, gave me the 'peel it, boil it, cook it or forget it' speech and set me free into the waiting city.

Surprisingly, there is a lot to do in Kabul other than get blown up and/or shot at. It has a golf course that contains real bunkers, a soulless zoo not worth visiting if you have any feelings for animals whatsoever, and a mine museum. I decided on the zoo. It has 116 unlucky inhabitants that are fed on handouts from Britain. In January 2002 the most revered resident of the zoo—Marjan the one-eyed lion—died. He had survived there for thirty-eight years through the Russian occupation, through countless rocket attacks, through the bitterly cold winters and dust-blown-faecal-matter stinking hot summers.

In the 1990s, when rival Afghan groups shelled the city into rubble, the zoo was on the front line. At one point a Taliban combatant scaled the wrong wall and ended up face to face with a waiting Marjan. The starving lion dispatched and ate the man. The following day the man's brother arrived, chasing revenge, and tried to frag Marjan by tossing a fragmentation grenade into his tiny enclosure. Marjan lost an eye and was lame for the rest of his life, but against the odds he survived. There are two new lions at the zoo now, 'Zing Zong' and 'Dolly', donated by China. I wish I could have paid my respects to Marjan though.

Driving in Kabul was almost as depressing as visiting the zoo. Kabul's streets are packed with four million people struggling to get from A to B in a heaving mass of dust, shit (human and animal), exhaust, and entirely too many people with guns. The inevitable gridlock happens every day. As soon as the car stopped moving, the peddlers appeared through the smoke, much like they do in so many other countries. Over the years I've been talked into purchasing all kinds of crap I didn't need, by old women, kids and one-legged, one-eyed people whose final option is to try and eke out an existence by lane splitting in static traffic and selling everything from peanuts to guns.

Warfare has turned most of Kabul's former middle-class apartment buildings into weird shapes; most were bullet riddled to the point of producing a dimpled golf-ball effect in the concrete, with virtually every single square inch having sustained small arms fire. Others had 'surgically removed' balconies where RPGs and mortars had impacted.

This place put me slightly on edge. It was like Afghanistan was watching, watching and waiting like a wild animal, like a wounded, hardened, one-eyed lion. I knew I needed to treat it with respect, keep my actions introverted, my voice even and calm, and only show my teeth in a smile.

Tom was in the front passenger seat with his armalite, muzzle down, between his knees. I sat in the back, looking out into the dusty street. Each passing minute one foot of forward movement rolled by in an excruciating test of endurance. You're not going to get out and run, not in Kabul, so you may as well accept it, even it if means missing your flight, meeting, appointment, whatever. Through the hot dust a figure emerged, a boy around eight. He had big sad hazel eyes.

'Spandi,' said the driver and lowered his window. The boy walked over to our driver's door. I'd seen them on the street before in Kabul, these young kids, peddling tin cans of smoke like little chimneys. I had no idea what they were up to. They just arrived at your window enveloped in thick spicy blue clouds. The driver handed the boy ten Afghanis and let the smoke billow from the can into the car, then the window went back up and the boy was gone, on to the next car.

The cans, much like the children holding them, all look the same: charred, dirty and too fragile for their purpose. They hang awkwardly from rusted handles resembling old bent clothes hangers, and the smoke . . . what was with that smoke? I thought it might have been hash, tea or a funky decongestant.

After half an hour of discussion with Ali, the driver, I discovered that it came from 'spand', a herb that can be found in markets across Afghanistan. One who sells spand is referred to as 'spandi' by the Afghans. When the herb is burned, the smoke produced is believed to ward off evil spirits and misfortune. The practice goes back centuries, buried deep in Afghan tribalism that revolved around animism and ancestor worship. The spandi eking out an existence on the streets are desperate, so they play on the superstitions deeply rooted in the collective psyche of the Afghan people.

There is a lack of basically everything in Afghanistan. The country is living on a meal ticket supplied by everyone else, and progress is about as fast as a tectonic plate. The 4.6 billion dollars it was promised by the international community has come up very short, thanks to a never-ending daisy chain of bureaucrats who pass paperwork around in a giant merry-go-round of red tape from one side of Kabul to the other. So what does it have apart from more dust than a British rail seat and a lot of poppies? Not much. Perhaps by some miracle in, say, thirty years it will have all the things we take for granted. Changes have been made for the better, compared to Afghanistan circa 2002, and there have been improvements in new construction, roads, power supply and medical aid, but by our standards it's still a mess.

Already two days had passed. I flopped down on my hotel bed, stared at the ceiling fan and let my brain go numb. And slept the heavy deep sleep you get after a long journey followed by Kabul belly and a nice day at the zoo.

It was lunchtime when I finally woke up. After a call to the boys and a quick bite to eat in the hotel, I was again stuck in Kabul traffic. Chris was next to me in the back, Sami behind the wheel and Tom in the front seat next to him. I could just make out a spandi working his way through the dust and exhaust fumes, down perpetually nervous and impoverished streets.

Sometimes we saw a car, usually military, with a big round disk on the roof. The disk is plugged into a bank of batteries in the back that provide the power for it to pulse out multiple signals to detonate any IEDs (improvised explosive devices) that may be buried in the road ahead. Once a disked car is spotted by the locals it creates a parting-of-the-sea effect, as no-one wants to be ahead of it if a bomb does go off—especially when the IEDs are becoming more and more advanced. Indeed, simple IEDs are giving way to what Tom calls 'off-route mines', devices that are hand-turned on a lathe, packed with explosives and capped with a concave steel or copper plate. The mine can be concealed and detonated horizontally or vertically, triggered by remote, infra-red or command wire. The explosion turns the concave plate into a molten jet or EFP (explosively formed projectile) moving at two thousand metres per second. It can penetrate up to ten centimetres of armour plating at one hundred metres. It creates a very effective killing ground and injects real fear as no-one is safe.

Suddenly the traffic started separating, everyone pulled onto the kerb in an effort to get out of the way, and a disked-up car ploughed past, leading a convoy of four vehicles at high speed through the city centre. The cars were big expensive four-wheel drives with blacked-out windows and armour plating. The spandi was caught in the mayhem of traffic, he dropped his can, for a second he was enveloped in a blue cloud, then in a blur the four cars sped past us. Every driver instantly tried to fill the hole the convoy had made in an effort to get an extra twenty yards down the street. Our driver did the same. I looked to my left just in time to see the boy; he was down, his burning spand smoking all around him. One of the convoy vehicles had driven over his left foot, smashing it to a pulp. He just sat there in shock. In seconds we were turning down a side street. I tried to get out, but it was too dangerous: the repercussions of the hit-and-run would soon send the people who saw it into a frenzy, and our driver wasn't stopping no matter what I did. Tom swivelled in the front seat, his face was blank, 'Can't stop, mate. You don't want to be there, it'll get nasty.'

Sami pointed the car down tiny parallel back streets, expertly navigating the maze laid out in his head. He is former Mujahadeen and has forgotten more about Kabul than any of us will ever know. I think my bum spent more time in the air than on the seat as we ploughed on, over small boulders and through potholes big enough to have a party in. My whole spine felt it, as any contact with the seat seemed to have the padding of Victoria Beckham.

Later that evening we set out into the city to relax and have a drink. My stomach was doing cartwheels again, thanks to the roads, but after a couple of tablets the German doc had given me I had regained control and was ready for 'Samarqand'.

'This place is the wild west, mate,' said Chris as we bounced down another Kabul back street. High walls topped with razor wire surrounded every structure, and there were big iron gates and armed guards who always made eye contact and tracked your uneven progression past their post. Tom was grinning in the front seat, but he was the one with the pistol on his hip and an M4 armalite in his hand. It was getting dark; random lights broke through the thick dust but visibility was no more than thirty feet.

'Put your game face on, mate,' said Chris as I jumped out of the big four-wheel drive and straight into a deep pothole full of grey sludge. The boys had a good laugh. Luckily for me this bar didn't have a dress code rule regarding being covered in shit from the knees down.

I was asked for ID at the entrance. It's best to wear shirts and jackets with huge breast pockets here, as reaching inside your clothing tends to look a bit like you're going for your Magnum, and digging around in your pocket does tend to send armed men frantic even if the only thing you produce is a Mars Bar. I always give the doorman a massive tip when going into rough clubs in rough countries. I tell them if they see me running out pursued by some pissed-off punter, I'm the one they let back in.

When we walked in, it became apparent that if there was a rule it was that there were no rules. Everyone looked like an extra from *Gladiator*. All sorts of shady characters were hanging about, expatriates from all over the world, diplomats, UN staff, soldiers, ex-soldiers, spooks, dealers in opium, arms and worse. I fixed myself on a spot near the back with good access to the rear entrance and not too much light. Okay, I thought, I've been in places like this before. Don't make eye contact unless you're shaking some bastard's hand, don't bump into anyone, don't talk about the War on Terror, or 'OBL' as he was known, don't get drunk and, for fuck's sake, don't talk to any of the women.

Chris appeared with a round of beers, sat down next to me and rattled off the names and backgrounds of two-thirds of the men in the bar, every one sounding as disturbing as the last. Some were what the boys called 'Walters', short for Walter Mitty, meaning someone who talks it up; some were 'Bongos', or business-orientated NGOs, who were there for charitable reasons but got paid more than Somalia's national debt. The only attractive woman in the room was as popular as a naked prom queen handing out free beer at the footy; she was slowly backing away from a conversation with increasingly overt 'someone jump in and save me' looks to the room. The guy she was talking to had obviously changed from the dark handsome stranger to a fanatical big-mouth with a serious chip on his shoulder.

The bar started to fill with more and more guys; the full ensemble and cast of the ubiquitous 'don't ask me why I'm here' consultancy company, some exchanged close quiet conversation, others roared in loud backslapping stories, chasing endless shooters with jugs of beer and cigars. It was a Thursday night, party night as the Islamic weekend is Friday, and by 10 p.m. it was packed, loud and everyone was having a good time. Then suddenly an explosive fight broke out. Two guys traded blows for a few seconds but were quickly separated. The fight was over the good-looking woman, who had, by all accounts, been with both of the men, and now hard stares across the room just didn't cut it anymore. So in the true tradition of drunks with guns, these two men decided to settle their dispute over the woman by stepping outside and having a good old-fashioned duel. You know, ten paces, turn and fire.

They dropped the mags from their pistols, leaving one round in the breech, re-holstered their weapons, stood back to back, swaying, then staggered apart; no-one was counting as everyone was either hiding or looking for cover. The younger of the two spun around, but in his rush he put his only bullet into the ground before his pistol had cleared the holster. Realising his predicament, he spun round the other way and took off down the street, zigzagging in all directions. While all this was going on the older and, as it turned out, more experienced of the two took his time and carefully aimed at his frantic, sprinting opponent, but missed. He actually looked genuinely disappointed and wandered back to the bar. The woman had gone; everyone just went back to their conversations, picking up right where they had left off.

Chris and Tom kept a low profile, and their people were also very quiet, blending into the walls so well they were almost forgotten. Most of them are ex-Gurkhas and can dissolve into an Afghan street remarkably well. The boys play their cards close to their chest, but it's obvious they are very good at what they do; even when they get drunk they remain aware of everything.

Everyone in Kabul can drink, and if you come here you'll want to, you'll need to. No-one here is without a horror story, and if you stay long enough you'll hear them all. The nightlife in Kabul is surprising. When everyone and his dog has a gun, and you never know what's going to happen next, it adds a certain moment of satisfaction to every meal you eat, every sip of whisky, every new day. The conversation is better, the jokes are fucking hilarious, and the drinks are never ending. For a moment it could have been another Kabul, the best version, the one from the 1960s, the halfway house in a righteous passage through a spectacular dope-filled wonderland en route to Kathmandu and enlightenment. One hit of edible opium goes for less than a dollar here, while I'm paying more than I do in Sydney to drink whisky. As far as good hash, opium and bad roads are concerned, Kabul has not changed that much since those halcyon days.

The drinks kept on coming, the night rolled into a full-blown drunk, it was spectacular and so was the hangover.

I woke up with a beauty the next morning. Chris and Tom were having breakfast in their office with a map laid out on the table.

'Morning,' Tom said and smiled the way you do when you know you stopped drinking early enough the night before.

My mouth felt like an Arab's sandal, but there was a lot to talk about; not the rosy-cheeked scamperings of the previous evening but about the following day's three-car convoy to 'Camp 87', a cement plant and road works eighty-seven kilometres from Kabul, past a few thousand landmines and other assorted unexploded ordnance, near the town of Gardez, right on the Peshawar–Pakistan border. It was a routine visit, so I jumped at the chance to go along and see the front line of Afghanistan's new infrastructure.

'Do you want a weapon?' asked Chris, rather like you would ask someone if they wanted an umbrella before a country walk. He knew I had used firearms before, but this time was different, I was here of my own volition and, more importantly, I was free to run away. 'It's like having a condom,' he went on. 'Better to have it and not need it, than need it and not have it.'

'No, mate, I'm not going to shoot some bastard,' I replied and gulped down my coffee. As much as I liked his analogy,

I struggled with the mental picture of myself running to a twenty-four-hour chemist, as opposed to finding myself unarmed while someone empties an automatic weapon at me.

'Okay, there'll be plenty of support if something does happen.' Chris went on to describe our route and the day's events at a pace that was way too fast and detailed for my brain to retain. He showed me on two different maps at the same time, then suddenly stopped when he looked at me and realised that I'm no former fighter pilot like him, and given the amount of whisky I'd necked the night before he was talking to someone with the mental retention capacity of a wet piece of toilet paper. At one point, I think I may have even gone cross-eyed.

Tom sat at his desk reading something, then the phone rang, he answered and instantly sat forward with his free hand cupping his left ear. Chris stopped talking and we looked on, as the call was obviously not good news. Within moments I was sprinting down the hall trying to keep up with Tom, who was heading straight for the car, while Chris jumped on the phone. Tom relayed what had happened: one of his staff, an Afghan man who works for CTG, had been stabbed repeatedly outside his home in what appeared to be a random robbery. He was at the UN hospital and was waiting for transport to the bigger hospital.

The stark UN building seemed deserted except for the occasional small group of Afghan workers huddled in a corner and whispering together. Tom broke into a run, rounded the last few corners and burst into a room where Mr Nazari lay on a gurney, tears streaming down the sides of his hollow cheeks. Mr Nazari is a real person; he is a forty-five-year-old man, with a wife, a brother and no other family. He loves both his wife and his brother dearly. Mr Nazari could not understand the Spanish military doctors conversing with each other, but knew that his life was hanging in the balance. I stood unnoticed in the corner; the room was organised chaos. I could see Mr Nazari's eyes: he couldn't believe he was in this situation. He had lived through the jihad against the Soviets and he had survived the Taliban, only to get shived in his own front yard. He was aware that there were so many things he may never get to say, so many goodbyes.

The tears rolled down the side of his face and slowly over his ears. He looked around, slowly, his movement constrained by both an oxygen mask and a central line drip that was secured by a cannula inserted into his clavicle. He saw Tom, their eyes met, and there was a glimmer of recognition. Tom knelt down beside Mr Nazari and felt for a pulse. Mr Nazari mumbled something under the mask, Tom leaned in.

'Mr Tom, please find my wife and my brother, please,' he whispered. Tom's eyes said it all. A former captain in the British Parachute Regiment, he has seen men lose their life for cause and country but he wasn't going to let Mr Nazari go for this. The private exchange between the two men in front of me was intensely moving.

Mr Nazari was transferred into an ambulance. The arriving medics knew the prognosis wasn't good, they knew how much damage a human body can absorb. Just forty-eight hours ago they'd lost seventeen of their friends in a helicopter crash. The flags in the compound were still flying at half-mast.

The UN doctor was from Romania and the military doctors were Spanish. Together they went through the handover. One of the Spanish doctors directed the UN doctor's attention to the various entry wounds, and clinically cast aside the sheet under which Mr Nazari was lying, exposing his modesty. Mr Nazari was 'the patient', this was purely business for the doctors, but

Mr Nazari was a devoutly Muslim man. Semiconscious, he tried to move the sheet to cover himself. He was aware of the Spanish nurse and was humiliated by his exposure. His movement was pathetic, there was no strength left in his arms and even less coordination. He continued to stare into the hard sun, his eyes never shifting, his pride never wavering once, his dignity eternal.

There are occasions in life to be amazed by the physical and mental courage of the human animal under stress. This was one of them. Later Tom would quietly relax, expressing himself with a kind of fatalistic humour and simplicity that both comforts and disarms. He leaves you with a warm heart in the end, perhaps because you know he doesn't really care what you think.

The next day we left the centre of Kabul and headed south-east. I was in the middle car with Chris and Tom. No-one spoke, everyone was focused on the road ahead. Routine trip to Camp 87 or not, it was still a dangerous journey. Mr Nazari was still fresh in my mind so I paid close attention to Tom.

Wherever you want to go in Kabul, it's important to depart early in the morning. Those of us who complain about 'peak hour' have not seen Kabul traffic. There are no traffic lights. There are traffic cops, though, but don't pay any attention to them, as they are quite keen on waving you into the path of a semitrailer full of bridge parts.

The chaos and dense brown haze slowly gave way to clean crisp air. The new road we sped down cut a black line straight through the middle of massive snow-capped mountain ranges, leading us into the Panshir valley and on to Gardez. The predominant colour changed from light brown to green, and beautiful grassy hillsides lit up my window. Farmers dodged mines to plant opium, their land still pepperpotted by gun emplacements or the occasional howitzer or burned-out Russian tank with its turret still pointing towards a long-gone enemy. They were far too busy cultivating opium to fuck about with the remains of another foreign invader.

Twenty-eight of Afghanistan's thirty-two provinces cultivate massive amounts of opium—89 per cent of global production or more than four thousand metric tons that year. The farmers used to grow raisins, saffron and pomegranate for its oil, which was exported for use in the cosmetic industry, but there is too much money in drugs. Each province has a warlord, some of whom, I am told, are payrolled by the CIA as anti-Taliban allies. The regional warlords command militants numbering seven hundred thousand men.

Is anything going to change in Afghanistan? The Afghans are extremely long-suffering, which is why they've been able to survive so much. Perhaps that is why the country has not changed faster despite the foreign aid dollars. To the Afghan, we are just another occupying power. Having said that, the current, albeit undermined, Karzai Government appear to be giving Afghanistan a temporary artificial boost in development. But for how long? Compared to the stale developmental limbo it experienced under the Soviets in 1979–88, the minor development under the Afghan Communists in 1989–92, the fearsome civil war under the Mujahadeen in 1992–96, then the horrific oppression of the Taliban years 1996–2001, now it's new and improved, with minty fresh faecal matter and far too many guys with guns looking to make a fast dollar. Outside Kabul, Karzai is mercilessly nicknamed 'the mayor of Kabul'. He's trying to change the drug trade with the introduction of the 'Afghan Irradiation Force' who are 'fighting the drug war' in the provinces; that's a bit like trying to teach a monkey how to perform brain surgery with a pipe wrench.

But the Irradiation Force has been put to good use on a few occasions. Such as when one farmer was having problems with his bull and couldn't plough his fields, so he placed an anonymous call to the Irradiation Force telling them the location of a huge, freshly sown crop. They arrived with brand new farming equipment and ploughed the shit out of everything in the area looking for opium seeds. So the new system of Western-style democracy has only brought an organised framework to old corruption. And besides, some say the biggest drug dealer in the country is the president's brother, with the second biggest being the deputy minister of the interior. It's just too big and too profitable to stop, no matter how benevolent the next dictator may be or how powerful the next liberating superpower is.

All this bounced about in my brain box as we bounced past the huge razor-wired gates of Camp 87.

'How was your run in?' asked Don Rector, the man in charge at 87, as he shook my hand.

'Just fine, Don,' I replied and smiled, trying not to notice the smorgasbord of weapons casually decorating his office.

'Hell, just last week someone took a shot at me.' He leaned back in his chair. 'Three rounds entered my vehicle from two shooters, one was on a rooftop, the other was dug in level with the road.'

Don is in his sixties and is probably fitter than me. He is tall, broad and looks every part the veteran he is. He has an impressive military background, and three sons all serving with US forces in other parts of the world. He explained how the system works. His company protects the guys who are rebuilding the roads. His men engage the Taliban in fire fights on average twice a week. They regularly find IEDs planted on or near the new roads. So in order to help Afghanistan's infrastructure take hold through new communications, roads, bridges and construction, you need all these guys with guns to stop the Taliban from killing all the engineers and workers who are building it all.

A metal bucket full of coiled up .50-calibre belt ammo sat by the door. I asked Don how often he uses it. 'Well, now and again they shoot at the camp, so I grab my bucket and head up to the roof,' he said casually. 'The fifty puts a stop to just about anything.'

'Oh right,' I smiled, thinking this man would be a pensioner at home.

He saw me eyeballing a bent RPG warhead sitting on the floor near my chair. 'Oh that reminds me, I must get rid of that.' He picked up the big green rocket and put it down on his desk.

The radio on Don's desk crackled to life and soon I was shaking his hand again, saying bye bye and hoping no-one was going to stitch up our unarmoured car on the way back to Kabul.

It's impossible not to be impressed by Afghanistan's rugged beauty, not to mention the Afghans themselves and their determination to get on with their lives despite their daily suffering and adversity, and what appears to be only the slimmest chance of finding peace. Ironically, this is one of their most enduring characteristics, as the Afghan culture reinforces the ideal of stoicism and obstinacy in the face of hardship. That must get frustrating for all these well-intentioned NGOs who want to help by implementing change.

The Panshir Valley is beautiful. The Soviets tried nine times to capture it, but it remained too strong. Now it's the one part of Afghanistan that has the glimmer of a new life shining in its mountain streams. There is food in the roadside market stalls, and the kids are wearing smiles as they tear arse up and down the road. Everywhere else ethnic conflicts flare up enough to keep people fearful and indoors.

The drive back was incident-free, apart from one road block where we had to stop as some rocks had fallen onto the road from an overhanging cliff. Everyone had their fingers on triggers and shifted nervously in their seats, scanning for a threat. I noticed a giant old billboard by the road. Left over from the Soviet occupation, it depicted two hands, one full of opium, the other full of money, and on the opposite side figures handing over a rocket. It was the international sign for 'We'll give you drugs and money for stinger missiles'. The stinger turned the tide of the war, and the Afghans shot down hundreds of Soviet Hind gunships with that simple shoulder-fired weapons system.

The boys dropped me off outside my hotel. I walked through the obligatory metal detector that beeped loudly. I have walked through metal detectors on my way through every door in the country. They almost always beep, but no-one cares; if the detector didn't beep, I'd be asked, 'Where's your firearm?' Back in my room I had a shower. I felt dirty, but still, the amount of brown muck that came off my body was surprising, as was the result of blowing my nose. I wrapped a towel round my waist and opened the balcony door.

It was already dark outside. Kabul lay directly below me, thousands of headlights and horns jostled through the dust in the fight to end another day. The bottle of Macallan on my desk looked at me and said 'I can read your mind', so I poured a big one, straight up, no ice, there wasn't any. The single malt bit into my mouth and I savoured the heat of its slide into my belly. The rich taste made me homesick. I picked up the phone to call Clare, but she was still at work. I looked at my watch; I'd usually be enjoying a whisky with my friends Sally and Simon in their nice happy safe Sydney garden. The gentle sound of small-arms fire broke my moment and slammed the reality of where I was back in my face like an angry slap.

I turned off the light and closed the curtains; it would be just my luck to catch a stray round while necking a scotch in my hotel room, especially after spending the day as a bullet magnet on the road to Gardez. The young spandi boy's face flashed into my mind. He was probably dead. It was obvious he'd suffered since birth. You recognise that unmistakable look, all of humanity's pain resides in that look.

It's hard sometimes to get to grips with what's happening here—is it just one giant power struggle to gain control of the region? Oil is the lifeblood of our modern world, and Afghanistan is becoming more and more important in the global struggle to get and move oil as we slowly, inevitably, and at any human or environmental cost, struggle to find more.

For now the only thing everyone appears to agree on is how bad the Taliban are. Sorry, I can't. It's just too hard to go through the huge pile of scribbled notes and things I've written on pizza box lids and cocktail napkins, hours of garbled recorded conversation with Afghans and expats who all end up sounding like Col Gaddafi on speed, just to punch out three quotes on what a sack of complete thundercunts the Taliban are.

In Afghanistan the war machine is stretched to its limit, like it is everywhere else in the Middle East. So the time will come when the job of soldiering is contracted out. It's happening now, soldiering to protect future oil, as well as liberating

Afghans and Iraqis from tyranny—it's that simple. They call it 'security of supply'.

The numbers involved are mind-boggling; the United States has spent more than eighty-seven billion dollars conducting the war in Iraq alone, and probably the same amount on petrol, domestic beer and acne medication. Talk to the UN people and they will tell you that less than half that amount would provide clean water, good food, sanitation and education to every individual on the planet who needed it. Meanwhile we sit back in our new BMWs and wonder why there are terrorists.

Afghanistan could be more important to global oil supply than even Saudi Arabia. In 1997 'BBC News' reported that the American–Saudi oil consortium UNOCAL tried to negotiate pipeline deals through Afghanistan from the Caspian Sea. The Caspian Sea is a California-sized body of salt water—the world's largest landlocked body of water—that may sit on as much as two hundred billion barrels of oil, which would be 16 per cent of the Earth's potential currently estimated oil reserves. At today's prices, that could add up to three trillion dollars in oil.

As the world's quest for new oil reserves intensifies, so will the 'war on terror'. And the use of PMCs will only become more prolific as well. Guys just like me have been full-bore drilling for a century, but keeping up with the insatiable demand is daunting; current production (the number of barrels pumped per day, BPD) is falling each year, while in thirty years we will need more than twice the oil we need today. Imagine what it will be like in thirty years. 'Hell, I can remember when petrol was only two dollars a litre,' you will say. You might have faith, or belief in our system of government, or even lots of money, but everyone will feel it on every level—the end of affordable fuel brought about by our own belligerent superpowers and, of course, the inconvenience of upsetting everyone's weekend road trip plans in the West. But apart from that, it's all just fine . . . What time is the next appalling reality TV show on?

Afghan TV needs a show called 'Who Wants To Be a Normal Person?' followed by 'Survivor: Kabul', then another riveting re-run of 'Mass Murder She Wrote'. Can you imagine breakfast TV, with your appropriately jovial and upbeat presenters faking smiles and doing the daily 'faecal matter' count and car bomb traffic updates? Interviewing celebrity-obsessed Western visitors, and crossing to a guy who will show you how to disarm a landmine, and sell you today's special offer on the new 'Kevlar second chance' bulletproof vest. Just be one of the first ten callers and we'll throw in a prosthetic limb of your choice.

I had finished half the bottle, my head was swimming; it was like trying to understand free-to-air TV. The age of cheap oil is over; what we are doing is the long slide into post 'peak oil' propaganda. What kind of future will Clare and I leave for our children if we are lucky enough to have them? Within their lifetime it's possible they could slowly see the world end up in a kind of permanent energy crisis, a 'forever war'. If we're not careful, hydrocarbons and warfare will go hand in hand to define human life.

8 LEARN OR BURN

I woke to the sound of an argument in the corridor outside my room. I did the worst thing imaginable and had a cigarette, sat at the formica desk, turned on my laptop and listened to the argument escalate into a fight as my computer booted up. The perfect background music to try and make sense of this place. The phone rang; today I was going to the hospital. In order to see the result of warfare, the most obvious place to go to is the hospital. There is no darker place in Kabul than a trauma ward.

You might think it's strange that I would go to a Kabul hospital, or that the hospital would have the time to waste with someone who to all intents and purposes was 'visiting'. But, you see, as with all places around the world where conflict is tearing people apart and where there is a great deal of suffering, they welcome outsiders because they want you to witness what they are going through, they need you to witness what they are going through and to tell as many people as you can about it, because one more person knowing just might make a change for them. I was simply compelled to go.

'We'll be there in halfa,' said Tom. I put down the phone, showered, dressed and was side-stepping the 'What? No firearm?' metal detector half an hour later.

The main hospital in Kabul is operated by 'Emergency', an Italian organisation. The organisation has three hospitals in Afghanistan—in Kabul, Panshir and Lashkar Gah—as well as twenty-six clinics scattered throughout the country. On top of this, it also provides free healthcare to the three thousand-plus inmates of Kabul prison, and the orphanage where there are eight hundred kids aged from five to eighteen years old.

The building itself was a welcome change; as one would expect it was spotlessly clean and white, and within the walls in the centre was a beautiful garden with benches and rows of flowers. There to greet me was Dr Marco Garatti, an immediately likable man. He shook my hand and offered me tea. I could see he was tired and I asked if I should come back another day.

'Oh no, I'm fine,' he said, smiling. 'I was up all night in surgery, we had five patients come in, all with penetrating trauma.' He flopped down on a sofa next to his office. 'Just another day in Kabul,' he added, then scratched his greying beard and offered me a cookie.

Having already been in Kabul for two years with his wife, Dr Garatti was somehow managing to make a difference against a never-ending stream of civilian casualties, about 350 every month. He seemed to have an inexhaustible energy for his patients and staff. I felt guilty for using up his time, that would otherwise no doubt have been spent sleeping. He politely explained how much penetrating trauma is inflicted on his patients, from car accidents to mines and other unexploded ordnance. Three of the five individuals he and his staff spent the night trying to save were children who had triggered mines.

On the road to Gardez the previous day we had driven past Kuchi farmers carefully ploughing in the hope that they didn't go bang. There are an estimated ten million mines buried under Afghan soil, and to my utter dismay fresh mines are still being buried by 'Area Commanders' (warlords) in the provinces. How does one hope to try and stop all this carnage?

Dr Garatti is superhumanly optimistic, and in his position I guess you have to be. 'I have six beds in "intensive care", and we try to keep a patient's stay in that bed down to three days,' he explained, frowning into his tea. 'In a Western hospital you would be there for as long as you needed, but here we have to try and move them back home. We train the family to take care of the patient, we have to because there is always another person who needs the bed.' He put his cup carefully back on the saucer, but the tea still spilled a little as his hand was shaking. He sat forward, rubbing his hands over his eyes.

I reached for my cigarettes in the silence, a knee-jerk reaction to feeling unable to say something positive. The packet was in my hand and Dr Garatti looked up. 'Oh, I'm sorry,' I apologised and put them away.

'By all means, let's go outside, I'll have one too,' he said and smiled.

I think short of jumping up on his coffee table and taking a crap, not much offends Dr Garatti. He produced his own smokes and we walked down through the centre of the courtyard garden. Here is a man who has devoted all his time and energy into saving lives that should never have been in jeopardy. His finger is stuck in the dyke, stopping the flow of blood from the Afghan soil. But he is under the gun.

Dr Garatti also has the only CT scan in the country, so at any given time there is a mile-long queue at the front gates. On a daily basis, Pashtuns wait alongside Tajiks and Hazars for a consultation; everyone just sits down and quietly waits their turn. No-one gets turned away.

We walked back around to the main wards and I asked Dr Garatti if there was anything I could do. 'Follow me,' he said and took me into a 'clean room', where I put on a big blue coat and special covers over my boots. We walked through another white door into a ward full of children. Every one of them had stepped on a mine. Some were just toddlers, ripped apart but somehow alive. Three hundred and fifty children a month arrive here in pieces, and a quarter of Afghanistan's children die by the age of five. One little boy's face was completely unrecognisable as human; his eyes blankly stared through me. My heart fell into my boots, I could feel the blood drain from my face, my mouth went dry.

At the end of the ward there was a playroom filled with old wooden toys, half-deflated balls, and dolls also with missing limbs. Half a dozen children were there spending time with their parents. One toddler sat motionless next to a nurse. I watched him for a full five minutes. He just looked at the other kids playing and ignored the nurse's attempts to read him a story, although his gaze occasionally darted to the entrance. 'He's waiting for his mother to arrive,' the good doctor quietly explained. When his mother appeared through the door her eyes found her baby instantly. She dropped her basket, spilling fruit and precious milk across the floor, and ran to her little dismembered boy. The child launched himself from the chair and tried to run to his mother on what was left of his legs, then he suddenly floundered and ducked behind a chair. He pouted, angry with her for abandoning him. She stopped and fell on her knees, her arms open, her fingers trembling, tears streaming down her cheeks. The sheer force of her emotions almost sucked him across the room; he flew through the air into her arms, burst into tears and wrapped everything he had left around his mother. Safe in the warmth of her love, the familiarity of her hair and everything that makes a mother special. They sat there, oblivious, moulded together. Men with guns could not have separated them. I had to move away, as I realised I was crying.

We left the gut-wrenching children's ward and Dr Garatti introduced me to a boy on crutches. He was around twelve, his right foot had been blown off by a mine. The boy smiled and politely engaged us in conversation. His English was excellent. On a bench next to him sat his mother and sister. He was waiting for his prosthetic foot to arrive. I was amazed at how quickly he had already started to overcome his disability. He was just happy to be alive. With ten million mines littered around the country, it's inevitable that when kids are playing or just moving around they are going to set them off.

I had taken up enough of the doctor's time, and as we walked to the main entrance he put his hand on my shoulder and said that if I knew any doctors who had experience with 'penetrating trauma' and wanted more, I should direct them to 'Emergency'. 'The salary's not bad, and you would learn more in a week about gunshot and shrapnel cases than in a year in any major Western hospital. We also need anaesthetists, gynaecologists and midwives,' he beamed and shook my hand. Then another doctor came running up, his stethoscope swinging wildly. He rattled off a lot of high-speed Italian, and with that Dr Garatti was off, shouting 'Ciao' as he sprinted down the hall.

I wandered outside the hospital, rewinding the last few hours in my mind the way you do when you're walking out of the cinema. Did I just absorb all that? The street was full of people waiting to get into the hospital; clouds of dust kicked up by passing traffic had turned everyone into the same shade of light brown.

The car was waiting, but I wanted to take a bus. 'You what?' said Sami the driver.

'It's okay, Sami. I'll be fine.' I smiled, gave him my best 'I know exactly what I'm doing' look and walked across the road to the bus stop. The buses basically go from one side of town to the other, so all I had to do was get off near the centre and I could walk to the hotel.

Kabul has 108 public buses and more than four million people. Crowded does not begin to describe it. I waited for five minutes, long enough for the dust to paint me in the same way it had everyone else. At home where people are truly free, a crowd waiting for something will automatically form itself into a queue, a single line incorporating almost military precision where personal space is respected and no-one pushes. But in parts of the world where the people are mostly free only to get shot or blown up or run over, a line for anything is more like a mosh pit.

Then through a giant cloud of diesel fumes and brown air lumbered the bus, its brakes making the mosh pit cringe in unison. The driver pulled on a lever to manually open the door and gave me a blank surprised look. He said something to the man standing behind me. 'What the fuck is he doing here?' I presumed. The man smiled at me and moved forward, there was a brief debate between the driver, the man and everyone on the bus, with occasional hand gestures in my direction. As it turned out, the debate was over whether or not I should pay. Afghans, when they're not queuing, are gentle, generous people, and given the opportunity will extend every imaginable courtesy, including free bus rides for random bald foreign guys. I got on, nodding thank you to the packed bus's passengers, who all smiled and pointed towards the back of what looked like a dusty version of *Dante's Inferno*. There at the back in the middle was a free seat, next to an old man who was, remarkably, fast asleep.

After less than a kilometre I realised why the seat was free; the old bloke was letting go with the most horrendous farts. I nearly gagged. A pothole sent him careering into the roof. He landed back down on his seat, awake, but with his headgear pushed down over his nose. He rearranged his 'shamag', and in doing so retrieved a big fat joint, then he licked the end and winked at me. He's going to fire that up, I thought, and he did. By the time we were in the city centre, I was quite stoned from the various fumes he happily wafted around the bus. We had come to a grinding halt in the standard traffic-jam nightmare that is the centre of town.

A couple of passengers got off to grab a kebab from a roadside vendor who also sold bottled water and bags of mixed nuts. The more I inhaled my new pal's smoke, the more the water and mixed nuts caught my eye. Finally, after what seemed like an hour, I had the munchies. With a fist full of Afghanis that say in bold text across the top 'Da Afghanistan Bank', I walked towards the front of the bus to get off, but suddenly two men stood up and stopped me. It's unusual for Afghans to touch you, but these two guys were physically restraining me. Both were talking super-fast Dari, then one pointed outside and made throat-cutting gestures.

The penny finally dropped. It wasn't a place for someone like me to get out. I thanked them and went back to hide under my seat. After a few moments the bus started moving and I got up and shot a quick look out the back window, seeing what looked like six or seven cops in some kind of scuffle over an accident and some kind of protest march being led by the Kabul Municipal Post-Traumatic Stress Disorder Marching Band. To my surprise, Sami was following the bus; he saw me trying to look straight and grinned at me.

I spent the rest of the day taking out-of-focus photos in the highly depressing and totally deserted National Mine Museum. With the compassion of a cluster bomb, every device designed to maim and kill was laid out on tables. Perhaps I should have come here first, either way I was left with the same lingering hollow-fist-in-my-gut feeling.

I had a quiet simple meal in the hotel that night. I thought about the lucky ones who have no idea what they have, and struggled to fall asleep against my mind's need to unfold the day's events and somehow make sense of them. Feeling truly philosophical distended into myriad real and humbling emotions that in the end just made me angry. Tomorrow my alarm would go off at 4 a.m. Sleep eventually came through Kabul's confusing dust.

It was still black outside and surprisingly cold as I stood by the hotel entrance, rubbing the sleep and dust from my blood-shot eyes, my breath making clouds under the fluorescent lights. It was Anzac Day. The car pulled up, its windows clouded over. The boys were quiet as we made our way to camp 'Eggers', the US base located in the centre of town.

'Good morning, gentlemen. You're here for the service,' said the guard at the main entrance.

We were processed through and freely moved around within the walls. The service was about to start, so I found a spot off to the side and waited for the soldiers to parade.

The 'Last Post' hung in the air as the sun crept towards the top of camp Eggers's razor-wire fence. The thirty or so men and women from Australia, New Zealand and America's armed forces stood rigid in the morning light as flags snapped overhead. A small group of men stood motionless in the corner. Dressed in old fatigues, not showing any rank or unit, all sporting big bushy beards, they watched then quietly left. 'SF—Special Forces—guys,' Tom later explained.

Afterwards the Americans laid out a generous breakfast that included rum and coffee. I heard just how bad it was getting in Helmand, and more than one person advised me to stay in Kabul. I was told that within a week riots would break out in the city. This 'insurgency' is not a simple black-and-white struggle of fundamentalists versus foreigners. I had as many conversations with as many different people as I could. It was confusing, and even the name 'Taliban' may be misleading as it has now become a 'tag line' for a super-complex dynamic of narcotics, oil, corruption, tribalism, warlordism, PMCs, Arabs, Iranians, Chechens, NATO and, in the middle of it all, the West shovelling Western precepts on a postmedieval economy. No-one knows what's going to happen, no-one ever will. The only certainty, as in life itself, is that people will die for all the wrong reasons.

Two days later I was at the airport. It's a lot easier to get into Afghanistan than get out, especially when the city is rioting. Getting through customs and immigration is like 250cc motorcycle racing: all knees and elbows. After a few well-placed dollars and weird hand signals to a man in uniform who held my passport upside down, Sami and Tom had me at the stairs to the departure hall. We said our goodbyes, short and sharp, the best way. The passengers nervously boarded as random people were pulled from the queue and questioned. I kept my head

'Blitzkrieg' reigning supreme.

Blitzkrieg lying in wait … the owl never knew what hit him.

'Fantasy Island', Sakhalin, Russia 2006 … spot the ex-con.

'No Fighting' sign.

A well test, flaring in full swing.

Training centre with Calvin the ex-boxer; he can push his nose into his eye socket.

Erwin—not a rig in sight.

Dad in 1960; what goes up ...

El Adem, the Libyan desert, 1964.

Death or even worse!

Thirty years' worth of damage to Bob the driller's hands.

The billboard that says it all.

No room service, no minibar, no mint on the pillow.

How to buy your fuel in Kabul; make sure you pay before you pump.

Over ten million mines in a country the size of Texas.

One of Kabul's prettier boulevards.

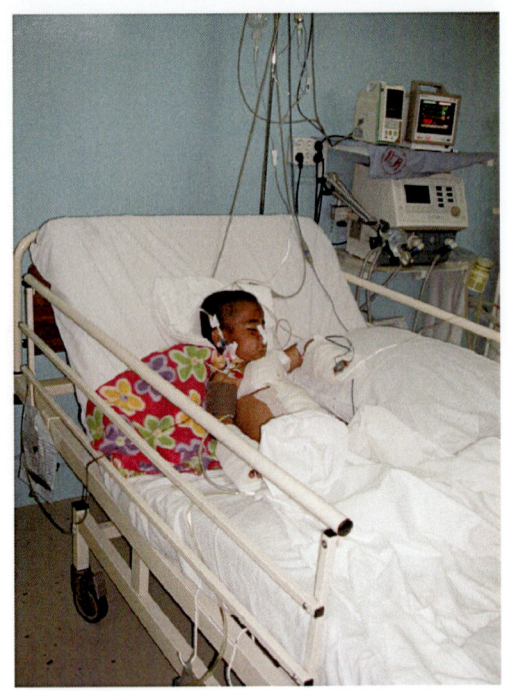

A little man in the fight for his life.

An opium field, Afghanistan.

down and shuffled along, my eyes fixed on the first step of the boarding ladder to Clare and home.

Only after our aircraft was over water and descending into Dubai did I start to feel my shoulders relax. What did I learn from this? I sat there and let what I could replay in my head. I reminded myself of human dignity, resolve, compassion, fear, hope. Afghanistan reminded me that it changes you, more than you change it. It's sitting in freedom's nursery, but learning from all the bad kids. The man sitting next to me shifted in his seat and folded his newspaper; 'Kabulseye' said the headline.

9 TURNING MARGARITAS INTO SWEAT

Coming home to Clare after Afghanistan I felt like the luckiest bastard in the world. Even packing my bags for the next gig in the Philippines, I felt lucky. That's what happens when you've been to the other side, to the places where you're lucky to make it to puberty.

We arrived in Manila without incident, the flight was great and so was the hotel. It was late so everyone just went to their rooms and hit the sack. The following morning we gathered in the lobby after breakfast, as our instructions had us checking in on a 7 a.m. chopper. Ambu had three croissants shoved in his shirt pockets and was slurping coffee while trying to read some businessman's newspaper without him noticing. I had phoned the rig at 6 a.m., they filled me in on the operation and, according to them, the weather was perfect for our scheduled flight offshore. It was a quarter to seven when the concierge came up and handed me a fax. I read it then turned to Ambu. 'Never mind that nice man's newspaper. Now's your chance, mate,' I said, handing him the fax. 'Aloud if you please.'

Ambu handed me his coffee, wiped the crumbs off his

mouth and cleared his throat. 'Chopper cancel no go rig today,' he said and smiled.

There was a mixed reaction. 'Yes!' Don was happy. He was going back to bed so he could go out tonight and play; he has the sex drive of a gorilla in mating season. The others went back into the restaurant with Ambu. I sat down with them.

'Why's it cancelled?' Erwin asked me. I handed him the fax. 'Weather?' He looked out the window. 'It's perfect here. Did you phone the rig?'

'Yup, and it's perfect out there too.' I shrugged my shoulders and ordered coffee. It's like all things men plan when they're single. The plans are perpetually tentative because, no matter how big or serious the plan, if there's the slightest chance of getting laid, all bets are off. It's the unwritten rule between men and it's been that way since the dawn of time. If you hear, 'Nah, let's go for the summit tomorrow' or 'The launch has been delayed due to technical difficulties' or 'The captain has to turn back to port to take on more fuel', you know that's not really what's going on. I was guessing that one of the pilots met someone on his way to the chopper. He was probably out there on the tarmac, with his sunglasses on, leaning against the cockpit, talking to her.

That night we all decided to go out with Don. He had been offshore for a few months on another job before this one, and it was his first break in what must have seemed like years so he was only interested in getting laid. As we walked into the 'Firehouse' he made a beeline straight for the toilets. I just parked myself at the bar, ordered a margarita jug, and waited for the dancing girls to slide down brass poles and land on a fire truck behind the bar, hence the name, and shake their moneymakers at me, small pleasures. For now they were playing some God-awful country song, you know, 'She peed on my carpet, She shot ma horse, She left me with nothing' and so on.

Don came out of the toilets with a lump in his pocket, sat down next to me, and eagerly rubbed his hands together while looking at the girls who had just descended the brass poles and started lip-syncing to a Madonna track.

'Why the dash to the toilet? Have you got the shits, mate?' I asked Don.

'Nah, I just took off my boxers—easy access.' He pointed at his crotch and winked at me.

'Oh Christ, put on a fuckin' rubber!' I handed him a margarita, but he was in a world of his own.

Don is my age, but he looks younger. He grew up in Texas, the son of a disturbed alcoholic father, and a mother who resorted to self-medicating with painkillers. That in turn transformed her into a reclusive shut-in, and as an only child he grew up fast. Don initially did very badly in school, the product of a desperately unhappy home. He was a loner labelled as stupid by the system, until his teachers gave him an IQ test as he was slated to be held back a year. That's when they discovered his triple-digit IQ, realised he was a fucking genius and put him in a school for gifted kids. Don excelled in chemistry, art and mathematics. He's a social chameleon, able to blend into any group and look like he was born there. He can go from brawling with wharfies in a harbour bar to attending a dinner party in town. I've sat there fascinated while he was being anecdotal and getting laid. Don is intelligent, resourceful and thoroughly ruthless. As an adult he is the one I have to watch, as Don could have done anything he wanted to in life. I think he's in oil because, on some base level, he likes the lifestyle. A global transient, he's independently wealthy, has no real fixed address and he's free of any ties to anyone—there is no surviving family, his father died in prison, his mother passed on back in the 1980s. He's moved in and out of places around the world on the back of our modern oil addiction, sometimes places sealed off to everyone. Don is fit and good-looking in an indifferent way. He can turn on the charm with anyone if he wants to, manipulating a situation as easily as you or I order a burger. Sometimes I think Don's a serial killer.

The rest of the crew wandered in over the next half-hour and we all sat at the bar, drinking margaritas and swapping stories. Don finally settled on one of the dancing girls and called over the mamma-san to talk price. She clapped her hands and pointed at Don's new girlfriend, who came down faking a smile at Don. She must have been half his size, poor girl; Don is a skip-the-foreplay kind of guy.

Twenty minutes later Don was back on the stool next to me. We all gave him a hard time but, hey, Don is single and in need of female company. Another half-hour went by, we were all enjoying ourselves, and a few other guys also waiting to go offshore came in and joined us. They had just flown in from other parts of the world so we asked them all the usual questions about what's going on with the well and who had done what to who and why. I noticed Don had been scratching his arse for a full ten minutes. 'Have you got fuckin' fleas, Don?' someone asked him.

He just smiled, but ten minutes after that Don's right hand was buried up to the third knuckle in his backside and he was scratching like an old dog. We were ignoring Don's mad fishing in the back of his pants when his new girlfriend came running up in her boob tube and high heels, the tassels stuck to her nipples propellering around in hypnotic circles.

'Honey, honey, I loose,' she said to Don.

We all stopped talking and looked at her. She held up her right hand; on the end of each finger was a huge talon-like false fingernail with glitter, palm trees and other assorted shit painted on it—except her middle finger, it was missing its fingernail. Don's face dropped in complete horror, he banged his glass down on the bar and bolted out the door.

'Oh fuck. Run, Don, run!' yelled John. 'Should I go with him?' he asked me.

'No.' I was laughing so much I could hardly speak.

Don's new girlfriend was already back on the fire truck waiting for another punter to ask her to poke her finger up his bum.

Three hours later Don came sheepishly back and sat down at the bar. He received a standing ovation. Don's new girlfriend was waving like a lottery winner at him from the fire truck. He pulled a small biohazard ziplock bag from his pocket and waved it at her, there was her bloody glitter-clad fingernail.

'I'm going to pin this to her fuckin' liver,' he said, grinning through clenched teeth.

'Now, now, Don, that's what you get for making that nice girl do sick things to your butt,' John said and slapped him on the back.

'How's that sock fetish going for you, dickhead?' Don was ropeable. I was on the floor again, laughing so much my margarita was coming out my nose.

A few days later we were on the rig. The entire crew had heard about Don's new girlfriend and the poor guy was copping shit from everyone.

A month later our job was pretty much over, we were just starting the last section, and the crew had finished checking over our tools and equipment. I wandered up to the drill floor as I knew the driller on tower from Shell's 'Iron Duke' campaign years earlier. Mike had just come in on the afternoon chopper. I found him standing behind the brake. Like so many guys on rigs all over the world, we stood on the drill floor and played catch-up. I noticed Mike was limping a bit as he moved around. 'You got a parrot to go with that limp, Mike? What's up?'

'I got clipped by a drunk driver on my Harley,' he said. 'Motherfucker put me in a ditch and took off. I was in there for hours before someone found me. My leg was a mess, I woke up in the hospital and realised they had amputated it.'

I looked at him in disbelief. 'Come on . . .'

'No shit, check it out.' He pulled up the leg of his coveralls and there was a metal shaft coming out of the top of his Red Wing boot.

'Oh fuck, Mike. I'm so sorry, mate,' I stammered, feeling awful.

'It's okay, bud, you weren't to know. The company really looked after me, paid for all of it.' He propped his leg up on the railing and pulled back his coveralls. 'It's titanium alloy, best you can get,' he said proudly and rapped his knuckles on the shiny tube. 'Eighteen thousand bucks.' It looked like it belonged on the side of a space shuttle.

Mike was a tough bugger. He had to learn how to walk again as well as dealing with the loss of his leg, and to his credit he was back at work six weeks after the accident. He poured a cup of coffee from a thermos and handed it to me.

'Cheers, Mike.' I was about to change the subject when Mike went on.

'So I'm all groggy after the op and the fuckin' surgeon is standing there. I thought my leg was still there, but when I looked down there was only one foot poking the sheet up.'

Mike was telling me this rather like you would tell someone a joke. 'Then he says, "Would you like us to forward your leg on to your home address?" I'm laying in a fuckin' hospital bed in Singapore and this guy wants to know if I'd like my cremated leg sent to my mom's place in Canada. Jesus.'

There was a moment's silence as I was left speechless. What do you say to a man who's lost a leg? Fortunately, Mike kept going.

'What's your problem tonight? Busting for a smoke, huh?' he asked and smiled slyly.

This particular rig had decided to ban smoking, and before we boarded the chopper to go offshore we were searched for 'any source of ignition'. They turned our bags inside out and removed all our cigarettes, lighters, matches, the lot. After a month I was starting to get more and more agitated.

'It's been a month, man,' I moaned. 'I should be over it by now, but I'm not.' I was biting my fingernails and eating too much, which made me feel bloated and added to my already wicked mood.

Mike wandered closer to me. 'Listen,' he whispered, leaning in, 'after your shift, come by my cabin and I'll get you a smoke.' I looked at him in confusion. 'Don't worry, it's cool,' he said and went back to work.

Later, after we finished at about two in the morning, I knocked on his cabin door, he answered and I stepped inside. 'Here,' he said and handed me a Styrofoam cup, a box of matches and a pack of French smokes. 'You wait till the guys in your cabin are eating, then get up on the top bunk, pile up the pillows, turn off the lights and slide the ceiling panel above your head over to one side, then sit on the pillows and stick your head up through the hole and light up.' I must have looked vacant. 'Are you getting all this?' Mike asked.

'Yeah, won't someone smell it?'

'Just blow your smoke into the air-con duct, put some water in the cup and ash into it, leave all of it up there, and just put the panel back when you're done. See ya.' He slammed the door.

And off I went to break the rules. Everyone was still in the TV room, so I went through Mike's routine, sitting on three pillows in the dark with a smoke dangling from my mouth while sliding the ceiling panel back and debating whether or not I should do this. I'll end up getting caught and I'll get run off—fired—and all because I can't go without a fuckin' cigarette.

When I stuck my head up through the hole and peered about, all I could see was a long line of glowing red smokes going as far as I could see in both directions; the whole rig was up there, all puffing away without a care in the world.

'Took you long enough, Pauli, you shithead,' Mike said from halfway down the line. Everyone burst out laughing, bastards.

The next night I was on the drill floor with Iron Mike. We were running pipe in the hole using a power tong, a kind of giant hydraulically powered wrench. It has two hoses plumbed into the back of a hydraulic motor, one hose being the supply line and the other the return line. When the tong is spinning pipe together, the volume of hydraulic oil circulating through the motor is considerable. It was while making up a joint of pipe that the motor seal blew on the tong, covering the drill floor in hot oil. I ran over to the power unit to shut it down while Mike sorted out the roughnecks to pick up the backup tong.

He came out from behind the drilling console and was walking over to me, no doubt to give me a hand, when he hit hot oil. Both legs shot out from under him, in that classic banana peel slip. We all watched as Mike's new eighteen thousand-dollar titanium alloy leg, as if in slow motion, flew through the air, did a nice little pirouette and bounced straight over the side. Mike had gone down hard, his hard-hat stopped him from knocking himself out, but he had seen his new leg disappear over the side. We all rushed over to help him.

'Get back!' he yelled, furious. 'Haven't you seen a fuckin' one-legged driller before?' Mike hopped over to the railing and peered into the night, his empty trouser leg flapping in the breeze. 'Motherfucker!' He was off, hopping down the stairs, to look for his leg.

The rest of us exchanged blank looks.

'Well, go and give him a hand,' I told Ambu, who grabbed a walkie-talkie and went after Mike.

After only a few moments Ambu was on the radio. 'Hello, I have Mike leg.' That was fast, I thought. The boys were crowded round the radio listening, and we could also hear Mike swearing below us. 'I come back drill floor now,' said Ambu.

'No, Ambu bring the leg to the galley, okay?' The boys looked at me. I had an idea. 'I'm going to hide it,' I told them. There was a lot of laughing. 'Ambu, bring the leg to the galley.'

A long pause. 'Okay, come we go.'

Ambu was waiting for me with Mike's leg dangling over his shoulder. I had a quiet word with the camp boss who laughed when I told him I wanted to hide Mike's new leg in his freezer.

Poor Mike was distraught; he finished his shift on one leg and cursed all the way through his shower, his meal, the movie afterwards, and breakfast the next day. That's when we told him where his leg was. 'Bastards!' He threw a cup of coffee at me, and was off hopping towards the freezer. An hour later Mike was still not on the drill floor. I found him with a paint-stripper heat gun blowing hot air into his new leg. 'Can't get the motherfucker on, 'cos the cold contracted the metal, you fuck' and another cup of coffee was airborne.

That afternoon we touched down in bad weather at Manila's Ninoy Aquino Airport. The pilot shut down and we all hurried through the rain into the hanger to wait for the ground crew to bring in our bags.

'Just beat the weather,' the pilot said as he ran up to us, shaking the rain off his head. 'I'd hate to get stuck in Busuanga.' Busuanga is one of the larger islands in the Philippines, where choppers refuel en route to the rig. It's a lush green paradise, though sparsely populated and therefore, I must admit, lacking in amusements.

'Why?' I asked. 'It's not so bad.'

'I've got a date tonight,' he beamed.

Where did you meet her?' asked Erwin.

'Right here at the airport actually.'

Erwin looked at me, I started laughing.

'What?' The pilot looked annoyed.

The bad weather turned out to be the start of one of those Philippines typhoons that shuts off the power and transforms the streets into rivers. We ended up in a small bar that had this excellent seafood restaurant out the back and settled in for the rest of the night. It was pointless trying to leave; the whole place was in gridlock. It was close to midnight when the lights went out. We were the last group in there, all drunk, and the manager who had been sitting with us doing tequila shots staggered off to get some candles. Ambu continued eating.

'He's a machine,' said Erwin. 'Keep your hands away from his face when he's feeding.'

Ambu can see in the dark and poured himself another tequila. I was three feet from him and could only just make out what was going on. It must be one of his jungle skills or something, like his complete lack of fear. If Ambu is wearing his 'power belt' then, as he puts it 'Ambu cannot die.' I've seen him work over guys twice his size. I've also read his medical file, or rather read it to him: the official diagnosis is abbreviated as NAFOD, meaning No Apparent Fear Of Death. To Ambu, the belt is his power. He believes in it and wears it everywhere. 'It's magic,' he says. Unfortunately, since airports have started dissecting us before a flight Ambu has been forced to take off his 'power belt'; he was causing small riots in the departure lounge when a security guy pulled a two-metre long leather belt, with human teeth and other assorted charms dangling off it, from inside his pants.

Jimmy, the restaurant manager, returned with a box of candles, a flashlight and a bottle of premium tequila. 'This is the best,' he said and went back to the bar for a tray of glasses.

'Keep away from children.' Ambu was reading the plastic bag the candles were in.

We had been doing shots all night—the salt, the sticky glass and a wedge of lemon pushed into gritted teeth. We did them all: the 'Body Slam', the 'Depth Charge', the painful and completely stupid 'Tequila Stuntman'. If memory serves, that's the one where you snort the salt, take the shot, squeeze the lemon in your eye, and eat the worm. A great many of us have spent the early hours of the morning projectile vomiting into a taxi while your mates remind you about the worm you ate after that last shot.

Tequila was never meant to be downed in one, with salt licked off various body parts, lemon was never part of the equation, and the worm was simply a marketing gimmick introduced in the early 1980s to sell more bottles to people who were so coked up they thought a preserved slug (that's got nothing to do with the drink whatsoever) was neat. Sipping it and enjoying the flavour, rather like one would savour a cognac, is the way to drink tequila. Mexicans drink it that way, or in the form of a margarita.

Still, we drink it, the new way or the old way, we will dance, laugh, throw up, fall over, but only ever on the surface. We all look after each other, even Don.

The bottle Jimmy was pouring was shaped like a big 'X' and it did taste great. 'Cheers!' he yelled and went off to get his guitar.

'Did you know tequila comes from the blue agave plant?' Erwin was holding his glass up to the candlelight.

'Yeah, it's a cactus.' I was really drunk.

'Not a cactus, buddy, but in fact a relative of the lily.' And he was off.

Erwin is a remarkable man. While the rest of us are telling fart jokes and chatting up the waitresses, he can focus and tell you something other than drivel. 'It takes roughly fifteen pounds of blue agave cores or "pinas" of the plant to produce one litre of tequila.'

Ambu stopped eating. 'Penis,' he said.

'No, *pinas*, Ambu. It's Spanish for pineapple.'

We then spent the next five minutes explaining to Ambu that the Spanish don't call the penis a pineapple.

Don was dancing with his other new girlfriend behind the bar while Jimmy played his guitar. The others were either passed out or chatting at the bar. The storm outside raged on, the water slowly starting to lap at the front door.

Erwin went on. 'Tequila's origins are a combination of conquest and necessity, with mankind's need for war and getting hammered. Circa mid-sixteenth century, what you had were a bunch of Spanish conquistadors arriving in Mexico and running out of beer.' Erwin poured us another round. Ambu had finished his fifth crab and settled in for what was to be his bedtime story. 'Having an intimate knowledge of the distillation process as well as warfare proved useful in between brawls in the sleepy town of Tequila. They discovered after long chats with the locals that the blue agave produced a sweet sap that, once fermented, was a knockout beverage. The native Indians had been drinking it for nine thousand years, but once the conquistadors had finished with it, the fun really started, and there you have it. "Tequila" the town had produced "tequila" the drink. Tequila is also the name of the volcano overlooking the town and probably the name of the dog that lived in the pub where it was first poured.' He sat back smiling, Ambu had started snoring.

'This is so much better than the crap we've been drinking all night,' I said.

'That's why I didn't join in.' Erwin had been on light beer up until then. 'Understanding the difference between the two can get complicated, so first, in case you were wondering, there is no "mescaline" in mescal. The word "mescal" is often used with tequila as roughly translated it means "cheers". It's part of Mexican culture, a social icon, simply a toast as well as a drink. The best way of describing the two is to say that they are made from different types of agave plant and different amounts of sugars.' He leaned in and pointed at his glass. 'They are distilled in different ways, but to put it bluntly it can be likened to the difference between single malt, and rye or sour mash whiskies, or if you prefer cognac and brandy. I love this one.'

The difference between Erwin and Don, I thought, is much the same. I looked over at the bar where Don was licking his tequila off his other new girlfriend's thigh while Erwin sipped his in the corner and laughed. Erwin is the boss, his depths are a complete mystery, but he can handle the roughest crews with a skill I could never match, even when they get really wild, close the doors of the bar, turn the plane upside down and cut their toes off.

At some point Don was in the kitchen helping Jimmy with the crabs for the next day, when he got the idea to have crab races down the hall between the bar and the restaurant.

'Sheeet son, this'll be fun,' he beamed. The crabs were massive, each had a body the size of a frisbee. Their huge claws were tied up with string, but their legs were going like the clappers.

'C'mon, I've got the three biggest ones in the sink.' Don was leaning on his other new girlfriend who looked suspiciously like a man.

We taped different coasters to the back of the three crabs and set them up in the hallway. Erwin, Don, Ambu, Jake, John, the waitress and Don's other new girlfriend all sat on the floor on cushions, their backs leaning against the far wall with their legs stretched out under a big glass coffee table where the drinks sat. I was up the other end of the hall with Jimmy, who giggled so much he nearly fell over trying to control three pissed-off giant mud crabs. Jimmy had pulled out three drawers from a wooden desk in his office and we had a crab under each upturned drawer. They were so strong that if you stopped holding the drawer it would take off down the hall.

'Okay, you ready?' Jimmy was all set. 'On three.' I struggled with the drawers. 'One, two three!' We flipped up the drawers and the crabs bolted. Team 'San Miguel' climbed over the drawer and straight onto my foot, then back into the kitchen. The other two were neck and neck down the hall, going straight for the coffee table. Ambu was waving his arms and slapping his thigh like people do at horse races. Don's crab, Team 'Heineken', crossed the line first, his other new girlfriend rolled over onto his lap and kissed him.

The race over, Ambu and John went after the second crab, who had made a break for the door, while Jimmy was in the kitchen putting 'San Miguel' back in the crate. Don's winning crab was under the coffee table with Don's bare feet.

'Okay, who's drinking?' He suddenly stopped, his eyes locked on his other new girlfriend's—they may have been separated by countless cultural and socioeconomic barriers, but the look on Don's face crossed them all instantly. I'd never had a small Asian woman fired across a table at me before.

There was the most blood-curdling scream. The crab, with the bigger of its claws free of the string, had latched onto Don's little toe and, being not too happy with the whole crab-racing thing, it had decided to cut off Don's toe altogether. Don kicked over the glass coffee table, smashing it to pieces, grabbed a huge round glass ashtray and beat the crab into pulp, while his other new girlfriend screamed and ran on the spot with one high heel on. By the time Don finished, the claw was the only thing left; still attached to Don's toe, it lay there among all the broken glass. The place looked like a Tom Waits song. Don refused to go to the hospital. Besides, in our state we wouldn't have made it to the end of the street. Eventually, he opted instead to cremate his toe on Jimmy's barbeque.

10 HURRY UP AND WAIT

Three months after Clare and I were married, we finally got around to our honeymoon. I had six weeks off so we went to visit Europe and my family, and hopefully not get into any trouble. It made a nice change when we got to the red line at the airport. I hate the red line. Usually Clare stands right on it, we go through our goodbyes, I would cross it, walk a few yards, stop just before the barrier where immigration starts, and look back. Clare would still be standing on the red line, waving, tears rolling down her cheeks. We had done that so many times, but not this time. This time she was crossing the red line with me.

Airports throughout the Western world are, I think, designed by the same firm. Each is just a slight variation on a theme. If you get hungry after you have gone through immigration, you get nailed twenty dollars for a very average cup of coffee and a bun. It's like you're in a limbo state, temporarily a citizen of no country, you're in airport land where they can charge whatever they want.

The good ones give you a trolley for free, like Singapore's Changi Airport, but in most of them you have to pay, why?

They make so much money, why do they think they can get away with stitching you up two dollars for their crappy little trolley. This is especially annoying when you discover, after arriving in a foreign land, that the machine dispensing the trolleys only accepts local coins. Japanese trolleys are free and by far the best ones I've used; they have a flip-up bar at the front that springs up as you pull the trolley out and stops your bags from falling off, and they have brakes, suspension and no mind of their own. British ones also have brakes, and a sticker on the lever that tells you to apply the brakes on a gradient. However, every time I'm at Heathrow I witness a hilarious trolley prang, usually involving an elderly person who has suddenly lost control of their trolley on a slope and embarked on a slalom down towards some unlucky punter coming the other way.

So Clare and I crossed the red line together, went through the current improved security check—screen, pat-down, sniff test, strip-search—and wandered into the labyrinth that is an international airport departure building. This one is like a shrine to last-minute consumerism, another award-winning design by architects 'Can We Cheat 'Em, and How'. It could fit like Lego into any other airport terminal in the world. While Clare went off to arm herself with magazines, I found a spot in the corner and sat quietly watching. The airport is a good place to observe the human animal under stress. Travellers scampered in that hurried way like migrating hedgehogs across a busy road. Backpackers walked past, almost floating after having checked in their massive backpacks that always look like they weigh twice as much as the owner, who has to lie down to get the pack on, only to realise they can't get back up. Tourists in 'Bondi' T-shirts were going home after getting various degrees of skin cancer.

For once, I wasn't dreading the flight. We were flying business class; I have done my time in economy. The airlines discovered ages ago that they can physically cram an adult human into a space barely comfortable for a chimp as long as they tell you beforehand that you may lose all feeling in your extremities after the first hour. This could be permanent, and if you're unfit, diabetic, fat, a smoker or just unlucky it could lead to deep vein thrombosis and kill you, but only after you're enjoying your first day on the beach. For me, there would be no elbow brawls over the armrest, no fake smiles from cabin attendants whose teeth are so bright that I need sunglasses just to look at them, no mini-meals with a metal fork and a plastic knife, or some crappy pre-made cheese sandwich getting dumped on my tray table for $12.98. Instead our flight was remarkably nice; we had a whole human-sized seat each.

Sixteen hours later we landed in Paris. During the hour we waited for our luggage to appear I went off to get a trolley. The French trolleys are free but look like reject designs for a light aircraft undercarriage, they career off in random directions much like the supermarket ones do, and they always seem to have one wheel that appears to be having a fit of some kind.

We had a fantastic ten days in France. We visited my mum and John, her second husband and an all-round legend. They threw a party, inviting their friends. Sitting down to eat with a dozen retired people, I was surprised to find that they knew how to party. It was like being at a 'Bond Villain' convention.

Afterwards we went up to Scotland to visit Klaas, an oilfield mate who was the company man on my first job offshore. He was with Shell and I was there to learn how to inspect pipe. Klaas saw his opportunity to completely mess up my head. He called me into his office, Erwin was there too, keeping a straight face. I had been working for a full day and all night, trying to make a good impression, but in the early hours of the morning Erwin had come out on deck and told me to go to bed. I wasn't working for him yet, I was with another outfit who had sent me out there on my own. Erwin certainly didn't need to take over from me, but he did anyway, and did a better job in the end. Mid-morning, I had just woken up and was standing in the company man's office. 'So, Paul,' said Klaas, 'did you inspect our pipe last night?'

If he knew Erwin had done half the work then I was in big trouble. 'Well, Mr Van der Plaas, you see, I was getting tired, and Erwin here was nice enough to take over for me . . .'

He cut in, 'Does Erwin have the right pipe inspector's tickets?'

I looked at Erwin, who shrugged at me.

'He doesn't even work for the same company as you.' Klass looked really serious. 'Take a seat,' he said and nodded towards a chair in the corner. I sat down. I'm going to get run off, I thought.

Klaas picked up the phone on his desk and began banging his index finger down on the buttons while he glared at me through the smoke rising from the Marlboro dangling from his bottom lip. Erwin just sat there, pulling all the right faces. I was shitting myself.

Klass suddenly launched into a high-speed Dutch conversation. Occasionally I heard my name, some bad language, my name again, oh God, now the company name; he looked at his watch, glared at me again, then he was talking about choppers. That's it, I thought, he's got me on the next chopper, the end of the shortest oilfield career in history. He banged down the phone, leaned back in his chair, had a long drag on his smoke and exhaled, his eyes hard and fixed.

I was waiting for it, indeed now fully expecting it. He sat forward in his big company man's chair and started laughing. Erwin jumped up and was out the door, laughing all the way down the hall. 'Ya, it's okay buddy, we're just fucking with you. Go and get some sleep.'

I got up and turned to go, then stopped and asked, 'Who did you call?'

Klaas was still laughing. 'My wife. I just bullshitted about who's out here, and what she's cooking for dinner tonight.'

Fifteen years later and he's not changed a bit. Klaas is bright and has done well in his career. I went to a work function with him and ended up sitting next to some ambassador's wife making polite conversation while Klaas pulled faces across the table at me.

The next day I ran into another guy, at Aberdeen Airport. I was leaving for London, walking towards departures. He had just arrived from a rig and was walking towards arrivals. We approached each other, glanced, made eye contact for a second, then continued on our paths. Then we both stopped about three meters apart and turned around at the same time.

It was Donald, I hadn't seen him in years. When I knew him, he was a driller. Now he was a company man; everyone has moved on, done well and become successful in oil, except me. I'm still doing the same shit I was doing ten years ago. But he was just as I remembered him, and within five minutes we had abandoned our respective plans and were sitting in the airport bar.

The last time I saw Donald, he was getting fired. A new tool pusher had come out to our rig in a quiet corner of the South China Sea and took a disliking to Donald. This escalated over the next few weeks, culminating in an explosive display of what happens when you wind up Donald. All I remember was the tool pusher getting punched, falling over and Donald casually picking him up by his ankles and dangling him over the side of the drill floor. The guy was beside himself, screaming while the contents of his pockets spiralled down to the sea some two hundred feet below. Donald eventually put him down and walked off to the locker room, as he knew the chopper would be en route within the hour.

That's one of the things that never ceases to amaze me about the oilfield: you could be sitting in some God-awful backwater on your way to or coming from a job and run into someone you worked with years ago, and you pick up right where you left off. If it doesn't happen that way, then it will on the job. Once I was standing on the drill floor on a jack-up rig in Asia, sucking on a boiled sweet and thinking about a workover job we were about to start, when a Baker fishing-hand marched up to me. Fishing-hands are specialists, like directional drillers who speak their own dialect that revolves around the language of drilling. They retrieve lost 'items' from a well. They are skilled individuals who use various 'fishing tools' down an open or cased hole, and they can fish everything out from a drill pipe to hand tools or the occasional unlucky roughneck, but that could be a myth. He was older than me by about twenty years, and had strong features and a purposeful stride. He took off his safety glasses when he was standing right in front of me, gave me a hard look and said, 'Spit that shit out, Paul. If your mother saw that, she would kick your arse.'

I was completely bamboozled and quickly looked around. Is this guy mental? I thought. So I cupped my gloved hand under my chin and spat out my sweet, totally taken aback and a little worried about what this guy's problem was.

'Oh shit. Sorry, mate, I thought you were chewing tobacco.' He gave me a huge grin, he could see that I had no idea who he was. 'It's me, you fuckwit, Tony.'

I was blank.

'Tony Lacey. Shit, you used to play with my kids, come over for barbeques.'

Finally I remembered. My parents worked with Tony when I was eight, but to him it may have well been yesterday. He recognised me straightaway. That's the oilfield.

Clare had to go home a few days before me for work. I didn't want her to go; I didn't want our trip to end. When my turn came, things got complicated, they always do. I departed London on the seventh of the seventh; exactly one year since I'd arrived in the middle of the bombings. The city was functioning as it normally would, but there were masses of people attending memorial services at tube stations, flowers and wreaths adorned station entrances, and all over London crowds had gathered. I took a cab to Paddington Train Station where I planned to catch the Heathrow Express to the airport. The cab ride seemed to take forever, and when I did get to Paddington I emerged from the cab into a sea of people. It was peak hour times ten, I've never seen so many people. The central staircase descending to the tube was a river of people. Moving against the flow was impossible; it was like trying to move through a packed nightclub, with luggage. I stood there for a moment, just looking into the void, then picked up my offshore bag and ran the gauntlet over to a café on my left. It was strangely unoccupied, so I ordered coffee and parked my arse in the corner, deciding to kill the next hour there before braving the hoards. There was an air of worry and concern in every face that went past, the horror twelve months ago still alive in their memories.

I pulled a magazine I'd nicked from the hotel lobby coffee table out of my bag and settled in, blanking out the millions around me. It was one of those blokey mags with a model in a bikini holding an automatic weapon on the cover. After forty pages of beer, sport and tits, followed by a sudoku puzzle, I was successfully distracted enough to relax.

That's when I noticed the black Samsonite suitcase under the table next to me.

It was one of those smaller ones that you can bring into the aircraft as hand luggage. The masses flowed past, ignoring the empty café and its unattended bag, as did the guy running the place. I sat there for a moment, then called him over and asked for a latte. 'Who's case is that mate?' I pointed at the suitcase.

He bent down to look. 'I have no idea,' he replied, and instinctively and cleverly backed away towards the shelter of his cardboard booth.

I got up and walked the few metres to his booth. 'Look, make my coffee and I'll be back with a security guy, okay?' He just nodded, keeping his eyes on the suitcase.

I picked up my offshore grip bag and stood on a chair. Throughout the tube stations and train stations in London there were posters to recruit new security staff, in a push to put people at ease. These new staff wear a luminous yellow vest and carry a two-way radio, but spotting one was proving difficult. Then I saw one, with his back to me, also trying to stay out of the flow of people. He was too far away to hear me, so I waded in. At first I was carried along with the current of people; no-one gives a fuck or gets out of your way so you have to just go head down and barge. Finally I got to him and explained that I'd found an unattended bag. He got on the radio, then said, 'Show me.'

The café now had a German family sitting at my table. They were oblivious to the suitcase, and the dad had also become fascinated in the beer steins, guns and airbrushed topless cheerleaders. The café guy was still in his booth with my coffee sitting on the counter in front of him.

I pointed at the suitcase. 'There it is.' I went to the booth to pay for my coffee, and by the time I'd turned around the German father was gathering up his children, one under each arm, and jumping into the mad faceless blur of people flowing past the café's boundary, his wife, struggling with the luggage, swept along behind him, their steaming drinks all sitting on the table untouched.

The security guy was back on his radio. I stood at the booth with the café guy and watched two more security guys roll up through the masses. One walked over to us. 'No idea who left it, mate?' he asked the café guy, who shook his head and began to look worried. The suitcase was nameless; it sat there looking more and more conspicuous. Two of the security guys very carefully lifted up the table that the suitcase sat under and moved it away. Then they all stood around it and talked. Finally, one leaned over to listen. Was it ticking? I thought. He casually booted the suitcase with his size-ten combat boot, and it slammed over on its side with a thud.

'Fuckin' hell!' The café guy was off, with me following right behind him. I walked all the way around the station to enter from the other side and get on the next Heathrow Express, waiting for a bang the whole time.

The last time I'd heard a bomb go off, a really big bomb, was in 2001 when I was working in Nigeria. Anyone who has worked in Nigeria will know the expression '419', after section 4-1-9 of the Nigerian Penal Code, which relates to fraudulent schemes. I drove in through the office gates, it was a lovely sunny day. The vultures were all lined up on the office roof—the base was only a stone's throw away from the Port Harcourt slaughter market—and were looking down at the office staff and workshop technicians, who were all standing outside in the carpark.

The first thing that jumped into my head was, 'Fuck, they've all gone on strike.' But no, I was told we had been robbed and that the security men had been found out the back, gagged, tied up and smelling of shit.

On entering the office we found the place trashed, tables and chairs upside-down, and the safe opened with the aid of a sledgehammer. There were expatriate passports all over the floor. The safe we had purchased locally some months earlier, and by the looks of things it wasn't the first time it had been broken into; lumps of car filler had broken off its shell. We didn't keep the petty cash in the safe—it came back to the staff house each night—so the thieves ended up stealing passports, the fax/copier machine and the company communication equipment, VHS and VHF radios.

Later in the morning the local CID arrived on the crime scene. They told us they needed a photographer, the loan of a car and driver, some money for food and drink or, as they say, 'minerals', before they could start their investigation and apprehend the criminals. The officers then took advantage of the car for the rest of the week, without coming up with a thing, so we decided to drop the case and get back to as normal a working life as you can expect in Nigeria.

One of the passports that got lifted was mine, which meant I had to go to Lagos to get a new one. I stayed in a staff house on a very busy, very dirty road. It had huge solid iron shutters on the windows and another for the front door, and every night the house was closed up like the dark ages, both to keep the locals out and us in. I was only going to be there for a few days so I didn't mind too much. My first night was spent chatting to the other two guys who were also temporarily staying there. One of the guys worked for a well testing company. He was in Lagos because his warehouse had been broken into and the thieves had made off with some very powerful high explosives which we use inside special tools that are sent down the well to fracture a formation.

The second night I was halfway through dinner, eating at the coffee table in front of the TV, when the whole house and everything in it, including me, appeared to go up a few feet then crash back down again. The TV fell forwards onto its screen and blew up, glasses and plates smashed on the kitchen floor, the windows flexed and shattered in their frames. The other two guys in the house came sprinting out of their rooms, one in his jocks, the other in coveralls. We all went for the front door. The lights had gone out, so we fumbled at the bolts on the iron door, then finally it swung open and we spilled out onto the street. Car alarms shrieked in the distance, I could hear children screaming. At the end of the street where an apartment building had stood a few minutes earlier, there was a big pile of rubble. A giant cloud of concrete dust roared down the street, swallowing up everything. We ran back inside and bolted the door.

'How much of that shit did you lose?' I asked the well tester.

'That much,' he replied.

The following morning the sirens were still wailing up and down the street as I got in the car to go and get my passport. By the time I had done that and jumped on the next flight to Port Harcourt, the story was on the news. It was the well tester's high explosive that went off the night before. Some would-be bank robbers had stolen it, improvised a device using all of it, put it in a car and parked the car in the basement carpark of the apartment building; it was supposed to be a distraction from the real drama, the bank directly across the street, which they had planned to knock off. Not realising how powerful the explosive was, and not doing a very good job of rigging it up, they all went bang in the car and vaporised at two thousand feet per second, as did the whole building.

Our base in Port Harcourt was a five hundred-square metre concrete compound, with various workshops and two single-storey office buildings, all surrounded by a high concrete wall festooned with razor wire and protected by armed guards on duty twenty-four hours a day. Every morning we would run the gauntlet of impoverished locals waiting for our car to arrive at the main gates. It took a few minutes for the guards to unlatch the lock and swing open the doors, and in that time the car would be surrounded with requests for a few *naira*, Nigerian currency, and sick babies would be pressed against the window. Begging with babies is, unfortunately, something I've seen many times in many parts of the world, and occasionally the infant is quite obviously dead. If there was time before the guards came out and pushed them all away, we would slip them a few bucks.

During a particularly hot still day, I was working on some equipment in the middle of the yard. We had so much equipment in the base at that time there was no more space left to work in the shade. So, using the forklift, I dumped everything in the open and set up an umbrella. Two guys were giving me a hand, and we passed the morning chatting about the usual stuff as we worked. Then around lunchtime I noticed they were shooting glances over to the far wall near the corner. There was nothing over there at all. 'What's going on?' I asked.

'Target practice' was the response. Then I saw a man's head and shoulders appear at the top of the wall; it was fifteen feet high so he must have been propped up on something. I looked closer. It was the handicapped guy I had seen begging at the front gates.

The two blokes I was working with suddenly produced slingshots from their pockets and began firing rocks with money wrapped around them at the poor guy's head. I stood there horrified. 'What the fuck?' A rock bounced off the guy's head, but he didn't go down.

'Do you want a shot?' One of the blokes, the bigger one, offered me his homemade slingshot.

'No, I don't want a fucking shot! Stop it.' They ignored me and went back to their fun. The rocks were small bits of dried cement wrapped with money, and occasionally they disintegrated against the wall in a puff of dust and paper. But every shot that went high would have sent the beggars on the other side into a frenzy. This had obviously been going on for some time, and all the people on the other side of the wall had ganged up on the handicapped guy and made him the target.

'Cut it out,' I tried to stop them.

'Make us,' said the big one without looking at me.

'You guys are fucked!' I wasn't getting into a brawl, but I had to stop them somehow without creating a problem. Then the handicapped guy dropped down and that was it. In the five minutes he was up there, they had fired off perhaps twenty dollars in small bills; the poor sod they were shooting at only got hit once and that, it seemed, was an acceptable reason for his pals to grab him and shove him into the line of fire.

The next day when I arrived at the workshop gates I saw him off in the background; he was sitting with his back against the compound wall and drooling while the others banged at the car windows. Later that morning I thought of a way to stop him from getting hurt, but still allow the money to keep coming in. I told one of the other guys about it.

'What are you going to do?' he asked me.

'Do you know who Ned Kelly is?' I said.

'Ned who?' He had just come from South Africa on his first job overseas so I didn't bother explaining it to him.

'Google it,' I said and went off to the paint shack to get a bucket. Once I found the right bucket, I washed it and cut out a little slot so that when Ned had the bucket on his head he would be able to see what was going on. Then I tied two rubber straps to the brackets that held the handle. I went out through the gates with the bucket and found Ned still sitting there in the same spot. The others weren't quite sure how to react to me and just watched. I stuck the bucket over Ned's head and ran the straps under his arms. He may have been sitting there in his own shit and drool but he knew that with his new bucket he wasn't going to lose an eye in today's session.

I went back to work on our tools in the yard with the two sadistic maniacs. Bang on lunchtime they pulled out their slingshots and loaded up. Ned appeared, his head rag-dolling from side to side, and they lost it, unloading all their cash at Ned and missing altogether. Ned was a hit. It went on for the rest of the week, and by then Ned was cashed up. On the following Monday morning he was sporting a new shirt, his bucket under his arm as he waved and howled at me through the window of the staff car, spraying the entire vehicle in spittle. Another week went by and Ned was in new shoes, and he'd painted his bucket and stuck bottle caps all over it. He was ecstatic.

Christmas that year was good for the crew, and everyone got a bonus. We got a cheque and the local guys got what they wanted; not cash, that was too simple. They wanted to be given a gallon of cooking oil, a twenty-five-kilo bag of basmati rice and a live chicken on Christmas Eve. So the company made sure it was the right type of oil the majority would expect, that the bag of rice did weigh twenty-five kilos and not nineteen, and especially, that the chickens were all alive and kicking; no Nigerian wants a dead chicken, with no electricity at home for a fridge. Christmas was good for Ned too. He got a new stainless-steel bucket with foam and rubber lining to reduce noise, and a slingshot so that if by chance his hand–eye coordination somehow returned, at least he could shoot back.

A good tip for anyone going to work in Nigeria is that you will be asked on more than one occasion, 'What have you got for me?'

The answer is, 'My blessing on you and your family.'

Trust me—it works every time.

11 THIS LITTLE PIGGY

Home in Sydney again after our honeymoon, Clare was back at work and I was sorting out my visa for my next job in Russia. This time the campaign was supposed to be an improvement on last year's shambles. I sat in my office remembering how miserable I got out there. But most of all I remember how hungry I was by the time we got from the rig to the hotel, a day later. I ate leftover bread rolls off room service trolleys in the hotel corridors on my way to go out and eat with the boys. That's hungry. Money before you eat when you've been offshore on a rig that serves dog food has no value at all.

Last year after a massive three-month Russian stint we gathered in some nice restaurant. As usual it was Erwin's choice—I think he instinctively knows where to go. We had each purchased one of those bargain-bin business shirt and nasty rayon tie combo packs, and we arranged ourselves around an expansive table adorned with pressed tablecloths and silverware as if we were the rulers of our own special empire. It was worlds away from shuffling along with plastic trays in our hands. Ambu clapped and read out the name of the company that printed the menus for the restaurant. We ordered an aperitif and read the menu with Ambu. It felt like we were about to have the greatest meal of our entire lives.

Before, during and after dinner we decided to drink, along with wine, a great deal of gin and tonic. Last time it was vodka, before that single malt, before that tequila and so on, from one end of the bar to the other in more than a dozen fine restaurants around the world. As usual everyone degenerated into 'male-violent' lunacy, everyone except Erwin; he always maintains control of himself and thereby us, which explains why we haven't been kicked out of more than a dozen fine restaurants around the world.

'Would this gin and tonic help me to avoid malaria?' I asked Erwin.

'No.' He was studying the label on the back of the bottle.

'What if I had another one?'

Erwin looked over at me. 'The gin and tonic, Pauli, was created as a way for Englishmen in tropical colonies to get loaded in the middle of the day while at the same time ingesting their daily dose of quinine, used to ward off malaria, right?'

'Right.' Excellent, I thought, he's off, he's going to tell me all about gin.

'Modern tonic water still contains quinine, though as a flavouring rather than a medicine. To answer the question of how many modern G&Ts would need to be consumed to deliver a preventative dose of quinine? Sixty-seven litres.' He was well and truly off. How does he know that? Why does he know that?

Ambu was loving it. 'I like gin,' he beamed.

'Let's have a martini, Ambu,' I suggested and grabbed the cocktail list.

Ambu started reading out the names on the list. 'Pink Slapper,' he said as his stumpy finger moved across the letters.

'Slipper,' Erwin corrected.

I found the gin-based cocktails, nudged Ambu and, doing my best Sean Connery voice, said, 'Why don't you slip out of those wet clothes and into a dry martini, young Ambu?'

He gave me a blank look. The waiter came over and we ordered three martinis, shaken not stirred.

'James Bond ruined the martini,' Erwin was off again. 'A martini is made with gin, and shaking gin muddles its flavours and clouds its appearance. Ambu, you could be a Bond villain.' Erwin was laughing. 'But you'd need a shaved cat and a collarless shirt.'

Ambu looked blank again.

'So where does gin come from, mate?' I asked Erwin, who was back to the label on the bottle.

'Oh, gin has a dark past, more daunting and evil than any Bond villain. It's steeped in black history, it fuelled a billion drunks through Britain's lowest moments. The Dutch started the whole thing in the lowlands of Holland. One Dr Franciscus de la Boë in the university town of Leiden created a juniper- and spice-flavoured medicinal spirit that he promoted as a diuretic. The new creation spread fast. It was the late sixteenth century. The Dutch christened it "jenever", the linguistic root of the English word "gin". Initially it was sold in chemists to treat stomach complaints, gallstones and—are you listening, Ambu?—gout.'

'I have gout,' Ambu replied, sipping slowly on his martini.

Much later, we were full, after the wine was gone and we squeezed in a cheese platter and dessert, and a glass of brandy, and one of those little mints, and coffee with its little cookie. My belt had gone back two notches and there was a cigarette butt in Ambu's mash potatoes. Erwin and John were talking Don out of cutting off his other little toe with a cigar cutter.

Don had his shoe and sock off, and was convinced he'd 'stop walking funny' if he removed and no doubt cremated it. Then they moved on to motorcycle header pipes. I was telling the others to share the cigar trolley, someone threw the cigar cutter at me, and that was when John made the international sign for 'the bill'.

Getting the waiter's attention can involve everything from making eye contact to discharging a firearm in some parts of the world. But then you do a pantomime of writing something on your palm while mouthing the words 'THE BILL' at your waiter, a sign recognised universally. When it does arrive it's passed around and everyone scratches their head for ten minutes, and inevitably it's shoved in front of whoever's turn it is to pay. The argument is that some countries are more expensive than others. But that's the system, it works out in the end; you could get nailed with a thousand-dollar bill in Japan and one month later its two hundred bucks in Thailand.

This year's Russian campaign surprised me. I was overjoyed to see that improvements had been made, and while the job was going to take three months again, this time we would get changed out with a fresh crew after six weeks. We had a great room on the rig, the shower had hot water, the toilet flushed, the food was edible, but best of all the people in charge were back again. Colin and Ann Smith are a remarkable couple. They are the only husband-and-wife 'company man' team I've come across (these are people who work on equal time rotation—month on, month off—with the 'back to back' person in the team doing your job while you're on your month off). I try to imagine having Clare as my 'back to back' on the rig and I can't. They are superb people to work for, and they have been working like that for years.

About halfway through my six weeks I was in Colin's office, having a chat, when he told me about a land rig he and Ann had worked on years ago in Colombia. The rig was in the Cupiagua basin, deep in the jungle. They were frequently attacked by local rebels, who would take a shot at the rig every few days and on a weekly basis try to blow something up. The location was completely surrounded by a high wire fence and security personnel were on patrol twenty-four hours a day.

Not too far from the rig was the tool pusher's cabin with the company man's cabin next door. The company man and the tool pusher basically ran the whole operation between them, making them highly desirable targets. The portacabins were very basic, just thin plastic over a metal sub-frame. Inside, the layout was just as simple—a desk, small closet and a metal-framed bed, with a foam mattress on top. The tool pusher hated the bed, and every time he crew-changed back to the rig he moaned about his bed to Ann and Colin. So with the tool pusher's birthday not too far away, Ann and Colin decided to get the onsite chippy to make him a fantastic new bed. The carpenter did a great job, making a huge frame with two massive drawers underneath, and Ann and Colin got him a big sprung mattress. The real motivation for the new bed, however, was for the drawers in its frame as the tool pusher was really keen on dirty magazines, and Ann was fed up with walking into his portacabin after he had been in there for a month and finding his cock mags all over the place. So a month later the tool pusher came back out to the rig, walked into his portacabin and discovered he had a huge new bed with two drawers full of porn—what more could a tool pusher want?

A few days later the rebels strong-armed one of the local guys who worked on the rig to plant a bomb in the tool pusher's cabin. They had the device in a box and the timer was set to go off in the middle of the night. The tool pusher went to bed at the end of his shift as usual, and in the early hours of the morning the bomb went off. The blast shook the whole camp, and the tool pusher's cabin disintegrated, but he survived. His massive collection of dirty magazines saved his life, they absorbed the shockwave and, along with the new bed and mattress, he was propelled through the roof and into the night sky.

The whole job went very well, even the Azerbaijanis avoided their usual brawling, and Mother Nature left us alone as well. My hitch was soon over. Erwin asked if Clare and I would like to go to his place in Perth for Christmas. Erwin's is exactly the kind of home you want to wake up in on Christmas morning. His wife, Lucy, produces meals that make you wish you could eat your bodyweight, and his kids, all four of them, are great fun. He has a living room not unlike Captain Kirk's bridge on the starship *Enterprise*: one big comfy chair and a plasma TV that fills the entire wall. There are motorcycles, dogs, cats, rabbits and a huge backyard with a giant trampoline that gives me head injuries every time I get on it. In all, I look forward to a Christmas at Erwin's place.

Most of all, I love the bikes. Erwin has the same fascination with motorcycles as I do. Whenever we get the chance and we're not both on a rig somewhere, we have track days. Erwin rides a Jap 500 single in a Norton wide-line featherbed frame. I, on the other hand, ride a Kawasaki 650 Twin; it's a modern bike designed to look like a classic, but he still rounds me up. The bike I'm riding now is my second after I dropped my first bike twice. Riding a motorcycle is total joy, right up to the point when your overconfidence causes your first big 'Get Off'. My first 'Get Off' was just plain stupid.

After a long flight home from West Africa, suffering jet lag and everything else that goes along with modern economy air travel, I arrived in Sydney in the early hours of a Friday morning. It was summer, I was happy beyond words to be home and away from the diabolical shit that you have to deal with in West Africa. I'd spent the last few weeks on the rig constantly thinking about riding my bike when I got home. And here I was at last. I hit the ground running and went straight to the garage. I didn't bother showering, or perhaps waiting a day so I could get some sleep and allow my body to adjust to being home. No, I was going for a ride. With the battery reconnected and a full tank of fuel, I checked the tyres, threw on a jacket and bolted down the street. I was free, completely free, no-one was going to give me any shit or ask for a bribe or shoot at me. I'm in Sydney, where the roads are made of tar not dust, where road rage is just verbal abuse not a loaded gun, where people will go to extraordinary lengths to avoid a fight.

The hours passed, and halfway through my second tank of fuel I stopped in Bondi for lunch. The girl waiting tables outside was nice, we flirted a bit as I paid my bill, she asked about the bike and we chatted about it for a while. It was turning into a typical hot crowded Bondi day; the street was full of people, all the cafés were packed. My bike was parked directly opposite the table I was sitting at. The waitress walked me over to the kerb and I pulled on my helmet and sunglasses. 'Ride safely,' she said and winked at me.

'Ciao.' I threw my weight down on the kick-start and the Staintune exhaust blew a wonderful note across the sidewalk, turning everyone's head in my direction. The street was clear, I gave her my best casual wave and she waved back with a white napkin.

Twisting the throttle wide open and dropping the clutch, I felt my back wheel spin off the kerb, the bike slid into the open street and I roared off—a whole two metres. Then the disk brake lock I had put on when I parked bit into the front fork, instantly stopping the front wheel and sending me on a long, unimaginably embarrassing flight over the handlebars, where I executed an interesting mid-air turn and landed on my back in the middle of the street. My bike flipped over, also landing on its back next to me. The entire street stood up and clapped.

Needless to say, I never again forgot about the disk lock.

My first motorcycle experience was at my mate Andy's house. All the other neighbourhood kids hated Andy because after we had all banded together to build the best billycart in history the year before, Andy crashed it into a parked car at the end of the steepest street in town. He sustained head injuries and lacerations to most of his body, he smashed his sister's horse-riding helmet and, of course, we all kicked the shit out of him for crashing the cart, so Andy was shunned from all things.

But Andy had a postie bike. The great Australian 110cc postie bike, a fine machine, delivered the nation's mail for decades. Built by Honda, it is in fact one of the bestselling motorcycles in the country; it's bulletproof. And Andy also had a big shed with a huge old couch in it, a fridge and, best of all, a ping-pong table. That was enough; I was fifteen and I would have been friends with Pol Pot if he had a ping-pong table.

Andy and I would pour his mum's olive oil over the bike's back wheel and 'smoke it up' in his driveway. Eventually, I talked my parents into letting me have one, and after months of chores and odd jobs I had enough for a bike. Andy and I would ride around the streets, blowing up people's letterboxes with firecrackers, ride around the local golf course at night and generally make bastards of ourselves. At that age it was the most fun I was going to have with my pants on.

Then I met Debbie, and that changed everything; there was no more time for Andy, I was far too concerned with the intricacies of one-handed bra release. One weekend my parents went away and left me in charge. So the first thing I did was talk Debbie into coming over. After a lot of fooling around I finally had her naked and bent over on our new couch, her head unceremoniously buried under the armrest. I had successfully negotiated a condom over my penis after several failed attempts that included actually looking at the instruction booklet. This was going to be fun. My mother walked through the front door on the first stroke. Our eyes met, my jaw dropped and I fell forward in slow motion, my hands slipping off the armrest and sending my spotty teenage face into the scalding hot iron pipe protruding from the top of the pot-belly stove. My mother was not happy, Debbie was not happy, and I had a huge round blister in the centre of my forehead and no chance of getting any girls naked on the couch in the near future, so I was not happy. The only person who thought it was great was John; he just winked at me and pissed himself laughing.

Ten years later, after getting off a rig, I was taking a break in Perth and decided to look up Andy. He had gone into his family's construction business and had done very well. Andy had stayed in touch with all the boys who grew up in the neighbourhood and we planned a big reunion. So I found myself standing in the pub where we had all had our first legal drink ten years earlier; it had changed hands a few times over the years, and its current guise was kind of upmarket and boring. We gathered in the middle of happy hour near the garden bar at the rear of the building. There was Andy, myself, Bob, Dave and Michael. Bob had turned into a degenerate gambling junky and had gained two hundred pounds; Dave was making surfboards for a living and looked happy; Mike was married, had two kids and ran a pharmacy in a shopping mall, he'd aged twenty years.

The pub was crowded. Dave fought his way to the front and started passing drinks back to us, but it was taking forever. I didn't mind as my alcohol tolerance was shot after a month on the rig, and my nephew could have drunk me under the table. But Andy was pissed off. 'I'll be back in ten,' he said and walked off.

'What's he up to?' I asked Mike.

'Oh, he's going to one of the other bars in here—there's five, but they're probably all as crowded as this.' He nodded towards the garden bar then added, 'Or he's going to shit somewhere public.' Mike finished off his beer and shook his head.

'He what?!'

Mike leaned in, fiddled with his shirt tails and gave me a strained look as if it hurt to tell me. 'Andy has a shit fetish.'

'Oh fuck off, I've known him since we were kids,' I protested.

'Mate, you haven't spent any time around Andy since you were in your teens. He's got a problem. He's a great bloke, he's done really well for himself, he's just into poo,' Bob said, backing Mike up.

Dave walked up with five beers. 'Good to see you, Pauli. Cheers, mate.'

We all had a drink, then Mike said to Dave, who was holding a spare beer, 'Andy just walked off five minutes ago.'

'Oh fuck, he's not that pissed already is he?' Dave asked.

'What?' I looked at Dave blankly.

'Mate, last time we went out, he gets blind and takes a dump in some guy's car. Yeah, he reckons the bloke stiffed him on a business deal last year. We saw him park his car on Loftus Street, and Andy jumps on the roof, pulls his pants down and drops one through the sunroof.'

I burst out laughing, but wondered if the boys were having a lend of me.

'He's sick, and he's got issues with women,' Mike chipped in.

Andy came back and the boys went quiet. 'I can't tell which one of you four looks most like my dick,' he said.

I looked him in the eye. 'So the boys have been telling me all about your shit fetish, Andy.'

'Oh bullshit, it's not a fetish. Here, hold this.' He handed me a shot glass.

'What's this?' I asked.

'One shot of Baileys,' he answered.

'You went over to another bar to get this?' I put it down on the table.

'No, I went to get one of these.' Andy pulled a vending machine condom from his pocket, opened it up, took the glass of Baileys and poured it into the condom. All four of us just stood there looking at Andy, who looked back at us like we'd just asked him to kick a kitten into a woodchipper. 'That fuckin' idiot behind the bar is useless, so I'm going to fuck with her,' he said, and marched over to the packed garden bar. We slowly followed, but no-one said anything.

Andy, looking perfectly respectable in his designer suit and silk tie, quietly waited in the corner, then casually tossed the condom onto the back shelf behind the bar. The whole bar was black marble, and within seconds someone saw it and freaked. Soon after, the entire crowd at the bar had stopped yelling 'two vodka Red Bulls' and instead had become transfixed on the condom.

The poor girl tending the bar didn't know what to do. She was young, probably in college, and I noticed she was flustered with the demanding punters. You have to lip-read orders and mix multiple drinks fast to work in a place like this, and she wasn't coping with bottom-shelf drinks. She called the manager, he turned up with the big set of keys hanging off his belt, took one look at the condom and said 'Clean it up,' before walking off. She went over to the corner and came back with one of those little pivoting dustbins on a pole that you sweep up cigarette butts with, and a small broom. After five minutes she had the condom grasped in the middle, using the dustbin and broom like giant chopsticks, then she dropped it, spilling some of the Baileys on the counter. 'AAAAAH,' the crowd jeered.

That was when Andy launched himself across the bar and grabbed the condom. He grinned at the crowd, stretched it out, tipped it up and poured the contents into his mouth. One girl threw up on the spot. I turned and walked straight out, telling the guys where I was going in case they wanted to join me. I didn't look back, the place went nuts, bouncers sprinted past me towards the soon-to-be-battered Andy as I walked out.

An hour or so later we had all regrouped in a nightclub in a different part of town. I was standing at the bar with Dave, looking at an untouched Andy. He had apparently bought his way out of trouble, and was now sitting in a booth with four women around him, ordering drinks, the centre of attention and loving it.

'He's turned into a twat,' I said to Dave.

'Yeah, well, he can afford to, I s'pose.' Dave was as easy-going as ever.

We stayed there for a while, milling around and enjoying ourselves, then Andy was there next to me. 'C'mon, we're leaving,' he looked stressed.

'Why?' I asked.

'No time to explain.' He pulled on my jacket.

'Hey, fuck that, Andy, I like this place,' I said. 'What happened to your ladies?'

He didn't answer, he just left.

Dave and I stood there watching the girls in the booth. One of them opened her handbag and took out a packet of cigarettes, then paused and looked into her bag. Her girlfriend leaned in and peered into the bag as well. Then from somewhere inside she pulled out a neatly wrapped paper towel and out rolled a six-inch turd. It hit the glass-topped table in front of them and continued rolling all the way to the middle where it sat among their drinks. Four high-pitched almost perfect Hitchcock screams completely blanked out the music, and kicked off a stampede that emptied the dance floor and threw half the place into a panic. And all because Andy's completely depraved, sick little mind had decided it was a good idea to hide a turd in a handbag.

The final straw for me came right at the end of the night. We were all very drunk and trying to get a taxi, a five-seater taxi, at four in the morning in the middle of town; we had about as much chance of finding one as catching a lift home in the Pope mobile. Then Bob had an idea. 'Dave, you're the smallest, hide behind that wall,' he said and pointed at a tree, but we knew what he meant. 'I'll get the next taxi that comes round the corner, he will stop 'cos . . .' Bob stopped to stare at the pavement, swallow and focus. 'There's only four people and not five and he'll stop, you'll see.' He slapped his hands on his big belly and smiled the way you do after you've had so many beers you've lost count at twenty and you've completely forgotten what you're talking about.

There was a pause as we all grappled to understand Bob's idea. 'What? So everyone's in the taxi except Dave, he's hiding behind that wall,' Mike said. 'Not that I care, Bob, look I'll hide behind the wall, I'm supposed to take the kids to the beach today after church. It's Sunday morning now.' He was leaning against a bus stop and realising he was very late.

'No no no no, sorry, when the taxi pulls up, I'll open the door and Dave'll dive in and lay on the floor, then we all get in 'n the guy won't see Dave, you see,' Bob explained.

'Aw fuck off, fat boy. You lay on the floor of a filthy taxi and we'll all stand on your head,' Dave protested. He had beer hidden in all his pockets and threw one at Bob. The can hit Bob square in the forehead. Nothing, no reaction, he just rubbed his head then took off after it.

'I'll do it,' said Andy.

'Fine, great idea, I'll get the taxi.' I stepped into the street looking for the light on the roof, and right on cue a taxi pulled up. Bob was honking about the beer, not the fact that it had been thrown at him, but because it exploded in his face when he opened it. The confused Bob distracted the driver, Andy slipped in and lay quietly in the foot-well and the rest of us piled in.

Bob was in the front seat. 'Fremantle, please,' he said and grinned at the driver, beer dripping down his drunk face, and we drove off. All three of us who were sitting in the back exchanged the same look, then Andy farted. Mike kicked him in the ribs and that was it.

The driver's hand shot up to the mirror and angled it down to see Andy's head rearing up to confront Mike. He slammed on the brakes, ripped on the handbrake and went bananas. In seconds he was out of the taxi, the door was open and Andy was getting dragged out by his hair. The taxi driver was big, Italian and obviously at the end of a bad shift. Andy came up swinging and missed, and Mike and I got in the middle of it and tried to calm the cabbie down. Bob was waving his arms in the air, and Dave can speak some Italian and joined in, but while we all collectively talked the driver down, Andy had gotten into the driver's seat, closed all the doors and locked them. The driver was the only one facing the car, and he suddenly stopped gesticulating and his face went red. We all turned to look. Andy was unscrewing the black buttons at the tops of the doors, the ones you lock the doors with, and eating them. He swallowed all four, then clicked the column shift into gear and just drove off.

The five of us stood there for a moment, then we scattered in four different directions, leaving the poor cabbie standing there; he didn't know who to chase, and this was before mobile phones or any of that shit. I felt awful as I ran up a side street. Andy had issues, and I was hoping he didn't shit in that taxi.

That was more than ten years ago, and I haven't seen Andy or any of the others since. Though I did hear through the grapevine that Bob had his stomach stapled, Mike is divorced, Dave is gay, and Andy is still Andy.

12 THE LAST STAND

'Do you realise what the human body goes through when you have sex? Your pupils dilate, arteries constrict, your core temperature rises, your heart rate and blood pressure skyrocket. Your respiration becomes rapid and shallow, your brain fires bursts of electric impulses from nowhere to nowhere and secretions from every gland. Muscles tense and spasm with enough force to move three times your bodyweight.

'So why waste money by joining a gym?' the doctor said, beaming back at me. 'And the best part is, you can make a baby.'

Good advice indeed.

'You're in good shape, Paul, just stop with the damn cigarettes.' This guy is good, he's been giving oilfield hands their work medicals for years, and his demeanour is a result of that. He's seen it all, guys walking into his office with everything from missing digits and broken backs to galloping jungle crotch rot. He's about fifty, Australian and looks a bit like a hippy crossed with a King Charles spaniel.

I was there because I'd just come off a rig that served a turkey at lunch the previous day that was so undercooked a skilled veterinarian could have saved it. I had casually asked if the doctor thought it was a good idea if I joined a gym, and he was basically telling me to spend my time at home in bed with my wife—nice one.

'Sorry, honey, doctor's orders.' I could see it now. Most guys after months offshore tend to leave their loving partners feeling like a seafront village after the Vikings have been through it.

The crew and I would be back the next day for our work medicals, and I didn't want to be throwing up while I was there. The doctor gave me some pills and I went back to my hotel to spend the rest of that day vomiting.

The following morning I was sitting in his waiting room again, this time with the crew. I hate waiting rooms; after all, it says 'Waiting Room' on the door, and there's no chance of not waiting, you have to just sit and wait. It's like standing in a long queue at the post office, it's infuriating and you end up thinking rotten things about the person standing in front of you. He's got dandruff, the fuckin' loser, or why hasn't she moved up in the queue, there's a huge gap, are you blind? The waiting room is even more annoying when you're there for a work medical—you don't feel sick so you really don't want to be there. And these days, it's not just touch your toes and read the board with one hand over your eye; it's full body scans, X-rays, blood, pee and poo in cups, climb this, run on that. It takes days.

I looked at the magazines on the coffee table in front of me. No matter how hard you resist, you will end up reading a three-month-old copy of *Woman's Day*, but that only lasts so long. I looked at the boys. Ambu's got gout, so I was hoping I would go in before him 'cos he'll take ages. Don pulled out the pages from copies of *National Geographic* and sniffed them 'because they smell like childhood', apparently, then he folded them into Japanese origami animals that were actually very good. Jake drew penises on everyone in *Newsweek* with a texta pen. Erwin has infinite patience, he just goes to his happy place or something, but then a Harley went past. A Harley Davidson exhaust note is like a dog whistle to Erwin: his ears twitch, his head cocks to one side, and he's up and over at the blinds to look.

My new guy was there cracking his knuckles. I hate that. John's a young American, hardworking, full of beans, keen to learn, and still copping endless shit for rubbing one out during a training course while wearing a heart monitor. He went in first, but came back out after only ten minutes or so. He sat down quietly and started thumbing through a magazine. We all wondered why he came out so fast. 'What's up, mate?' I asked.

But before he could answer, the doctor stuck his head round the door and said, 'Hey you, young guy, stop jacking off into your footy sox. You've got tinea on your bell end.' There was a long pause, and with that he called in Ambu. As soon as the door clicked shut we started laughing.

'Still thinking about that fuckin' nurse, John?' said Don looking up from his origami folding.

'Yeah well, at least I don't get shit stuck up my ass,' yelled John before he stomped off to the coffee machine.

Don furrowed his brow. 'That's an inherent contradiction,' he said and went back to his folding.

'You need to think about a plausible reason for your toes, Don.' Erwin looked serious.

'What, you mean just being a fuckin' sociopath isn't good enough?' John was getting past it.

'Screw the nut, mate,' I said. I could see this turning into a brawl. Don closed the magazine, his face turned to stone. He got up and walked over to John, who puffed out his chest and changed his stance. His voice also goes up half a dozen octaves when he's scared, whereas Don's goes down. This makes Don sound like he should be doing voice-overs on beer commercials. Don's jaw was set and he was wearing a smile, but behind it was John's first real beating and the young guy knew it. You see, John's a nice bloke, and that's where his problems start. Nice blokes with nice wives and happy children don't go toe to toe in a waiting room, but Don does.

'Fuck off,' said John in a high-pitched squeak, sounding about as frightening as David Beckham. John was backed into the corner, then Don held out his hand and gave him a beautiful origami bird.

'I'll give it some thought,' said Don and burst out laughing.

Almost an hour later Ambu finally came out, armed with lots of paper so he could go down the hall and give blood, and pee in one cup and poo in another. In the past, after receiving instructions to bring back a 'stool' sample, Ambu has gone off and returned with furniture, ice-cream, even cigarettes. The cups they give you for urine and faeces are the same size and dimensions; however, the main difference between them is that the one marked for number twos has a tiny shovel attached to the lid. So even if you had not yet mastered the English language, you should understand the purpose for putting the little shovel in the lid, thereby distinguishing the vessel's intended contents. This time Ambu got it right and he returned some time later, smiling, casually walking past us holding his cup that had an entire foot-long turd jutting out the top.

Two days went by, spent mostly in the Singapore workshop pretending to work, then we got the okay to go on our next job, in sunny Bangladesh.

If my career was a house, with Japan being the lounge room, then Bangladesh is the remains which stand in that muddy patch of the backyard.

The flight was average, only remarkable because Don didn't stab anyone, or make obscene hand gestures at old people, or ask complete strangers to pull his finger, or drink soy sauce, or push foreign objects up his nose and wander into first class, or stare at small children until they got paranoid, or push John's face into his lunch, or strike up a conversation with a pretty girl in one of five languages only to start faking a twitch, or sniff hair, or smoke in the toilet—I could go on for days. We landed in Chittagong, and we gathered around the luggage carousel to wait for our offshore bags to trundle by. An hour later they appeared, and we filtered through customs and into the arrival hall.

Usually we have an agent or representative there to meet us, someone who has all the local info. They would help organise transport to and from a hotel, and to the heliport, for example, or bail Don out of the local lock-up in time for him to make it to the job, or pay off the local heavies after he put someone through a window, that kind of thing. But here we had nothing organised, so we ended up pairing off and climbing into three equally diabolical-looking, three-wheeler tuktuk things. My first car, a Holden Torana, was much like a two-door V8-powered strip club; it could kill half the Amazon every time you floored it. My current car is also a Holden, only a new one; it trundles along on a shot glass of fuel and Chanel No.5 comes out the tailpipe. What we really needed right now was a 'Paris to Dakar' Land Rover, especially when getting to the hotel turned out to be one giant game of chicken.

In Bangladesh, the crap coming from the exhaust of our transport was black but actually cleaner than the air that went in. The air was so filthy that when the six of us walked into the hotel lobby, we looked like we'd just arrived for the Al Jolson convention.

Our chopper out to the rig was going to be early the next morning so we all shuffled off to our rooms to relax and get some sleep. The hotel looked like a derelict building would if you wallpapered it and put gyprock over all the holes. I kicked the door shut and walked across the room to dump my thirty-kilo offshore bag on the desk. On the floor there was a nasty-looking purple oval rug, and as soon as my right foot hit the middle, it disappeared into the floor. My bag combined with my bodyweight was too much for the old floorboards, so there I was, looking at my left leg jutting straight out from under me. I was surprised that I could hear Don swearing. I scrambled to get up, luckily the rug had protected my right leg from the splintered wood. I pulled the rug back up, got down on all fours and peered through the hole into the room below me. Don was sitting on a chair, smoking a cigar and looking up at me. We laughed for a full five minutes.

At the time, Bangladesh was experiencing some problems of its own. In Dakar the people were rioting and this had spread to the outlying areas, so to be on the safe side we all stayed indoors that night. Not that an upset local here is a big problem; if we were in Korea, I'd be worried. We were in Seoul once when the locals decided to have a riot, and no-one goes off like the Koreans. They all go at it like their hair is on fire, especially like the matching headbands. As we were about to leave, Don went missing. He'd gone out drinking the night before the riot started and never came back to the hotel. So eventually we packed up his gear—I had his passport and offshore pass—paid his bill and left for the harbour to jump on a supply vessel bound for the rig. At the last minute Don arrived at the jetty in the back of a packed ute, with his new friends chanting and punching the air. Don didn't have any of his original clothing on, he was wearing a headband and sporting a split lip, and didn't even know what the riot was about.

The Bangladeshi rig was a joke. It sat in the middle of a swamp, an old Russian jack-up that was more rust than anything else.

The company man was a perfect caricature of a company man. The brim of his massive plastic ten-gallon cowboy safety hard-hat came round the corner, followed several minutes later by a beer gut and a classic old-school oilfield attitude. They're thinning out now, these older guys; one by one they're retiring. They came up in the days when the rigs were hard as fuck, and they were screamed at, abused and tormented by tool pushers and drillers who would appear quite mad on a drill floor now. The ones who survived were the hardest, and it's these characters who you see now and again running a drilling operation. You can tell if they're old-school simply by the way they walk, and the way they will run off (fire) someone for no reason, but I like them because of what they say. And at least you know exactly where you stand.

'How's it going?' I nodded towards the drill floor, smiled and stuck out my hand.

The company man spat a wad of chewing tobacco on the floor, crushed my hand until my toes hurt and grinned. 'There's more oil in ma fuckin' hair. Check your tools.' He turned and sauntered off, packing a new wad of chew into his black bottom lip.

Two weeks later I'd lost nine kilos, apparently the average for anyone who ate in the galley. The rig had tried to kill us from the outside too, the main staircase simply falling off one afternoon, just after we had all used it. Then the next day a five-inch gooseneck fitting protruding from the floor exploded across the main deck with 2800 psi behind it. That's a bit like putting a landmine in the local park.

The whole operation was a mess, and after all the drilling was done, we didn't find a thing.

Things come full circle eventually; time catches up with all of us in one way or another. I'm happy, in all of the four dimensions. For me the rigs are an endless source of adventure and torture at the same time.

I'm sitting in a small crew room next to a land rig in the Japanese mountains as I write this. I've been up for more than thirty hours, the coffee is shit and it's starting to wear off. The blizzard outside the door has turned the rig white, and I can just make out the drill floor through the horizontal snow. Ambu and Don are asleep on the floor near the heater; I'll wake them up soon so we can help the guys on tower to rig down. We're all getting older—half of the crew are hitting their mid-fifties—and pretty soon it will be like running pipe with the cast from *Cocoon*. We'll shuffle in walking frames towards the rig and hope no-one puts their back out.

You get used to the oil patch, and you become used to white noise, to pain, to wearing huge industrial orange earplugs to bed every night because the big guy in the bunk above you snores like my mate Steve's French Mastiff being hot-waxed, and come to think of it you get used to the guy who looks and acts like Steve's dog. Now I'm talking about a gigantic drooling beast that lays all over the furniture, only gets up to eat and wets itself when you come home. Imagine a grown man that can do an 'excitement wee' after hearing the words 'chopper home'.

By tomorrow Don will be trying to drag Erwin and me out of a Tokyo motorcycle shop and into a bar, Ambu will be eating something that looks like it was rolled onto his plate by a dung beetle, and Jake will be getting new ink via a bamboo needle and the steady hand of a master tattoo artist apparently favoured by the Japanese mafia. The rest of us will fall back happy in each other's company.

Erwin just picked up the last stand of pipe to run in the hole. It's 2 a.m., Tuesday I think. The last stand, the last job for this year. I wonder what Clare is doing. She'll be happy to know I'll make it home for Christmas. I pick up the payphone on the wall in front of me and dial home, the sound of Clare's voice transporting me to a better place. For anyone who does what we do for a living, you don't need me to tell you how hard it is to maintain a normal relationship. Drilling rigs have been looming over my subconscious like a fat oilfield zeppelin ever since we decided to start a family.

'There's a letter here for you,' Clare says. I ask her to open it. 'It's good news.' She is smiling, I can hear it in her voice. 'You know that oilfield desk job you always wanted to have a go at? Well, I'm looking at it.' I'm ecstatic, I've been waiting for that letter for more than a year. My phonecard is about to run out. 'One more thing, honey,' she says, 'I'm pregnant.' The line beeps and cuts off.

Erwin comes through the door, stamping the snow off his feet and waking up the sleeping beauties. The wind snatches the door and slams it shut behind him, leaving the cabin looking like a pillow just exploded. No-one notices the blank look on my face. Erwin pulls off his hard-hat, and that smile spreads across his face through the melting snow around his upturned collar. He cracks his neck and rubs the back of his right knee—it gets sore in the cold after one too many bike crashes and thirty years on the rigs. 'Just another glorious day in the oilfield,' he says and grins.

13 THE WHOLE OIL THING

I wanted to round everything out, I wanted to have a conclusion, an answer. I set out to make something as smooth as the prime minister's bedsheets, but somehow I ended up with an oily rag.

Time is money in oil. Every minute, every hour, every single day, year after year, the BPD (barrels per day) must keep pumping life into the system, a system that since the end of World War II has grown into a monster with an appetite that redefines insatiable. Feeding the monster via our global umbilical network has given us ease of progression into a new disposable push-button life, but mother's milk is going to give us all umbilical whiplash that could take it all away forever.

Perhaps I have a jilted, somewhat negative view of human nature. After all, we're products of our environment. I'm free, I live in a free market economy, I have the right to choose everything from soap to government, I can make or lose money according to my individual goals or fuck-ups, and if I don't like any of that I'm free to piss off and live somewhere else.

The huge amounts of money we spend fighting wars for oil and building ever-smarter smart bombs could perhaps be spent on deepwater exploration. Instead we feed our lust for selective destruction; now there are bombs which discreetly enter buildings through the letterbox and vaporise anyone whose eyebrows are too close together. It's a lot like the space race in the 1960s, when the sheer idea of getting to the moon was unbelievable, back when bombs just went bang and history judged the military not by what they aimed at but by what they hit. Why is this Earth-bound frontier so formidable, or own inner space overlooked?

This is an ocean planet. It's so big and completely mystifying. Take the Pacific Ocean: it covers half the globe, and you can jump on a plane and fly non-stop for twelve hours and not see any land. How much oil lies out there? All of the offshore drilling so far has occurred around the edges if you like. The future is a race to meet demand by pushing the boundaries of deepwater exploration. And the open sea is a formidable opponent. Off the coast of West Africa at the moment we are drilling into the seabed without damaging the life that exists there, other than the hole itself in six thousand feet of water, and down to twenty thousand feet of real estate, but we are far from reaching the uncharted depths. Sixty per cent of the planet is covered in water more than a mile deep, and it's largely unknown; more people have been into space than have explored the deep sea.

To drill for new oil out there, within the most powerful force in nature, will take engineering like never before. There could be trillions of barrels out there, enough for us to stop killing one another long enough to find an alternative to fossil fuels that works. Out in the open sea, a rig is vulnerable; forget the sheer depth, the surface alone can slap a rig around with a savagery that's difficult to describe in print. I've been offshore in bad weather and felt real fear pulling at my 'what if' strings; anyone who has looked over the deck into a dark, heaving, white-capped, freezing liquid hell will know what I'm talking about.

Mother Nature is to be feared and respected like no other, but perhaps we have finally reached a point where we can beat her down. We are neither savage nor wise, it's our half-measures that are the worst of it for Mother Nature. Overharvesting, deforestation, habitat destruction, war and pollution will cause, possibly within a hundred years, the biggest mass extinction event since the end of the dinosaurs sixty-five million years ago. In the beginning Mother Nature reached our soil and made it hers. After only a million years or so of doing nothing, we have come leaps and bounds, especially in the last hundred years, a millisecond for her. Old greed and corruption dies hard, makes men blind, drives them mad enough to devour her heart and turn her into a memory walled up in a zoo. There is more life on our planet right now than ever before, more than one and a half million different life forms exist. These are remarkable times; this new century will mark either the greatest era of human discovery or the end of 50 per cent of our planet's biodiversity.

But that's just my opinion. Any questions you may have, please direct them to: god@theblindingwhitelight.com.

ACKNOWLEDGEMENTS

A great many individuals have my thanks this second time around: Clare, my wife and my universe; Erwin Herczeg, always in my corner, and his amazing family have my eternal friendship; the inspirational Sally and Simon Dominguez, and their single malt; Claire Atkins, a remarkable woman; Greg Waters, who underestimates the importance that his contributions make; Klaas van der Plas; Dave Sadler, a man who can really ride a motorcycle; Ross Luck; Steve Tunley; Vince and Sheman Moritti; Miranda Culley; Johnathan and Angela Catana; the De La Vega family; Geof Pacecca; Allan and Terri Cole; Steve, Pyneia and Anastasia Papal—legends all. My family Al, Liz, France, Elinor, Johannes, Callum, Rory, Alex, Mathew, James, Daniel, Carrie, Cathy, Phillip, Fingal and Tamsi (happy trails).

The lovely and completely brilliant team at Allen & Unwin: Jo Paul, your critiques turn what would otherwise be one long fart joke into a book; Lou Johnson; Catherine Milne; Alexandra Nahlous; Julia Lee—you all perform the literary equivalent of teaching a monkey how to perform brain surgery every time you take a manuscript off my hands, and you make it look easy. Thank you for going in to bat for me so many times.

All the Singapore crew, especially Drew, Les, Hiram, Myles, Adam, Ramat, JJ, Tahir, Fauzi, Joey, Bidin (who nearly cut his head off last year—glad you're still with us, mate) and Razac, rest in peace brother.

Ambu (take that belt off), John, Don, Jake (back in the big house), Avas, Barry Reilly, Dave 'The Seal Basher' Nordli, Vodka Bob, Fat Tony, Robin, Eddie, Ronny, Smithy, Colin Henderson, Ann Smith, Sick Boy, Well Head Willy, Donald Millar, Damian Forte, Pilso, Sam Leon, Wongy, John Logan, Chris Glennon, Cameron Westholt, Tony Lacey, Capt Tom Naude, Sqd Ldr Chris Boucousis, the manager of the 'Romper-Room'.

And Officer Young, sorry about the mess, and thanks for being gentle with me.

Special thanks to that Afghan guy near Gardez, by the side of the road somewhere between Camp 87 and Kabul on 21 April 2006, who decided not to shoot me—much appreciated.

All of you, lying in your bunks on a rig, we are multiplied and defused throughout the world, be safe, godspeed.

IS THAT THING DIESEL?

ONE MAN, ONE BIKE AND THE FIRST LAP AROUND AUSTRALIA ON USED COOKING OIL

CONTENTS

PROLOGUE 359
1. DERRICK THE MAN 361
2. COVER YOUR ARSE 369
3. WHAT COULD POSSIBLY GO WRONG? 374
4. PANIC FEST 379
5. BIO WHAT? 396
6. THE BIKE THE UNIVERSE LANDED 405
7. BETTY 413
8. GETTING TO KNOW YOU 421
9. THERE IS NO PLAN B 430
10. PPPPPP 438
11. TO ADELAIDE AND BEYOND 446
12. STAGE ONE: GREEN FUEL, WHITE KNUCKLES 459
13. STAGE TWO: SPIDERS 470
14. WALLET 480
15. STAGE THREE: LIFE CYCLE 488
16. STAGE FOUR: FOLLOW THE BLOOD-SPLATTERED BRICK ROAD 493
17. THE LONG REACH 510
18. IT ONLY HURTS WHEN I LAUGH 525
19. STAGE FIVE: UNEASY RIDER 542
20. STAGE SIX: NUMB 553
21. STAGE SEVEN: HARDER THAN YOU THINK 557

EPILOGUE 566
ACKNOWLEDGEMENTS 568

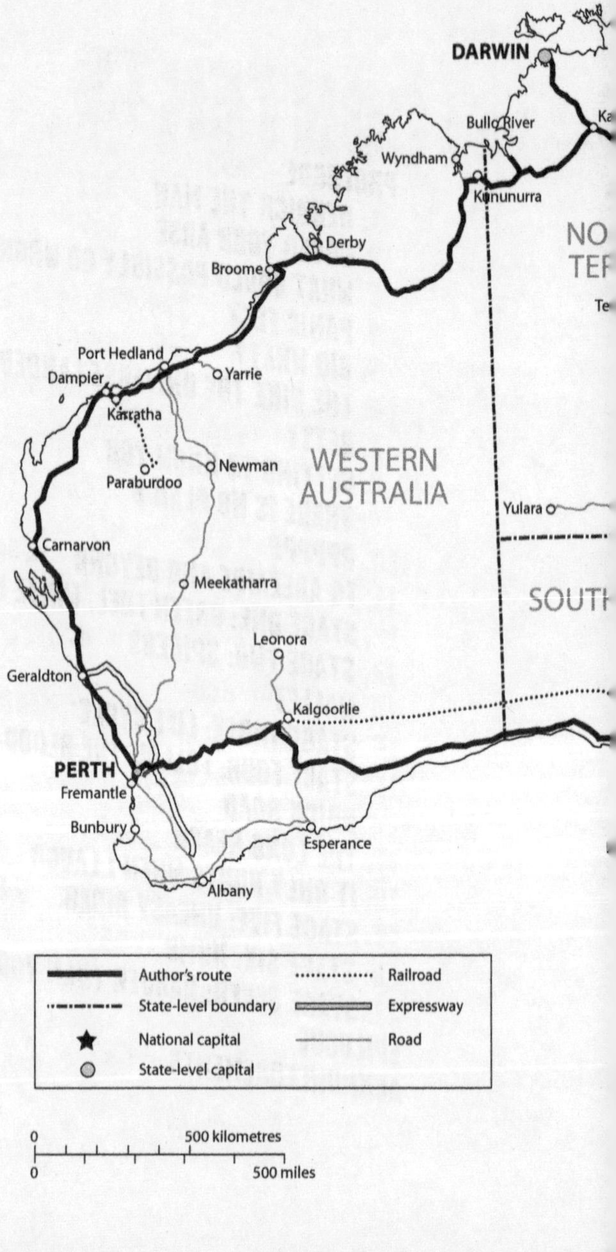

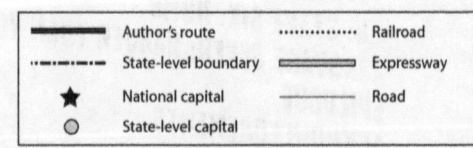

PROLOGUE

My name is mud, or at least it should be. Today I'm taking my cat to the vet, to have him put down. Not, I hear you thinking, the cheeriest way to start a book. But my cat Oswald has reached the end of his days, because his bladder recently reached the end of its days as a functioning organ. There's more cat pee than carpet in the house—it's like the blood in the *Alien* movies, burning little acidic puddles everywhere.

Dead cat walking.

My only regret, I never took him to Vegas.

You will in the course of reading this book—that is, if I can keep you interested beyond this prologue—hear tales of Oswald my cat, and of my life over the last few years. But before that happens I need to explain how I got to be here in your hands, on this bus, in this toilet, or wherever you like to do your reading.

I'm an oil man, I come from oil parents, and I spent twenty years working on drilling rigs, in sixteen different countries on three different continents, drilling for oil. Dirty, black, stinking, polluting, penguin-clogging, globe-turning, war-inducing, non-renewable, blood-of-Mother-Earth oil. I love it, and it's been very good to me. But now, at the age of 40, I take stock and look back.

From eighteen to 38 I had a ball. So much so I'm amazed I'm not dead. I worked with the same crew of men for fifteen years; they were my brothers. Some were amazing characters who showed me the way, some were sociopaths who should have been institutionalised, and some are now dead. After working and living with them, often in tough locations like jungles or deserts or offshore in the middle of a cyclone, I realise how lucky I am. In 1989 eight guys from my crew died, some in quite horrific circumstances, but I was lucky enough to walk away. Guys I know have had body parts lopped off, or had various things much bigger and heavier than them roll, pinch, crush or land on them while I was standing right there next to them. I have been shot at, held hostage, locked up in a Third World country and locked in the toilet by my own monkey. Many, many times I've found myself in situations that defy reality, but every time I managed to walk away. After twenty years I got spat out by the oilfield rotational life in one piece, my sanity, liver and fingers intact. Why, I have no fuckin idea.

My first book about living the life of an oilfield contractor, *Don't Tell Mum I Work on the Rigs, She Thinks I'm a Piano Player in a Whorehouse*, was published in 2005, my second book *This Is Not a Drill* in 2007, and quite by accident, my publisher tells me I'm an international bestseller. Like everything else in my life, I was in the right place at the right time. This phenomenon continues, as you'll discover if you choose to read on.

Why, I have no fuckin idea.

1 DERRICK THE MAN

'What's in Perth?' Dave Sadler stood in my garage in Sydney leaning against my Kawasaki, scratching his crotch and looking confused.

'Mate, we're moving to WA in two weeks. I've taken a desk job.'

'Oh,' he said. He knew about my promise to my wife, a promise I'd made years ago, that if we ever had kids, I'd stop working offshore on drilling rigs and stay in one place, stay at home and be a father. He knew Clare was six months pregnant, he knew I was worried about finding a stay-at-home job in a city like Sydney, and he knew I would probably move interstate, but he'd wanted to avoid the conversation as much as I did.

'Shit, mate.' He finished his beer. 'I'm going to miss ya.'

Dave had just given me a hand with a new set of exhaust pipes. We'd changed out the baffles, altering the note on a Harley-Davidson XR from a modest rumble to something like King Kong gargling battery acid. Dave grinned as he killed the engine.

I knew I was about to begin a new stage in my life, but I didn't want this one to end. I'd miss our regular motorcycle-maintenance and beer-drinking sessions and blats into the hills. Dave was a motorcycle journalist. We'd met years earlier. For a long time I'd thought motorcyclists in Sydney were a really friendly bunch; every time I was off the rig and belting around the eastern suburbs on my bike I'd get a wave during rush hour on the big lane split into Bondi. Turned out it was Dave every time, just on a different bike each month. When we finally stopped one day in the same place he explained he'd been waving to me for ages. 'Mate, I always had on the same helmet.' I hadn't noticed.

Though I didn't want it to, my time in Sydney was ending. Staying in our tiny flat and rotating out to a different rig every month just didn't fit into our plan now that Clare was pregnant.

We needed a house, with a garden. I needed a normal job, home every night, no more adventures; I knew I could no longer just roll up after a job and jump on my bike and disappear for a few days. It was time to get serious about our future. I had to grow up.

Shortly after that conversation with Dave, Clare and I packed our life into cardboard boxes, I freighted my bikes to a mate's place and had the obligatory fight with the real estate agent over repainting our flat, and a broken stove (it never worked properly anyway, all I ever did was light cigarettes off it). We had already found a great house to rent in Perth through the internet—compared to our tiny flat it was like Graceland. I had a desk job lined up with a drilling tool rental company in Perth. The move went like clockwork.

In Perth, Clare was blissfully happy. She'd wanted to be a wife and a mother since she was old enough to drape a pillow case over her head and pretend she was a bride. Now she was married and pregnant, and had me permanently at home. And when Clare is happy, she bakes. I came home every day from my new job to wonderful dinners and—I kid you not—cherry pie, unquestionably the sluttiest of the pie family. I couldn't believe my luck. After years of offshore galley dining at 'Chucks' in the Third World and then crawling off to a bunk in a four-man room smaller than my broom cupboard and smellier than the toilets in a cheap cigar factory, I was instead wiping whipped cream off my face and curling up each night in a bed like a sprung tennis court, with my gorgeous, pregnant wife; I was looking like one rabid, but very happy—and fat—dog.

Between all the cooking and the eating, Clare was nesting, so we went shopping, collecting all kinds of shiny new baby stuff. Let me tell you about baby stuff: there are strollers, big, fully integrated, multi-function, dual-directional, go-faster-James-Bond ones with better brakes and suspension than my car. Cots that are stronger, more comfortable and bigger than the bunks offshore. In fact, there are whole superstores that supply every baby thing imaginable. We made endless consecutive trips, collecting carloads of stuff that all needed assembling. We got a pram, a cot, and a baby monitor to wiretap our child's room. We even made the obligatory trip to the brand-new, brilliantly designed mega-Ikea store, joining up with hundreds of other shoppers at the bottom of the escalator like migrating salmon. Everyone had their Ikea face on, that 1000-yard stare into the wonders of modern Swedish pre-fabricated, flat-pack laminated furniture. Clare grabbed the brilliantly designed Ikea shopping trolley, the only item they produce that I actually like, and we entered the one-way river of Ikea zombies. Two hours later, the river emerged into a great feeding hangar—with your eyes shut it sounded like you were stepping into a lagoon full of flamingoes at dinner time. We waited in the brilliantly designed holding zone until a JCB deposited five metric tonnes of flat-packed brown cardboard boxes and an Allen key. All this for one very small baby.

With all the new things for the baby and the house we had to make room. Most of our existing furniture was pretty old, predominantly from the 1950s, but it was well made, so it seemed a shame to toss it. Having moved to Perth from Sydney I was used to just dumping unwanted items on the street. Bondi, where we lived, was for all intents and purposes a black hole where entire skiploads full of old junk evaporated overnight. Furniture moves so fast out there that all the homeless cats in Bondi have nothing left to piss on. (Seriously, you could dump a body on the sidewalk in Bondi and some backpacker would fuck off with it and turn it into a coffee table before you could say, 'Whatever happened to Grandpa?' I once left the most diabolical second-hand mattress on the street, just left it propped up against a lamppost. It looked like someone had shot a snuff movie on it. The next day—gone.)

But in Perth, in the refined environs of Nedlands, the items I left out—which I'll have you know were by no means crap—just sat there for weeks. Which left our house marked as the one moved into by trailer trash. Joggers would scowl at me while I watered the front garden; drivers would slow down and point. I found it quite annoying, although eventually I amused myself by standing in our messy front yard in just a pair of tracky pants and a stained wife beater, scratching my back with a toilet brush and belching my name. In the end, though, I had to pay someone to haul the stuff off just to stop us from being run out of the neighbourhood.

There's a strange kind of dynamic lethargy and indifference in Perth. People are almost snobby but not enough to piss you off. New luxury shops are springing up all over the place as the current mining and oil boom has injected billions of dollars into the local economy, lining the pockets of the real estate lucky and the people who work in the right industries. CUBs are popping up like mushrooms—albeit mushrooms with oversized status handbags and Armani sunglasses. CUBs: this was a new term for me—cashed up bogans. Blue-collar guys earning more than Somalia's national debt, and looking to buy new toys.

The family across the road had clearly benefited from the boom years. The dad was in real estate and had recently had all his tats removed. Their house was impressive, two storeys of limestone and marble with a manicured front lawn big enough to host the next Olympics on. Their daughter was around nine, and had more toys scattered over the front yard than I had ever seen when I was her age.

One morning I went outside and a bouncy castle bigger than the flat I grew up in was just sitting on their lawn. I couldn't help comparing it to the toys I'd had at that age.

When I was a lad I had to make do with improvised bits of shit I found on the street or hand-me-downs from my older sister. She hated having to share her toys with me. But hell, whoever said necessity was the mother of invention was onto something. Barbie, with her hair cut off and a texta-applied beard, in clothes made by my mum, made one hell of an action hero. The other kids had the real deal of course, GI Joe, Action Man, Stretch Armstrong, Big Jim, and Steve Austin with his mechanical arm and bionic eyeball. Austin was the best. You could peek out the back of his head through his bionic eye, and that was about as cool as it gets when it's 1979 and you're ten. I did my best to make my sister's former Barbie look manly: I took a bastard file to her boobs, and beefed up her arms with gaffa tape. I ran the edge of a hot knife down her cheek, distorting her right eye and leaving her looking like she'd been through the windscreen of a truck. I renamed her 'Derrick the Man', and convinced the other kids he was special and could breathe fire.

Still, I couldn't compete; one boy had the Evil Knievel action figure—it came with the Harley-Davidson XR750 and a ramp. We would have wars in the backyard, and every time, without fail, Evil would shoot through the air on his bike and save the fuckin day. Steve Austin, Action Man, Big Jim and GI Joe would cheer, while Derrick the Man just stood there looking like a tranny.

Until I put a hot nail through his pursed lips and filled his head up with lighter fluid. The resulting inferno nearly put the lot of us in hospital.

My reverie was broken by a bloodcurdling scream. The little kid from over the road was standing in the street screaming at her parents; listening in, turned out the bouncy castle wasn't the one she wanted. The dad was trying to calm her down, then he spotted me sitting there watching and waved the way you do at a neighbour you don't really know. He smiled, blindingly white teeth, bleached to perfection. My mind tripped and I found myself thinking about kids in West Africa expiring in the dust with perfect complexions and the whitest teeth you have ever seen . . .

I should have gone inside and forgotten about it, but I couldn't. There was a pitch-dark rage building inside me. I wanted to watch that bouncy castle burn. Just as I was thinking I should get the fuck out of there before I said or did something Clare would later bollock me for, the dad wandered over and tried to strike up a conversation.

I was sitting on the weekend paper; our front step was wet from the rain earlier. He made me squint when he smiled. He was clearly just so happy with his stuff: the big house, nice car, his wife, his toys, his kid.

'Are you reading that?' he said, still smiling, pointing at my newspaper.

'Yes,' I replied flatly. 'I have an eye in my anus.'

His smile faded and he asked me what my problem was. My anger deflated. He was right, I was being a jerk. I got up and handed him my paper.

'What happened to your ink?' I gestured towards his forearms.

'Not so good for business, you know?' He shrugged and smiled again, a bit uncertainly.

I smiled back. He once had a young man's tattoos. What now? What images could cover the scars left behind that would accurately capture impending middle age? Precisely how does one illustrate an irritable bowel and mortgage repayments? But I didn't say any of this. Just gave a non-committal wave and wandered inside. I knew I'd been a rude prick. I was missing the rigs, missing the old days, missing those giddy flat-out rides into the hills with Dave. For twenty years I'd been running all over the planet, rig-hopping from one job to the next, completely free, no ties to anyone or anything. Now my crew had moved on and I was in a suburban utopia more imposing and alien than any jungle I'd worked in. I told myself this was the new life that I so desperately wanted, but honestly? It was on the verge of blossoming into a real three-fingered prostate exam.

2 COVER YOUR ARSE

Having over the course of the last year got married, stopped working offshore, knocked up my wife and moved to the 'burbs of Perth, I was now officially middle-aged and boring. Let me tell you how I learned this.

Clare's brother Mathew came to Perth the first week we were there, in his role as manager of a band that was playing a gig in a city club on Saturday night. It was all a bit last minute and rushed but my wife is very tight with her family and it was her only opportunity to see her brother. So, even though she was eight months pregnant, we went along.

We got to the venue, parked out the back, and Matt was there, grinning. He told us the band was a breeze to look after. As well as managing a band, Matt also plays with his own group, The Drugs. The Drugs play hard and party harder. To give you some idea of just how hard, Matt's stage name is Ian Badly. After one of their tours, I once saw Matt with a laminated card around his neck that read: 'My name is Ian Badly. If I am drunk and/or wasted, not making any sense or passed out, I am staying at the Holiday Inn. Please contact our manager on . . .' By contrast, the biggest problem Matt had getting these other guys on stage was dragging them away from their hair-dryers and make-up.

Matt is the funniest and most disturbing of all my relatives and in-laws; his sense of humour is sharper than a new razor and equally dangerous. He often has pink streaks in his hair and most of my oilfield mates would assume on first appearance that Matty is gayer than two cocks touching. Matt's short stocky frame and boyish good looks often lead people into making benign assumptions about him, when in fact beneath his good looks and quirky charm is a head space that should have danger signs around it.

The three of us chatted for an hour or so, then the band went on and about a thousand chicks rushed the stage. I wandered to the bar to get a beer; pausing to look into the back of the venue, I saw a group of eight girls staring at me. I smiled, they smiled, and the cock-eyed optimist in my pants shouted up to my brain, 'Yup, you've still got it.' Then one of the girls broke free. She was around twenty, or probably not, and she was wearing a very short skirt and a push-up bra. My balls twitched; it was like a koi pond down there—I was doing my best not to clap.

'So are you with the band?' she asked, thumbing a Bic lighter.

'What makes you think I'm with the band?' There was no way she saw me talking to Matt, I told myself; I have so still got it.

She snorted smoke out. 'Well, you're either someone's dad or you're with the band.'

I was crushed. That's right, I'm thirty-nine. Where's my pregnant wife? What the fuck am I doing here?

IS THAT THING DIESEL?

On Monday morning I was sitting at my desk considering this same question. What the fuck was I doing there? I was the Rental Tool Manager; I'd been in the job for a week and already I was making quite an impression. The previous Wednesday I sent a quote to a drilling company for a bit of kit called a split bowl. Not a difficult task, and I certainly knew what a split bowl was. Problem was, my business writing skills were not quite on par with my equipment knowledge: I sent them a quote for a split *bowel*. And then I signed off as the Rectal Manager. Oh yeah, I'm the man. The drilling manager responded a few days later; a guy I'd worked with years earlier, he signed off by saying he always knew I was an arsehole.

Simple things that others took for granted mystified me. For example, on my first day the bloke at the next desk emailed me a request. I read it, looked to my left and said, 'Sure, no probs.'

He gave me a sympathetic smile and responded via email, explaining as a footnote that I needed to cover my arse by putting absolutely everything in an email from now on. This struck me as both good advice and a horrible thought. It didn't matter if the person you were talking to nodded and said, 'Yes, I understand, I'll do that today.' No, I had to follow up with an email, get T-shirts printed, and put post-it notes on the wall in front of me to remind myself not to let him forget so that I would have some proof when he *did* forget and so we could assign blame correctly.

What the fuck did we do before email? How did we assign blame? Or was the 'give a fuck' factor just higher then?

How many emails would I have to write, just to cover my arse?

I was not the boss anymore, this was not a drill floor, and my fragile male ego made me want to tell everyone politely just to fuck off. Instead I had to suppress my urge to kick people as they sleepwalked through their day doing just enough not to get fired. There was no work ethic like I was used to. On the rigs, the crew would back each other up in every way. But onshore, in a regular job, I was clearly on my own.

The drilling guys would quickly weed out the weak link in the work chain, or just refuse to go offshore with someone lazy or indifferent—they're too dangerous. Years ago, I was sent to work at a supply base for a month while the rest of my crew went offshore. I was being punished for destroying a hire car—but that's another story. I was on half pay, working seven days a week loading out drill pipe and prepping it for inspection. Buffing tool joints with an angle grinder in the sun for twelve hours a day and being made to work with guys I looked down on was a good head check for me.

That was the first time I experienced the kind of slack, hide-from-the-boss bullshit that made me rage—mostly in the slovenly form of Victor the forklift driver. One morning, I wandered into the workshop, and there was Victor floating around the entrance like a vegetarian turd. He was wearing an orange T-shirt that read 'Drink More Piss'. I vented at him simply because he was there.

'What the fuck are you doing, Vic?'

He looked at me. 'I'm waiting for the Jiffy slut,' he responded matter-of-factly.

'The fuckin what?'

Right on cue the Blue Jiffy Food Company van pulled into the car park.

'That lady is very nice, Vic; don't call her a slut, OK mate?' I said, trying to keep things civil.

But Victor was already mentally inhaling sausage rolls, visibly salivating as he meandered in a Jiffy trance towards the back of the van. He was a cross between Pavlov's dog and Homer Simpson, only more food obsessed. Every day before lunch he devoured two jumbo sausage rolls with extra salt and sauce, then choked down two smokes. Vic's colon must have been the size of the Hindenburg; his gut was so big that his belly still rubbed against the steering wheel even with the seat on the forklift racked back as far as it would go.

Like clockwork, at 10 a.m. the next day he was lurking in the shadows of the workshop entrance like a fat ninja. This time I snuck up on him.

'Who you waiting on, Vic?'

He turned, smiled and grunted, 'The pie mole.'

3 WHAT COULD POSSIBLY GO WRONG?

Nine months into her pregnancy, Clare started to get painful back spasms; she looked like she had been shot in the back with a nuclear submarine. At first I felt helpless, but after talking to her and asking lots of questions I rigged up a rope harness in the garage. Clare would dangle there in among the motorcycles, gently swinging, relief spreading across her face.

The day Clare finally said it was time to go to the hospital— 13 December 2007, the day Lola arrived—changed everything for me forever. It was like joining the Mob; I was in for life, no backing out. The fuzzy ultrasound image that I'd stared at in disbelief was about to breathe new life into my corner.

The birth was a lot like being in a Roman Polanski film: confidence seguing into terror, followed by an epidural, followed by an emergency caesarean, followed by a double Scotch. I knew my wife was mentally and physically strong, but Jesus. She comes from a long line of hard-core Catholic working-class ladies; her mother produced five children, in each case working full time until her waters broke, then she mopped the floor, knocked off and walked to the hospital.

I'll spare you the details of the labour, but suffice to say after being an observer I'm sure there must be a special thing that helps women forget the months of pregnancy and the delivery once it's over. I now know for certain that men would never have the balls to nut out a sprog; we would rather have sex with a bear trap. Here's to all the mothers: we men salute you.

Lola was perfect, a mini me: bald, blue eyes, with a breast fixation. Clare says the only reason she looks exactly like me is so I won't eat her. But I was in love, beyond smitten; I could have been the Dean of Smitten at Smitten University. Lola shat on me, threw up on me, peed on me, ate the buttons off my favourite shirt; it was like being in a country and western song, but I didn't care. This, as my fellow parents well know, is the way of the universe.

I struggled with the simple things, like trying to dress her, paranoid that I would snap off a finger or throttle her in an attempt to put on her jumper. Bathing her felt like handling a particularly slippery unexploded bomb, a scenario that made me sweaty and unsure about so much more than just cutting the blue wire.

I felt a wonderful new parental sobriety surround me. Lola had been there for the last nine months, the bulge in Clare's belly; each night I had talked to the bulge about my day. But now—when she was quiet—I had the privilege of talking to her face to face. My life would never be the same again. It was like there was a lamp in my head, and it had always been there, only Lola had just turned it on.

I'd been living the last nine months underwater and now I could suddenly breathe. I was about to turn forty, and finally I felt like I'd come full circle, from a happy-go-lucky arse wrangler, to a semi-functioning wino, to proud father and husband.

We took lots of photos—at first most were a bit reminiscent of Sid and Nancy—and within days whole hard drives were full. Floods of gifts arrived and the house started to look like the Myer baby department during a stocktake sale. My life was becoming textbook white picket fence; it was like living in a Hallmark card. I knew it couldn't last.

Indeed, while home was great, my desk job wasn't improving on closer acquaintance. And the sleep deprivation caused by a new baby didn't help. I came home from work late one Friday, exhausted after a really shit day. On any given Friday someone pivotal would not show up. On this particular day, it fucked me up royally.

We'd received a last-minute order—the only sort there is in the oilfield—and so I had spent the entire day in the pipe yard moving drill pipe from one rack to another, trying to sort out what was good to go. It was a stinking hot summer day, the dust, grease and sweat were staining my shirt, and the whole time I knew there were dozens of other things I had to get done. My mobile went off constantly, the receptionist kept paging me, the paperwork kept piling up; I worked through lunch, then through dinner, and finally left work at 9 p.m.

Pulling into the driveway I could already hear my daughter screaming inside the house. And I was in the car. With the windows up. And the motor still running. I took a deep breath and headed inside.

Clare was sitting on the couch in the living room. The day had been a scorcher, and even at this late hour the house we were renting—an old sprawling 1930s uninsulated heat trap—was stifling. She was lathered in sweat; I had never seen her look so stressed. Lola's screams penetrated my inner brain box like a 9-mm hollow point. Neither of us had the energy to do anything, but I told Clare to give me the baby so she could go and have a shower and take a break. Her response was immediate and vocal.

'The washing machine has flooded the laundry,' she screamed. 'I can't get anything done. Go and fix it!'

In these situations it's better to comply with instructions and just do as you're told, so I went to the shed, got the tools, and within ten minutes the washing machine was sitting on bricks with me lying in dirty, foamy water underneath. Now, I'm no washing machine mechanic, but a scan around with my torch soon revealed that the drain hose was blocked, so I stuck the end of the torch between my teeth, took off the hose clamp and pulled on the hose.

It immediately jerked free, shooting said blockage—a turd consisting entirely of pubic hair and congealed soap—straight into my waiting open mouth. Almost as quickly, I started to vomit. I tried to sit up, but I was under a washing machine, so instead I bashed my vomit-covered face into the side of the drum, leaving me with a deep gash just above my left eye. The large amounts of claret gushing from my new head wound were staunched by winding half a roll of toilet paper round my head.

It wasn't pretty, but some time later I emerged from the laundry, the machine fixed and running, floor mopped, vomit, blood, soap and pubes removed.

My head was throbbing in tune with Lola's screams, which hadn't subsided the whole time I'd been gone. Poor Clare was sitting in exactly the same spot with exactly the same stressed, sweaty expression on her face. I was so hungry I could have eaten dust, but I was far too fearful to ask what was for dinner. I instead suggested again that Clare give Lola to me so she could go and have that shower. This time she gave me a tired smile and passed the baby over. 'What did you do to your head?' she asked.

Lola was wrapped up tightly in a light pink muslin cloth. She was about a three and a half inch outside diameter, two feet long, with a shiny bald purple veiny head sticking out the end. Naturally I thought, 'Wow, she looks just like an erect cock.'

I sprinted into the study where I drew a Jap eye with crayon on Lola's head, tucked her feet into my pants, and re-emerged into the lounge room shouting, 'Hey honey, check this out.'

I stood side-on so Clare could get the full benefit of my genius. Lola was rigid and I was holding her around the waist. 'Get the camera, get the camera!' I was laughing so hard I couldn't see straight. Clare snapped, grabbed the baby and disappeared back into the bathroom, slamming the door behind her.

Sometime later they reappeared: baby fast asleep, Jap eye removed. Wife was weird-calm. She sat down next to me on the couch, where I was nervously channel-surfing. Without looking at me, Clare spoke in that slightly deeper voice that women use when they really disconnect, and are about to lift cars or kill you with a blunt instrument.

'Don't ever make cock jokes using your daughter as a prop, OK?'

Months later at a public speaking event a bloke asked me if I had learned anything since becoming a father. In front of fifteen hundred people I went blank, then said, 'Don't ever make . . .'

4 PANIC FEST

Not used to being so housebound, previously simple matters—like getting myself around the world at short notice—became surprisingly complicated. In one particular case, I had difficulty leaving the state.

As you'll likely have gathered by now, as well as having a full-time job, I'm also a part-time writer. And one of the things that happens when you're a writer is you get invited to speak at writers' festivals. I had done three; no matter how many times I do it, I still freak at the thought of talking to large groups of people. Then along came the Melbourne Writers' Festival. Even the invitation letter was flash. It's one of the premier writing events in the country—how the hell did I get an invite? I promptly phoned my publisher, who confirmed that I was indeed on the billing. So naturally I responded telling them I'd be delighted and thank you very much for thinking of me. Months later I got an information pack from the festival organisers, containing my flight itinerary, hotel reservations, books by the other authors attending, and information on where in Melbourne to get everything from a bikini wax to a good cappuccino.

When the festival dates rolled around Clare was visiting her family in Sydney with eight-month-old Lola. She phoned me the day before I was due to leave for Melbourne, asking if I had remembered to get her car registered. I had purchased Clare a small hatchback just before she left for Sydney, and of course I had completely forgotten to register it. If I didn't drop what I was doing at work and get to the licensing centre pronto, there would be all kinds of shit as a consequence, so I raced out the door and drove to the nearest one, took a number from the machine and sat in the packed waiting room looking at the big red digital numbers clicking over from 28 to 19998.

Several hours later my number appeared and I approached a spotty bored kid with ink all over his hands. He was however very helpful and explained that in order to register Clare's car I would have to give up my New South Wales licence, which he would cancel, then he would give me a Western Australian licence, and then I could register the car. So I handed over my Sydney licence, and he gave me this shitty interim piece of paper, as it takes a week to make a plastic licence in WA. I folded it up and stuck it in my wallet, walked out and rang Clare to tell her everything was sorted and wasn't I organised.

The next morning I woke up nervous; I had packed the night before but I double-checked everything. Hours went into thinking about what I was going to wear for my appearance on stage. I don't usually worry about such things, but at this event I was going to be in the sort of company that makes me anxious. People I've read and admire; gifted, intelligent, articulate writers, like the brilliant Clive James and John Clarke, who would no doubt be wondering what I was doing there. People who would think I'd feel overdressed if I was wearing a belt.

As I made last-minute shoe-change decisions, I paused to calm the fuck down. This is not that big a deal, I told myself, it's just fifteen minutes on stage. I think I know what I'm going to talk about, I know what I'm going to wear, and besides, when I get there we'll have a nice long meeting on who will go first and all that good stuff, so just relax and take your time.

I made myself a cup of tea and sat on the porch for a moment. My cat fronted up from inside a nearby bush and sat directly in front of me, smiling. Oswald is pretty much an outdoor cat; he's scarred from a million fights, and his face is contorted in a permanent scowl thanks to a stroke he suffered a few years ago. He's deaf, his left ear is completely split, his tail has multiple fractures, he's pissed more blood, drank more drain water, and lived through more attempts on his life than most people I know. But he's smart, very smart. I think he's even got his own website.

Oswald spent months checking me out from a safe distance before he decided he was my friend. At night I would see his reflective eyes watching me intently from under a bush or car, sometimes from the roof. Now he knows me as an animal lover and we have quiet moments on the porch together.

He wanders up and growls at me. His cat voice turned into a low rasp years ago; he sounds like a pack-a-day cat. I give him the odd treat, and he forgets himself and thinks he's human, rolls over and shows me his beer gut so I will make a fuss of him.

The family opposite us have a likable but stupid rottweiler, one of those bounding, relentless, totally undisciplined dogs that just does whatever enters its melon head. You know, piss on the car, eat the child, fuck that rubbish bin, rub your arse on the carpet. Oswald and I were enjoying our quiet moment when the rottweiler saw us sitting there on the porch and launched itself away from his owner across the street, coming at us full tilt, its tongue slapping the side of its head. Oswald sensed something was amiss. His head swivelled in the direction of the driveway where 200 pounds of mind-numbingly thick dog was hurtling towards us at breakneck speed.

The dog was ten feet away when it suddenly put the brakes on, skidding to a stop only inches from Ossy. He was barking madly, his spit flying into the cat's face. Oswald didn't move a single muscle, just gave the rottweiler the dead-eye stare. The dog looked completely confused: wasn't it in the cats' contract that Oswald had to shit a brick and run like fuck? But Ossy just turned his head back to me, looking bored. Utterly nonplussed, the dog started running in wild circles, barking randomly, until his owner came down my driveway apologising and dragged the dog off.

Here was an old cat showing me the way: he had just faced down a demented rottweiler and casually fallen asleep. All I had to do was picture the audience as demented rottweilers, naked demented rottweilers, and I'd be fine.

My phone rang; it was my publisher making sure I was ready to go.

I called a taxi and stood in the driveway. I've stood in the driveway a thousand times waiting for a cab to take me to the airport. This time it was not to an end destination on the other side of the world that involved a drilling rig in some swamp. This time it was as a writer. Me, a writer; I still can't believe it.

Perth Domestic Airport is always busy. I joined the queue to check in. My turn arrived and I handed over my ticket.

'Where are we off to today?' The check-in guy faked a smile.

'Melbourne.' I faked one back.

'Right, Mr Carter, I'll need to see photo ID please.'

My hand automatically went to my pocket and then I froze, pulling that face you make when you know you're stuffed.

The interim paper licence came out anyway. I showed him the formal invitation letter; I pleaded with him. He pulled the face you make when you don't really give a fuck. The APEC Conference was about to start in Sydney, a delegation of some of the planet's most important decision-makers—and George W. Bush—were about to fly in, so the security protocols required that everyone checking in for a flight needed to have current valid photo ID.

'Sorry,' he smirked, 'I don't make the rules.'

I was livid. Right, I thought, think fast. I ran to the taxi rank, jumped into the first cab and looked into the face of an ancient Indian man with glasses thicker than George W. Shit, I thought, this is going to be like *Driving Miss Daisy* all the way to my house.

'Get me to my house and back here as fast as you can, mate, and I'll look after you,' I said.

George hammered it. I was doing the right foot into the invisible brake thing all the way home. There was no way I was going to get back in time to make my flight, but there was another one departing in a little over an hour. It was the only flight left that could possibly get me there in time—and it would be tight.

I booked it on my mobile while George snaked in and out of traffic mumbling to himself, constantly pushing his glasses back up on his nose with his index finger. By the time we turned into my street I was starting to feel confident; George had done a sterling job.

'What number?' he asked, but I was staring in shock, my heartbeat had doubled. 'Oooh, there's a fire,' he casually pointed out.

'Stop the car,' I yelled at him. We pulled up in front of my house—my rental house, currently on fire. Neighbours had gathered on the lawn, peering through the front window. Flames were visible and smoke was billowing out.

I ran to the front door fumbling with my keys while the neighbours flashed their whiter than white teeth. 'We called the fireys,' they said. I suppressed the urge to run straight through the kitchen and into the study. No doors in the house were closed and smoke was filling the house from our high ceiling down to head level. I could see into the study from the kitchen; my desk was burning, as was the carpet underneath it, and half my bookshelf. Right, I thought, think faster. Working on drilling rigs, every two years we would do a firefighting course. First we'd practise assessing hypothetical situations and decide the best way to deal with all kinds of different fires, and then we'd spend the rest of the day setting things on fire and putting the theory into practice. After all these years, my first time ever fighting a fire, and I didn't even have time to enjoy it. Shit.

Propped up against the wall by the kitchen door was a nine-kilo dry-powder, big fuck-off industrial fire extinguisher. I grabbed it, pulled the pin, and pointed the nozzle at the bread bin to test it. The corner of our kitchen bench, the bread bin, the toaster, the kettle and a revolting embroidered hanging thing that said 'Clare's Kitchen' were instantly covered in white powder. Yup, it worked. I turned to my study and let fly.

The fire was out before the extinguisher was empty. My passport sat in the top left-hand drawer of my desk. As I pulled it out I heard the fire truck roll up outside. My heart was pounding and I was sweating like a pig. I shoved the passport into my hip pocket and ran out.

On the way out I passed the firemen, the real estate agent and the neighbours, still standing on the porch.

'You got keys?' I said to the worried-looking agent.

'You got insurance?' he replied.

The taxi driver sat there behind the wheel, engine still running. I jumped in and started doing a pantomime for 'get me back to the airport'. He couldn't believe I was just going to leave.

'But what about your house, my friend?'

'Just go,' I snapped.

'Don't you want to change your shirt?'

'No, just go.'

'Did you just use a fire extinguisher?'

'Yup.'

'You know that was very dangerous. What if you inhaled smoke and collapsed?'

'Airport.'

'Yes, I know, you want to go back to the airport. It must be a very important meeting you are going to then.'

'Yup.'

'Do you want me to take the tunnel or go through the city?'

'JUST FUCKING GO.'

George's finger shot up and shoved his glasses back up on his nose and we took off like a rocket. My phone rang. It was the real estate agent: the fire was well and truly out. Thank Christ for that, I thought, imagining the alternative, searching for a way to make myself feel better. All those years of working on the rigs, with endless flights, hundreds of charters, choppers, donkeys, commercial airliners—you name it, I caught it. I had only missed one check-in in twenty years. This time I was lucky I'd missed that flight. The agent was very understanding and said we would get everything sorted out in a couple of days when I got back from Melbourne.

I sat back, trying to relax, looking at my watch every few minutes. There were just too many variables. I had stacked things in my head the way you do when you're confronted with too much to deal with and none of it is really under your control. I stank, sweat was running down my back, my hands were sticky. Meanwhile George continued to drive like a maniac, and we pulled up at the terminal almost before I'd gathered my thoughts. He popped the boot. I slapped two green ones down on his waiting hand and he beamed. 'Good luck to you.'

I had arrived just in time to make the second flight. I couldn't believe it. Skipping the long queue I ran up to the guy at the desk. Same guy, same expression. He even said, 'Where are we off to today?'

'Melbourne.' I slid my passport across the counter to him.

He looked at it for a moment, then looked at me with a mixture of pity and contempt. 'This is expired, Mr Carter.'

My face must have dropped a couple of feet. 'What?' I grabbed it and yes, I had picked up the wrong one. When you get a new passport the government sends back your old one as well, but because it's cancelled they cut off a corner. I stood there for a moment looking at my photo, the top right-hand corner of my head chopped off. How had I missed that?

'Look, you can see it's me,' I said, holding the invitation letter above my face to block out the same area, but it was pointless.

'Sorry, I don't make the rules.' He faked a sympathetic smile and waved up the next person.

I went back outside the terminal and stood there for a moment, getting myself together. I've managed to get myself into and out of some remote corners of the globe, often really shitty parts of the Third World, sometimes countries where civil war was raging, but I couldn't get it together to get out of Perth to go to a writers' festival. I was shaking with anger, but there was nothing to be done; I'd blown it. At least the house hadn't burned down. All I could do was phone the festival organisers and let them know I would be a no-show.

After I made the call, I looked over to the cab rank; there was George reading the paper. The thought of getting in that cab again was too much to bear and I found myself wandering back into the terminal, towards the airport shop. The airport shop where they sell books, books with the author's photo on the jacket . . . motherfucker. I broke into a sprint, grabbed the first book of mine I could see on the shelf, stood in the queue feeling like a dick for buying my own book, then ran back to check-in guy and thrust it under his nose while people in the check-in queue protested. 'What the fuck?'

I ignored them.

'Excuse me, dickhead.' A deep voice spoke close behind me. I turned and the guy stopped mid-speech. No doubt I looked like your stock-standard bald, angry, control-seeking narcissist who's in receipt of some kind of mental benefit. Our eyes met. He took in the stench of a house fire mixed with dry-powder extinguisher, mixed with sweat, mixed with my best fuck-off look, and he took a step back.

I turned around to the check-in guy, who was studying the jacket photo. 'OK, Mr Carter, here's your boarding pass, good luck.' This time he showed teeth.

'Thank you.' I had five minutes. 'Thank you.' I ran towards the security section. 'Thank you,' I yelled over my shoulder.

Sitting in the departure lounge I felt worse than before I made the check-in. Now I had to phone the festival back and tell them I was coming after all. Hearing their confusion, I could tell they were convinced I was an idiot. Finally we boarded. I tried to relax. A quarter of an hour went by, then another. If we didn't push back from the terminal in the next five minutes I wasn't going to make it. If we got underway now, and landed on time, then I had just fifteen minutes to get from the airport to the stage. Christ. I turned my phone on and dialled the only man I knew who could get me from the airport to the festival at light speed. James Ward was my only hope.

James is an interesting guy, affable, funny, in his mid thirties and already the manager of the Supercar Club. He has at his disposal a frightening array of ridiculously fast and exotic sports cars, as well as the necessary driving skills to put a fast car into low orbit.

I'd met him a few months earlier, when a TV crew was in the process of casting the presenters for the Aussie version of the British motoring television show *Top Gear*. Out of the blue they'd called and asked me to audition.

'But I'm not a car guy,' I said, but apparently that didn't matter.

The next day I was on a flight to Sydney, and from there to a small town in rural New South Wales via a minibus. I met James on that bus. From the get-go I was the guy in that group who didn't know about cars. That is to say, yes, I'm a car lover; yes, I know as much as any regular guy who dreams of owning a fully restored 1966 Fastback Mustang, but the others were all walking auto savants who could rattle off every conceivable detail about any car. 'Mate, the GTO was faster than the ABC coz the '76 model had the blah blah plugged into the thingy, blah, blah, blah, blah . . .' was all I heard after the first hour. You can imagine the amount of testosterone in the room, ten guys in heated 'pick me' mode, every last one of them a dedicated car lover.

'Paul, what do you think of my new Ford Blah?' they'd ask.

'Very nice,' I'd say, while another guy jumped in with: 'I've got one, but what about their move over to trans blah,

blah . . .' Each question posed with a serious expression, as they tried to feel out exactly how much I don't know about cars. 'What colour is it?' I would respond. Another asked me what I thought about V6 compared to V8 and I told him I preferred apple juice. They must have hated me.

So James and I drank all their single malt, and bonded; James didn't care either.

We drove about in go-karts, racing each other while the decision-makers recorded everything. All I managed was some very average drink-driving, ending in a fairly unspectacular crash. The whole experience was lots of fun, but in the end they chose their presenters and the rest of us sobered up and went back to our regular jobs. James and I stayed in touch, and I'm glad we did. Now I was about to ask him for a huge favour.

He picked up the phone when I rang and without hesitation said, 'No worries, mate, I'll be out the front waiting.' As I turned off my phone and the aircraft finally pushed back, hope flickered alive once again. During the flight I pondered my situation. Why was this so hard? It wasn't like we were trying to breed pandas here, all I had to do was get up and go to the airport for fuck's sake.

The aircraft touched down bang on time in Melbourne; I had no check-in luggage so I bolted for the exit. Hitting the outer doors I spotted James instantly, leaning against a brand-new white Maserati GranTurismo.

Bingo. This was going to be fun, I thought as I ran up. I started thanking him and apologising, but all he said was: 'Jump in.'

I dropped into the low-slung car like you'd slide into a warm bath after a hard day. James took off like we'd just robbed a bank, concentrating totally while making polite conversation.

I tried not to look frantic as we passed other cars as if they were standing still. 'How's Lola doing?' James asked casually, taking the Italian V8 from a low growl to a fuel-injected feeding frenzy as he pointed my great white hope towards two giant semitrailers and shot out the minuscule gap between them like an Exocet missile.

'Oh, she's fine, mate.' Time slowed down. I think a little pee came out. I was pushed back into the ample black leather, feeling like a bum in a dinner suit, mesmerised by the number of buttons and dials on the dash.

If we had passed a cop, there would have been just enough time for them to report a UFO. James chatted calmly about everything from politics to soap operas as if he was driving the Popemobile sedately through Rome, not tearing down the Tullamarine Freeway at a million miles an hour. If I had been driving that car we would have ended up vaporised in the grille of a semitrailer full of bridge parts. Or the cops would have nailed me, and what would I have told them? After the day I'd had, I would have welcomed getting arrested. I could have popped open the glove box, and shown the officers the scarf I was knitting or given them a list of the top ten movies that made me cry. Jesus. I needed a tall glass of 'Harden The Fuck Up': there was no backing out now.

If the Nobel Prize Foundation gave out awards for driving, James would have won that day. It was like being on the set of *The Transporter*, but without the guns. We banked hard and darted into an exit. I glanced down at my watch. I had two minutes. 'Don't worry, mate, I'll get you there,' he said in that confident I-could-do-this-shit-for-a-living kind of way. Sure enough, he made it; I owed him one.

My goodbyes were fast. I had already undone the seat belt, and I sprang from the low GT as soon as he pulled up outside one of many entrances to the theatre. It was one of those utterly confusing modern buildings; I had no idea if I was at the right door or even the right building. Adrenalin forced me to run inside, my head darting from left to right as I looked for a magic arrow to point me in the right direction.

A young woman came around the corner in a festival T-shirt wearing a headset and carrying a clipboard, so I grabbed her. 'Hi, I'm supposed to be on stage,' I blurted out.

She scanned the clipboard. 'What's your name?' I told her and bang, we were off: down the hall, up some stairs, down some stairs, through a backstage corridor. I could hear a lot of people settling in on the other side of the wall, and nerves started pulling at my gut.

She stopped and motioned towards a small set of stairs that had to lead to the stage. 'Go out and take your seat,' she said, looking firm.

I stood there for a moment trying to gather my wits. As I took the stairs, time slowed down again; I rounded the corner and there they were, the writers, looking over their glasses at me the way parents observe other people's kids. To my right sat many hundreds of paying members of the general public. I looked like shit on a stick. I sat down in the free seat, sweat making its horribly dank and smelly way down my back.

Suddenly I was being introduced. Shit, I was the first cab off the writers rank today—perfect. I'd thought I'd get the chance to sit down for a few minutes and try to remember what the fuck I had planned to say to these people, but now there was polite applause. Finding my feet, I confidently strode over to the podium, smiling out at the bright lights. I cleared my throat, thanked the festival for inviting me, thanked the members of the audience for coming, and then I went completely blank.

I decided to explain why I looked like shit, and of course I ended up telling the story of my day so far. I had fifteen minutes to speak and it took fifteen minutes to tell the story. I didn't talk about books, or writing, or anything to do with literature. But I did explain that I am indeed the guy who manages to get himself in all kinds of shit just by getting up in the morning. They loved it, thank God.

After the session we all went to the green room where speakers were supposed to wait before going on, and had a drink. On the way I discovered that there was an area outside the green room where we each had a desk set up with our names on a little card, so audience members and festival-goers could buy a book from the bookstore and take it over to the author to sign or write obscenities in, etc. At the end of the row of desks was my name, and a queue of people all holding books. I wandered up as the staff ripped open boxes, pulling out copies of a book by Professor Paul Carter. 'Um, that's not me,' I said, pointing at the pile on the table.

'What?' said the young guy unpacking the books.

'This isn't my work,' I said. I confess, for a moment I thought about just sitting down and signing them.

'Oh, I'm so sorry, we'll get it sorted out.' He grabbed the books and disappeared, leaving me in front of an ever-lengthening line of people.

To my right I could see all the other authors making polite small talk and doing their best signatures on huge piles of books around them. More and more people filtered into the courtyard.

It was the entire cast and crew of the Melbourne literary scene; there were pearls and lots of air-kissing. The word 'darling' skipped across lips and reverberated as frequently as 'fuck' used to on the drill floor.

I saw a familiar face in the crowd: not someone I knew, someone I recognised. He got a bit closer. It was Geoffrey Rush, the actor, and he was working his way around the courtyard. Wow, I thought, I'm going to get to meet him. My books had turned up—perfect. I started chatting and signing, all the while closely monitoring Mr Rush's progress towards my table.

It was all going very well: the people waiting for me to sign their books were all very nice, the wine was very nice, the gentle tones of civilised conversation broken by the occasional laugh were all just very nice. The sun was shining and birds sang from trees nearby.

That's when I heard it, a rough voice that could have come straight from the oilfield, shattering the peace and my sensation of wellbeing. 'Oi, are you Paul Carter?'

Turning to my right I saw a six-foot, 300-pound, slightly drunk man with full-sleeve tats and wearing a VB T-shirt with sauce stains down the front, eyeballing me through more facial hair than I thought it was humanly possible to grow.

'Yup.' I smiled. I think he smiled back.

'I fuckin loved your book, hey.'

'Thanks, mate.' Just past his left shoulder I saw another familiar face approaching through the crowd; this time it was someone I knew.

'M'name's Dwayne hey.' My new fan stuck out a massive hairy hand. I dived my hand into his, making full contact with his upright thumb, enabling me to get a firm grip and shake. I looked him in the eye; he was pissed. I darted a look at

Mr Rush—his entourage was getting awfully close—at my friend, now waving and bounding through the crowd towards me, and then back to Dwayne, who was still talking at me.

'Lemme shout you a beer, mate,' he said, raising his other hand. Only then did I notice the stubbie neck just visible through the furry knuckles.

'Cheers, Dwayne,' I said. 'I'll just finish up here, mate, and meet you at the bar in half an hour.'

At that moment, my friend appeared next to Dwayne.

'Hi, Bruce.' I hugged him and we shook hands. Bruce is a truly gifted man, he's a very talented writer and filmmaker, a gentleman in every way.

'Why does this stuff always happen to you?' Bruce was laughing—clearly he'd heard about my day so far. Mr Rush was now ten feet away.

I introduced Dwayne to Bruce and they regarded one another carefully—it was like worlds colliding. Bruce, ever the gentleman, politely smiled and got his manicured hand crushed by Dwayne, who defaulted back to beer.

'I'll shout yas both a beer.'

Mr Rush was now just a few feet away and getting closer. Bruce was enjoying himself. 'Have you read Paul's books?' he asked Dwayne.

Dwayne looked at Bruce's perfect attire, his neat, clean, personable aura, and spoke loud enough for half the courtyard to hear him. 'Mate, I'm just like him. I know what it's like to work for a living hey, not like all these cunts.'

The second Dwayne dropped the C bomb, Mr Rush turned on his heel and melted back into the crowd. Bruce was loving it. 'Go on, Pauli, have a beer with him.' He nudged me with his elbow and gestured towards Dwayne's hand. 'Look, he's got a traveller.'

Dwayne looked at Bruce. I looked at Bruce. 'He's got a what?' I started to worry.

'You know, a traveller.'

At this point Dwayne stepped forward, and with his beard almost touching Bruce's face said, 'Mate, a beer you walk around with is generally referred to as a *roadie*; a *traveller* is when you crack a fat on public transport.'

'Oh.' Bruce nodded. 'I'll try to remember that.'

Dwayne stepped back, took a long swig of his beer and regarded the two of us. You could almost hear the penny drop: it was like a thought bubble appeared above Dwayne's head that read, 'Oh, they're a gay couple. Paul Carter's a poofter.'

This could not have panned out any better for me. Bruce registered all this and kindly helped me to embrace the horror by placing a hand on my shoulder. That cemented the picture for Dwayne, who got out of there so fast you would have thought his hair was on fire.

5 BIO WHAT?

Not long after the writers' festival, I started a new job in Perth with an oilfield supply firm, working in a small office not too far from home. The job was perfect; the boss was just like me, he'd worked in the field for years, and everyone we did business with was pretty much from the old school. Most of our business dealings were conducted over a single malt at lunch, very civilised.

By this time, I'd settled down a bit. My wife was amazing; my child was amazing, they made me dizzy with contentment. I actually enjoyed my job and we had purchased a house that ticked every box. I would stand in the power tool section at the hardware store, envisaging potential backyard projects. On weekends I pruned hedges and mowed the lawn. I made polite conversation with my neighbours wearing a silly hat to keep the sun off my bald head. I even got to know the postman—I never ever thought I'd know the postman.

After kicking and screaming all the way from the rig for the last twelve months, I had crossed over into the next stage of my life. Well, you can't stay in a bad mood forever. I'd turned into the grey man living the middle-class dream—there was even a white picket fence around my house. I bolstered my pension plan and life insurance, I stopped smoking, and before the rebellious voice in my head could say, 'Hey, what the fuck?', it was my fortieth birthday and I was in bed by ten.

Christ, I was middle-aged and happy about it.

For my birthday I got the regulation socks and jocks, a gift voucher for the hardware store, and a copy of *Long Way Round*, the documentary series on Ewan McGregor and Charley Boorman's epic motorcycle ride. When I did finally get the chance to sit down and watch it I discovered instead Lola's *Finding Nemo* disc inside, my sixteen-month-old daughter having put my DVD into one of the many cases piled up on the floor.

Whereas in my old life I used to play beat the clock on every job, I had even stopped marking time. Despite this, the year had blown by faster than I'd ever experienced before. There were reminders of what I now looked back on as my old life; for example, my friend Erwin, who still lived at a pace I couldn't comprehend from the 'burbs and was still working offshore. He'd come home to Perth on a crew change, and within 24 hours of arriving he'd ride his motorcycle over to our house and demand a long ride into the hills.

Erwin was my mentor: we had spent many years rig-hopping all over the world together. He's a larger than life character, he has the light around him—you know, anything could happen and he would walk away without so much as a scratch. Our friendship had literally kept me in one piece for the better part of fifteen years; I would have been eaten alive by the oilfield without his guidance. If Mother Nature wasn't trying to kill us there always seemed to be something else that was. The first time I went up in the derrick—that's the big steel mini-Eiffel Tower on the rig—it was Erwin who taught me how not to fall, get crushed, or cut any limbs or fingers off. Believe me, over the years a great many men have hurt themselves up there. If it were not for his patience and skill I probably wouldn't have the digits to sit here and type this.

These brief two-wheel interludes with my old friend became very important to me. Time spent on my bike put me in a mindset that I just couldn't replicate any other way. When Erwin and I got tired, we'd stop and rest and I caught up on all his latest adventures.

Even though I was getting used to life at home, something was not quite right. Maybe it was turning 40; maybe it was a lingering sense of loss, knowing that I had departed a life I had loved for twenty years and could never go back. I still missed being on the rigs. It was always fun working and hanging out with my crew; I had never laughed so hard or been so scared in my life. Or maybe what I missed was the sense in those days that adventure was a thing that just happened, without any planning or preparation, just random spontaneous life getting in the way.

In the weeks after my birthday I started to realise that I couldn't go on in the same way that I'd been living for the last year or so; I just wanted more from my life. And when I say more, I'm not talking about material goods. The arrival of Lola and the profound and all-encompassing impact of being a father had helped drown out all that chatter and white noise and worries that can make us slaves to our possessions. It's funny how your kids change your priorities overnight. So long as Clare and Lola were alright, you could set fire to all our shit (I had a bit of experience at that now) and I wouldn't bat an eyelid. I used to worry about my stuff, my special things, but not anymore. Doesn't matter if it's something really nice or valuable, in the end you're just the custodian of it for a while, then someone else gets it anyway. No, this restlessness was just about adventure.

The highway sat there out the window, waving a dusty invitation at me through the heat haze. Back in Sydney I had been able to indulge myself on my days off. If the urge got to me, all I had to do was wander into my garage and get on a bike. Not just a bike, an escape into a mindset of corners, faster each time; a heightened sense of awareness that blanks your troubled mind and focuses it on one thing only: the ride. No responsibilities, no life insurance, no five-year plan. It's not just a bike, it's a get-into-jail card, it's an unlicensed weapon and a fat bank guard, it's whatever you want it to be, as fast as you like.

I would leave the city and head south, to Araluen; sometimes I would just keep going, stopping when I got hungry or tired, buying clean jocks and socks in some small town, throwing the old ones in a motel bin, getting drunk with strangers and ending up in Melbourne. I missed those days, before I was a grown-up.

At the halfway mark during one of our rides to nowhere in particular, I looked over a roadhouse table at Erwin and announced, 'I'm going to ride my bike around Australia.'

He finished his mouthful of steak sandwich and beamed. 'When are we leaving?'

'How about now?' Obviously I was joking, but there was a time when that was exactly what we'd have done.

Erwin looked at me thoughtfully. 'You watched that *Long Way Round* DVD I gave you for your birthday?' he asked.

'No, not yet.' I was looking at the bikes in the car park.

During the ride home the idea solidified in my head. I thought, I'm not done, I'm nowhere near done. Somehow, I was going to get the time off work, talk Clare into giving me a leave pass, and get to have my cake and eat the bastard too.

The thought sat there in my head, bobbing about like a crouton in my brain soup for weeks—and it *was* soup, strained through months of paperwork, tender documents, pre-qualification questions. The detritus of business was weighing down my itchy feet, a paperweight of increasing responsibilities, increasing business lunches and my increasing waistline—all of which pushed me to broach the idea with Clare.

My wife, flat out dealing with motherhood, which is in itself much harder and more draining than anything I'm ever tasked with during the day, listened patiently while I blurted out my idea. I was nervous: I knew it was a big ask.

She surprised me. Apparently, Clare had been waiting for me to do this for a while. She said she knew it was only a matter of time before sitting behind a desk and living in Lego Land would turn my life into a cage with golden bars.

'You're going to write about this, right?' she asked me. What can I say, she knows me well.

'Well yeah, why not?' I replied, wondering where she was going with this.

'Honey, anyone can get on a conventional motorcycle and ride it around Australia. You should find a machine that's different.'

The more I thought about it, the more it made sense. After all, Ewan McGregor and Charley Boorman had punched out two books and two TV series about riding around the world. (Which reminded me, I still hadn't found my copy of their DVD yet.) Motorcycle travel/adventure has been done to death.

So, how would I jump on a bike and have an adventure without replicating what's been done before? I knew I couldn't get anywhere near what those guys did. Ewan McGregor is a movie star, they had limitless funding, an army of people in support, and the ability to make shit happen on their custom-designed, top-flight BMWs. And that's the point: I'm about as far removed from their end of the spectrum as humanly possible. Whatever I did, it had to be different.

And then a light bulb went on over my head. I couldn't believe I hadn't thought of this earlier. Enter Mr Greg Quail, aka Quaily—an old mate, a prince among men. Greg runs a successful television production company based in Sydney; he's animated and insightful, but above all, when he's armed with an idea he likes, he won't let go. He's like a greyhound chasing after a stuffed rabbit. Earlier in the year, one of Greg's staff, Warwick Burton, had called me to discuss the idea of Quail Television making a show about a ride on a bio-diesel motorcycle. I had thought it was brilliant, and perfect for me: I'm the oil guy—what else should I ride but a bike that runs on bio-diesel, environmentally friendly fuel? It had sounded redeeming, and at the time, was a nice alternative to going back offshore. But the idea never made it past conception, and I'd put it out of my mind.

Now, when I reminded her, Clare said I should call and find out how far Warwick got with his research. I practically knocked her over in my rush to get to the phone.

But Greg and Warwick didn't have good news for me; apparently the TV networks in Australia, while interested and enthusiastic about the concept, thought the idea was too expensive to make. The networks are generally more interested in something 'reality'-based, something that's cheaper to put on the telly. You know, 'Find My Bogan' or 'World's Silliest Bogan', or a group of people trying to lose weight, or dance or sing or cook or renovate another fucking house, or a bunch of celebrities between gigs dissecting the news on a panel. That kind of stuff is cheap and very simple to produce. But above all, it's what we want to watch at prime time, isn't it? Not a bloke riding a motorcycle around, especially if he's not overweight and not trying to dance, sing, cook, renovate a house or find a long-lost degenerate alcoholic sibling.

I just don't understand the way the TV game works. Greg is a good mate, and whenever I'm in Sydney or he's in Perth we get together and, as mates do, we discuss work. But I have neither the patience nor the ability to try to comprehend how Greg gets an idea for a show, makes a pilot or reel and then sells it to a network. Sounds simple, doesn't it? Well, as far as I can make out, quantum physics is simpler. Essentially, the 'bio-diesel bike ride around Australia' idea was too much of a hard sell, and Greg had to shelve it.

However, I was only concerned with the ride, and Greg was only too happy to pass on the info they'd compiled on the bio-diesel motorcycles currently available. Armed with Greg and Warwick's research, I started my own hunt for information. There are several bio-diesel motorcycles commercially available in the world, but none of them are for sale in Australia. I found a great bike made in America, another in Holland, one in Japan, and a really good one in Germany fabricated by a former uber-lieutenant from Porsche who had packed in his job and started building bio-fuel bikes. (Germany, I learned, has over 1600 bio-diesel fuel stations.) His bike was perfect and completely capable of doing the ride. But no matter where in the world I found a bike I liked, I couldn't get a compliance plate on it or get it legally registered and insured so I could ride the bastard round Australia.

This mad hunt for bikes went on for months. Several times I came close to nailing it, but in the end, as everything does, it boiled down to two basic problems: time and money. I had planned to set off on the first of September to get the best weather and wind direction, heading east. But it was May and I was running out of options. As far as I could make out, getting the Batmobile for a blat around Australia would be a whole lot easier than getting hold of a bio-diesel bike. I could see why no one had done it before. I wanted to be the first rider to circumnavigate the country on a motorcycle running on used cooking oil, but good old-fashioned bureaucracy was pulling the rug out from under me.

Another potentially big hurdle was that I would also need to convince my employers to let me go and do 'the thing with the bike', as it would become known.

My immediate boss, Craig Voight, is based in Queensland; like all the other area managers, I report to him, and Voighty in turn reports to Peter West—Westy—who reports to the owner of the company. I had to ask Voighty first; if he said yes then I could ask Westy (I know it's getting silly, but the area manager in Adelaide is called Rossy). Craig was as calm and laid-back as ever; I, however, was nervous. I was a new employee, I'd been there just on a year. But all he said was: 'OK mate, run it past Westy.'

I'd known within minutes of meeting Peter West that he was a character. He stands out in a room, not just because he's a big man but because he has presence. If Westy was at the obligatory Thursday night oilfield drinks, then I knew the conversation would be good. Westy looks like he should be either a cop or a crim: he has that face; he's seen life, and people listen when he speaks. His hair is cropped short and neat, and he's always in a suit. But he can, when he's in the right mindset, carry himself in a way that makes you think he's just come from his millionth parole hearing. He has the demeanour of a man who's at peace with himself, but he also gives off the vibe that he's capable of anything. In reality, though, he is a gentle man who needs intolerable provocation to become violent, and you always know exactly where you stand with him.

Bearing in mind all that makes Westy Westy, I walked into his office one morning and asked him if he'd have a problem if I took off for three months to ride a bike—a bike I hadn't actually found yet—around Australia.

There was silence. Westy sat back in his chair and pondered. My heart pounded.

'OK mate, we'll work something out.' That was it.

So, Clare, Craig and Westy—the most important people, who could make or break the plan—were OK with it. Now I really had to do it.

6 THE BIKE THE UNIVERSE LANDED

The search for the bike went on. Whenever I wasn't working or sleeping I was thinking about it. What the right bike might be, how to get it, how to pay for it. Another month rolled by with no result. I turned over and over the problem late at night, a constant chain of repetitive, relentless thoughts without conclusion. With all the bureaucratic negotiations and wrangling, I'd over-complicated things and backed myself into a corner; I just couldn't see a way out of the maze.

And then, in the way that women often do, my wife one day just casually solved the problem that'd had me stumped for months. Yeah, she googled it.

Within five minutes she'd found an article somewhere in cyberspace from a South Australian newspaper dating back to 2007 about the University of Adelaide winning the Greenfleet Technology class of the World Solar Car Challenge—an annual race from Darwin to Adelaide with vehicles using alternative energy. The University of Adelaide's mechanical engineering team, led by a Dr Colin Kestell, won the Greenfleet class (for fuel-efficient and low-carbon vehicles) on a motorcycle called the Bio Bike. As my eyes scanned ahead on the article, my heart jumped. The winning bike ran on . . . used cooking oil.

That's it, I thought. If the University of Adelaide was involved then you could bet the bike was properly registered and insured. I brought up the phone number for the university and called them straightaway.

'May I speak with Dr Kestell, please.' It was only as my call was being put through that I realised I'd never even met an academic before, and I had no idea what I would say to this guy.

The call was picked up and a distinctly English voice said, 'Colin Kestell.' I immediately launched into my introductions, but I could tell he thought I was another of the dozen crackpots that probably rang him up every month with ideas for bio-diesel washing machines and golf carts.

With impeccable manners he politely went about the process of getting me off the phone so he could get on with his day. I left my number with him and hung up, convinced that he thought I was full of shit. Much to my surprise, an hour later he called me back. He said he'd mentioned my call to some of his students who, luckily for me, had read my books. He'd then called my publisher to confirm I was legit. Now he asked me how he could help.

Our conversation was perfect. Colin Kestell was an academic, but he certainly understood guys like me. Within ten minutes we had worked out a plan for getting the university to lend me their Bio Bike in such a way that I could legally ride it right around Australia and do it while properly insured, with no dire consequences to the university if I decided to ride it into a semitrailer or a school bus.

Excited, I then rang Greg Quail to tell him I'd just obtained the use of the only properly road-registered and insured bio-diesel motorcycle in the country. Greg was typically animated; he said he'd film it even without a TV contract.

'What?' I was stunned.

'Fuck it, Pauli, it's too good an idea not to film.'

'What about the cost?'

'Mate, if you can find the sponsorship to do the ride and provide a support truck, then I'll put a cameraman in the truck and cover the cost of all the filming and my guy's expenses.'

That was it. Greg was as good as his word: not only did he enlist the services of a cameraman, he also set up a website to promote my trip (www.thegoodoil.tv). The next day I called Colin back to arrange a date for me to fly to Adelaide to trial the Bio Bike—which was apparently named 'Betty'.

'How about next month?' said Colin. I could hear him turning pages in his diary.

'Sounds like a plan, Colin.'

Next, I called my lawyer, Mr Digby or 'Diggers'.

I'd always liked the idea of having a lawyer—to help with this kind of thing, mind you, not to get me off because I just stabbed someone with a pitchfork. Diggers came recommended by a couple of friends who swore by his rabid legal mind. If Diggers could deal with *them*—and they *were* the kinds of dudes who might stab someone with a pitchfork—then a guy like me should present no real problems. As usual, he wrapped his head around my situation in one phone call. The contract and all the relevant paperwork was in the mail to the university's lawyer that day.

The next day, I leaned back in my chair, the office air-conditioning whirring quietly in the background. Westy was at lunch and mine was sitting on the desk in front of me looking sad and a little soggy. My computer blinked with an incoming message and I focused on the screen. Colin had just received

Diggers' paperwork and had emailed to say there should be no problems at all. Wow. In 24 hours I had landed a bike; now all I needed to do was get over to Adelaide and ride it.

Colin's email included a few photos of Betty the Bio Bike. I sat there holding my sandwich and staring at the bike, imagining the ride. It looked uncomfortable. But something about it felt so right. This trip was about me, a former rig worker, sponsored by oil service companies, riding a bio-diesel-fuelled bike around Australia. At the end of the trip, after I'd recouped my costs, I planned to sell the support truck and give any leftover funds to charity. Everyone wins. Perfect.

I heard the tyres and gearbox of a powerful car clatter over the asphalt and pull up outside. The car's door slammed shut, closely followed by the large voice and banter of one Shaun Southwell. Shaun is the Western Australian manager of a large oilfield supply and fabrication firm we do business with. He's a tall, good-looking, completely confident, swaggering kind of Aussie bloke. I like Shaun; he's only in his mid thirties and has worked his way up from scratch; he knows his job, and you can rely on him. Above all, he's always got a smile on his face and rarely knocks back the opportunity for a laugh. It's as if he's aware that so many men at his stage of their career take themselves too seriously; having some fun in his day is the yeast that fluffs Shaun's mind.

He flopped himself into one of Westy's high-backed tub chairs and demanded a coffee.

'What can I do for you today, Mr Southwell?' I asked. 'Apart from explaining the circle work in the car park to Peter when he gets back.'

Shaun grinned. 'Where is he?' Tipping his head towards Westy's empty chair.

'At lunch with the boys.'

'Ah,' nodded Shaun. 'So he won't be back any time soon then.'

'Dunno, mate.'

His coffee arrived and I watched him study our receptionist's backside over the top of his mug as she walked past my desk.

'Anyway, it's not about what you can do for me, numbnuts.' Looking excited, Shaun dived his hand into his jacket pocket and produced an envelope. 'It's what I can do for you today, mate.' The envelope landed on my deck. From the look on his face I knew this had nothing whatsoever to do with work. He was grinning and making car noises while I opened it up.

I looked up from the ticket inside. 'What's the Clipsal 500?'

Shaun nearly fell off his seat. 'For fuck's sake, Pauli, that's like saying, "What's footy?", you pommy girl.'

Obviously the Clipsal is an important event in the Aussie Man Calendar. I continued to look blank.

'The V8s, mate. In Adelaide. Four days of intense piss-drinking, V8 supercars 'n tits, fuckin man nirvana, you muppet. Westy can't make it this year so you get to go compliments of us, everything paid for.'

'In Adelaide, next week.' I couldn't believe it.

'Yup. If you miss this and want to retain any street cred with the boys you'll have to be in prison, overseas, clinically insane, or already there waiting.' Shaun leaned back and drank his coffee.

'Well, I'd love to, mate.'

Before Shaun had finished dropping another burnout in our car park, I was on the phone to Colin. He was as surprised as I was.

The universe was lining up for me. A bike, airfare, hotel, booze, food and V8s 'n tits in 24 hours. Wow, I must have done something right in my last life.

That week went by excruciatingly slowly. The uni sent me the factory manual on Betty's power plant. Basically she was an eight-horsepower irrigation-pump single-stroke diesel engine made by Yanmar in Italy, mounted in the only bike the uni's 2006 mechanical engineering class could get, a now twelve-year-old Cagiva W16, coincidentally also made in Italy. The bike now looked a little odd to say the least, but she was a proven performer.

She had certainly proved her mettle during the World Solar Challenge in 2007. Her vitals were impressive: 2.9 litres per 100 kilometres while emitting only 71 grams per kilometre of carbon dioxide—that's over 75 per cent less emissions than a standard diesel engine. Her average speed was 70 kilometres an hour.

Betty looked good on paper, and in a diesel kind of a way she looked OK in pictures as well, although she had been painted a revolting lime green. I looked forward to meeting her, riding her, and painting her another colour. I was starting to sound like Captain Kirk. But as stupid as it might sound to someone who's not a bike rider, it's important to have a bond between rider and bike.

To a rider the bike is everything. It's an extension of the body, an expression of the last shred of rebelliousness still possible within the confined pigeonhole of suburban reality. But it's not an easy thing, a long motorcycle journey. The long-distance motorcycle rider has to challenge unknown roads in new places where anything can happen. Lots of people told me not to ride alone; I would have liked to do this trip with my mate Erwin, but there was only one bio bike. The two of us used to sit in crappy motel rooms between offshore jobs

IS THAT THING DIESEL?

watching old motorcycle movies—*Easy Rider*, *Stone*, *Mad Max*, *On Any Sunday* and the unmissable *Wild One*. Brando's character Johnny is cheesy 1950s bad boy perfection ('What're you rebelling against, Johnny?' asks a girl. 'Whaddya got?' says Johnny). Ever since Mr Brando pulled on that leather jacket and mumbled his way through Lee Marvin's earwax, I have wanted to do that endless motorcycle journey, and there was no one I'd rather do it with than Erwin. But, as much as he wanted to, I knew Erwin couldn't do the trip with me. Which just left me mumbling Marlon Brando lines all by myself.

Brando was by and large the first mainstream Hollywood star to look really good in his leather jacket, and when he wasn't doing that he was busy looking good walking around in his underwear, and thereby started a trend of looking good in leather jackets and underwear. Brando gave birth to the wife beater as a top to be worn by a sweaty man beyond the parameters of the home, while drinking a Stella, while hurling abuse at Stella in his wife beater. You know what I mean. Post-war America could not get enough of the romance of the motorbike.

I remember older guys in the UK talking about the veritable wars that kicked off between the Mods and the Rockers in Britain through the sixties and seventies. Huge two-wheeled hordes of bikers perpetuated the dark outlaw ethos. How bizarre that a form of transport could be linked so tightly with music, sex and crime—all the bad and all the good. The motorcycle will forever seduce a young rebel's mind. When I think about what made me fall in love with bikes, I think about my joy at watching *Easy Rider* for the first time, *Mad Max*'s evil bikers, Steve McQueen's (or rather Bud Ekins's) jump over that fence. The first time I went to the speedway, I stood so close to the track that oil and mud splattered my trackside face on the first turn. My first bike was a second-hand Honda C90. I was fifteen and spotty. Twenty-six years and several bikes later, I still can't get enough.

I've had years of only really being at peace when I'm sitting on a motorcycle with nothing but time to kill. For my ride around Australia I could have had any bike on the Aussie market. But Betty was going to be my ride; she would be the one. An experimental bike, built on a shoestring budget, by students. I knew this was going to pan out, there was just too much synchronicity about it: there was no way I could be a BMW tourist now. No, this ride was going to be about me and Betty.

7 BETTY

The flight to Adelaide was about to board. I got there just in time, the last in as the crew shut the door.

My window seat near the back was the only empty seat on the entire aircraft. It looked impossibly hard to fit into from the aisle. The guy in the aisle seat got up to let me do the sideways shimmy thing, breathing in. It's an interesting challenge to try to get into an economy class window seat without touching the headrest of your seat or the seat in front of you. Either I've grown or economy has shrunk in the last ten years.

I parked my arse, did up the buckle, looked out the window and contemplated how long I had to sit there. Only a few years ago I had been a real air traveller from one job to the next, racking up huge distances all over the world. It took many years to get my platinum frequent-flyer card. By that time I was only flying business class. Then I stopped working on the rigs, and before I knew it, bam, I was demoted. Just a few months earlier I'd finally got a crappy entry-level green card, back to where I'd started over twenty years earlier, and back in economy.

The realisation that I could no longer afford to be an airline snob came crashing down as I leaned forward to scan the contents of the seat pocket and discovered that the seat in front of me could recline into my face. The guy sitting beside me gave a sympathetic nod. 'Just as well it's not a long-haul flight.' He smiled, and stuck out his hand. 'Stephen,' he introduced himself.

'Paul.' I shook his hand, or rather jutted my palm out from my armpit and waved it up and down. We looked like two grown men attempting an impromptu impression of two tyrannosaurus rex thumb wrestling.

It turned out he knew of my books. 'What brings you to Adelaide?' he asked.

'Well, it's research.' I explained my plans, and his smile broadened.

'Well, I'm the Deputy Lord Mayor of Adelaide. I know the university well. How can I help?'

At the end of the flight, I stepped off the plane with Stephen telling me the lord mayor would probably be happy to wave me off at the start of my trip. This promised coverage on the local news, which would be great for my sponsors. Again the universe was surprising me.

I checked into the hotel, left my bags with the concierge and crossed the road. There in front of me was the University of Adelaide. I walked slowly through the campus grounds. The place was a joy to take in. Wonderful old buildings mixed well with their younger, more modern counterparts, generously spaced out with manicured tree-lined pathways. Bespectacled students hurried past me clutching folders and looking worried but intelligent. I called Colin on my mobile, and he directed me to his office.

A small group of students was standing in the doorway when I got there. As I approached they dispersed, filtering past me and out the door. Colin was standing in the middle of his office—which was exactly as I'd imagined it would look. Opposite the door was a large desk facing a window with masses of paper stacked on every surface; a coffee machine and a keyboard could barely be seen under all the books and paper. Across from the bookshelves on the left was an old well-used couch. A large whiteboard hung on the wall covered in technical drawings that looked to me like a map of the London Underground.

'Paul, welcome, I'm Colin Kestell.' Unlike his office, Colin did not look anything like I'd imagined. He was of medium height and build, looked younger than his years and was wonderfully frank in his conversation, spoken in that London accent. He was a lad at heart, one of the boys; I was instantly at ease.

Over the next few hours we went over my plan, then he suddenly stood up and said, 'Look, all this is just academic.' (I couldn't help smiling.) 'You need to ride the bike. Follow me,' he said.

On the way to see Betty, Colin took me on a brief tour of the mechanical engineering building. They had a vast array of resources, from full CAD design level to fabrication. If they'd wanted to, they could have built a bus from scratch, or a Transformer, or both.

I wish I'd had the chance to go to university when I was young, but that opportunity never presented itself. Where I came from, going to uni was not really an option; anyone who wasn't doing serious time or addicted to heroin was considered a high achiever.

We entered a large open-plan workshop full of milling machines, lathes, all manner of welding, drilling and cutting gear immaculately presented for the keen young student to play around with. Colin stopped by the open doors of a small window-lined room and stretched out his arm as if to make a formal introduction. 'There she is, Betty the Bio Bike.'

I walked into the room and stopped to look at her from a distance. She was bigger than I imagined.

'We had her stored in the basement,' Colin said. 'I asked the workshop guys to bring her out and prep her for you.'

I approached her the way cats do a new home. Then, circling her frame, I started firing questions at Colin. Soon I was on all fours poking my fingers inside the frame, and in less than a minute I was lying flat on my back looking at the drive system. The engine was bolted directly to the modified frame, which had to be widened to take the extra width of the heavy diesel single. There was no gearbox; to comply with the tight fabrication budget the students who built her three years earlier had opted for a Comet 500 series CVT (constant variable transmission) drive system instead of an expensive gearbox. The drive is transferred from the engine shaft by a spring-loaded round cup that extends towards the bike, squashing a rubber drive V-belt. The more you open up the throttle the faster the cup spins; the faster the cup spins the more the rubber drive belt is squashed; the squashing of the rubber belt expands it open, stretching it to the outer diameter of the spinning cup and thereby rotating it much faster. The rubber belt is connected in turn to the drive sprocket via a custom-made idler shaft system and from there via a conventional chain to the sprocket on the rear wheel.

Much like a golf cart or many modern scooter drive systems, Betty was simply twist and go; she looked like the easiest bike in the world to ride. Colin explained to me that the bio-fuel is corrosive and over time eats the fuel lines, so these were made from a very heavy-duty hose. She had a custom-made fairing and instrument cluster displaying speed on an old-school cable-driven analogue gauge that also contained an old rolling mechanical odometer, engine RPM, oil temp and battery voltage. Everything else on the bike was as per the original 1997 Cagiva W16.

The bike had been donated to the uni, as was the L100AE-DE Yanmar industrial engine—Japanese design but Italian built. It's an extremely common engine, found on irrigation pumps or in boats. Finding parts would be easy, as would troubleshooting on the side of the road. In terms of consumables everything was off-the-shelf gear available from major suppliers. She was running Pirelli MT90 tires, again Italian, 21-inch on the front and seventeen-inch on the rear.

Next I met Rob, Steve and Phil who worked in the uni's workshop—great guys. What a fantastic place this must be to study; I envied the students the opportunity to learn from people like Colin and men with real industry experience like the workshop guys. I thought teaching must be very rewarding, too. Colin was completely devoted to his craft, and after meeting some of his students I could see that they were impassioned by his method. 'His lectures aren't boring,' one student told me. I heard later that Colin once walked into his class dressed as a gorilla.

Colin had a helmet, jacket and gloves ready for me, and we rolled Betty out of the workshop. 'Off you go,' he said. 'Take it for a good run, Paul.'

I slotted the key into the ignition and turned it: the little red glow light came on; I hit the start button, and her starter motor sprang to life, the single piston pumping, her big round steel impeller spinning beneath its cover. As I twisted the throttle to get more fuel through the injectors I had to pull on the front brake to stop from lurching forward. Then it hit me, the most amazing aroma of cooking oil. It was an unmistakable food smell, a combination of fish 'n' chips and greasy fry-up. I turned in the saddle and looked down at the light grey smoke puffing in time with the engine's KA DONK, KA DONK, KA DONK.

I took Betty out of the university grounds and we cautiously circled the block, before exploring further afield. Her riding position was very upright. The foot pegs were low, and directly under my knees, like riding on a Vespa. Sitting there with my legs at a strange angle, I felt as if I were sitting in an office in a typing pool, rather than on a fairly big Enduro bike. Betty's handling characteristics were like nothing I'd felt before, but then again this bike was one of a kind. Her 160 kilos fell into corners halfway round on the right side, responding to minimal handlebar pressure more than any weight transfer. I assumed this was due to the big heavy impeller spinning at her centre of gravity. The opposite effect on the left had me hanging over and pulling her round. It wasn't until I got onto a highway that I really started to worry: the vibration through the entire front end was massive, like holding onto a jackhammer. But having said all that, she worked, and worked well. Her top speed was 70 kph, not too bad considering that on this first ride I travelled 100 kilometres on just 2.9 litres of used cooking oil and waste animal fats.

I pulled back into the university grounds that afternoon feeling both euphoric and more than a little worried. I was hopelessly out of my depth; even the janitor in that place had a better knowledge base on this stuff than me. Plus, Betty was only designed to get from Darwin to Adelaide. Now I was going to push the envelope and attempt to take her all the way round the continent. I knew it was a long shot, but what else was I going to do: fly home, forget the whole thing and mow the lawn? No way, this was a challenge.

There was no real choice for me anyway. This motorcycle worked, it was registered and insured, and most importantly, it was free.

I didn't need to be at the Clipsal until the following morning, so I suggested we go and have a celebratory drink. 'Sounds great,' said Colin. One of Colin's students, Kelly, came with us, as we wandered into the city. After a few drinks, Kelly had to leave; I grabbed a single malt and sat down, keen to talk more about Betty with Dr Kestell.

He was direct. 'Mate, Betty's a good bike. The kids who put her together got the right learning curve constructing her, the race they won from Darwin to Adelaide was just icing really. She was never intended to cover that kind of distance.' I sat back and said nothing.

'Look, from what you've told me, she's the only bike available. With enough spare parts you could make it.' He flipped over a coaster and pulled a pen from his top pocket. I shifted around to see what he was doing. *Total distance, roughly*, he scribbled. 'Average speed, right, that's less than half the working life of the engine.' I smiled. 'Just keep the oil topped up, order enough drive belts, sprockets and filters, and the rest is easy to get. We can even give you a spare engine and CVT drive.'

'What about the vibration?' I asked, and he shrugged.

'That engine is bolted to the frame, there's no quick cheap fix for that. You might want to think about changing the seat too, mate, there's no quick cheap fix for your arse either. Good luck to ya, cheers.'

This is possibly the silliest thing I've ever tried to do, I thought.

During the course of our conversation, I found out that Colin used to work for British Aerospace. 'What did you do there?' I was fascinated.

'I was on the team that designed the Exocet Missile System,' he said. Even I had heard of that. 'And the Martin-Baker Ejection Seat.'

I couldn't believe it. 'My father used one of them,' I said, and we sat there talking late into the night, the bar emptying out around us; only a few punters parked on stools bar-side sat nursing beers and what looked like troubled lives.

It turned out that Colin was far too interested in bikes to stop at Betty. 'Well, we're in the process of designing a bike to break the bio-fuel land speed record.'

I sat forward; the hairs on my arm stood up. That would *definitely* be the silliest thing I've ever tried to do. 'That's getting a bit serious, mate,' I said.

He smiled. 'Well, every aspect of it will be overseen by myself, and it's a great experience for the students—they get right into it.'

'Who's riding it?' I asked.

He could see the look in my eye. 'Well, no one yet.'

'You're in charge.'

He sipped his whisky. 'Mmm.' He nodded.

'And you used to be a rocket scientist,' I said.

'Well, I suppose you could put it that way.'

He knew what I was going to say way before I said it. 'I want to do it,' I said.

He finished his drink and eyeballed me through the bottom of his glass. I sat up straighter, and tried to look like a man responsible enough not to crash a bloody fast experimental bio-fuelled bike in a land speed record attempt. He leaned across the table and shook my hand.

8 GETTING TO KNOW YOU

The Clipsal 500 hit me the next morning. Southwell was wound up like a kid in a toy shop. He led me up into a private stand trackside, handed me a cold beer and beamed. 'You're gonna fuckin love this, mate.'

By the end of the first day I was happily pissed. I was also surprised at the sheer number of really hammered middle-aged guys I saw staggering about with empty beer cartons on their heads. One guy had a huge Holden flag tied around his neck; running flat out in his underpants across an open stretch of grass and yelling wildly his cape flapping behind him, he looked like a semi-naked overweight superhero. He was closely followed by 'Ford Man', also in a cape and underpants.

Shaun was in his element. We looked at the strippers, drank too much, put on silly hats, smoked cigars, and talked about cars, bikes, tits 'n shit. Clipsal might as well be called Man World.

'You know they limited everyone at Bathurst to one carton per day this year,' he leaned in to yell at me over the roar of the cars, spit hitting my inner ear. 'Heaps of blokes snuck in at night and buried cartons all over the place, then the next day there were hundreds of piss-heads wandering about with those collapsible shovels looking for their beer.'

I looked at him. 'That was you, wasn't it, mate?'

One day at the races was enough for me, though; the next day I was at the uni again, this time with my head in the High Performance Diesel Motorcycle (HPDM) project. At this stage it was physically nothing more than a car engine and a rear swing arm sitting on a big table, but the plans were impressive. The wiring harness alone spilling out of the engine was intimidating, like rainbow-coloured spaghetti hanging out in every direction. Each individual wire would have to be dealt with in order to get that engine started. I heard later that after weeks of testing, the students finally got it going by wiring up the cigarette lighter.

On my last night in Adelaide, Shaun and I sat down in a great little restaurant and actually had an intelligent, mature conversation. I was as surprised by this as he was. He was extremely supportive of my plans for Betty, as mad as it must have sounded to him. It was good to sit there and talk about our lives and futures; I saw a side of him that I suspect few people do.

The next day Colin saw me off back to Perth. We had made a plan for me to return in two weeks so I could spend a few days with Rob and Steve in the workshop getting familiar with Betty: practising changing out filters, lines, sprockets, injectors, blown tyres, chains, the idler shaft setup and the CVT drive—basically everything. I already had an extensive list of parts and consumables as well as complete detailed manuals for the bike engine—both would be put to good use after my next trip to Adelaide as Betty would then be freighted to Perth so I could get down to the business of pulling her to pieces and putting her back together again. I could practise changing out the entire engine if need be. For the first time since this idea raised its head and poked me in the eye, I was confident I could make it happen. I'd then put her in the back of the support truck, along with the spare parts, and drive from Perth to Adelaide, from where I'd start my journey the next day.

The two weeks dragged while I waited to return to Adelaide. On my first day back in the office I tried to remain focused on my job, and resisted the urge to jump on the phone and start organising; I couldn't wait to start planning. I came home from work to find that Clare, bless her, had gone to a specialty map store in the city and come home with an excellent, detailed map book of Australia as well as a giant fold-out map.

After supper I disappeared into the garage, opened up the fold-out map and lay on the floor looking at it. I had a rough idea of the route I wanted to take, but now I started to mark it out and break it up into various stages. I reckoned there would be seven in all, so I would need seven different support drivers, as no one person could take three months off work to accompany me. I listed some names in the corner of the map, opened a beer and picked up the phone. Now was as good a time as any to enlist my helpers. Six of the guys were old mates from the rigs, and then there was my father-in-law, Phil—he had to be there. We hadn't spent much time together other than the odd weekend visit, but I'd been sleeping with his daughter for the last seven years—it was about time I got to know the guy.

By the early hours of the morning I'd almost worked through my list. Waking guys up got me a great response: 'Do you know what fuckin time it is, Pauli?' But once they'd calmed down, they quickly got interested. There was a lot of laughter, a lot of 'You're gonna *what*?', but without fail they said yes.

Now, yes was good, yes works, but when it comes to guys who work in the oilfield, yes means shit. Not because the guy who says yes doesn't mean it, it's just that in the oilfield shit happens. In the last ten years I was working offshore I said yes to everything—weddings, Christmases, birthdays, funerals, armed hold-ups—but didn't actually make it to any of them. So the yes from the six who work in oil was taken with a bucket of salt.

Still, I was so grateful for their enthusiam; I would think that most people would consider themselves lucky if they could count on one hand the people that would do shit like this with them. During the course of my life I have managed to hold on to a small community of friends that will not only do this kind of shit with me, but often; without knowing it, again and again these guys save the day.

My support truck driver for the first stage—from Adelaide to Melbourne—was a bloke called Howard Fletcher who I met in Brunei back in 1995. He was now based in Brisbane, still in drilling but deskbound. Howard and I are the same age, same height, same build, and we've both got the same mad-keen motorcycle thing going on, but that's where the similarities end. Howard is quiet, calm, and doesn't fly off the handle like I do. He's also sound with mechanics and has bags of experience driving trucks, which is why I wanted to line him up first.

Second stage, Melbourne to Sydney, was supposed to be Neil Boath, a rig manager and rider, a typical hard-core drilling hand. I met him on a jack up in Bangladesh and we've been mates ever since. He said yes, but before the month was up Neil was sent to the Middle East and Shane Edwards stepped in. Shane is 40 years old and fitter than I was at twenty, another crazy rider. Shane's not oilfield, he doesn't take drugs, smoke, swear much, or fart in public, but he is one of the funniest blokes I've ever been drunk with. He's also one of those super-capable guys who can fix anything or anyone; he's generous to a fault and never late for anything. Most weekends Clare and I have breakfast with Shane and his wife Katrina, who's in possession of the most distracting cleavage in Western Australia. Her sense of humour often makes coffee come out my nose. Another friend at these breakfasts is Jools, who runs a funeral home, always looks amazing, spoils my daughter, and always has a story to tell. She's the woman you want to deal with you when you die; the thought of getting burned or embalmed by her sits well with me. I've always had a Sophia Loren fantasy that involved a bit of cooking and pain; it's just a shame that when it does finally happen, I'll be dead.

My father-in-law, Filthy Phil as I call him, was on board for stage three. He was only too happy to drive for me, which was great. I've got to set the record straight, though: Phil is only known as Filthy because every time I go over to visit him in Sydney he's in the back shed with his head in an engine and grease up to his ears. Filthy's shed is bigger than their house and goes beyond the realms of any man's world-shed scenario. It's a real working man's shed, with a classic vintage Plymouth project and enough spare parts, tools, and bits of man stuff to make Steptoe himself develop a man crush. He's even got his own forklift. Filthy is a talented man: he works as a panel beater, truck driver, mechanic and rebuilder of all things with wheels and engines. He knows the roads like the back of his filthy hand. He would get me from Sydney to Brisbane, no worries.

There's a driller who appears in my first book, a young, well-built maniac of a Scotsman by the name of Donald. Everyone else calls him Alistair. After sixteen years of knowing him, I still don't quite know why I call him Donald, though I really should know considering he's one of my closest mates. Once on an offshore drilling rig Donald was having a bad day on the drill floor and in a memorable moment picked up the tool pusher and attempted to throw him over the side and into the South China Sea. We managed to stop him, and that was the last time I stood next to Donald on a drill floor.

We had however remained close over the years, in an oilfield kind of a way, and by that I mean he'd be on a rig in Norway and I'd be on a rig in Africa and never did the twain meet, unless they happened to crew change from different sides of the planet through the same airport on the same day at the same time in the same departure lounge. Yes, you'd be surprised how often that happened. And once we'd rebooked our flights after missing our connections, sobered up and paid for any damages, we would go back to our different corners of the world until the next time the universe wanted a laugh. Much to my amazement, the last time we bumped into each other was one year ago right here in Perth, the most isolated city on the planet. I walked out of a lunch meeting at a Japanese restaurant with Westy, full of sake and with no memory of the business we'd sorted out in the first five minutes, and bumped straight into Donald. He had just arrived in town, and was working as a rig manager of a new build jack-up drilling in the northwest of the state. I was so happy to see his face, right there where I lived, and not in a blank airport in some shit hole. I knew that if there was anyone who would be fun to hit the road with, it would be Donald.

When I called him he said yes, and to his credit he did everything he could to get the time off. But through a chain of events that was beyond Donald's control, while I was on the road he had to push the button a man in his position never wants to push. The rig was evacuated as the well lost control and a sub-sea blowout crippled his operation.

My brother-in-law jumped in at the last minute to drive for

Donald on stage four, Brisbane to Darwin. I've already told you about Clare's older brother Mathew—musician, band manager, music lover and filmmaker. He's not at all what you're thinking: he's much, much worse. That's all I'm going to say about Matt for now.

Stage five—Darwin to Broome—Gavin Kelly. 'Fuckin Pauli, it's a bit fuckin late, mate.' He coughed for a full minute; Gav could smoke for Scotland. 'You better be on fuckin fire or some shit, mate, eh. What's gan on?' I ran my spiel past him, asked him the question. There was a pause. 'You want me te fuckin what?' I repeated my request, and there was another pause. 'Eh, what fuckin truck?' I told him again. 'Aye, OK, ne bother, mate. Hey I've got a fuckin truck licence as well, man.' I was happy. Even though he works in oil and is away a lot, if Gavin said yes, I just knew he was going to be there.

Southwell was a yes for stage six, Broome to Perth, but had to pull out because of—you guessed it—the oilfield. Again Clare's family jumped in to help; this time it was Clare's younger sister, Carrie, who's in the navy. She's a physical training instructor—still very much a lady but hard as fuck, and not what you're thinking—much, much better.

Last but not least was my old mate, Erwin Herczeg. I wanted him for stage seven, Perth back to Adelaide. Of course he said yes. Erwin's a company man now, a drilling manager; of course he was still offshore when his turn came.

By daybreak, the seven stages were marked out on the map, complete with dates, distances, places to overnight and get the truck serviced, and each of my seven support drivers. With Oswald making the odd visit, I had been in the garage all night, and now the morning sun cracked through the gaps between the door and the floor. I had worked it all out, or as much as I could.

I stood up, stretched, and drank a mouthful of cold coffee. I had to be at the office in two hours.

Clare came down the stairs carrying Lola and looking bemused. 'All night, honey, you need to rest.' She set Lola down and walked around the mess of paper and maps on the floor, my scribbles on everything; she could see I'd had some kind of breakthrough.

It had already been decided that Clare and Lola would come with me on the next trip to Adelaide as I wanted them to see what I had been doing. I'm truly blessed, my Clare is supportive and infinitely patient with me. I also love how she doesn't skirt around the edges of anything, she just dives right in. I often ask myself how I got so lucky.

'So we're going to Adelaide so you can practise on the bike,' she said now.

'Yup, the boys will walk me through everything, and I'll also get a good look at the HPDM project.'

She looked thoughtful. 'That's the speed bike for the salt flats, right baby? I don't like the speed project, it's too dangerous.' She looked over at Lola, who was busy fitting her dummy into the cat's ear.

'That bike is nothing like Betty,' I reassured her. 'It's very well engineered. I trust Colin, he's not going to hand over a machine that's not up to the task. Don't worry, everything will work out fine.' That's what I thought she needed to hear.

'I don't like it: you don't have any salt-flat riding experience and that bike is experimental.' She had that look in her eye.

'Look baby, it's going to be perfectly organised and as safe as we can make it.'

Safer than what? I thought privately. Putting on roller skates and strapping an Acme rocket to my back? Which reminded me, after our trip I had to fly from Adelaide to Sydney to sit down with Diggers and draft a will that would cover all scenarios.

Fortunately, Clare switched her attention back to my other crazy project. 'So you'll be going with the bike from here to Adelaide once you're ready?' She sat down on a box of oil filters.

I nodded. 'That's right.'

Lola, having successfully inserted her dummy into the cat's mouth, now picked up an axle bolt and stared beadily at poor Oswald's anus.

'Can we come with you in the truck instead of flying to Adelaide?'

I was pumped. 'That would be great, honey—are you sure?'

She laughed. 'Yeah, it'll be fun, our first family roadie.'

At that point Oswald let out a howl and then shot past us, Lola with the axle bolt in pursuit.

9 THERE IS NO PLAN B

The flight to Adelaide was soon upon us. Clare loves the place, and spent the two days we were there exploring with Lola. I liked Adelaide too. I could live there, even if for no other reason than it's closer to Sydney than Perth.

If I add up all the years on the rigs, I've spent two-thirds of my life somewhere else other than Australia. Staying in one place is a treat for me now, because for too many years I was just another expatriate, living in a country that wasn't mine. Living in the oilfield means living on the no-man's land of the rig and moving to a new country with every job. It does broaden the mind and your perception of life, and it puts a great deal into perspective. But after the crew has scattered it can leave you feeling alone and a little out of place at the ten-year oilfield family Christmas dinner.

Wherever I was, I would miss home, perhaps because of the way the oilfield and some cities just hem you in. I miss the open spaces and rich colour of Australia, and the vastness that you know is only a two-hour drive away if you need it. That empty space is there, it's big enough to swallow up all of Europe. That longing to be home would come into my mind and run on the hamster wheel for hours, I think because I spent so much of my life in the boxed-up world of life on a rig, where space is a valuable commodity.

In Adelaide, while Clare and Lola were sightseeing, I was back at the university. I was happy with the preparations for the ride. Thanks to Rob from the workshop, I had fuel filters, CVT drive belts, and a new battery.

Steve then walked me through his fabrication process on the HPDM. The bike was going to be a monster. Its frame weight was 75 kilos, the wheel base was 2.4 metres, with a Holden Astra turbo diesel engine plumbed into a Harley Dyna gearbox. The frame was—in a word—perfect; the engine sat balanced with only a few millimetres of clearance. I had already joined the DLRA—the Dry Lakes Racing Association. 'You're going to need proper leathers for the salt, mate.' Steve smiled.

The DLRA scrutineers would have to make several trips to the uni, making sure the bike conformed to their rule book. The plan was that the bike would go to Speed Week in March 2011 and start speed trials at Lake Gairdner, South Australia.

I was captivated by the amount of enthusiasm and skill behind this motorcycle. The students were as fascinating to talk to as the staff. They sat me down in a huge room filled with computers and showed me the computational fluid dynamics software that produced the fairing design. I couldn't wait to ride this thing one day.

Colin and I talked through the HPDM project, his office coffee helping my brain to keep pace with his stream of motorcycle consciousness. We slowly worked out a plan for our week on the salt in two years. Then he took me back to see the engine running on a dyno test setup operated by his students. The engine looked strange mounted in a steel jig in the test room. We were all wearing industrial hearing protection, staring at it from behind glass. 'Increase rpm, more air.' One of Colin's students sat in front of a bank of computers turning dials, his eyes darting from one screen to another. 'Max power,' he said. The engine was screaming in its frame. Their calculations—encompassing the distance I had to get up to speed before the speed trap in the flying kilometre, versus the bike's weight, drag, max power, acceleration, gearing—had me getting to 260 kilometres per hour at best, not enough to beat the American who currently held the land-speed record for a bio-diesel motorcycle at 267 kph. I thought about going on a diet.

The class was unfazed by this, however; everyone simply focused on working through the problem, charging into conversations I couldn't keep up with, so I nodded and smiled, fiddled with the change in my pocket and ended up thinking about naked cheerleaders cavorting in jello with a giant beach ball.

Whatever the outcome would be, I was just happy to get the opportunity to spend time with the students and guys like Colin and the fellas in the workshop, especially Rob. He was a fountain of knowledge and couldn't do enough to help me with my preparations to ride Betty. On our last night we all had a beer together. The spares were boxed up and Betty was ready for her freight trip over to me in Perth. 'See you in a month,' I called as the cab pulled away that night.

From Adelaide, we flew to Sydney, where Clare and Lola caught up with her family and I went to see my lawyer to draft my will.

Diggers' office was comfortable. Soft light from the warm sunset spread an orange glow over his bookshelves; I could smell the sea. He gathered up some paperwork and offered me a drink. 'Just a coffee, thanks mate,' I said.

'I'll be right back,' he said.

I had my eyes closed for a moment, tired from the week's running around; a wind chime nearby made my lids heavier. When he came back in, the smell of fresh coffee filled the air. He sat down, crossed his legs and regarded me. 'Let's begin. I'm going to ask you some direct questions, Paul. I want honest, direct answers, is that OK?'

The process took a few gruelling hours. His manner was relaxed but you could tell the wheels were turning. Designing a will is important for everyone, and I didn't find any of it confronting, but it raised my buried worries about the element of risk in what I was planning to do. What if something *did* happen? I thought about the risks I was taking in riding Betty and leaving my girls alone for three months. I thought about the danger of the speed trials, the possibility of serious injury or death. The shadows in Diggers' office filled up with doubt.

I rubbed my eyes. 'I'll take that drink, mate, if you don't mind.'

'Not at all,' he said, and poured me a whisky. 'We're almost finished.' He went over the paperwork between the university and me, then closed his file and sat back. 'You're all set. If something goes wrong now, is there a plan B?'

I laughed. 'No mate, it's plan A or back to work.'

'Right. Well, good luck and be careful.' Diggers raised his mug.

'Cheers, mate.' I finished my drink.

'Don't mention it.'

He had brought up every possible scenario and we'd talked each one through. I was at ease now. I knew that no matter what, my girls would be OK.

The next morning I had a few hours to myself, so I jumped on a bus and headed off to my mate Dare's motorcycle shop. Well, shop is not the right word; 'complete mecca for bike enthusiasts' would be more appropriate.

It'd been about five years since Dare went into partnership with his mate Rod and opened Deus Ex Machina (God From The Machine), two storeys of homage to all things motorcycle. I remember the day he first acquired the building, formerly a furniture store covering a whole corner block of Sydney's busy Parramatta Road. Dare had also just purchased what would be the shop's main countertop—an entire intact ten-pin bowling alley lane. It weighed a ton; a huge group of us staggered across Parramatta Road with this gigantic wooden thing, and getting it through the front door was a nightmare. But now it looks fantastic, sitting proudly in the middle of the shop.

Between them Dare and Rod have carved out a nice niche in the bike world. Whenever I visit I always end up spending the whole day there. After a few years they opened an excellent instore café, so now you don't even have to leave for lunch. One half of the main shop sells clothing; they've also got an extensive bookshop, and as far as the bikes go, well, they sell stock machines, full custom builds, classic bikes and bicycles as well. Like I said, it's heaven on a stick for motorbike fanatics like me.

Sooner or later, I always end up in the workshop. The man then running the show was another mate of mine, Matt Bromley. He was a Perth boy, a doting father and a complete genius in front of a motorcycle. I've learned a lot from Matty; he's patient and methodical, his machines are perfect in every way.

This was a typically busy midweek day in Deus. I wandered in and ran straight into Dare and Ben, the store manager. We had coffee while I ran through my plans for the trip. They both jumped in with their usual enthusiasm for anything a bit different.

'When you pass through Sydney, make sure you stop by. Matt will service the bike and Taka can organise any spares you need,' said Ben, smiling.

'Why don't you have a chat to Taka and Matt now?' added Dare. His relaxed aura is palpable. When Dare's not messing about on bikes he's all about surfing, and he's got that surfer's calm about him. He reminds me of Erwin; they both have that vibe of appearing to be completely relaxed and yet capable of anything at the same time.

Following their suggestion, I made my way over to see Taka. Taka is Deus's one-man parts encyclopedia. A Japanese national who made Sydney his home some years back, his English is faultless and his brain box goes at a million miles an hour. As soon as I started telling him about Betty he knew exactly what I was on about, and asked to look at my spares list. He pointed out several items I hadn't thought of and was off like a shot to order them for me.

Matty Bromley was exactly where I expected to find him, out the back with his head in a frame and a coffee perched on his workbench. He was full of good advice as well. I was very grateful to know if I did have any problems during the trip I could count on help from the Deus guys. Matt asked about Betty's fuel and air filters; we talked about the oil, the tyres, and he gave me the number of a guy who sells these amazing air cushion seats. 'Mate, you're going to need to get one of these seats, that Cagiva will shred your arse before you get as far as Sydney.' He paused and placed the end of the ratchet he was holding against his chin. 'What's the vibration like?'

I laughed. 'Horrible.'

'Hmmmm.' He walked back to his workbench, past the other mechanics zoned into their work. 'I could go to town on it, mate, but it's going to take some time; what's your budget like?'

I knew I didn't have the time or the funds to get the bike over to Matty to play with before I set out, and I also knew he'd end up building a whole new bike once he started. 'Nah mate, can't do it.'

'Well, no worries, Pauli, we'll look after you when you come through.'

I told him about the website Quail TV had set up, and we tapped into the web; Matt laughed when he saw the picture of Betty on the laptop screen, then leaned in to get a look at her engine. 'Jesus, Pauli, you're keen, mate. Is this some sort of payback for all those years on the rigs or what?' I smiled. 'What's the top end power like, lots of torque from that diesel?'

'It sits on 70 at 3000 rpm on a flat road.'

He was deep in thought. 'How many teeth on the drive sprocket?'

'Forty-four,' I said.

'OK, we'll order you a 39-tooth rear sprocket—it'll be here in an hour or so. Take it back to Perth and see if it gives you more speed.' He explained that if we changed down a tooth on the drive sprocket the CVT drive might start to slip, but five teeth down on the rear drive sprocket should give me perhaps ten kilometres per hour more speed. We had some lunch and talked bikes, babies (he's a new father too) and the HPDM project. I asked Matty if he was up for a trip to the salt to have a go on the speed bike. 'Mate, I'm in,' he said. 'They're all nutters at Speed Week.'

We shook hands and I jumped in another cab to the airport, sprocket in hand, feeling good about everything. I'd put some fears to rest, faced down some internal dragons, been warmed by the generosity of old friends, and even better, had possibly gained another ten kph.

10 PPPPPP

A wise man once said: Proper Planning Prevents Piss Poor Performance.

Two weeks after we got back from Sydney, Betty turned up at my house. I wheeled her off the back of a truck and into the middle of my garage. She sat there surrounded by motorcycles and shelves of bike gear. I prepared to disassemble her, and Clare's car was relegated to the driveway. Each night after work was wholly devoted to this, while my weekends were spent drafting letters to potential sponsors. During the two weeks I'd been waiting for Betty to arrive I'd written reams of emails and letters.

Right at the beginning of the worst global financial crisis since the Second World War, I was running around asking the oil industry for money. Yeah, I know, excellent timing. Our government was about to start handing out free money, calling it a 'stimulus package'. I lay on the garage floor under the bike and listened to late night radio, stunned. When not on the drill floor, I've lived in this marvellous country for the last 25 years. Whether here or overseas Australians are doers, we get things done, we can deal with anything. Why was the Rudd government giving a nation famous for its adaptability and hardiness a giant cash dummy?

I'm not qualified to ramble on, but I also couldn't believe the power brokers who head up the world's banking systems had let it get to this. My cat could offer better guidance on the merits of lending money to people you know cannot repay it, but these people—who, I assume, hold MBAs, earn seven-figure salaries, and have a corner office—thought it was a great idea. We were all going to pay for it, one way or another, further down the line. But this particular financial pandemic was causing me problems right here and now. Suddenly, no one was interested in backing me. I thought about selling one of my bikes to help pay for the project, and my publisher offered to give me an advance on future book sales, but I was reluctant to go down those paths. I was despondent. All I had was an idea and the bike.

To do this trip I'd worked out I needed to raise $100,000. I had to find a support truck and rig it out with a cage, ramp, wheel brace, shelves, two 400-litre custom baffled fuel cells with proper electric fuel pumps, separate power, cover it with a good tarp, then get appropriate signs on it. Add to that bike-repair tools, a mountain of spares for Betty, including a spare donor bike, communications gear, insurance, accommodation, flights, food—the list went on and on.

Then to my complete surprise, during the week I spent in my garage pulling the bike apart each night, I landed seven sponsors totalling $85,000. The oil community in Western Australia got behind me—not the big players, but the smaller firms. I was amazed and humbled, especially since I knew giving that much was a big deal to them. To a big multi-national that's not a great deal of money—their budget for paperclips would be bigger than that. But to these small service companies and third party firms it was a significant outlay.

Still, it was going to be tight; everything would be second-hand but it had to look decent. The donor bike was the hardest thing to find. Cagiva sold very few W16 Enduro bikes in Australia twelve years ago. Eventually I started looking overseas but had no luck. In desperation, I wrote to Cagiva asking for the landed cost of a frame, front forks, triple clamp, bars, controls, levers, swing arm, wheels, tank, seat and a partridge in a Cagiva tree; the sum they quoted me was horrendous.

I gave up and started looking for a truck, all the while organising agreement letters, accommodation bookings, flights, ordering spare parts plus patches for my jacket and stickers for the truck and bike with all the sponsors' brands in the right size and format, and managing negotiations between my publisher and the production company. As well, late into the night I tinkered on Betty until she was completely disassembled. On occasion Lola helped by picking up a nut or bolt and eating it.

A support truck was proving tricky to find too; it had to be a dual cab to accommodate the driver, the cameraman and the large amount of filming gear he'd need to access from the cab. It also had to be over three tonnes but registered to drive on a car licence because only two of my seven support drivers had a truck licence. All in all, my requirements meant finding the right truck was as likely as finding a clean signed pair of Jeremy Clarkson's favourite driving panties in the specials bin at Coles.

But I couldn't let it bog me down, I couldn't stop, because the minute I did it would all look too hard, especially with a full-time job, and a wife and child to spend time with. During this period, there was no time for anything other than work, family, trip. I missed everything else, especially sleep. My garage looked like someone had set off a bomb in a bike parts warehouse.

Lola was now eighteen months old, and already displaying character traits that I found so familiar. Her new doll, a present from her aunty Jools, was abandoned in the corner; she was more interested in how fast her pram would go. Lola would often join me in the garage, handing me spanners and bashing things while chattering to me. None of it made real sense yet, but it was her sweet voice and interest in what I was doing that cracked me up. 'Daddy, Nemo, Wiggles, Dada, HEY, BIKE DADA BIKE, no, no cheeky . . .' BANG, BANG, BANG. I'd look around and she'd be swinging a wrench down onto her mother's new car. As soon as I turned around again she'd be off, her legs a blur as she races down the hall waving my wrench over her head. I'd come back later to discover sultanas, crayons and a dummy shoved up the car exhaust. I know she has my temper, but I hope as the years go by she also has my internal early-warning system and bullshit detector. I hope she takes life by the balls, and any boys that come around too.

Right when I needed it the most, it happened again: in one week I found both the perfect truck and a pristine Cagiva W16 garaged since new with only 3000 k's on the clock. Even better, both were in Australia and both were available for the right price. The truck was ex-council, downgraded and registered to drive on a car licence, four-tonne capacity, dual cab, with a nice flat tray. I picked up the bike for half the cost of the spares quote from Cagiva. It arrived, again on the back of a truck, and again I wheeled it into the crowded garage next to its environmentally friendly Frankenstein counterpart.

I stood there with a cold beer looking at the two bikes. Just to know what it felt like I threw a new battery into the spare-parts bike, changed out the spark plug, flushed the lines and carby, cleaned the filters, siphoned out some fuel from one of my other bikes and started it up. The Ducati-built four-stroke 600 single thumped to life; I waited till early the following morning to take it out for a thrashing. It was a good bike—pity I had to pull it apart for parts.

An old oilfield mate, Ross Luck, jumped in with an offer to fabricate the cage to cover the tray. I rolled up with the truck and sat down in his office. Ross doesn't mince his words; he instantly knew what I wanted and began drawing out the finished unit on a pad before I could say, 'Where should I put the fuel cells?' He spaced everything out for optimum weight distribution, and included rubber-lined brackets to brace the fuel cells, and side-lockable ports to pull the bowser-style pump handle through, so I could fill up the bike without having to open up the back of the truck and turn on the pumps. All I would have to do is pull up on the left or right side of the truck, open the port, reach in, flick on the fuel pump, pull out the bowser handle and fill the bike up. 'Don't forget to alternate your sides, so the tanks drain at equal rates,' Ross instructed. He included shelving, and even a special swivel seat that Dan the cameraman could install so he could film safely from the back of the truck. The doors lifted off and stowed down one side. The seat had a heavy welded shaft that slotted into what looked like 3½-inch tubing welded directly to the chassis; it had a safety chain and a four-point harness.

'You could tow another truck from the back of this chair, mate,' said the welder, another Paul. He did a remarkable job;

every aspect of Ross's design was faithfully reproduced down to the finest detail. I was overjoyed.

Next I rode Betty to Ross's workshop, and we pushed her up the ramp into the wheel clamp. It was a perfect setup, custom made for the bike. Five minutes later Ross and Paul had pulled the brakes apart and remade them, boosting my angle on the pedal and beefing up the steel. Ross took her for a blat around the block. He came back laughing—he usually gets around on a Harley Night Train. It must have been like sitting on a lawn mower.

Practice makes perfect, provided of course you have the right parts. I drilled myself over and over again on changing tyres, chains, sprockets, filters, the whole lot. Betty and I went for ever longer rides from Perth. I was getting to know her, and discovering that many of her character traits were—how can I put this?—less than ideal. Betty was loud, so loud people walking down the street 50 yards away would turn to see what was making that bizarre noise. This was often followed by an open-mouthed stare and the question: 'Mate, is that thing a diesel?' Riding Betty past a group of people waiting roadside for a bus was a cringe-making, loud, smelly and smoky experience; the combination of her rank green colour, noise and exhaust fumes was as repellent as you could imagine.

I also did my research on riding gear. I was going to encounter rain, wind and temperatures ranging from freezing up to 50 degrees Celsius, so I needed a good full-face helmet, gloves for the cold weather and the heat, fully armoured boots and riding pants. The choice out here is literally mind-numbing and shop assistants do my head in. In the end I settled for a combination of the gear I've always used and trusted and some new gear.

One evening I came home with the CB radio communications, a simple setup consisting of three hand-held CB units.

One could be plumbed into the helmet via Velcro flat speakers with a mouthpiece and a small push-to-talk button that would go on the left handlebar grip. There was one unit for the truck driver and one for the cameraman to use when he was in the back of the truck or filming by the side of the road; that way we could all talk to each other all the time. I'm usually one of those guys who has to play with the new thing before examining the instructions. 'RTFM,' Erwin used to say after I'd complained about some new toy not working: Read The Fuckin Manual. This time I did. Standing on my front lawn in pyjama pants and a new white full-face helmet with carefully attached communication wiring, a shiny new CB radio in my hand, I pressed the push-to-talk button. 'Honey, can you hear me?' Clare was in the living room halfway through another classic episode of *So You Think You're Too Fat?* and wasn't replying. There was nothing, just static. I pressed the button again. 'Hey babe, you hearing me, over?'

Nothing. A bus went past, full of people staring at me. 'Hey love, baby, come in.' I cranked the volume knob. 'Hey baby, I've got my helmet on, can you hear me or what?'

'I CAN HEAR YOU, MATE.' A deep man's voice came booming into my head. I doubled over in pain, fumbling for the volume knob. 'SO WHERE'S YOUR HONEY?'

Clare came on: 'Hi love, over, who was that, was that you?'

'THE NAME'S EARL, SWEETHEART.'

I'd forgotten it was a regular open CB, so anyone on channel 44 or scanning would have heard me. No doubt he was some truckie, probably rolling down the freeway behind our house. 'Arggh, make him go away,' Clare groaned. She was standing at the window laughing at me.

The last few things came together quickly: the tarp to cover the cage, a two-tonne trolley jack, an extra spare wheel for the truck, plus a few small items like a GPS and a mini fridge for the cab. Mates from the oilfield started calling with offers to help, and thanks to them I was able to keep my costs down. Doing some experimental filming, we discovered that Betty's rank lime-green colour was overpowering my sponsors' stickers on screen, so my mate Goldie jumped in with an offer to re-spray her. I had stripped the spares bike by then so he did the whole lot, two black sets of everything, perfect job. Black Betty was reborn with a new diesel heart transplant, ready to take on a whole continent.

11 TO ADELAIDE AND BEYOND

Dan Stevenson, the cameraman, arrived in Perth four days before our scheduled departure. Dan is in his early thirties, and has loads of experience doing this kind of fly-by-the-seat-of-your-pants filming. He's calm, creative and thoughtful but, as I was to find out, very, very forgetful.

I knew everything worked, but what I didn't know was if it would all work together. We needed to practise, Dan in the special filming seat, camera harness and comms on, me riding behind the truck, and both of us in communication with the driver. I called my mate Dave and asked him if he could spare the time to drive the truck all over the place while we got used to the gear. He came straight over. Like most of my mates Dave's an oil man. He's mad on his car, a brand-new Audi R8; the truck must have been punishing for him in comparison.

During our run-through we had a few dramas. At first I couldn't hear Dave but Dan could. Dave would brake while I was too close to the back of the truck and I almost ended up in Dan's lap several times. But eventually we made it work.

The next day I had to drop Ossy the cat off at the cat hotel, his new home for the next three months. We had taken him to the vet a few weeks earlier as he was doing some seriously weird shit. He was starting to look a bit haggard as well, like an elderly bum had just been reborn as a cat. It was $600 worth of blood tests and check-up.

When we returned with Ossy to get the results, the vet gave us that sympathetic smile. Oh dear, I thought, he's gonna give us the sleepy needle speech. But no. Ossy's blood work had come back revealing the bastard was built like a freight train. 'He's a big boy; when he was young he must have looked more like a dog disguised as a cat.' The vet strained to lift Ossy's bulk up onto the counter. 'He's around nineteen, but could last another five years—all his organs are working fine. Considering his history he's in great shape physically, but his hearing is very impaired. Also, his erratic behaviour and night terrors are classic signs of cat dementia.'

'What?' I looked down at Ossy. A small string of cat drool was about to connect his head to the countertop.

'Cognitive dysfunction syndrome,' the vet said.

'OK, so he's going mad,' I said.

Clare jumped in. 'He's just an old man, honey.'

The vet smiled and stroked the back of Ossy's head. 'Look, he could settle down or stay the same, or it could get much worse. Just monitor him and come back if you think you need to.' Ossy was now crashed out next to the fax machine on the counter, looking like a bum next to a dumpster. We took him home.

Let me explain what the vet meant by erratic cat behaviour. Ossy would wake up at 2 a.m., walk into our bedroom, come over to my side of the bed and let go with a series of howls that our neighbours could hear. This was dementia cat speak for:

'WHAT THE FUCK AM I DOING HERE? . . . I DON'T KNOW WHO I AM . . . NO, WAIT, I'M A WELDER FROM NEWCASTLE.' I would wake up with a start, and in the meantime Ossy would walk into Lola's room, and let go with another howl—'WHAT THE FUCK'S GOING ON WITH ALL THIS GIANT FURNITURE?'—from directly underneath her cot, so she would start howling too, and now the two tenors would begin their impromptu sold-out concert. Clare and I took it in turns to deal with it.

Calming my daughter down involved the search and retrieval of one of her two compulsory sleep dummies. She's got a hell of an arm on her, so I never found them in the cot, but on top of her wardrobe or pegged halfway down the hall. While I was rocking her on my shoulder in the dark and looking for said dummy, Oswald would see me, stop mid-howl and say to himself, 'Oh . . . that's right . . . I'm a domestic cat, I live here with this bald idiot and his mental family. Shit, I'm going back to bed.' I've seen his face at this moment; you could see the realisation come crashing down. He'd walk off slowly towards his bed. 'Fucking humans,' he mumbles under his kitty-cat breath. Two hours later the whole thing would start again. 'WHY IS IT DARK? . . . WHO THE FUCK AM I?'

That's not to say he wasn't affectionate, though he chose his moments. One night, after working on the bike till very late, I found myself asleep on the toilet at 3 a.m. I woke up, my eyes struggling to focus, and looked down to see the old cat curled up in the nest of jocks and trousers between my ankles, his bulky frame spilling over the edges and his drool everywhere.

So you'll likely sympathise when I say I had a twang of separation anxiety as I pulled away from the cat hotel. Even in the car with the aircon on and the engine running, I could hear Ossy protesting from his new digs. The cats next door to his fenced room were considerably smaller than him, and they all had the same reaction to his arrival, scooting off to hide under their beds. I hoped the crazy old bastard would still be around when I got back.

I could hardly believe it was 1 August 2009, but the time had finally come. Dan was ready to film us leaving. He would then fly back to Sydney and six days later come to Adelaide with 200 pounds of filming gear, ready to spend the next three months on the road with me, poor bastard. I had a good feeling about Dan: he could go the distance, and most importantly he had a great sense of humour.

Now he quietly went about assembling his huge pile of kit while we ran around trying not to forget things. One of the last-minute jobs was properly tethering Lola's baby seat to the back seat of the truck. There was a portable DVD player mounted behind the driver's headrest so she could watch her movies and hopefully not scream the cab down all the way to Adelaide. By mid-morning we finally had everything squared away. The truck was clean and organised, with everything in its place, everything accounted for and working. I would never see it like that again.

This was it: departure time. I wasn't going to see my home again until I rode Betty through Perth on the way back to Adelaide. Our neighbours came out to see us off. Nick and Gorga are great people, we're lucky to have such a cool couple living next door. They would keep an eye on our place while we were away, empty the letterbox, mow the lawn—the usual stuff. Nick and I had sat in his backyard the night before, drinking whisky and talking till late. He's a good laugh, always the optimist. 'Don't worry about the house, mate, we're going to turn it into a roller disco next week, I'm gonna flog your bikes and have sweet rave parties in your garage.'

Right, had I thought of everything? I went through my list, mentally ticking things off in my head. Standing on my driveway, the sun beating down on me, I knew that everything that could be done, had been done. Lola was in her seat already plugged into The Wiggles, Clare was hugging Gorga, and Dan was standing on our front lawn patiently holding his camera. I was ready, the truck was full of fuel, spare tyres, food, water, the sat phone, CB radio, sat nav, and enough spare parts and tools to give MacGyver a boner.

Finally, the first part of this journey was beginning. As we pulled out into our quiet street, I felt my sense of adventure flare up; my pilot light was back on.

Perth's suburbs drained away fast. Clare and I talked and talked, our conversation going all over the place. Before long we had trundled past Southern Cross. We both stopped talking simultaneously at the crest of a hill. The straight road rolled under the truck's cab in silence. Ahead, blacktop line into infinity. The heat haze washed it with mercury silver sheen. Even though it was bumpy and we were doing 110 kilometres an hour it felt like we were standing still. 'Shit babe, it's a long way to Adelaide,' Clare said, turning to check on our daughter. The Wiggles had put Lola out cold in the back.

I know about riding a bike in the heat, but driving an air-conditioned truck at the speed limit is an entirely different experience. Betty was going to be the slowest thing on the road and that would be frustrating and dull. Plus riders like corners and hills, and the Great Eastern Highway is short on both.

We rolled into Norseman that evening off the Coolgardie–Esperance Highway, checked into a motel, and all three of us fell into a vast still sleep; the 700 k's had zapped our energy. In the morning Clare got the coffee going while Lola climbed onto my chest and prised open an eyelid. 'Cheeky Daddy,' she said. I had to get up and start the day. After a daybreak roadhouse breakfast, a refuel, and a quick check of oil, water, tyre pressure, we hit the road again.

If I'd thought the previous day was a dull prospect for a motorcyclist, well, the second day was worse. The Eyre Highway was the road equivalent of a doctor's waiting room without the two-year-old copies of *Woman's Day*.

We stopped to refuel in Balladonia; Lola made friends with a puddle of diesel—clearly she's my daughter—and then we spent half an hour cleaning her up. We ate petrol station sandwiches that had an interesting diesel aftertaste, and climbed aboard for more of the same. This particular stretch of the Eyre Highway, around 150 k's, is Australia's longest straight road. I was so happy to have my girls there with me; doing this journey by myself would have been painful otherwise. There were some drawbacks though. Lola by now had watched *Finding Nemo* close to six times and she was nowhere near bored with it. As a consequence, Clare and I can recite that entire movie verbatim—that, and we know every song in The Wiggles' repertoire.

Somewhere between the end of the long straight bit and our destination for the night at Madura Pass, Lola had a massive freakout. She went from fast asleep to ballistic in a nanosecond. I would ordinarily just put this down to what we had heard other parents describe as the 'terrible twos'—those times when your sweet little toddler is smiling and chatting one minute, and seconds later is possessed and biting, arms thrashing wildly. Our little girl is no exception: I was starting to consider shaving her head to look for the three sixes. But this time I could sympathise with her.

We pulled over and discovered her slumber had been disturbed by a cockroach. It had probably crawled into our open cooler bag last night in the motel. While Lola was passed out in front of *Finding Nemo*, the insect had made an attempt at circumnavigating the top of her head. Now, Lola's usually unfazed by insects, and picking them up for a closer inspection is normal. This often progresses into a simple hand crush to see what they look like on the inside, or she goes full Bear Grylls mode and just flat-out eats them, with all Bear's facial expressions. (We love watching Bear Grylls' TV show *Man vs Wild*; Lola in particular loves it, especially when Mr Edward Grylls eats insects.) However, this was her first contact with a cockroach. She had woken up, managed to grab the beasty, and then gone bananas.

It appeared that along with a love of diesel and axle bolts, Lola could have inherited my fear of cockroaches. We all have a thing, don't we? You might be freaked by snakes or rats or sharks, but my freakout is the humble roach, closely followed by spiders. I can deal with everything else, and over the last twenty years I've woken up in various Third World jungles to find all manner of beasties biting, burrowing or feeding on me, both externally and internally. But it was a cockroach that caused my record freakout.

After my wife had dealt with the roach, we climbed back into the cab and pushed on. Clare was laughing, clearly reminiscing about a horrible moment in my past. 'I'll never forget that night . . .' She smiled at me sympathetically.

'Hmm.' I shifted uncomfortably behind the wheel and started brushing off imaginary roaches.

Four years earlier I was working a rotation in Japan, on a land rig in Hokkaido. I had just flown back into Australia for my days off, ready to have some fun. We had accepted an invitation to spend a night at a friend's parents' holiday home an hour out of Sydney. Simon and Sally are always a great laugh, so Clare and I were really looking forward to a good catch up, no doubt an excellent meal, and some very fine wine. Our evening unfolded as expected. Simon cooked, Sally had me laughing so much I got hiccups, we all hammered the wine and ate too much, and ended up around a huge fireplace with Simon's 25-year-old single malt before wandering off to bed at midnight, happily pissed.

The house was massive, and our room was on the ground floor, near the kitchen. I was still pissed but woke suddenly in fright, kicking the covers off the bed. I can't remember much about it, but Clare said I was on all fours and completely rigid, my eyes wide in panic.

'There's something in my head,' I apparently screamed.

Right, so you get the picture. She's thinking, 'Oh perfect, now I find out he's actually completely mental.' I'm still blurry on this part, but somehow she ascertained that I wasn't having a psychotic episode.

I was by now rolling about on the floor, both hands cupped over my head, demanding something I could poke into my left ear. My frantic wife took off down the hall, doing the Tom Cruise sock slide into Simon's parents' holiday home kitchen where she started madly riffling through drawers. I was by now completely sober and in ridiculous amounts of pain. The horrible realisation that something had crawled right into my ear, and was now attempting to burrow through my eardrum and into my brain, was making me crazy.

Clare burst into the bedroom with a meat skewer in her hand. 'WHAT THE FUCK BABE, I'M NOT JAMMING THAT FUCKING THING INTO MY EAR,' I screamed. I was convulsing and slapping my hand against the left side of my head. The insect or whatever it was seemed intent on moving forward. It was, in a word, terrifying.

'CALM DOWN, I NEED TO WAKE UP SALLY,' Clare shouted at me. I must have looked out of my mind, because she took off again. She reappeared next to me with a fistful of uncooked spaghetti, and was off up the stairs to wake our hosts.

I shoved the end of a stick of the spaghetti into my ear. This made whatever was in there only more determined. I could feel lots of sharp legs madly scrambling, and every few seconds something hit my eardrum. You know when you're fiddling about in your ear with a Q-Tip and you push it in just a bit too far, and it bloody hurts? Right, well imagine hitting the end of that with a hammer, and that's what it felt like. I was beside myself with fear, pain and spaghetti. Simon and Sal came running in, wearing what looked like each other's underwear. 'Jump in the car mate,' Simon said, trying to sound sober.

I ran out to the dark winter driveway, twitching wildly. Sally rang ahead to tell the local emergency room there was a disturbed bald man in his underwear about to arrive with something digging a hole through his head.

The drive was only a few miles, but it might as well have been to the moon as far as I was concerned. Panic started to shoot waves of adrenalin through my body as we pulled into the small hospital, the two main doors and big red emergency sign flooding the car park in fluorescent light. Simon leaped from the car and ran inside. Clare opened the car door for me and I sprang into the cold like a wild man. The doctor on duty that night was waiting just inside the entrance; he simply gestured me towards an open doorway. Clare sat down in the waiting room with Simon, who looked drunk but appropriately concerned.

I stood in the little examination room staring at the eye chart on the opposite wall and nervously hopping from toe to toe while the doctor sauntered in and casually closed the door, regarding me with a whimsical look. 'Right, you've got an insect in your ear then.'

I twitched, my eyes big and crazy. I closed the gap between us, put both hands on his shoulders. 'Get it out, for fuck's sake.'

He straightened up instantly, all humour gone. 'Don't worry, Mr Carter. Over to the bed and sit down, please.'

I leaped onto the bed. 'Call me Paul. Just get it out, Doc.'

He produced one of those black trumpet-shaped scope things with the little light, pulled down on my lobe and poked in the scope. As his head drew close to the lens he jerked back. 'Whoa,' was all I heard.

'What the fuck is it?' I asked.

He put down the scope. 'Well, there's a big cockroach in there, but don't worry, first we're going to drown him with oil, then we can remove him.'

'Whaddya mean *drown* him? It doesn't need to look like an accident—why don't you send in a hit man? Drown him in oil, what do you mean in oil? I work in oil. What kind of oil? Why fuck about with a drowning? Just use a gun—even better, there's a meat skewer back at the house . . .' I was raving, but he was already gone. I sat there for what seemed like forever. My new friend, sensing he was in real trouble, began scratching around even harder. The doc came back with a giant turkey baster full of warm vegetable oil. He had to sit on my head to keep me still while a nurse squirted the oil into my ear.

The roach went into his death throes while he slowly suffocated. The doc held on while I screamed and bucked wildly. The nurse held the examination bed down while the doc enjoyed his first human-head rodeo; he rode for the full eight seconds before dismounting and straightening out his hair. I lay there twitching in unison with my newly drowned friend.

His oil-covered cadaver came out in two pieces. Rejoined, he was an inch long. I took him back to the house in a biohazard container to show everyone.

Just before I went back to the rig, Clare and I were getting ready for bed and I wandered into the bedroom and stretched out on top of the bed. Just as she came in and turned off the light a Bondi roach flew through the open window like a bronzed hockey puck with wings, and landed on my chest. I lost him behind the wardrobe twenty minutes and several failed attempts to kill him later. Sleep came eventually after stuffing my ears full of toilet paper.

Back on the road to Adelaide, we made regular stops to stretch our legs and point at nothing. The odd dingo mooched about looking for a handout. There was a roadhouse every 200 kilometres or so. Clare fell asleep; Lola was still fixated on *Finding Nemo* and I let my mind wander. There was going to be a lot of this to come, I thought. It's a hard barren place out there. I don't know what triggered it, but having my girls in that truck with me sparked my instinct to protect them. The sky turned to stone as dusk approached, then from nowhere it started pouring with rain.

We ascended through the Madura Pass at nightfall, with rain still falling hard, and pulled up at the motel there. 'Try the quiche, it's really good,' said the motel manager as I checked us in. I glanced over to the driveway; Clare was waking up in the cab outside.

The manager was a big man with a shaved head, a goatee and a lazy eye. On a night like this one, my first impression was that he had probably just finished digging three shallow graves out in the bush in anticipation of our arrival. It didn't help that the motel was a big spread-out complex at the base of the pass. Other than us and the manager, it appeared to be totally empty. Our room was at the end of a wing that stretched into darkness.

'This place is creepy,' said Clare, looking through the rain as lightning lit up the wet landscape.

We unloaded our bags and ran back to the main building for something to eat. The motel manager was there. 'Try the quiche,' he grinned. 'It's really good.'

We sat there in the restaurant alone, not another soul in there. 'This place is like an Aussie Bates Motel,' I whispered.

Clare looked worried and put on Lola's bib. 'He's scary,' she said.

'Are you going to have the quiche? Apparently it's really good.'

She pulled a face. The manager returned a moment later with a pad.

'I'll have the quiche,' I said, smiling at Clare. Clare had a salad and Lola demolished a big piece of fish.

The quiche was horrible, our night was long, the door had a flimsy lock on it, and Clare was convinced the motel manager was going to burst through the door and hack us up with a fire axe. She was ready to pile up the furniture against the door, but in the end the night was uneventful. The manager was in fact a perfect gentleman with a dry sense of humour and bad taste in quiche.

We crossed the border into South Australia the next day. I watched an electrical storm brewing over the Bunda Cliffs on the northern side of the road, rain cascading down in liquid sheets across the highway and out to the southern ocean.

The rest of our journey played out in much the same way, with two more days of driving. Crossing the Nullarbor Plain is, well . . . plain, especially the part called the Treeless Plain—that's *really* plain. But eventually the plain gave way to grassy rolling hills and the outskirts of Adelaide.

12 STAGE ONE: GREEN FUEL, WHITE KNUCKLES

I hadn't really slept the night before, but day one, stage one, had me out of the hotel at 6 a.m. and over to the uni's workshop. Howard, the support driver, was due to arrive in an hour, and then we had to get the truck over to the MoGas holding yard and fill up the tanks with 800 litres of bio-fuel that had been waiting there for me for weeks. Then all we'd have to do was wait for the lord mayor and the media to arrive before we could take off. At 6.30 a.m. I stood there in the workshop with a mug of coffee, the huge roller door opened to a big, almost empty car park surrounded on three sides by the university's buildings. The truck was parked next to Betty, and everything was packed, ready to go. Only a few people were around; it was the calm before the storm. I had the time and the quiet to reflect on the last four months.

What was I really trying to do, I wondered, other than ride a bike around Australia (which had been done many times before?). Well, it was the fuel and the bike that made this ride different, and that was the bit that excited me. The uni had built Betty as a prototype, but Colin and his students hoped that once this ride was over, she could be used as an example, perhaps in a first tentative step towards the production of an Australian-made motorcycle for the farming community to use on their properties, powered by the same diesel fuel used in tractors, pumps and all manner of motorised farming machines. As with any other ag bike which would only be used on a farm, it wouldn't have to be registered to run on the road. More ambitiously, though, this first-generation agricultural motorcycle could run just as effectively on bio-fuel. Every rural community has a roadhouse or a pub that each week discards around 20 litres of used cooking oil. One roadhouse could provide enough fuel to run one bike for over 500 kilometres of travel a week. I had discovered in the course of my research that the farming community in Australia is more than willing to embrace the concept of a bio-fuel ag bike, as for many farmers the cost of running a standard fossil-fuel-burning quad bike, in terms of fuel and maintenance, is on par with running a car. Fuel is one of their biggest costs.

And then there was its potential application in the city. Could you imagine all those people who ride cheap scooters to work every day instead riding a version of Betty to the office, no longer paying for their fuel at the service station in the city? Though the loss in fuel tax revenue alone would have the bike taxed in some other way before it even left the factory. Bio-fuel could also have applications in public transport or industry.

Transport contributes some 16 per cent of Australia's greenhouse gas emissions. Seventeen per cent of that is from the burning of diesel fuel. Fuels made from used vegetable and animal fats are renewable, and the costs involved in production are very moderate; production of bio-fuel, called transesterification, is not a hard process. When bio-fuel is used it produces 60 per cent less carbon monoxide and total hydrocarbons than fossil fuels. It's also non-toxic to animals or marine life. If there was ever a spill, after three weeks it would degrade to sugars and starches; it's ten times less toxic than table salt.

No, this wasn't just another adventure. This entire project revolved around the effective use of waste cooking oil, and it was crucial that I didn't fuck it up. There was a lot riding on this, apart from my arse; it wasn't just about me getting from point A to point B and having my jollies. There was a purpose to it, and a responsibility as well. I drained my coffee, feeling good about the prospect of getting on the road.

Rob and Steve, the workshop guys, arrived. They gave me a supportive slap on the back and wished me luck. Rob even lent me his personal generator and a full jerry can of fuel. Howard called from the airport; he was on the way. The lord mayor's office called to tell me the TV networks and press were also inbound, as was the lord mayor. Last and most importantly, my wife and daughter were on their way. It was time.

Howard got there first, followed by Dan. We jumped into the cab and we headed off to pick up the fuel. You'd think getting the fuel would be relatively simple, but no. We got lost on the way—incidentally, our directions included a line that said we had to turn right at a sex shop, brilliantly called Beaver World—and then I had a freakout when we got to the bio-fuel storage yard and discovered that the fuel was kept in a special vessel and my tanks were bolted to the floor in the back of the truck, and there was no way of connecting one with the other. I didn't have a hand pump or any hose or funnels to transfer the fuel into my tanks; conscious of time ticking on and the assembling media, I started to sweat. Howard, being calm and capable, had a scout around and soon came back with funnels and a hose. We picked up the vessel using the on-site forklift, plumbed in the hose he'd found and funnelled fuel into one tank, then transferred fuel over into the other tank using the internal pump. Perfect.

We got back to the workshop, where Howard put on the CB headset. I got on Betty, continuing to talk to him over the radio. Colin gave me the nod; we had to drive around the corner and pull up out the front of the uni where I was to chat to the media people, shake the lord mayor's hand, kiss my wife and daughter goodbye and peel off into the waiting city like a bio-fuel poster boy.

And, thank Christ, that's exactly how it went. It was a perfect departure, all smiles and camera flashes, proud wife holding waving baby daughter, cue wind tussle of hair as wife looks happy but concerned.

But just two blocks down the road I stopped, realising I'd just spent half an hour telling the country's media that people could check out the journey online by going to www.the goodoil.tv, yet this website was not emblazoned on the truck, or anywhere else for that matter. How did I miss that? So we detoured to the nearest Bunning's and picked up some stick-on letters and fixed up my mistake.

Our first night's stop was due to be Mount Gambier via Keith. My initial joy at finally being on the road was ephemeral to say the least. The first thing that hit me—again—was how slow Betty was. The second thing that hit me—on a highway surrounded by trucks—was the shockwave of wind right after each truck has shot past. My hands were totally numb from the vibrations coming through the bars. Now that's a weird feeling: you know you're holding onto the handlebars, you just can't feel it.

Betty's riding dynamic was like no other bike I'd ridden. She didn't like hills and hated cross-winds. I had experienced this before but this was fairly tough riding. The Coonawarra hammered me with a sudden freezing wind, blowing the bike all over the place. When the sun started to set the temperature plummeted, the wind picked up again and the rain set in. We were only halfway to Mount Gambier, and I was getting fatigued and a little scared at the thought of riding at night, when Betty's CVT belt suddenly let go. We pulled over by the side of the highway. The trucks shooting past kept knocking Betty over, so I decided to ride her up the ramp into the back of the truck where I could put her in the wheel brace and work on her out of the wind.

That was my first mistake. I had previously ridden her successfully up the ramp at home; you needed a good run-up as she didn't have the torque to get up without it. But with all my riding gear and a full tank of fuel she was so heavy that the bottom of the frame slammed into the back of the truck when I got to the top of the ramp. I fell backwards, the bike landing unceremoniously next to me, smashing its tail-light and indicators. With me in the back seat of the truck, we pulled into Mount Gambier late that night. Howard crashed; I had a whisky and moaned to Dan for an hour about being a shit rider.

I crawled out of bed at 5 a.m. and spent two hours fixing the tail-light and indicators and replacing the CVT drive belt. Dan was late getting up. I didn't know it yet, but Dan is not a morning person: he likes a lie-in. Before the week was up Howard had renamed him Mattress Man. Poor Dan: half-man, half-bed.

We fuelled up, pigged out, coffee'd up, and took off into another cold wet day. Next stop was Melbourne, and we had two days there to figure out how I was going to make this bike go all the way round the continent without it killing me. Twenty minutes after setting off we crossed into Victoria. I wouldn't see South Australia again for over three months—that is, if I ever saw it again.

We stopped briefly in Warrnambool, where I pulled on a few more layers. During the following leg frustration really kicked in. Bike after bike flew past me on the Great Ocean Road; *everyone* flew past me, even little doddery grannies in ten-year-old Honda Civics with their noses one inch from the windscreen. I got abused by all of them because I was so slow. They could not understand why this guy on a big motorcycle was only doing 80 kilometres per hour. I was in the slow lane, where you can legally do 80, but this just wasn't good enough for the average mild-mannered motorist, most of whom simply defaulted to giving me the finger and/or a verbal serve on passing.

I'd had enough, so we turned off the coastal route at Lavers Hill, heading northeast. This country was much better for an underpowered bike. Betty cruised over the Otway Ranges through some really pretty country. The sun came out, the road traffic was light and I started to enjoy myself—that is, until the sun went down and we hit the Princes Highway. Back to the road rage and abuse—again with the hand gestures—from fast-moving cars; trucks blew by threatening to suck me from the handlebars. It was impatient driving at its worst. One bloke even threw a kebab at me.

We finally hit the last long artery that would plug us into Melbourne. The sun had well and truly set behind me. All I had to do was hold the throttle open and avoid getting pummelled in the traffic. At one point we traversed a series of big hills that came out into a huge sweeping run; the wind suddenly picked up on the eastern side and got behind me, and the highway fell away, descending sharply out in front as far as I could see. Betty hit a ton and I was happy. Tucked in behind her fairing, I optimistically changed into the middle lane for the first time since leaving Adelaide. Betty cracked

110, and I started ranting, 'LOOK AT ME FLY NOW, YOU FUCKING WANKERS.'

Howard got on the radio. 'Pauli mate, did you pull over? We can't see you.'

I started overtaking the left lane. Kebab guy in his big manly red penis of a ute was in the right lane ahead of me, but was now stuck behind a truck. Betty hit 125; I couldn't believe it.

'Pauli, come back, over.' Howard sounded concerned. 'Where are you, mate? Over.'

I pressed the little red transmit button on the left grip. 'I'M DOING 130 K'S MATE, THIS HILL AND THE WIND, AWESOME—130! OVER.'

Howard came back on the radio, laughing. 'Just keep going, we'll catch up.'

I shifted my weight back and lay over the tank, tucking in my legs and elbows. She was still picking up speed—I stared at the speedo: 140 now—her wild vibration making the front end speed-wobble. Ute guy was level on my right side. He heard the tiny diesel engine shrieking in agony next to his phallic red turd. I was getting close to losing control of Betty; her vibrations were so intense my bum skipped forward on the seat.

'ONE HUNDRED AND FORTY ON COOKING OIL AND AN EIGHT-HORSEPOWER PUMP ENGINE, YEAHHHHH.'

He looked over, and his jaw dropped open.

'FUCK YOU, CUNT.' I gave him the finger with my left hand; my right hand was holding the throttle on full and completely numb. In fact, both my arms were completely dead from the elbow down, and I realised I was waving my index finger at kebab guy. He gave me a quizzical look, leaned forward in his nice warm comfortable seat to see what I was pointing at, then returned me the finger, stomped his foot into the firewall and disappeared, just as Betty's CVT belt flew apart again.

It was freezing cold as we crossed over the Bolte Bridge into Melbourne much later that night. I was in the middle lane following Howard; he was acting as a weather shield. The traffic was horrendous, bumper to bumper; I was boxed in between a bus on my left, a cab on my right, and a semi right on my arse. I heard the truck getting close. I fired a quick look over my shoulder—the bastard was two feet from my back wheel, all I could see in the mirror was chrome grille. Howard could also see what was going on. 'Pauli, how close is that truck?'

I was waving my left hand at the cab asking him to back off. 'Too fuckin close mate, I'm boxed in.' This was getting really frightening.

We reached the highest point of the bridge, hundreds of feet up in the air, the cross-wind buffeting Betty, when the big truck applied the pressure again. I looked back: he was right there on top of me. I turned my radio over to channel 44, the one the truckies use. 'Hey, truck on my arse halfway over the Bolte Bridge, back off.'

He came back to me straightaway: 'Get out of the way then.'

'I'VE GOT NOWHERE TO GO. NOW BACK OFF MATE, THIS IS DANGEROUS.'

Howard managed to pull into the right lane and slow down, creating a gap for me to cross into and get out of this idiot's way. It was right at that moment that Betty started coughing and lost power.

I pulled into the right lane just in time. It was so close, I thought the truck was going to go straight over the top of me. If Howard had not acted when he did and made that gap, I would have been stuffed.

Madura Pass, crossing the Nullarbor.

Lola maxing and relaxing in the back of the truck.

Pre-ride anti-vibration training.

Matty's pre-ride survival training.

Gavin Kelly and myself on the Victoria River. We're supposed to be fishing.

Dan Stevenson—full-time camera man, part-time lunatic.

Dan and Dave Henry getting the chopper shot.

Gav making friends with the locals, Bullo River, NT.

It's only bad when they overtake you.

Riding into the sun, central Queensland.

He died just after I got there.

The bush at dusk—hard to beat.

'So Pauli, how are you feeling?'

Too much glare, do it again. Too much noise, do it again. That truck's in the shot now, do it again. Where did that eagle come from? Do it again. I need to pee, do it again. Where's the long lens? Can you do it again? Okay, almost there, no wait the battery's flat, do it again.

It's a big bite.

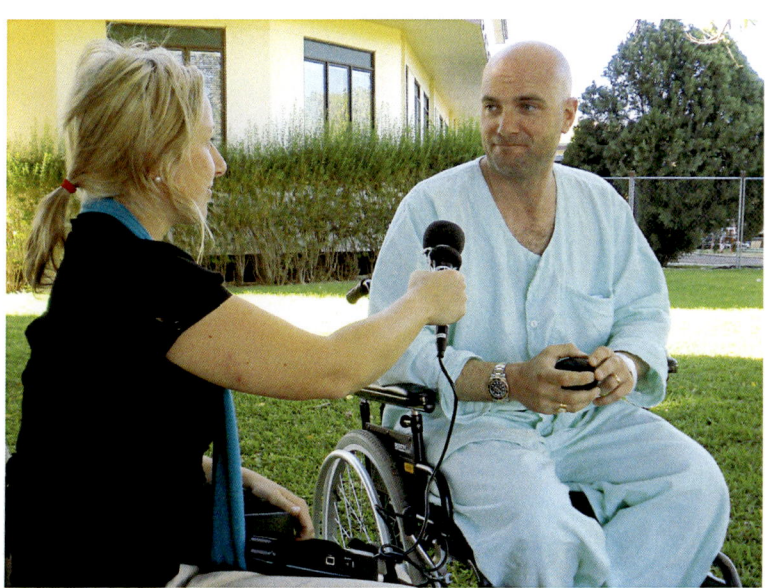

Longreach Hospital interview.

Betty's donk now resides in the Australian National Motorcycle Museum.

Betty's big bad sister the high performance diesel motorcycle awaiting final stages of fabrication at the University of Adelaide's Mechanical Engineering Department, ready for a land speed record attempt on the salt flats during Speed Week 2011 at Lake Gairdner.

'GET THE NUMBER, GET THE NUMBER,' I screamed over the radio. I was ready to kill that guy, no question.

A few seconds later, Betty's power came back; I didn't know why it had dropped out—could have been a blocked fuel line or a clogged injector. We descended into the city. I was fizzing, full of adrenalin, but it passed. The safety of the city streets put me at ease.

I had rented a small terrace house in Richmond for three nights, only a block from my mate James' Supercar Club building. He had offered me some space to work on the bike, so I could spread out all my tools and take my time. However, I had not been able to raise him on the phone over the last few days. As it turned out he was overseas, so we made straight for the rental house. I was shattered.

The tiny garage had once been full-size but had been converted into a bedroom; only the first metre was still garage, and it now housed a small laundry and two bins. There was a door leading from the garage into the bedroom, so we just opened it and parked Betty half-in, half-out of the room. Howard and Dan were as tired as I was, so we all had a beer together then called it a night—but not before I made a call on that truck.

Melbourne is a wonderful city, and we had two days to relax. Howard had to bolt first thing in the morning; he was moving house the next day and his wife didn't like the idea of tackling that alone with two girls under five in tow. He jumped into a taxi, job done; I couldn't thank him enough.

Dan has mates in Melbourne so he was off as well, intent on chasing all the things that a young single man chases on weekend pass. I pulled the tools out of the truck and lay in the street under Betty to do an oil change. The radio in the truck was on, the city came to life as the sun rose over the terraces, and people ambled past with strollers and dogs. Oil change done I replaced the CVT belt, then worked on the rest of the bike, which took up most of the day. That night I went out for dinner with my mates in Melbourne, the Jacobson boys (of *Kenny* fame) and their wives. As always, the two brothers had me in stitches, and the night was over way too fast.

The next day Shane Edwards arrived, full of energy and boundless enthusiasm. Shane does marathons and triathlons and jogs every morning. He eats right, works hard—a real clean-cut Eddie who never has a bad word to say about anyone. But that boy can drink . . . 'Let's get on it,' were the first words out of his mouth.

'Er, OK,' I said, and we went straight to the pub, where two of his mates joined us.

Ten hours later Fast Eddie was walking on footballs and slurring his words, as we discussed whether to go clubbing or move on to another pub. We were in the corner of a pub somewhere in the city, a nice place, not too crowded for a Saturday night. 'WHHOOOO,' Eddie said suddenly, with his arms in the air, 'we're going to the Black Spurrr, me laddy.' He raised his eyebrows to emphasise this and grinned.

'What's the Black Spur?' I asked. 'And why are you talking like a pirate?'

Eddie's mates picked up on the pirate thing. 'Beware the Spur boy, it'll swallow ye up like a prawn, so it will, arrr.'

I started laughing. Eddie was on fire; he stood up and did a little drunk jig. 'The Black Spur be no place for a bio-gay bike and a baldy-headed fool. Lucky for you I'm just the man te get ya there, 'n no bones about it.' He flopped back into his seat and laughed.

'OK lads, what the fuck is the Black Spur?'

'BEWARE THE BLACK SPUR,' they all joined in.

I finished my drink. 'It's just a hill mate, the black spur,' said Eddie. 'BEWARE THE . . .'

'SHUT THE FUCK UP.'

'That bike is never going to get up it. Let's get a taco.'

Our night went on into the morning. At one point Dan called me; he was as smashed as I was and wanted to meet up with us at some club but that was never going to happen. Eddie, his mates and I ended up in a random horrid little bar, more like a public toilet with a bouncer; from the smell of the place it was bang in the middle of Melbourne's urine district. I spent an hour doing shooters and sticking to the carpet.

When we got back to the house, I was worried about the truck getting tagged by some kids we'd passed on the corner, so I went out to move it closer to the house. Bad move. My attempt to drive twenty metres down the road started and finished with the truck lurching forward straight into a streetlight, and that's where I woke up several hours later.

13 STAGE TWO: SPIDERS

Bags packed, our laundry done, a decent breakfast, the bill paid: it was time to depart Melbourne and make for Sydney via Canberra.

'All set, mate.' Eddie looked and sounded like he hadn't even sniffed a drink last night. Bastard. Dan looked the opposite, just like I did. I filled up the bike, pulling the hose through the little flap on the side and flicking on the fuel pump; the smell made me gag.

'What was all that pirate talk about last night?' asked Dan. 'I called you to see if you guys wanted to join me and all I got was "Arrr this" and "the Black Spur that".'

'BEWARE THE BLACK SPUR,' yelled Eddie from the cab. I shot him a smile. 'Pauli spent the night in the truck, it smells like a brewery in here,' said Eddie.

Dan looked puzzled. 'What happened?'

Eddie described my drunken mission to rescue the truck from some taggers.

Dan looked at me. 'It's still parked in the same spot.'

'Not quite.' Eddie pointed at the front left side. 'He managed to shift it all of five feet into that streetlight.' Dan walked around to the other side and started laughing.

Not too much damage, just a dented ego.

The rain started as we pulled off and kept on going for the rest of the day. My head was thumping in perfect time with Betty's donk. I sat behind the truck for ages, riding on autopilot, until we hit Healesville. *Whap, whap, whap.* Sports bikes blasted past us as we began to climb. This must be the start of the dreaded Betty-crushing Black Spur, I thought.

Eddie swiftly confirmed this over the two-way. 'THE BLACK SPUR,' he announced. 'You're never gonna make it, sucka.' I overtook the truck and put-putted into the most amazing high country forest. Two brand spanking KTMs pulled alongside and Betty got the once-over. There was some pointing, lots of laughing, then they barked the engines, down a gear on the throttle, front wheels effortlessly airborne—wankers—and off up the straight on the balance point through the gearbox.

I couldn't do that; I just didn't have the power or the gearbox. But I could enjoy the scenery, hairpin after hairpin straight up into the Yarra Ranges. Betty was doing about twenty kilometres an hour, much to the annoyance of all the cars behind me, but there was nowhere to pull over with any degree of safety.

The ride down the other side was a joy, all the same swervery but no longer underpowered so I could finally keep up with all the other bikes enjoying the run. The KTM duo were stuck behind a caravan, deep in conversation, doing twenty. I thumped past, rushing a really silly overtake on the apex of a right hander—no oncoming traffic but an overhanging tree nearly took my head off. Don't look back, just hold her wide open and go.

The game was on. I caught flashes of their headlights in my mirrors; Betty's footpegs touched bitumen for the first time. I rode as hard and fast as the bike would let me. We duelled, always within our lanes, measured, experienced fun, ripping through turn after turn, the bikes well over, jittery on the lean from the leaf litter on the roadside, into the centre line and back, always thinking ahead, always looking towards the exit point and the next setup. No looking back, or they'd know I was trying, no glancing down at gauges or mirrors. We were flying. At the first straight section we came to the duo pulled up, one on either side of me. I was hopelessly out-gunned, out-wheelied and out-braked. We rode on, three in a row down the straight, no hard-faced manly nods or piss taking, just big happy grins.

'Nice one, mate,' said KTM One; thumbs-up and he was gone.

'It's a diesel, hey?' KTM Two asked.

'Yeah.' I smiled.

'Where you headed?'

'Doing the big lap,' I said.

His eyes widened. 'Really? You're game. Good luck.'

'Cheers,' I said.

He lifted the front end again and blasted away in a spectacular display of proper motorcycle hoonability. Melburnians are truly blessed to have such a great choice of rides to occupy their weekends. Eddie was smiling when we stopped at the bottom.

'Mate, how good was that?' I couldn't stop grinning.

We sat on the Maroondah Highway headed for a small town called Taggerty, where Eddie grew up. 'Mum and Dad's is next, mate, there's gonna be a good feed on.' He sounded excited to be visiting home.

IS THAT THING DIESEL?

As predicted, Eddie's folks were hospitable beyond words. Dan and I pigged out on Eddie's mum's lasagne, then we got the tour of the property. Eddie's dad, Murray, is the area's deputy group officer, a volunteer firefighter. He casually walked me through a shed to rival my father-in-law's. Guys from that generation know how a man's shed should be: no comfy seats, no designer shelving or super clean floors, just tools—heavily used tools. Power tools, tools with big engines, half a tractor here, half a big-block V8 there, and in the corner an old fridge that looks like a car door packed with man beer, not imported Italian stuff. These men have the man caves that my generation should aspire to. Murray talked casually about the Black Saturday fires that ravaged the area one year before, Australia's worst fire disaster. As he talked, I got a glimpse of the type of men he and Eddie are, just flat-out hard-working, decent blokes who will risk their lives to save people and property from turning to ashes.

Everyone else headed inside for a cuppa and I went to check Betty's almost shredded CVT belt. She was going through these drive belts at an increasingly rapid rate. I wandered through the shed, straight into a waiting spider's web the size of a bed sheet. At the last nanosecond I saw the spider, right in the middle; he looked like he could bench press Spiderman. And right there in the semi-dark wooden shed I did what my wife calls 'the spider dance'—the interpretive instant spin/strip that you do while hopping up and down and wildly rubbing your hands over your head. You know he's holding on somewhere, ready to plunge his white-hot fangs into you. Thank God no one was around to see me do the spider dance—except the spider, of course.

After lunch, we ambled on from Taggerty past Bonnie Doon, made famous in the film *The Castle*, but the lake was dry. We stopped to refuel the truck in Benalla, passed Wangaratta, then got on a minor road to Wodonga on the Victoria/New South Wales border. This little back road was almost as direct a route as the Hume Highway, and there were no trucks or hell-for-leather near-death experiences. I was back to riding relaxed again; my only lingering worry was the CVT belts—I had only one left.

We crossed the border into New South Wales at dusk, Eddie leading, and got a bit lost looking for the motel in Albury. 'I'm chuckin a uey at the lights, mate,' he said over the radio, while in the background the GPS in a clipped English accent said, 'Execute a legal u-turn at this intersection.' I watched Eddie take out a traffic-light shroud with the side of the truck as he turned around. It rattled down onto the road, so I hopped off and picked it up. I had an old milk crate strapped to the back of the bike where I put my helmet and gloves whenever we stopped, as the wind had been blowing my kit all over the place. Eddie's carnage was placed in there, and I caught up with him still looking for the motel.

'Mate, you nailed that traffic light back there,' I laughed over the radio.

'Bullshit,' said Eddie, so I pulled up next to him waving the shroud at the driver's window. 'Oh shit.' He looked worried.

We found our digs for the night and I was asleep before my head hit the pillow.

New South Wales is my old stomping ground; there's some great riding in this state, but on this trip, it was only on the downhill side. The next day we were off to our nation's capital

IS THAT THING DIESEL?

Canberra, again taking the back roads. We left Albury via the Murray Valley into Corryong, a nice little goldrush town, and then into a valley.

The road was empty so I had a chance to take in the landscape. Shadows spread across the road, and the place felt palpably creepy. 'Good location for a horror film,' Dan said over the radio. He wanted to stop and do some filming against this backdrop. Five takes and ten passes later he was happy.

The road snaked round the foothills of the Snowy Ranges and on to Tumut, then we doubled back on the highway, heading south through Kosciuszko National Park and Australia's highest town, Kiandra. We took a left turn at Cooma and then drove back up north towards Canberra. The day's riding was spectacular. I felt light and happy. It had been a risk, I guess, to ride so far with only one belt left, but the riding was worth it.

About an hour before Canberra we pulled over for a break. I brewed up some tea and lay back under a tree, looking up at the branches swaying. Dan found inspiration in the landscape and bounded off with his stills camera. Eddie was in good form, so we fell into conversation. Before I realised it, we'd burned too much daylight and it was late afternoon.

Off again, me in front this time, and I focused on the road ahead, the bike thumping down the highway. And that's when I felt it. Only a little at first, a light pressure at the back of my head, and then the horror set in. It was like a small hand slowly crawling from the back of my lid to the front. Something big and hairy with long legs was inside my helmet, looking for an exit point.

I checked my rear and slammed on the brakes, locking up the back wheel. A blue streak smoked off the burning rubber as the bike slid off the road. I sprang off, letting the bike fall over like a doddery toddler, and did the Roadside, One-Night-Only,

Helmet Spider Dance. It's not unlike the standard spider dance, but this one involves the high-speed removal of gloves and a mad thrashing at the chin strap, followed by helmet soccer and the traditional rubbing of hands over your head.

The truck pulled up just as I was composing myself. Eddie wound down his window. 'Everything OK, mate?' He looked over at the bike lying on its side, the motor running.

'Oh yeah, fine.' I ran over and stood Betty up, smiling at the boys.

We continued on. It was getting dark and really cold, just above freezing; I was wearing all my gear now, almost too many layers to do up the zipper on my jacket. I ran out of fuel less than a kilometre from the motel. Running out of fuel is a prick on Betty; she's hard to start in the cold, and even harder to start with the lines and filter empty.

Canberra was a dark, empty meat locker. We found our motel eventually. I left my bike-maintenance ritual for the morning; it was too dark, too cold, and besides, Eddie had bought beer.

The sun broke through the next morning while I was working on the bike. My last CVT belt had to get me all the way to Sydney, where I could pick up some more. Today, we were going to a tiny little place called Majors Creek to see my old mate Nigel Houston Begg. Majors Creek is a jewel nestled in wonderful country among the rolling hills behind Araluen Valley, where another friend had a place which would be our stop for the night.

I was excited about seeing Nigel. He's quite mad, a dedicated motorcycle man who eats, sleeps and breathes everything bike-related. He used to be a daredevil of sorts, once jumping a mountain bike over I can't remember how many buses—let's just say there were lots. That was back when mountain bikes were just regular bikes with slightly wider tyres. Over the course of his life he's had many passions; his current one is all about getting back to the basics. So some years ago he sold everything, purchased a large chunk of Majors Creek land onto which he put a 40-foot sea container full of motorcycles, and moved in. The container has no power or running water, in fact no amenities whatsoever, just Nigel and his bikes. I thought he had finally cracked back when he did it, but I was wrong: I've never seen him happier.

That could have a lot to do with the young lady from Belgium he rolled up to meet us with—on a tandem bicycle—outside the Majors Creek pub later that day. From there we followed him out to 'the container'. It was spectacular; Nigel had made it very comfortable. There was a creek running past the front door. Nigel pointed to a clump of bushes near it. 'There's our laundry,' he grinned. I got the tour of the inside. 'Feel the temperature drop when you walk in?' he asked, and I nodded. 'That's the nature of tin box.' He had a generator for power, a gas stove, everything you might need (on a basic kind of Nigel level).

We swapped a few stories, had a whisky and decided to go down the back road from Majors Creek to Araluen. I love that track; it's just a small dirt road but it's fast, steep and a lot of fun. Dan climbed on the back of Betty to film, and Eddie drove the truck round the long way to meet us at the Araluen pub.

'I've never been on the back of a bike before,' said Dan, looking a bit worried, more for the brand-new thirteen-thousand-dollar camera in his backpack than anything else.

'Don't worry, Danny, it's all downhill mate, just hang on,' I said. Nigel rode beside us. The track was a blast, Dan letting go with a few screams on some tight hairpins when I let the back wheel slide out near the edge, giving him time to look over and realise there was no railing, just a sheer drop a few hundred feet down a cliff.

We were on our third beer at the pub in Araluen when Eddie showed up.

After that it was on to Gail's place for the night. She was away in Sydney at the time, but being the legend she is, she'd left us a roast in the oven, apple pie in the fridge and cold beer in the esky. That night was like every night I've ever spent on that property, just brilliant. With a full belly and the peace and quiet, I slept like a baby.

In the morning Eddie got up early and fixed us a full cooked breakfast. Dan wanted to go for a ride to get some shots, so he jumped on the back of Betty again. We plodded through a few paddocks, cresting a big hill to pull up right in front of the biggest bull I've ever seen. He was magnificent. It looked like someone had stretched a hide over a drooling city bus. The big beast blew snot out of nostrils you could fit a fist in.

'OK mate, we've seen the giant bull, let's move on,' Dan said nervously.

The bull turned and started walking towards us.

'Pauli, let's go, c'mon mate,' Dan said.

I pulled off very slowly. Dan didn't think it was funny.

By lunchtime we were past Batemans Bay and heading for Kiama and a great night with another old friend of mine, Jane De La Vega.

About twenty k's out of Batemans Bay, I was going down a hill sitting on 90 when Betty's back wheel suddenly locked up. She bucked wildly, her back wheel sliding then freeing up again. I nearly came off. The idler sprocket, shaft and housing had sheared off, flying into the main sprocket and chewing everything to pieces. This was a big repair, not something I could do roadside. I needed a new chain, sprockets, shafts and bearings.

Betty went into the back of the truck for the third time. I sat there, worries filling my head. I had to get the bike to Matt Bromley in Sydney; once he'd worked his magic on it I could relax, and hopefully spend no more time sitting there on the back seat. We rolled into Jane's driveway two hours later, to be met by a great home-cooked meal, hot showers, and lots of good conversation.

The next day we got an early start for the last run into Sydney, another two hours down the highway. I called Matt at Deus; he was ready for us to bring Betty straight into the workshop. This whole leg had seen me relying on mates to get me through; sometimes friends make all the difference.

14 WALLET

Clare and Lola would be waiting for me in Sydney. My dad, who had flown all the way from the UK, would be there too. He was going to join Phil and Dan in the truck up to Brisbane on the next leg. The time I spend with my father is great now, though it hasn't always been that way. We were separated for a long time by my work and a lack of communication that lasted far too long. I was looking forward to seeing his face when he finally laid his eyes on my daughter for the first time.

I was a little apprehensive about getting the bike fixed, and having my family shacked up in a hotel while all this was going on. I would be busy every day helping Matt with the bike, plus I had to find spare parts, and I didn't have a clue how long all that was going to take.

Betty rolled into Matt's workshop on Thursday afternoon. I had Friday to find all the spares; on Saturday I had a racing suit fitting and Clare had to go to a funeral so Dad would have to look after his new granddaughter.

The racing suit fitting was important. Through Deus I had been put in touch with Rory, the Australian supplier of Gimoto racing leathers, world-class Italian-made racing suits. That gear is normally well out of my reach, however Rory had heard about the HPDM project for the Speed Week flying kilometre and very generously offered me a set of leathers for the salt. I was stunned. 'Mate, I think it's great,' said Rory when I called him. 'We love to get behind this kind of thing.' He was going to meet me at Deus on Saturday at noon, and Dan wanted to film the fitting for the show.

At Deus, Matty was as keen as ever. 'So, this is Betty,' he said, and he looked her over. 'Mate, if you're going to keep punishing yourself on this thing, we need to rebuild the whole sprocket and shaft system. How much time do you have?'

'Not much. Money's tight too.'

He sipped his coffee. 'Well, I'll get started. Don't worry, mate, we'll look after you. Now go and see your girls.'

A great sense of relief washed over me as I handed Betty over to Yoda. Fix it, he will.

The other two mechanics looked over the top of the bikes they were working on. 'Is that thing diesel?'

On the way out I stopped in the café for a brief moment with Eddie. His wife Katrina was there, so I got a chance to say thanks to them both. They're good people, the kind that make the world go round.

When I got to the hotel, Dad was already there with my girls. Everyone looked great. I had missed my father's first contact with the next generation, but life is like that. It didn't matter, I was just glad to see him there holding Lola, so very happy. I hadn't seen him in two years, but we picked up right where we left off. He would be with me for the next week, supporting me—he'd even brought the single malt.

I stayed at the hotel for an hour and then went back to help Matty. He had already stripped the shit out of the bike. 'OK, mate, we need to replace all that, but with bigger bearings and shafts. You're going to need the same sprockets but they need to fit round the bigger bearings.' He pointed to a box of stripped parts.

Taka was there too. He'd already ordered a new chain but the drive and idler sprockets were not off-the-shelf items as I had been told. 'No, not available off the shelf, I'm afraid.' He picked up the smashed idler sprocket and held a vernier to it. 'Custom size.' Taka may be as laid-back as it gets, but he still has that wonderful Japanese sense of precision and efficiency. He's probably on the ball even when he's asleep. I've got nothing but time for Taka.

I called Rob at the uni's workshop, and told him what we needed. 'Not a problem, mate,' he said. 'I'll courier the lot up to you today.' He would also make, from scratch, new shafts and sprockets all properly hardened and ready to go; however this would take four days, which meant that I'd get back on the road by next Thursday if I was lucky. My other problem was the CVT belts. In the three years since the uni built Betty, the firm that fabricated her CVT belts had gone out of business.

Rob couldn't believe I'd gone through the lot. 'You've got none left? I'll try looking from my end.'

I started ringing around every drive-belt supplier, importer and manufacturer in Australia. The belt had very specific parameters, as nothing on the bike could be moved to fit the belt—the belt had to fit the bike. I had some luck with CBC Bearings, and fixed a time to go out to their warehouse the next day. That evening was spent chatting to Dad, but by eight o'clock I was falling asleep, exhausted.

On Friday morning I had coffee with Matty at 7 a.m. He was busy with several other bikes, so Dan and I went out to CBC Bearings and met Steve Hudson, the Senior Applications

Engineer, and the New South Wales General Manager Lou Amato. They listened as I described my problem, then walked me into a warehouse big enough to park two 707s.

On huge racks stretching to the ceiling were thousands of drive belts. 'Right, what size do you need?' asked Lou. I told him, and there was a moment of hope. I was standing there, surrounded by millions of drive belts; surely there wasn't a drive belt on the planet that they didn't have. But guess what? They had drive belts that were close to my requirement but not exactly the one I needed.

I was stunned. They saw the look on my face. 'Don't worry, we'll get the right belts, Paul,' said Lou. Steve offered to come all the way across Sydney to Deus and have a look at the drive system on the bike. He couldn't believe that the belts we had access to would not work, so we drove back to Betty with a box of belts. Matty and I reassembled the bike and for the rest of the day we tried all the belts, one by one.

There was one that was almost the right size, and would work at a pinch. 'I can get a slightly smaller version of this belt in from Mexico in a week; it should work fine,' Steve said. He had saved the day. 'We have enough of these to get you going, and the rest can be sent on to meet you. Just let me know by phone where you are and I'll freight them to you.' Steve even sold me the belts and bearings to match the new shafts and sprockets at cost. I was stoked and mightily relieved.

Matty was getting ready to knock off for the weekend, and he handed me a beer. 'Mate, we're not coming in this weekend, but here's the key—you make yourself at home and use all my tools. With any luck we'll have the shaft sprockets on Tuesday, whack 'em in and you're off.'

That night I walked across the street to the hotel doing the maths in my head. I was rapidly going over my budget for spare parts, but there was no backing out now. All I could do was move forward. Tomorrow I would finish changing out the nuts and bolts on the bike, then pull the front end off the spare bike and fit it to Betty.

Saturday found me in the workshop at 6 a.m. with a coffee, the radio and more tools than I'd ever seen. Meantime in Adelaide, Rob had received via courier the parts we'd pulled off Betty, and he spent the weekend machining new sprockets and shafts. I continued pulling every nut and bolt off Betty and replacing them with high-tensile steel ones, nylock nuts and lots of thread lock. She had shaken herself to bits. The front end was a mess, the triple clamp was worn; the forks vibrating had taken its toll. Everything was stripped and replaced.

The morning passed quickly. At midday Rory called me to say he was waiting for me in the Deus café. I washed the grease off my hands and ran around to meet him. 'Can't thank you enough for this,' I said, and shook his hand.

'No worries, Paul.' Rory was very relaxed and easy to talk to. Dan arrived with the camera and set up in the middle of the shop, and Saturday afternoon shoppers and bike nuts milled around watching.

Rory had obviously done this kind of thing before. He talked easily to the camera, he spoke well and knew exactly what he was talking about. He described the ideal fit of a riding suit for professional racers and amateurs, and explained the difference from a rider's point of view in the different suit designs as well as different types of leather. 'Right Paul, if you could hold out your arms like so,' he said. I did as I was told, and Rory started taking my measurements, then entering them into his laptop. I was rather enjoying the whole thing, until Rory got to the crotch measurement. 'OK, Paul, I need to get the tape directly on the skin here, so I'll need you to hop out of your jeans.' There was a pause while my mind raced for an answer.

Rory grinned. 'You're not wearing underwear, are you?'

I shook my head. Dan looked up from the camera. 'Mate, who goes to a racing suit fitting jockless?'

I tried to look penitent. 'Sorry, guys. I've been on the road and just ran out of clean undies.'

Dan was laughing. 'There are many subtle refined stages in the cycle of a man's jocks on a roadie,' he said, adopting a declamatory stance, placing one foot on his tripod case and leaning forward with an elbow on his knee. Shoppers gathered closer to listen. 'Obviously, after the initial soiling your first step is to simply turn them inside out and soil the exterior; next, depending on any skid activity you can wear them back to front, or burn them and go straight to the final stage . . .' he gestured towards my crotch, 'where Paul is right now, the free ball.' Dan smiled in a knowing way.

'Deus will lend you a pair of shorts, mate,' said Rory, nodding towards the clothing section. I asked one of the guys working there, grabbed a pair and raced off to the change room and was back on my spot ready for Rory to stick a tape measure into my boys.

'All done.' He shook my hand, we traded business cards and that was it. Dan packed up his camera and was off to enjoy the rest of the weekend in his home town.

I changed back into my filthy jeans and went back to pulling the bike apart. By 4 p.m. I was getting tired. We were supposed to be heading out for dinner that evening with Dad. It had been very dull in the workshop without Matty to bounce off and learn from.

I called Clare to tell her I was shutting it down for the day. Dinner was booked for six so Lola could eat without passing out in her food. Just before I left I did the pat-down thing: watch, wallet, glasses, keys—no, wait, wallet . . . wallet . . . WALLET, WHERE'S MY FUCKIN WALLET?

A horrid pang of doubt ripped into my brain. I started a mad search around the workshop but found nothing. Panic started to fill me. Everything was in that wallet: all the funds for the trip on a Visa card, my personal cards, licence, all the usual suspects. I called Clare.

'Calm down,' she said. 'Now, when did you last see it?'

'When I got my coffee this morning.'

'Did you eat lunch?' she asked.

'No.'

'Honey, no wonder you get so tired, you can't keep skipping lunch. Right, start retracing your steps and call me back when you find it.'

I retraced them out into the shop a billion Saturday shopping punters had traipsed through. My heart sank. I bolted into the change room, but it wasn't there either. Perhaps the cash got lifted and they tossed the wallet? Eight bins and a dumpster later, I called Clare back. It was now 5 p.m. and dinner was in an hour.

'OK, sit down, have a glass of water and go over your day again slowly.'

I forced myself to stop racing and just sit. I thought hard about every step of my day. Then it hit me: when I'd got back to the workshop after meeting Rory, I pinched some chewing gum off Matty's desk, and went to the toilet. But the shop toilet was busy so I used the one in the workshop . . . so . . . I was the only one who's been in there all day! BANG—I slammed the toilet door open and was on all fours round the back under the plumbing quicker than a refugee in an airstrike, peering over half a dozen copies of *Just Bikes* and *The Picture*. There was no sign of it. I sat there on the floor of the toilet and thought about getting on the phone and cancelling everything. Was it too late already? Had all my accounts already been handivacked?

I stood up and stared into the stained porcelain. Fuck it, I had to check. I rolled up my sleeve and dived my hand in, right in, up to the elbow in, and had a bit of a gag when my chin nearly hit a yellow pee stain on the side and . . . wait a minute, my middle finger was touching the unmistakable corner of a credit-card-sized single-fold, polished black leather Dunhill wallet. 'YOU FUCKIN RIPPER!' A bent coat hanger finally got it out. I was so excited I called Clare immediately, toilet water still dripping down my arm.

'That's great, honey—where was it?'

'Oh, on the floor by the workbench,' I lied.

Having said all that I can assure you, had I not found my wallet, this book would still be in your hands now, but you would not know that I fisted a public toilet.

Dinner was a dismal affair in a nasty, cramped vegetarian restaurant. There were ten of us, we ordered, and an hour later I went for a walk with Lola who was getting very hungry and angry. We got two Subways and stood out the front eating them, then went back inside, waited for another fifteen minutes and finally gave up and went back to the hotel.

On Monday afternoon the bike was almost ready. All it needed now were the sprockets, shafts and new bearings. Matty had seriously beefed up the frame and brackets that made up the drive housing, he put on a set of highway pegs, and another set above the originals, so I had a choice of three different positions for my feet. All I could do now was wait. Rob's custom-made parts arrived on Wednesday afternoon and we put them straight in. I repacked the truck and got everyone organised for our departure the next morning.

15 STAGE THREE: LIFE CYCLE

On Thursday we were out the front of Deus, waiting to go. Dare, Taka, Ben and Matty had all come out for a chat. Again I had been saved by my mates.

Saying goodbye to Clare and Lola is never easy, but I pulled on my helmet, climbed on the bike, had one last look, gave a wave and we pulled off. My father-in-law, Phil, was driving the truck, Dad was in the passenger seat and Dan was in the back. Phil has driven trucks from Sydney to Brisbane for the better part of 30 years, so I just followed him out of town. Dan wanted to get a shot of the bike going over the Sydney Harbour Bridge, so we pulled over, stowed the doors, strapped him into the shooting seat in the back and made for the bridge. Everything went well—well, almost everything. Betty's CVT drive fell apart, but that was because I'd forgotten to tighten up the bolts.

A massive dust storm had blown up from the desert the day before, sandblasting the city and turning everything orange. There was still a weird hue in the sky as we broke free of the traffic and headed north.

Stage three was a straight run up the Pacific Highway through Newcastle with a brief detour through Bucketts Way. It's a popular run for riders. Some parts of the road are not so great to ride on but at my speed and with all the vibration it didn't really make any difference. We meandered along with the Karuah River past wide paddocks and shaded forest, then turned left at Gloucester and on to Nabiac and the National Motorcycle Museum.

Our stop for the night was a small house in a paddock directly behind the museum. As usual we arrived late. Dad and Phil had spent the day on the road chatting and both looked tired, so Dan and I wandered over to the main entrance of the museum in the dark. A massive bike was displayed out the front. Dan lit up the camera, and its beam cut through the pitch-black interior, bouncing off hundreds of neatly lined up, polished handlebars. 'Wow.' It was an Aladdin's cave in there. I was like a drooling kid outside a toy store window at Christmas. I pushed on the door as if somehow by magic it would open and automatically all the lights would come on, beaming me through the looking glass and into Bike Nirvana.

The door of course remained locked, so I had to wait till morning, but as soon as the museum opened, I was there hopping about like a cartoon rabbit ready to spend my morning soaking up bikes, bikes, more bikes, bike stuff, bike trivia—bike everything. The place didn't disappoint. I have never seen so many bikes in one place. Imagine the *Titanic* was stacked entirely with bikes, that's how many bikes there were. Or you know those offshore firefighting vessels with their massive water cannons? Imagine they shot out liquid bike, that's how many bikes there were. My mind melted, I didn't know where to start. Every machine I'd ever wanted to take a gander at was there, but soon Phil and Dad were gently trying to wean me off the bike drip I'd so quickly become addicted to. 'Mate, we should think about heading off,' said Filthy.

'He's right son, let's go.' Dad had to drag me out of there to my own bike—my bio, no-power cement mixer of a bike. It was a bit of a comedown.

We continued on the Pacific Highway. Just outside Kempsey I shredded the last of the original CVT belts, so we put on the first of the new make-do ones I'd got from Steve in Sydney. Getting the bastard on proved to be a nightmare. An hour later we were back on our way to Grafton, where Clare has family. Her mum, Cathy—or as everyone calls her, 'The Cath'—grew up around Grafton. Filthy told me about Cathy's cousin, Don Walker—'Great songwriter,' he said. Over the years Mr Walker has penned an astonishing array of chart successes for the likes of Cold Chisel and others. 'You know the song "Flame Trees"?' asked Filthy as we entered Grafton.

'Mate, I love that song.'

'Well, that's about some trees here in Grafton,' he said. We stopped for a quick visit with the family and then continued on to Ballina, our stop for the night.

'There it is, mate.' Filthy's voice woke me; I had gone catatonic on the bike again.

'Where's what?'

'The Big Prawn,' he said. Yup, there it was, Ballina's pride and joy, looking a bit run-down and scary. Usually all the big things, like the Banana, the Pineapple and so on, are a bit polished, they look kind of soft and familiar to the eye, but the Prawn looked like a dirty alien and certainly didn't make me feel like diving into a big plate of prawns.

As it happened, it was time for dinner. 'I think I'll have steak,' I said. Later, my belly full and the beer icy cold, we sat around talking until my lids started to droop. A hot shower and a soft mattress beckoned.

By 8 a.m. the next day we had passed Mullumbimby, where my good mate Erwin has a property. Four years ago, Clare and I stayed there with Erwin and his wife Lucy. He's worth visiting just for a trip to his toilet; called 'The Long Drop', it's just a little outdoor dunny in a shed with no door, set right at the crest of a hill that gives you an amazing panoramic view down a valley. I was just sitting there, minding my own business, when yes, you guessed it, I did the 'Exposed-Arse Spider Dance'. This version differs from the others, but only in the most subtle ways; essentially it's just a flat-out sprint and roll.

By mid-morning we had crossed over into Queensland. By then we were back on the Pacific Highway and I was back to feeling silly each time a big, ballsy, hairy-armed biker sidled up for a look. As I sat in my upright bio-fuel typing-pool riding position, hairy-armed bikers glanced over at me with a mixture of pity and amusement. Seated astride their Harleys in that laid-back, reading-the-weekend-paper-in-the-armchair position they travel past me effortlessly, their bikes sounding like several howitzers going off in unison. Even when bankers, lawyers and brain surgeons skip a weekend shave, get up early, saunter into the garage and throw a leg over their Harley, they get that face on, that look-at-my-bad-arsed-substance face. When they go past me, I can practically hear what they're thinking: 'I'm cool today baby, but next to this thing I'm really cool. Hey, I think it's a diesel.' I knew that for the entire ride I was never going to bump into another twat riding an irrigation pump, I was never going to go fast enough for anyone to want to ride with me, unless I befriended a retired biker in a golf cart. I was never going to hear someone say, 'Hey, you have a slow bio-diesel Frankenstein special, so do I—let's be friends.'

Lunch in a gas station, a quick pee, then a final push into Brizzy, where we dropped Dan and Betty off at a hotel in the city. Filthy had to grab a cab to the airport, and the old man and I drove across town in the truck to spend the night with John Lloyd, an old Air Force flying mate of Dad's, and his wife Glenda. John's a great guy; I ran into him at the Brisbane Writers' Festival last year. He had me in stitches with stories about Dad, and told me lots of things I didn't know about him. John's memories of those days, long before I was born, were clear as a bell, and by the end of the night I started to look at my father in a new light, like a veil had been lifted. They were like two young blokes again, bouncing off each other, laughing. I hope Erwin and I will be like that in years to come.

16 STAGE FOUR: FOLLOW THE BLOOD-SPLATTERED BRICK ROAD

Mathew Downey, Clare's big brother, is not physically big—in fact, none of Clare's family is big. But what they lack in height they compensate for in character, and Matty is no exception. He was waiting for me with Betty and Dan in the city centre, his bag packed and the obligatory Downey silly hat parked on his head. We stood around outside his hotel for half an hour. I said my goodbyes to Dad, John and Glenda; Dad looked good standing there with his old flying mate. I was itching to get going. Soon Betty was shuddering away under my arse, the Sunday morning traffic was minimal, and we peeled off into the city, waving. I got lost a couple of times, eventually hitting the Warrego Highway en route to Toowoomba.

Truth be told, I was feeling a little shitty. A few riders I'd chatted to before Brisbane, including Howard, had told me about an amazing ride through Brisbane Forest Park to a place called Mount Glorious; apparently it's a world-class blat. Once they'd stopped laughing at Betty they all said the same thing: 'Don't bother on that thing, mate, come back and do it on a real bike next time.'

I tried not to think about it, but it was a still, gloriously sunny morning, and soon huge packs of Brisbane riders were swarming in my mirrors then shooting past me, *whap*, *whap*, *whap*. Dozens of big sports bikes vaporised into the distance doing three times my speed, no doubt on their way to Mount Glorious for coffee. If I lived there, that's what I'd have been doing that morning. A few riders, puzzled by my smoky slipstream, pulled up level with me on the highway, flipped up their visors, eyeballed Betty's shuddering frame—dry-humping me violently at 80 kilometres per hour in the slow lane—and at the top of their voices fired off the standard: 'Is that fuckin thing diesel, mate?'

My ride eventually went from 80 to zero. There's this giant hill outside Toowoomba and Betty didn't stand a chance. Back in the truck she went; this time I managed to get her up the ramp without stacking her. Even our truck struggled to get up that hill, doing the last few kilometres in first gear.

We stopped in Toowoomba for something to eat. Matty had a good laugh at just how slow Betty actually was, and asked whether I enjoyed the humiliation of all those riders zapping past at light speed. He wondered out loud if Betty was in fact not a motorcycle but rather a machine for destroying drive belts cunningly disguised as a bike. I took it all, knowing that Matt, a strict vegan, had his coming. We were approaching the outback—no place for a vegan. Sure enough, every time we got hungry, poor Matty went through the inevitable horror of trying to find something to eat. People just don't get vegans; I heard countless roadhouse employees rattle off what they could do for him, but, oh, that's got mayo in it, or ham, or egg—sorry mate, how about a bread roll? On the trip his standard meal three times a day was any fruit he could find, fresh or tinned, and a salad roll, and by that I mean a bread roll with no butter and two lettuce leaves, perhaps some tomato or cucumber if he was lucky. Failing that it was a bucket of hot chips for breakfast, lunch and dinner.

By Toowoomba, Betty had chewed through four of the interim CVT drive belts. We only had one left. We decided to take a punt and push on to Roma; I called Steve and asked for the belts coming from Mexico to be delivered out there. We pushed on. The new belts should be in Roma tomorrow, and fingers crossed, so should we.

I'm not sure where the outback begins and ends in Australia. We passed signs now and again telling us we had just arrived in the outback, but I preferred to gauge this based on when road signs started warning me about getting clobbered by kangaroos, cattle, sheep and camels—and let's not forget the local armed outback Queenslanders; I definitely knew I was in the outback when I saw signs peppered with bullet holes. That, and my body was slowly cooking. This was the first of our long, dry and painfully slow stages into the red heart of the country. Matt hung back about a kilometre behind me, occasionally giving me a heads-up via the radio on a fast-approaching road train. This gave me enough warning to stop the bike and get off the road. Without Matty's warnings, I would have been in trouble; with all the vibrations my mirrors were effectively useless. The alternative was a road train—a massive thing that looks like a building with wheels—barrelling up behind my back wheel doing 130 kph and with no intention of stopping. Even pulling over had to be done with great care, as the shoulder was soft, and littered with dry sun-bleached animal bones that could puncture a tyre.

Roma was the goal; Roma was a place to rest for the night. I focused on the road ahead, and forced myself to pay attention. You live inside your helmet on a long-distance ride, but it becomes Wally World after a while. You drift, way off into other times, other places. While I rode I made lists, thought about tits, planned extensions to my house. I thought about the past a lot, revisiting childhood streets and alleyways in Scotland, like a morbid Google Earth. I jumped forward and backward through my past, made lists of people I wanted to catch up with, then crossed off the ones who were dead.

The problem is, if you let your brain box wander, your bike will eventually follow, likely straight into an oncoming road train. Rule of thumb, as I was repeatedly told by mates who know, guys who are long-distance riders: expect the worst, plan for the worst, and know yourself before you go. I have spent long isolated times away overseas with only my mind for company, so I knew hour upon hour, day after day of riding alone with only my thoughts rattling around in that helmet would be OK. Sometimes it would be a little dark, perhaps a little sick, but always within the realms of sanity. And of course I knew there was a truck a few k's behind me, so no matter what, I had back-up. That made all the difference. Attempting a ride like this on Betty without back-up would have been foolish.

When we stopped to refuel and drink some water, Dan would hop out of the cab while I was filling up Betty and ask me questions with the camera rolling. The answers I gave him were not always decent, polite or civil, or even comprehensible. But he rolled anyway. It helped keep me sane.

I ran into other riders along the way, guys chucking The Big Lap like me. I tip my hat to all of them: they were out there alone. Some had gone bush, tackling the likes of the Gun Barrel Highway, the Canning Stock Route or Gibb River; some were just mad, having completed the Finke Desert Race—basically, about two hundred k's of old railroad service track through the bush from Alice Springs to the town of Finke. Not too bad, I hear you thinking, but this track is hell on earth; you would be safer thrashing your bike across a minefield. There are corrugations deep enough to park a car in, and there's no maintenance done on the track—ever. But that's OK because you're doing 140 kilometres an hour; at that speed you're just planing over the top of everything and hanging on for dear life. So I listened while Geoff, the rider I chatted to during a break in the town of Jackson, told me how the Finke nearly killed him. Then he turned his attention to my steed. 'Is that fuckin monstrosity a diesel?'

There are countless disadvantages to riding an experimental bike like Betty around Australia, lack of power being paramount. Close behind is the lack of comfort—the vibrations had my arms feeling like they had just come from the dentist; I kept dropping things—and at this point, the lack of spares. We were down to the last CVT belt, and Roma was about 80 k's away. I waved to Geoff and took off, praying to the god of spare parts that my drive belts would turn up safely in Roma, all the way from Mexico.

Soon after Jackson, the road up ahead changed colour. I call that colour 'Hint of Death'; it's not quite brown, more of a reddish-brown mix. If this stretch of highway on my map was scratch-'n-sniff, then most people would vomit when looking at it on the way through Queensland. Plus, it looked like I was about to cross the frontline into some kangaroo civil war; littering the road before me were hundreds of stinking smashed carcasses in various stages of decomposition, from just splattered to bleached skeletons. I could smell it before I could see it, that rotting stink. Everyone else on the road was moving fast enough to rip through the pong before it made them gag—for other riders sitting on 130 kph it was just a matter of picking your way through the carnage and missing a breath. For me it was half a dozen breath mints and a prayer to the CVT belt: 'Don't fail me now.'

Australia relies heavily on the humble truck, the road trains that snake through our major arteries, but they don't stop for anything, especially the wildlife. Some parts of the road resembled streets I'd seen in Kabul right after a bomb had gone off. There were bits of bodies all over the place, and with the bits come the birds. But here it's not the odd crow, it's packs of crows, big ones, and the formidable wedgetail eagle.

Those birds are masters at playing chicken, no pun intended. Many times during the ride I came around a corner to find a giant wedgetail enjoying the never-ending all-you-can-eat roadkill smorgasbord. They would have heard me coming a mile away but just sat there motionless in the middle of the road, giving me the 'one day soon' look before reluctantly moving off at the last second.

Our ride into Roma was very tiring; the sun had turned my helmet into a convection oven. Finally we reached the town, and Matty got on the GPS and navigated us to the motel.

Roma is where Australia's oilfield started; the first wells were drilled out here in the late 1800s. I knew there would be enough oilfield hands milling about to make the next 24 hours interesting.

We pulled in to the motel, truck first, at dusk. I hopped off Betty and tried to cross my numb fingers while I asked the motel manager if a courier bag had arrived for me. Nothing. I tried to fill in the registration card, but my dead hands couldn't form letters so Dan had to do it. The motel was laid out in a big U shape and we had to drive past all the rooms to get to our room for the night. The place was full of oilfield hands, who sat out the front drinking in small groups. They tracked our slow circle round the car park, pulled the standard squint at Betty and wandered over as I got off and slid my sweaty head from inside my baked helmet. 'Mate,' said a big fella sporting a roll-up that dangled from his bottom lip and a sauce-stained, hard-yacka work shirt. 'Is that fuckin thing diesel?'

We all chatted for almost an hour, swapping stories and drinking beer. Then I got on the phone to try to find out where the CVT belts were. Steve was as encouraging as ever. 'You'll have them tomorrow, mate, late afternoon.'

I hung up. Dan looked at me enquiringly. 'We're going to have to stay here for two nights, mate; the belts won't get here until tomorrow afternoon.'

Dan looked tearfully happy at the thought of a lie-in the next morning. 'I'm gonna get some beers,' he said, and took off. Matt departed in search of food he could actually eat.

I couldn't relax though. I had a routine, it had to play out every night, no matter how tired I was. The bike needed a going-over in preparation for the next day. I had a bad case of 'equipment anxiety'. I'm used to planning everything down to the last detail, but with Betty there were daily issues. Overcoming them was just part of the game played out each day. It was psychological warfare at times, a war of attrition between Betty and me. The wicked vibration from the diesel single shook lots of things loose, so I would lie there in the dirt with a spanner and cast my eye slowly over the bike, checking her from front to back. I had a little white paint pen to mark bolts so I could see if they had backed off. I changed her oil, cleaned her air filter, checked the fuel lines and oil filter. I checked the tyre pressure on both Betty and the truck, lubed up everything that moved and polished everything that didn't. Like many riders I have an obsessive compulsive bond with my bikes. In Betty's case it was a pure love/hate relationship.

Matt came back with Dan. They had bought a slab of beer, two burgers with the lot and a salad roll. We settled in for the night, talking to the drilling hands in the cool night air well into the early hours.

Morning saw Matty putting a new sign on the back of the truck; he'd been down to the hardware store in town and come back with all the kit to make his own contribution to the ride: 'Caution Slow Bike Ahead'.

He was standing on the porch with a coffee when I came out to squint at the truck in the daylight. 'Nice work, mate.'

Dan was still asleep; all that running around with a big camera in the bush had taken its toll on him. 'Get the fuck up, you lazy cunt.' Matty leaped onto the bed and started jumping up and down until Dan got up.

After breakfast we decided to check out the Big Rig, an outdoor museum of sorts dedicated to the history of drilling in the area. We met the manager and got the full tour, and ended up spending the whole day there talking oilfield. Roma was very friendly to us, not just another outback town but one with a rich oil industry background. We pulled into the motel car park later that day. I ran in to reception, and there on the countertop were my CVT belts—all the way from Mexico. 'Yes!' I ran out waving them at Dan and Matty. We could hit the road again at first light. I was beaming as we rounded the car park.

This time some new faces milled about and there was a lot of laughter. A big bald Canadian guy sauntered up: 'Hey man, are you Paul Carter?'

I pulled off my helmet. 'Yeah.' I stuck out my hand, he shook it and started laughing.

'Dude, call your mom.' Everyone burst out laughing.

'You what?' Then the penny dropped. I'm not very good at staying in touch with my family; it's not unusual for a month to go by between phone calls to my mum. She lives in France in a tiny village—not that it makes any difference where she lives, she could live on another planet and still find me. I knew she didn't like the idea of me leaving my girls behind to go gallivanting around Australia on a motorcycle, and when Mum wants an update, she gets an update. She worked in the oilfield for 30 years and knows how to find people. I've been on rigs in really remote Third World toilets, where a two-way radio is considered top-notch, high-tech communications, and my mother has tracked me down.

This time she'd surpassed herself. 'G'day Paul, how's yer mum?' said the guy in the next room as we passed on the porch. I discovered that Mum had tracked my slow progress as far as Queensland and decided that Roma was an obvious place for us to stop for the night, so she got online and found the numbers for all the pubs and motels in Roma and simply started calling. It didn't take long for everyone in Roma to hear that the oilfield writer—and by all accounts, mummy's boy—Paul Carter hadn't called his mum for a month. Matty and Dan found all this hilarious. For the rest of the night as different guys knocked off work and returned to the motel, they each gave me a huge grin and asked how my mum was doing, and it went on for the next two days. 'Is that fuckin thing diesel—and have you called yer mother yet?' Finally I gave in and called her. 'Hi, Mum, I'm fine.'

The next morning Roma trailed off in the distance behind me: no more mum jokes, just a nice easy run on the Warrego Highway to Morven. I felt upbeat and well-rested. For people who don't know, riding a motorcycle for extended periods can be physically and mentally hard.

I heard a lot of shit before I left to go on this ride. I thought about that for a while as we slowly rolled towards central

Queensland. There were many people who supported me, but there were also lots of punishers, the sort who stay safely within their comfort zones in suburban bliss and feel compelled to make comments like: 'Why would you bother to ride a bio-fuel bike round Australia? What's that going to prove?' or 'You girl, with your support truck' or 'You're not even going up to Cairns or off-road properly' or 'Mate, I've been round ten times . . . in the nude.' Several of them said, 'Your truck burns conventional diesel so what's the point?' I would go through the motions of explaining that if I did convert the support truck to run on the same fuel as the bike then I would need to haul more fuel around than the truck could carry. You can't just pull up and get bio-fuel at every service station. Besides, I didn't have the funding to do all of that; I only had enough to cover the basics. Anyone who manages to tee up a big ride is doing well in my book, and I have huge respect for the adventurers who actually get off their arse and do it. In fact, none of the riders I met on the road made comments like that; there was only mutual understanding and curiosity about the ride ahead.

A few hours out of Roma, we pulled into a tiny smattering of buildings and a roadhouse. Matty filled up the truck and I parked across the street in the shade, quietly sitting on Betty. I began to take off my helmet when the ground started shaking and I heard the roar: dozens of Harleys rounded the corner; the riders braked and backed their bikes in next to me in a long row, back wheels to the kerb. Pulling off their helmets and gloves, they dismounted and slowly gathered around me and Betty. My backside puckered. They all looked like real bad-arse bikers, with full-sleeve tats, big greying beards and dark wrap-around shades. Oh fuck, this is the bit where I get to find out if Betty fits up my arse, I thought.

'G'day mate,' said a particularly big biker with gold teeth and a black bandanna.

'Hey fellas.' I tried to sound confident, but to these guys I must have looked like a lost schoolgirl on a Vespa.

'Is that fuckin thing a diesel?'

Well, thank God for that, they were actually really nice guys. We had a good chat, then they all had a beer in the roadhouse and we continued on.

Matt came on the radio as we pulled out. 'Mate, I thought you were going to get proper fucked then,' he laughed.

'So did I, Matt.'

Next stop, Morven.

It took time to get from point A to point B each day, partly because Dan is a perfectionist. Several times a day the truck would speed up and overtake me, then Matt would pull over, and Dan would spring from the truck and set up his camera. When he was ready, I would ride past, so Dan could film me approaching and passing the camera. Then Dan would jump back in the truck, and Matt would start the process again. That, or Dan would get me to turn around and ride past again so he could shoot the bike riding off into the distance; this often involved having to do it a third time so Dan could shoot the ride with his long lens, or a fourth, fifth and sixth time because of light, weather, traffic, or some other problem.

Sometimes they would scout ahead looking for a good spot to shoot, and this was when a road train would usually come out of nowhere and scare the piss out of me. Sometimes we would pass something that Dan liked and both Matt and I would leave Dan by the side of the road or he would take off up a hill or into the bush with his camera, tripod and a two-way radio to set himself up for the shot. Then we would backtrack a few k's and sit there in the 45-degree heat slowly cooking, waiting for

Dan's voice to tell us he was rolling. Once we'd ridden past, he would come over the radio saying, 'Shit, I didn't get the shot, do it again', 'Shit, there's a fuckin snake chasing me', 'Shit, my battery's dead', 'Shit I forgot the long lens', 'Where's my stills camera?' or 'Have you guys left me here? Come back . . . Hey, come on . . . this isn't funny.' Sometimes he took off into the bush and forgot the two-way radio altogether. This all added to my frustration; I had no idea how hard it is to do a ride like this on film.

Past two in the afternoon, we were heading into the sun, and the glare was directly in our eyes. I was riding with sunglasses, tinted goggles, and a tinted visor and I still struggled with the glare. We pulled into a dusty little place and stopped outside the pub, where I toe'd out Betty's kick stand and got off. A dozen or so young blokes were sitting under the verandah, knocking back beers and laughing. As I turned I realised they were laughing at me, but I nodded and smiled. One young man stood up, looking a bit pissed and sunburnt. He ambled over, puffing up his chest and grinning. Here we go, I thought.

'Is that piece of shit diesel?'

I smiled again—a bit thinly this time—and left my helmet on, just flipped up the visor. 'Yeah mate.'

He looked over my shoulder at Dan, climbing out of the truck with his camera. I turned around and thumbed the comms. 'Get back in the truck, lads, and go.'

'Are you fellas makin a porno?' the young lad asked. Interesting angle.

'No, why do you ask?'

'Well, you look like a big cock to me.' He had a laugh to himself, and his mates joined in.

'That's a coincidence,' I said casually. His brow furrowed, waiting for it. I glanced over at the boys sitting on the verandah;

they were just pissed enough to go for it. Oh, well, I've come this far . . . 'Coz you look like a giant cunt to me.'

Game on. It didn't get that bad really; the bike was the first thing he went for, he missed on the first swing, and I was long gone.

Morven finally loomed up on the horizon ahead, being met by the sun on its way down. 'Let's go straight to the pub, I'm hanging for a beer.' Dan's voice over the radio sounded relieved.

We pulled up directly outside the small-town hotel and wandered in. I was pulling off my lid as I walked up to the bar; a middle-aged woman serving sized me up as I approached. 'Bald head, motorbike, you must be Paul.' I stopped, nodded. 'Call ya mum, there's a good lad.' She walked off. Dan was pissing himself and Matt handed me his phone.

We fell into our usual evening beer-swilling banter, and had a counter meal. Afterwards, I went through my ritual with Betty, and by the time I walked into our shared room wiping grease off my hands with a rag and talking to myself, the boys were already fast asleep.

The ride to Tambo the next day started with sore heads and no breakfast or coffee. Dan wanted to film the scenery, or 'go all Spielberg' as Matt said over the radio. It was just too hot and tiring to wait around, so I pushed off. The arid flat landscape went on and on. This was the first time I had strayed well beyond the truck and the radio's range; I felt weirdly free, like I'd been released. I wanted to go back and do the whole trip again, but alone, like a few of the riders I'd met along the way. I thought about Clare and Lola, and I wondered how Oswald was getting on; I hoped he was still alive. Then I thought, if he'd gone surely the cattery would have called me on the sat phone.

Last winter he walked up to the front door of our house and announced his intention to go to the toilet. He has kitty litter, but prefers to poop in the comfort of the front garden. So I got up and let him out, and then my mate Gavin Kelly dropped by. I was standing on our front porch drinking beer and chatting to him when Oswald had one of his absent moments right behind Gavin's heel. 'MMMMAWWWW,' yowled Ossy.

Gav jumped about two feet into the air. 'What the fuck's up with your cat?'

Oswald was sitting between the roses howling that late night, psychopathic howl: 'WHAT'S GOING ON WITH THESE GIANT ROSES? . . . WHAT AM I DOING HERE? . . . WHAT THE FUCK ARE YOU TWO LOOKING AT?'

'He's got cat dementia,' I explained to Gav.

'MMMMAWWWW.' Oswald started digging out huge scoops of earth. It had started raining, but that didn't bother him.

'Where's he going mate, China?' said Gav.

'Well, either that or he's remembered why he's digging a hole in the rain.'

'He's down to his shoulder there, how big does your cat shit?' Gav finished his beer. 'That's a bit optimistic, don't you think, Ossy?'

I shrugged. 'He's an oilfield cat, mate, he'll be running casing in that hole next.'

Gav smiled and we were about to walk off when Ossy suddenly puckered up and nutted one out about a foot away from his perfectly vertical hole. Then he turned around and filled in the hole, patting down the earth fastidiously. He sprinkled leaves over the top and everything. He turned to go and stopped dead in front of his turd.

'Fuckin hell.' Gav was in hysterics.

Ossy looked up at us as if to say, 'Now, how did that happen?' and sat there in the rain looking at his poop.

Clare came out onto the porch to get us. 'Come inside, guys. What are you two doing out here?'

Gav said the obvious: 'Watching your cat.'

Ossy followed us in, soaking wet. We sat down and got talking. After a while, our conversation was interrupted by Ossy. He'd passed out way too close to the gas heater and was now on fire, running through the living room screaming 'MMMMMMMMMAAAAAAWWWWW.' He left a burnt-hair vapor trail down the hall.

'Jesus, the cat's on fire.' We put him out. Luckily only the top layer of hair was gone, and now so is the gas heater.

Back on the highway only static came back to me over the radio. Matty and Dan must be well behind me now, I thought. I put my feet up on the highway pegs Matt Bromley had installed, taking the vibrations off my knee to my back. Towards the end of the day a dust storm began brewing off to my left. There were flashes of lightning, and sudden violent wind gusts buffeted the bike. A huge willy-willy formed up ahead, spinning a curved cylinder of red earth into the brooding clouds. I was just happy not to be riding into the sun.

Every morning I calculated how far we had to travel that day, against my average speed, with a Dan ('Where's my . . .?') factor built in. I had become obsessed with watching the odometer ticking over: the first ton of the day was easy, before the sun got up there and cooked me. The rest of the day was agonisingly slow, the old mechanical wheel slowly rolling over. That afternoon, though, I knew I was less than twenty k's from town. Hopefully I'd get there before the storm got me.

'Paul, are you there?' Matty's voice crackled over the radio.

The radio's range was good for two k's so they couldn't be too far away.

'Hi Matt,' I said.

'Mate, we'll see you soon in town, at the pub, over.'

'Roger that.' I thought longingly about a big steak dinner sitting on the countertop waiting for me with a cold beer.

Soon I was rolling down the town's main street. No one was about and the wind was hammering dust and tumbleweeds across the road. I parked Betty around the side of the pub and walked into the main bar; it looked very comfy inside and the locals gave me a smile. I could smell a roast. Ten minutes later Dan and Matty stumbled through the door.

'Dan's made an executive decision to get shit-faced tonight, mate.' Matt put his hat on the bar and rubbed his hands together.

The girl tending bar came over. 'Hi, guys, what would you like?'

'One Pale Ale, one Guinness, a whisky 'n soda, two steak dinners, and a salad roll no butter with chips please.' Matt smiled.

'She's hot,' said Dan, watching the girl walk off to put the order in with the kitchen. 'So's she.' Another young blonde walked past. 'And another—they're all hot.'

Not only did the manager have a very nice pub, he also assembled a bar staff entirely of cute backpackers. 'Watch and learn, gentlemen.' Dan put his camera on the bar and within five minutes two of the girls were flicking their hair while Danny was being cute and anecdotal.

'I guess they don't get too many TV cameramen through town.' Matt regarded the scene and then his salad roll and chips. 'Yummy.' He lifted the top off the roll and started laying chips down in a row. 'If I never see another shit salad roll . . .'

We had a ball that night. Dan was hammered and very, very funny. Matt and I spent the night talking to a local guy who spends the day removing all the dead animals from the road. There's that much carnage out there on the highway that a guy has to drive up and down it all day in a truck collecting bodies. Now there's a tough job. I sloped off and did my bike ritual before I got too pissed.

'Tomorrow we ride to Longreach,' Dan announced later in the bathroom while trying to brush his teeth.

The morning presented itself in white-hot blazing hangover napalm heat. Squinting and cursing, the boys dragged out their bags and loaded up the truck. Betty was good to go, all I needed was a new set of ear plugs to block out Betty's racket. Without the ear plugs I was deaf after an hour. Sometimes I stopped for a pee in the middle of nowhere in total, outback middle-of-the-day silence and my ears were still shattering the peace and quiet. The residual ringing would last for hours, drowning out a leading question from Dan, filming me while I tried to urinate in peace.

'Sorry?' I'd say, and he'd repeat it. Still couldn't hear it. 'Say again, mate?'

'YOU LOOK LIKE A DISGRUNTLED STORM TROOPER IN ALL THAT RIDING GEAR, HOW DOES IT FEEL?'

'WELL, IT FUCKIN STINKS DAN, COS IT'S 48 DEGREES OUT HERE TODAY, BY NOW IT'S ONLY THE STUBBORN UNDERSTAINS THAT'RE HOLDING THE WHOLE LOT TOGETHER. LOOK AT MY PEE—I DRANK A LITRE OF WATER THIS MORNING AND IT'S THE SAME COLOUR AS THE BIO-DIESEL.'

We needed a mental health day.

We did the usual ten retakes of me riding past a particularly interesting tree, while Dan, Matt and I hurled abuse at each other over the radio. Finally Longreach arrived. We had a fine meal, lots of water, and an early night.

17 THE LONG REACH

The heat radiated hard invisible waves, zapping my energy. Today was going to be long; the truck was about one k behind me, but Betty's hellish vibration distorted the image in the mirror, turning one truck into four. No matter what I tried, there was simply no conventional vibration dampening system that would make a shred of difference to the mirrors.

I flipped open my visor to wedge a Minty into my mouth. The air was like a slap in the face—imagine sitting in a sauna while someone holds a hairdryer an inch from your eyes, that's what it was like. 'Fuck a pig,' I often swore out loud, or I'd sing, or have long conversations with myself like a mad person with Tourettes. A corner came looming up with a triple banking hard around it, always on the apex. You could sit on the bike for hours on the straight with nothing and no one passing you, then the minute you hit a blind corner, a road train the size of Brussels would be coming directly at you. There was no time to react, other than just blindly hang on and hope for the best. Because of Betty's very upright riding position, the invisible wall of air displaced by a truck doing 130 k's would hit me hard. It was often like catching a sack of flour in the chest, while the bike got blown across the road.

I'd just got settled back in the saddle, the truck was in the right place behind me, my Minty was doing a fair job of removing the rotting road-kill smell and we were purring along at 90 k's, when the bucket of coffee the French woman made me that morning hit my bladder in a latte tsunami. The usual deal with stopping for a pee was to wait for a proper bay where I could take off the helmet and gloves, unplug the comms, and have a slash at my leisure and in relative safety. But this morning I told the boys over the radio to drive past me and keep going; I would just pull over, hop off, pee, hop back on again and catch up. No removing helmets and gloves; I just wanted to keep going. I checked my right mirror as the boys sped up and moved across to pass, Matt gesticulating mid-story while Dan pointed the camera out the window and angled his head into the viewfinder. As they drew parallel with me, I got off the throttle and slowly applied the brakes together as I pulled onto the dirt. The shoulder was as wide and flat as the road; it looked like it had recently been graded. Betty was about two metres off the road when she slammed to a complete stop.

Time and adrenalin put you in a weird place. I wonder if there is a word for those moments in your life when accidents happen: that out-of-body parallel universe you enter when you realise you're going to crash, just before you actually hit something. Time slows down; adrenalin transforms you from a disposable camera into a microscope.

The information I processed in those split seconds was astounding. If only I could make my brain perform like that all the time. For me, the initial horror—like the spike of a needle—then dissolved into calm hyper-awareness like I'd had a giant hit of Berocca. I was suddenly as calm and detached as at any quiet moment. As my head went through Betty's windshield, I noticed the odometer read five kilometres; I'd reset it when we left Longreach. 'Five k's,' I thought, 'that's not very far out of town for an ambulance to travel.' My body was thrown forward and to the left; I was obviously getting high-sided and was about to get slammed down on my left side, head first. I thought, 'It's OK, the airbag vest will go off now,' and then my mind flashed to an image of me throwing the vest on the back seat of the truck as we left the coffee shop not ten minutes earlier. 'Oh fuck.'

Thomas Mann said it well: 'We never really learn anything, we just become aware of things when the time and the potential in us coincide.'

I hit the ground.

There was a lot of ragdoll tumbling. The brain stopped processing, shut down and rebooted seconds later. I was looking through my visor at a very worried Matt; he was bent over me, slowly lifting the visor open. Warm air rushed in but I couldn't get any into my lungs. The impact had knocked the air from my body; I could feel my right leg and arm but nothing else. Usually when a rider stacks it, the normal reaction is to spring up instantly and stand the bike up. But I could not raise my head off the dirt. I suddenly felt very self-pitying. Visions of me throwing a ball to Lola from a wheelchair wandered through my mind like a stray dog. 'Now look what you've done to yourself.' My sanctimonious common sense spoke up at last. 'Fatigue, not paying attention: cry me a river, you hedonistic wanker.' Oh God, what the fuck have I done? I tried again to get up but nothing worked.

Matt put his hand on my shoulder. 'What are you doing, mate? Lie still, the ambulance is on its way—ten minutes, OK?' he said calmly.

I became aware of Dan next to me. I grabbed his hand and squeezed. 'Don't worry, mate.' He faked a smile. It was bizarre to see Dan at this angle without a camera pressed up against his eye. I was grateful the boys were there.

The ambulance crew arrived, named Mel and Kim, much to Matt's amusement, then a fire truck, then the police. They were all completely brilliant, and fast. Suddenly there was a tarp between my head and the baking sun, and I heard the bike being carried off. My helmet was removed and all my gear. It was a frenzy of well-trained people, all of them knowing exactly what to do, unlike me and Matt. Once the ambulance arrived, even Dan got straight back to work and picked up his camera. Then came the pain relief, a big green tube, and whooooo the fuck am I.

Longreach Hospital's emergency entrance soon loomed up, reflected upside down on the ceiling of the ambulance. I was engrossed in that detached feeling you get with shock and strong pain-relief meds. This was just a movie I'd been watching; I'd seen this bit a hundred times—the gurney passing through several big swinging doors and pulling up next to the machine that goes *ping*.

The doctor marched up and said something doctor-ish like: 'So we've had a bit of crash then.' The green tube was removed and just as fast as I got happy the reality came thudding straight back, accompanied by fear. I was terrified I'd done something to my spine. The doctor asked what happened, and both Matt and I launched into the story while Dan filmed in the background. Suddenly Dan stopped and raised his hand. 'Excuse me,' he said. Everyone stopped talking and looked over at him. 'I've got the whole thing on camera.'

'Really,' said the doctor.

'Yeah, total fluke.'

'Well, let's see it then.' The doctor, Matt, Mel and Kim, a nurse, and the dude in the corner who'd been mopping the floor all crammed their heads over Dan's shoulder to peer into the camera's little video playback screen. There was a unanimous sharp intake of breath through clenched teeth, then everyone looked over at me flat on my back. The machine that goes *ping* pinged.

Longreach Hospital, although abundantly stocked with hot-looking nurses and extremely friendly doctors, unfortunately has no big expensive imaging machines with which to look into the human body for damage. They do however have a radiologist, who wheeled me away to X-ray my entire body. I was then wheeled into a semi-circular room at the end of a long corridor, and a few hours later the doctor reappeared with the good news: I had not broken any bones, though I had cracked two ribs, and torn my rotator cup, a groin ligament and my favourite riding pants. 'So in many ways it would be easier and less painful if you had just sustained a straight fracture.' He smiled and flipped over his clipboard. 'You're going to be with us for a few days. You'll have to eat prunes because the pain medication can cause some constipation. We're also concerned about any internal damage you may have sustained, so for the moment, it's all about you moving your bowel, OK Mr Carter?'

I looked over at the hot nurse who had given me morphine about 30 minutes before the doctor arrived. I knew I was grinning like a fool. 'So I can't go anywhere till I poop?' She looked at her shoes.

'Well, yes,' said the doctor. 'Remember to try to move about. You're going to be in a great deal of pain tomorrow, so we've given you sufficient pain medication to help you deal with that, and you've been admitted as a private patient so you have the whole room to yourself. The boys tell me they're going to bring some DVDs back for you later.' I looked over the doctor's shoulder at Matt, who was nodding and blowing kisses. Dan was doing that thousand-yard worried stare into nothing, the one he pulls when he's forgotten something. *Wait for it, wait for it . . .*

'Mr Carter, are you OK with all that?'

Dan's going to do it. Any moment now, wait for it.

'Mr Carter.' The doctor raised his voice and snapped me back.

At the same moment Danny said, 'Where's my phone?'

Right on time, Danny.

'OK, doctor,' I said. He could have just finished telling me I was going to develop a third eye and webbed digits; I had gone to morphine heaven. Gone. That is, until it wore off.

There was no self-medicating for me; I had to wait for the hot nurse to squeak her way down the hall to my pain-filled concrete room and jab that vein.

I woke up suddenly in the middle of the night from a dry, open-mouthed, drug-induced dreamless sleep. For the first few seconds I thought I was in another random donga, back on the road. It was like waking up inside Tupperware, all memory of the fall blissfully blanked. Until I tried to move, that is. The pain I felt in that dark room was more intense than anything I'd ever experienced, and I've broken bones before. For a second my eyes saucered as searing, all-powerful pain stopped me from sitting up. I couldn't even reach the little call button thingy to get the nurse's attention. Panic shot up and down my spine for a second, so I just lay there in the dark and focused on my breathing. Then I heard her shoes. I think I squealed a little like a Japanese schoolgirl in a Hello Kitty store. Thank God, she heard me, she's a hot nurse on her way, she's a fuckin angel, a morphine angel ready to jump on my midnight morphine roundabout, all the way to breakfast. I pictured perfectly poached farm-fresh eggs on toast with bacon and real coffee.

Instead, as the fluorescent light blinked on I looked up at a different nurse, older and grimmer, Skeletor in a white dress, who promptly shoved a pill in my mouth the size of a breeze block, followed by a straw. She took my temperature—for a moment I thought it was going to be the baby way from the look in her eye—she checked my blood pressure, scribbled on the clipboard at the foot of the bed and marched out, flicking off the light with a curt 'Try to get some sleep.'

The morphine kicked in eventually; I could feel it creeping around in my head with a pillow, smothering the screams.

The morning arrived with a gentle voice and a wheeled table gliding across the floor, pulling up over my waist. 'Breakfast,' the voice said, and a finger pressed the button to raise the back half of my bed. Someone opened the curtains to another hot sunny Queensland day. I looked up to see a homely-looking middle-aged woman; she smiled and slid a plastic tray onto my table with various round plastic containers no doubt housing a feast. But no: there was cold toast, fruit, corn flakes and yes, a big bowl of prunes. The doctor had said I would feel worse today and he was right. I couldn't see it but there was definitely an invisible elephant sitting on my chest, I was sore and felt completely crippled. My muscles just didn't want to work, I had no power; I was in a blackout on the left side of my body from my shoulder to my toes.

The hot nurse appeared. I could make out her underwear through her whites when she crossed the big round windows. 'How are you today, Mr Carter?' I was conscious of the fact that I looked and smelled like a bum. 'Enjoying the prunes?' she asked. I watched her young professional disinfected veneer closely. Where are you hiding those pills? She crossed the room again to refill my water cup, and I automatically checked again for the VPL. It's not that I'm a complete perv or anything, it's just what men do. Cleavage has the same effect, like looking at the sun or pulling on that little bit of skin next to a fingernail; every shred of your body says, 'Don't do it,' but you just can't help yourself.

She took my blood pressure and temperature, and brought in a huge purple Zimmer frame with retractable wheels which she parked beside the bed on my stronger right side. 'When you're ready, Mr Carter, use this to get yourself to the shower, it's just outside the door to your room. The toilet is next door.' I smiled, and yes, finally, there it was, the magic pill. 'The doctor will be starting his rounds soon, he'll be here by the time you've finished breakfast.' With a big smile and a quick retucking of bed sheets, she turned on her heel and squeaked out of the room. I could hear some loony shouting down the hallway.

God, I wanted to shower, shave and hopefully shit, thereby getting my departure ticket. But to what, a bike that I couldn't ride? I needed a plan. I had to call Clare; it had been twelve hours since the crash and I knew the boys hadn't made the call. This was on Dan's request—he wanted to film it. It's the call I never wanted to make, to tell her I've dropped it, to tell her to come to Longreach with Lola. The thought of my girls pulled hard at my gut, the morphine helping to produce crystal-clear images of Clare holding Lola, their faces happy, full of love, big as the sky.

Dan and Matt arrived with junk food, DVDs and real coffee. Dan did an about-face and walked out again, clearly having forgotten something. Matt's stocky purposeful stride stopped level with my head; he knew the first thing I would ask and he beat me to it.

'The bike's OK, mate; the front end's a little bashed in, the bars and the left foot peg are bent, the mirrors, tail-light and rear indicators are broken, but the frame is sweet.' He sat down and took off his hat.

'Where is it?' I asked.

'One of the fireys dropped it off in a ute at the motel this morning. How are you feeling? How are the drugs workin'?'

On any given day, all I have to do is look at Mathew and I'll smile, but on morphine I was grinning widely.

'Good stuff morphine, you look pain-free. That nurse is cute, she washed your balls yet?' He reached into a plastic bag and produced half a dozen DVDs. 'Now, the choices were limited, mate, this is the best they had.' I picked up the pile and in the process shifted my bum three inches to the right, causing me to wince in pain.

Dan reappeared. 'Where's my tripod?'

Matt looked at him and placed his index finger against his pursed lips. 'Hmmmm.' His other hand burrowed wildly into the back of his pants. 'Well, it's not up my arse—have you had a good look in yours?'

Dan smiled and put his camera bag down in the corner. 'Mate, local ABC Radio want to come by tomorrow and do an interview, is that cool?' I nodded. 'OK, I'll set that up.'

Matt's DVD choices were good considering he got them in a petrol station. Hitchcock's classic *The Birds*, *Ghostbusters*, an old Sean Connery sci-fi movie from the eighties called *Outland* and, God love him, Ewan McGregor and Charley Boorman's *Long Way Round*—just what I wanted to see. I'd rather rub Deep Heat on my balls and staple my tongue to a burning building.

Dan handed me my phone. 'Thanks for waiting, mate, I'll just roll.'

I called Clare. I didn't want to tell her I was in a hospital, that I'd dropped the ball. So I lied, telling her we'd decided to stay a couple of extra days in Longreach. She saw through my lie in a second, though, even over the phone. She was straight onto me, and got all the facts. She wanted to fly up straightaway, but in the few days since we'd last talked my daughter had developed a bad inner-ear infection that had just ruptured her eardrum, so they were temporarily grounded. Clare talked to her brother for a while, then Matt handed the phone back to me. 'Honey, I'll see what flights are available and call you back,' she said.

'Have you had a shit yet?' Matt didn't look up from his newspaper as he asked.

'No,' I said.

He shook the paper so the TV guide fell into his lap. 'Pity, this place sucks.' He put his feet up on the end of my bed. 'When did you have your last shit then?' He turned a page.

'Yesterday morning.'

'Right, that's 24 hours; you'd better punch one out for the team, champ, or we're all going to Darwin to get you scanned.' He tossed the TV guide onto the bed.

'What?' I looked at him and threw it back.

'Dr Feelgood and Nurse Ratched said yesterday you need to drop one within 48 hours or you're flying to Darwin to have an MRI.'

'Really?' I didn't remember that.

'Pay attention, 007,' said Matt, getting up. 'Now get your arse out of bed, have a shower, eat another prune-fuckin-McMuffin and poop for Uncle Matty or I'll wait till you're drug-fucked, get that crazy old cunt from down the hall, take out his teeth and make Dan film him with your cock in his mouth.'

That galvanised me into action, though I waited until they were gone to get to it. It took me twenty minutes to get out of bed and on to the Zimmer frame thing; the 50 feet to the shower was agonising. Hot nurse's voice came at me through the door: 'Everything OK, Mr Carter?' I must have been in there too long. I prayed she wouldn't poke her head round the door and see my pale, pathetic Zimmer-frame shower scene. I'd been trying to reach the back of my legs, and of course I dropped the soap.

'Fine, everything's fine, no problem, be out soon.' I overdid it; now she probably thought I was wanking. I brushed the socks off my teeth, shaved, and spent the rest of the morning pushing my pain threshold.

Dan arrived in the afternoon with Miss ABC Radio, and filmed her interviewing me in a wheelchair on the grass in front of the hospital. That was the first time I saw Dan film with his free eye open. Usually Danny keeps the eye not peering through the lens clamped shut, but now his free eye was wide open and wandering all over the ABC Radio journalist's gentle curves and blonde hair. Dan can do a great job of capturing the moment on film while having a good perv at the same time.

Later that night, while waiting for Skeletor to pill me out, I could ignore Ewan and Charley no longer. I could see the DVD cover on the chair next to the bed, the two of them sitting on their BMWs looking like a million bucks. I thought about my one bike, smashed up and stowed in a motel car park, and my leaky ten-year-old second-hand ex-council support truck. And then there was my support crew. Matt, well, he wasn't into bikes, he was neither sporty nor fit-looking—although he used to bowl when he was an alcoholic—he wasn't into road trips, he hates people, and every time Dan put the camera on him he spouted the most vile, disturbing, stream-of-consciousness rant, albeit delivered with real venom and wit; stuff that would peel the enamel from your teeth, make the hair on the back of your neck stand on end, if you were weak, old, or mentally challenged, would fuck you up. Yep, that's my support team right there. I wondered if Ewan and Charley had a Matt on their team.

In the end, alert from too much sleep during the day and still waiting for Skeletor, I gave in to the white-toothed allure of Ewan and Charley. It would have been easier to ignore blood in my urine; I just had to see what they did. I really enjoyed it, but I couldn't finish it. Not to detract from Ewan and Charley's efforts—I was fascinated—but I flaked out about halfway through.

That's when I met Bill—at least, I think his name was Bill—the crazy old gentleman from down the hall. My room was dark and cold, with invisible monsters hiding under the bed; I slept still aware of the crazy man down the hall, I was locked in the cell next to Hannibal Lector ready to swallow my tongue. I started to stir. Something deep in my subconscious was pressing an alarm bell. I woke with that disturbing sensation that you're being watched. I forced my eyes open. His nose was two inches from mine; I caught his cabbage breath in the same dark instant. 'Whoa.' My head jerked back hard into the pillow.

The TV still flickering with Ewan and Charley backlit his wild grey hair and creased leathery skin; he was babbling insane gibberish at me, nonsensical crazy talk, right into my face: 'Do you know the human head weighs eight pounds? Do you know that bees and dogs can smell fear?' He looked maniacal.

'Fuck off,' I said. I was scared for two reasons: one, because for a second there I was looking around for Dan and Matt in case Bill had indeed just been gumming my penis on film; and two, because even though I was to discover that he was very old and considered harmless by everyone, if he'd wanted to, this frail old bastard could have seriously fucked with me.

The light blinked on overhead. 'Out, back to bed, mate.' I'd never been so relieved to see the grim face of Skeletor. She gently but firmly shouldered Bill around the bed and out of the room, rather like a sheep dog nudging a lamb out of harm's way. Hot nurse no doubt had to deal with Bill's loose misfiring bowel and cabbage-breath-delivered bullshit during the day, and Skeletor had the task of rounding him up at night. This was not to say Skeletor was a dog; she just looked bad in that light at that hour of the night, when a man was seriously in need of more drugs. Soon she came back and hooked me up with the good stuff, thank God, so my pulse rate calmed down and I settled back into the BMW duo's well-planned ride. I need to watch it again one day when I'm not on drugs.

After my morning prunes in prune sauce with a generous side of prunes, I hit the Zimmer for an hour, then the hospital physiotherapist came by. 'Lose that girl's frame, mate,' he said. In his early thirties, he was tall and had a good sense of humour, he reminded me of Southwell. The frame got pushed into the corner while I stood in the middle of the room with my weight on one foot. The green hospital PJs were about three sizes too big, I just hobbled there like a big bald leprechaun.

'Hold on to my arm, we're going for a walk.' It really hurt, but slowly, very slowly, it did get easier.

Afterwards, I was in bed watching Oprah give another lesson in the real use of power, while crazy old Bill shouted nonsense from his room down the corridor, when suddenly that 48-hour back order of prunes hit exit point. Time was going to be critical. I don't know if you've ever seen a sloth panic; I did once, it's a super slow motion event—their top speed is fourteen kilometres an hour. You know the poor animal thinks he's doing 100, he's pulling all the right faces, it's just that he's going well under half speed. Well, today I was doing about five and needing to do about 105. That morning I had gone from sporting oversized PJs to one of those green reverse gown things that leaves your butt horribly exposed to the elements. At the halfway mark I realised I needed the Zimmer, so I had to make a brief diversion to the other end of the room, wasting valuable time. Clenching wildly, I angled the giant Zimmer towards the nirvana of clean cold porcelain, my already naked buttocks heading directly for docking. The music for *2001: A Space Odyssey* began to ring in my ears.

I focused on holding the clench, my balloon knot under increasing pressure as I reversed through the spring-loaded saloon-style doors to the toilet. The loud internal blitzkrieg in my bowel caused me to yelp in fear. I backed up to the throne as fast as my hobbling would take me, my knees started to bend, angle of impact looked good, five seconds to touchdown, stand by, stand by. As I reached the point of no return, I was no longer able to support my body weight, and I had to let go of the Zimmer and hope that I landed well. The inside of my right knee touched plastic and I let go. There was a sudden jolt of pain, easily a ten on the pain scale, as my weight came down directly on the middle of the seat. Shock combined with joy, combined with the knowledge that this—provided no internal organs were about to see daylight—could be my ticket out of here. Hallelujah.

In the meantime, hot nurse's desk was only a few feet away from the toilet door. The violent rapid bowel movement I was desperately trying to do quietly could in fact be heard in the Qantas Museum two k's down the road. 'You OK, Mr Carter?' Oh fuck no, her head popped round the door.

My voice went up ten octaves. 'Close the door.'

I sat there shaking and twitching for five minutes, then realised the roll of toilet paper was a good five feet from my useless left arm. The big red call button was two feet from my nose. All I had to do was give up and hot nurse would come in and really give me something to write about.

I stretched for the toilet paper, struggling against the pain, but fell short by an inch. I looked around for something else to wipe with. If I didn't sort this out soon, hot nurse would be back. I even contemplated ripping the arm off my backless green robe.

I finally bridged the gap—the long reach in Longreach—between my right hand and the petal-soft, fluffy white roll by using the toilet brush I found behind me. I discovered that if I smacked the brush down on the roll to make the paper spool out and waved the bristly end in the air, I could wind layers of paper around it. I was triumphant! But I was sprung. Hot nurse's puzzled face appeared once more in the doorway; I sat there looking at her, clutching my fairy-floss stick of toilet paper. There was nothing to say, so we both went back to work.

Why does this happen to me? It's not like I want to write about shit, but I'm the guy who loses his arse. In public. At least Matt will be happy.

18 IT ONLY HURTS WHEN I LAUGH

We are ready to leave Longreach. It seems miraculous but in four days I've gone from the bed, to a wheelchair, to the Zimmer frame, to the sloth hobble. Each transition was drug-assisted but still horribly painful. The hospital said I could go if I wanted to, but suggested I stay for a few more days before getting in the truck.

'Being here is getting easier for you now, but don't get ahead of yourself, Paul.' The doctor moved to the window and looked out at our old truck parked in the car park below. 'Sitting in that thing on our outback roads isn't going to be pretty.'

He knew I was going anyway; every day I was pushing my body closer to getting in that truck.

'What you need is time—you're going to be sore for weeks,' he said, looking doubtful. I must have looked like he'd just asked me to push a kitten into a blender. He sighed. 'Make sure you stop regularly and move about. I've organised some pain relief medication for you to use over the next two days till you get to Darwin. You need to sign for it, though.'

I hobbled over to him and he shook my hand slowly. 'You shouldn't go near that bike of yours for at least a month,' he said.

I smiled at him and hobbled off down the hall.

I could have hobbled onto a flight home, and spent the next month healing; the doctor and my body were both telling me I wasn't ready yet. But I was out of time and budget and full of pride and ego; there was no plan B, no backing out. The next 2248 kilometres to Darwin would be the fourth and last time the bike would be in the back of the truck, totalling 2427 k's travelled with the bike in the truck.

'The cherry picker can't lift a Jag,' yelled Bill as I passed his room. And goodbye to you too, Bill.

The elevator had a mesh folding door, the old-fashioned kind that you needed to close yourself. It took me five minutes to close it, and I was covered in sweat. I was as weak as a kitten, but somehow I had to climb into the truck and sit there for three days, so we could reach Darwin. I thought about the ride beyond Darwin. We weren't even halfway, we were just stuck in the middle of nowhere. I had to get to Darwin, get the bike repaired and repair myself, had to keep to some kind of schedule. Already we were two weeks behind and I was well over my budget. I had to push on. I'd found an excellent physiotherapist in Darwin who was willing to do nothing but work on me for a week, so at least that was organised.

To fix Betty, Matt Bromley, God bless him, had squared me away with a mate who ran a motorcycle dealership and workshop in Darwin. I could fly Clare and Lola up there to be with me for the week as well. I focused on that while I climbed into the cab; the seatbelt felt like it was made of lead. Lola's ear was on the mend; Clare had said on the phone the night before that she was taking her back to the doctor today for a check-up and hopefully an all-clear for the little one to get on a plane.

Heading out of Longreach, we stopped at that same coffee shop that we were in before the accident. I had another bucket of latte, and it hit my bladder at almost exactly the same place where I had dropped the bike four days ago. Matt slowed down as we passed the spot.

'We should do a piece to camera here,' Dan said from the back seat.

'Keep going,' I said. I didn't want to stand there looking at it. Matt nodded and got back on the throttle and back into the story he was telling.

Dan didn't say anything; he was very tolerant of me, even though I knew he would be worried about the lack of footage now that we were all in the truck. Poor Dan was now stuck in the back seat with his small mountain of camera gear. The back seat was shocking: you couldn't hear anything over the engine noise, and the air-conditioning, which was barely enough in the front seat to lower the temp a few degrees, was just about non-existent in the back. He was also sitting on top of the engine, and that barbecued your backside after the first hour.

Soon, however, I wasn't thinking about Dan's comfort anymore. By the time Matt pulled into Winton, 180 k's later, I was in agony.

Queensland's crappy outback roads would throw the truck's cab into the air every few minutes; my arse would leave the seat and come down hard, shooting waves of pain up and down my chest and shoulder. Because I could make out the potholes and bigger undulations up ahead I started tensing up and holding my breath just prior to the jolt, but this just made it worse.

As we pulled out of Winton the wheel directly under my side of the cab slammed into a bottomless pothole and I lost it. The next 2068 k's was feeling more like 10,000, and I still had over 8000 k's to ride after Darwin—that is, if I could ride after

Darwin at all. It was a dummy spit to end all dummy spits, but it made me feel a bit better. After all, there was no other option, we just had to keep going.

During this nightmare of a drive, Matt was my source of light. Even at times like this he could make me laugh so hard I cried. His rants go way beyond my toilet humour and into a place that you reserve for the wrong stuff that on rare occasions pops into your head and leaves you wondering if you're actually mental and just don't know it yet. And because Matt's stories are so out there, Dan couldn't even think of filming us, much to his increasing annoyance. Matt would start out fairly fast and loose into his story or whatever he was talking about, enough to completely sucker you in; then he unleashes the Matt you didn't see, the one hiding under his mild exterior, the Matt that I call Bad Matt. Dan would throw himself back into the rear of the truck's boiling cab with his camera in his lap. 'Right, well, thanks for that, I can't use any of it.'

The Matt rant could occasionally get scary in the cab of a truck doing 130 kilometres an hour. At one point while spouting a story about anal sex, he was looking straight at me, gesticultaing with both hands off the steering wheel: he was so entertaining I almost got comfortable, until a pothole threatened to re-crack my ribs.

My morphine reserve was helping. Around the halfway mark, I opted to lie down flat on the back seat, and the magic pills put me away. I was in limbo, when the truck suddenly stopped.

I heard Matt talking to someone and slowly sat up. There, in the absolute middle of nowhere, at an anonymous crossroads in central Queensland, was a group of eight lost backpackers. I got out of the cab; the drugs had me in their grip, and I wandered about on the baking hot road without a hat, looking at this group of carefree young backpackers. I don't remember where they were going, but one of them, a Canadian dude with a goatee, crazy hair and an eye patch, was playing a piano accordion.

My head was light as a feather, and Matt started dancing about in the middle of the road while Dan seized the opportunity to get some filming done. We all joined in. It was totally bizarre and very surreal, dancing a jig with the backpackers in the middle of the road in the blinding heat. Only in Australia.

The Canadian stopped playing, and his keen young eye spotted me as the one on drugs. He walked up smiling, with his eye patch and hair all over the place. 'Got some for me, man? I'm Carl.'

'Sorry brother, I'm a drug pig. It's morphine, I've been in an accident.'

'Oh, too bad, are you going to be OK?' He flipped up his eye patch and looked me up and down. 'Hey,' his finger came up and pointed at me, 'I know you, man.' I still had that feeling that perhaps I was still asleep and none of this was happening at all. 'Did you write that book about the rigs?' he asked.

'Yup.'

'No fuckin way. Wait here.' He bolted, and I turned to see him open the boot of their van and hurl all manner of crap into the road.

'What's the seal basher doing?' Matt walked up.

'I think he's got a copy of one of my books in that van.'

'Bullshit.' Matt threw his head back and laughed. 'Way the fuck out here. You serendipitous bastard.'

The young Canadian came bounding back with a yellowing, dog-eared copy of my first book. He'd hauled it all the way round the world to get it to exactly this point, where drug-fucked author met drug-fucked reader, at a crossroads in the middle of nowhere in the Australian outback.

I fumbled with the pen, tried to focus and wrote something profound and purposeful, the most encouraging, thoughtful, indeed inspirational thing I could think of at the time, a golden nugget of truth. Here's this guy, all of 22 or 23 years old, out on his first big adventure, eyeballing me and grinning like I'm a naked prom queen handing out free pot at a beer convention.

I have a responsibility to make this count, I thought to myself. I slapped the book shut and made him promise not to look until we had disappeared into the heat haze in the opposite direction. 'OK,' he said, and pushed the book into his pocket. We all shook hands and parted company.

I swallowed another pill and dragged myself into the back of the truck. Matt picked up right where he left off in whatever story he was telling as he pulled off the side of the road and headed towards Darwin.

'What did you write in his book, mate?' Dan was leaning over the front seat, his bearded face rocking from side to side with the truck.

'Dear Craig, avoid the clap, love Paul.'

Dan's face disappeared, leaving me dreamily gazing at the truck's roof, the hundreds of tiny dots in the fabric which gradually merged into blank sweaty sleep.

Mount Isa came and went. I know I spent the night there, I remember staggering out of the truck in the dark, in pain, and falling in a heap. I remember calling Pia, a friend who works in Tennant Creek, to tell her we would be there the next day. I remember Matty helping me back into the truck in the dark, in pain, the next morning. More pills please, Mr Brown Paper Bag from the Longreach Hospital. I don't remember crossing the border into the Northern Territory, but I do remember pulling into Tennant Creek. There I had a brief interlude of clarity.

We parked outside the first pub, as Matty always does, walked in and sat down. Within five minutes Dan nearly got into a fight with a bloke over his camera. Then Pia arrived; she hadn't changed a bit, she was full of life. We proceeded to get drunk, which of course is a really sensible course of action when you're full of morphine. While I was staggering about in the beer garden—well, more of a dusty shambles than a beer garden—Matt Bromley called to tell me he was leaving Deus.

'Oh shit, mate, what's going on?' I asked.

He told me he'd been offered a job on the team of mechanics hand-picked to build the bikes for the upcoming *Mad Max 4* movie. I could hear how excited he was over the phone.

'You lucky fucker,' I said.

'You're pissed, aren't ya.'

'Yup.'

'How ya feelin?'

'Well, put it this way, I'm not in any pain right now, brother.'

We bullshitted for ages. Matt was so happy; I was happy for him, he deserved it. Damn right. I wandered back into the main bar. Pia, Matty, Dan and another ten people were sitting there drinking and talking. My head was full of nonsense and morphine. I couldn't really join in; all I could do was listen and smile. Drinking in the Territory is like a professional sport; men seriously hit the piss there. Finally, we opted to bow out of the booze fest and get a pizza across the road. I waited in the outdoor dining area out the front with a bottle of water. Pia, Matt, Dan, a woman we found out was the drummer from the band The Go-Betweens, and another guy were all standing about chatting. By that stage I'd lost the power of speech and basic hand-eye coordination, but hey, I was in no pain.

The pizza arrived, and we were about to dig in when a car full of Aboriginal guys rolled up. A moment later another car full of Aboriginal guys rolled up. Everyone looked at each other. I know I looked like a wasted new graduate from some Nazi deportment school, so I hoped no one was looking at me. One guy from the first car asked where the guys from the second car were from. The answer came back—apparently from somewhere near Alice Springs. 'Well, fuck off back there then.'

The less aggressive second-car guys were outnumbered two to one. They took one look at us, pizza triangles dangling in front of our open mouths, and said, 'Hey, don't carry on in front of the white people.' All I remember was this huge booming voice from the first car right behind me. 'W-W-W-WHITE PEOPLE, FUCK WHITE PEOPLE.' The fence came down; it was on. I grabbed two slices of pizza and crawled under the table. Within a minute the pizza shop owner was out trying to separate them, and in another minute the police turned up.

'You right there, mate?' Dan was peering under the table at me, but my mouth was full so I couldn't answer.

The drummer from The Go-Betweens got me out from under the table and into her car. She dropped me off at the motel. 'What are you on?' she asked. I told her. 'Hmm, better stay in tonight then.'

Matty woke me up at 5 a.m. and we stumbled out to the truck. Dan fished out the last of the morphine from the hospital bag. 'Thousand k's today mate, all the way to Darwin. You're going to need these, that's the last of them.'

I pulled my sore arse into the truck. In the early hours, with no drugs coursing through my system, it felt like someone had been going at me with a baseball bat. Matt drove flat out, only stopping for fuel and hot chips. We drove into a miserable-looking, one-camel town somewhere before Katherine. I slowly sat up.

'It's weird here.' Dan was looking over to our left; there was a dust storm going full tilt outside, and everything was the same shade of light brown. There wasn't a soul to be seen, no cars, no signs of life.

We slowly made our way down the main street, and pulled into a service station. Matt hopped out, shielding his face with his hand against the sandblasting, and ran around to fill up the truck.

'Pump's not on.'

I staggered out and we ran over to the main entrance, rather like people do when they're caught in the rain, and stumbled through the open door. No one was there. We called out, but no one appeared. All you could hear was the wind howling outside. Dan came in, looking as perplexed as us. He shut the door, grabbed some bottled water from the fridge and plonked the bottles down on the dusty countertop.

'Hello,' Matt shouted. 'Anyone here?' We all leaned across the counter together to get a look into the back room around to the right. The door leading from there out to the back was banging against the frame in the wind, letting in intermittent plumes of dust.

For five minutes we just stood there, the wind flipping the pages of magazines on the shelf behind the counter like a team of invisible speed readers. 'You know, this is a bit like an Aussie horror movie,' said Matt. '*Wolf Creek* meets the Griswolds.' Dan was hooking into an ice cream, and I opened a bag of salt and vinegar chips.

'Actually, more like a zombie movie,' Matt said slowly, peering out into the street. We moved over to the window next to him, Dan with a face full of ice cream and me munching on more chips than one would consider polite to stuff into your mouth.

At first I saw nothing in the billowing dust, but then I noticed movement in the bush across the road. A figure moving forward, not in a normal fashion; they were doing a stop-start shuffle, arms a bit too rigid. 'Fuck,' said Dan, and stopped eating. So did I.

'There's another one.' Matt had his face pressed up against the window, trying to see through the dust and random airborne debris. Sure enough, another figure appeared, also moving towards the service station.

Maybe it was the previous night's drinking session, maybe it was the morphine, maybe it was just three overactive imaginations. Or maybe it was real; given the way my life had panned out up to that point, I could accept anything.

Dan let go with a nervous laugh. 'This isn't happening,' he said, and started to back away from the glass. 'Morphine or no morphine, they are not zombies, and this town is not deserted and I am definitely imagining all this,' I said.

Matt looked really excited. 'I hope they are zombies,' he said, eyeing a tyre iron by the fridge.

'AARGH.' Our heads snapped back to the window. The first figure was now passing our truck, still stumbling, hands outstretched; we could now see its face, covered in blood.

'Zombies.' Matt was up on the balls of his feet, as if realising this situation was ridiculous but ready to do something anyway. Dan's ice cream had melted down his hand, making a mess on the floor; he looked like a gay-porn-movie fluffer. I just stood there, waiting for an adult to come in and tell me what to do. We were all frozen to the spot.

The first zombie, a middle-aged woman in a ripped blue dress, pushed the door open, walked up to the empty counter and demanded a pack of Winfield Red cigarettes. At the same time a young guy came running through the back door. 'Bloody weather.' He stopped at the counter and took in the scene. Three out-of-towners obviously on drugs, and a zombie.

'WINNIE RED,' said the zombie.

'OK, OK, keep your hair on. You've been fighting again?'

The zombie ignored this. 'WINNIE RED.'

The guy put the pack down on the counter. The zombie opened its mouth, stuck its thumb and forefinger in up to the knuckle, and produced a gooey blood-soaked ten-dollar bill and some change.

'I've told you before about this, we don't accept money that's been in your body,' said the service station guy.

The zombie snatched up the packet quick as a flash and stumbled out.

'Any fuel, fellas?' asked the service station guy, switching his attention to us. He looked at Dan. 'Something wrong with the ice cream, mate?' he asked pointedly.

Dan snapped back to attention. 'Oh, sorry.'

'No worries, I'll clean that up,' the servo guy said.

'We need diesel on pump four.' I smiled, and went out to fill up the truck.

As we drove out of town Matt laughed for a full ten minutes. Every now and again I'd hear 'WINNIE RED' and he'd start laughing again. We stopped again in zombie-free Adelaide River for chips and diesel, finally arriving in Darwin in the late afternoon.

Matty had done a sterling job: he'd driven 1000 k's in one day, evaded zombies, done Dan's head in, and successfully taken the non-stop piss out of me the whole time.

I was so happy to see Clare and Lola, who were waiting for us at the hotel. I couldn't hug Lola enough. It was a good hotel too, the Holiday Inn, not a sweaty donga, or a flea-bitten motel room with stained carpet. This place had stars after its name. There are two Holiday Inns in Darwin, right next door to each other; Matty and Dan were in the same one as us, and Gavin Kelly, incoming support-truck driver and steadfast Scotsman, was flying in the next day and would be staying in the one next door. I spent the first night telling Clare all about the trip from Sydney while trying to ignore the pain that was slowly creeping back as the morphine left my system. But that night the pain was persistent and I had trouble sleeping. I concentrated on making it through the night. Tomorrow was a new day in the Top End, and would bring a 9 a.m. appointment with the physiotherapist.

It took me half an hour to hobble the two blocks from the hotel to the physiotherapist's office, Darwin's heat and humidity already making me sweat. I sat there in the waiting room, and waited. I picked up a five-year-old copy of *National Geographic* and pretended to read, but I was too nervous: this session was going to hurt, no question. A door opened down the hall, and the receptionist swivelled her head to look, turned to me, made eye contact: this was it. 'Mr Carter, you can go through now.' I faked a smile and slowly stood up. Rounding the corner I nearly bumped into the physio.

'Hi, my name's James, come through.'

I hobbled in behind him and he gestured towards a seat next to his desk.

'OK, you've asked for five days of physiotherapy following a motorcycle crash in Longreach about a week ago.' He flicked through some notes and looked me in the eye. A clean-cut guy in his mid twenties, he seemed well briefed and genuinely concerned. 'Did you bring your X-rays from the hospital?' I had them with me on disc.

After taking a good look he asked me to stand up and strip. I told him where it hurt, turned my head here and there, bent my arm up and down, did the hokey pokey and turned around, got on the bed and put my face in the hole. So far, so good: he was very thorough and explained what was going on in my body.

'OK, James, when can I get back on the bike?' I asked.

'That's hard to say. If you stick with the swimming exercises I outlined, we'll see how you are in a few days.'

'So when's it going to hurt?' I asked.

'Now,' he said, and pressed down on my shoulder.

At first impression he was all about a warm handshake, but this turned into a cold kick in the balls for the next hour. 'You do have a high pain threshold,' James said happily, making my leg fit into my ear while I spat phlegm at the ceiling and slapped my hand down on the vinyl. I know I piss and moan a lot; it's one of my coping mechanisms.

The next three visits to James—or The Painmonger as I came to call him—were intense. But the guy was good, and every time I left his office I felt better.

I said goodbye to Matty on the second day; he was flying back to Sydney and work. I was really going to miss having him around. On the same day I called Matt Bromley's recommended bike workshop, Precision Motorcycles in Berrimah. Matt had already phoned to let them know I was inbound, and he'd given them a rundown on Betty's particular needs. Tim Walker couldn't have been more helpful.

We got the truck over to them straightaway and I watched the workshop guys unload Betty. That was the first time since the accident I'd had a chance to look at her properly; the crash had done a fair bit of damage. The workshop manager, Darren, was straight onto it. Next the truck went in for a service.

At this point I didn't know if a week was going to be enough time for my 40-year-old body to climb back on Betty, or indeed if Betty was going to make it. One thing was certain: my funding had all been used up. Clare didn't know it yet but I was hacking into our savings now.

I found Gav poolside, sucking on a beer. He had flown his wife Jhovana and daughter Leonie up to Darwin to spend a few days with him before we left—that is, if we left. Leonie is an uber-cute, ridiculously polite eight-year-old; she loved playing with Lola. Clare and I loved that she loved playing with Lola, because it meant for a few hours each day we could sit in peace without taking endless turns at putting a stop to Hurricane Lola's vandalism. Jhovana is in many ways the perfect match for Gav: she's got the same wicked sense of humour, the same can-do attitude; like him, she can deal with anyone and any situation. I think it's got a lot to do with being an oilfield wife. But unlike Gav she doesn't possess the fast-food eating skills of a golden retriever, nor is she capable of sniffing out cold beer where there's no cold beer to be found; Gav could put a cold beer in your hand if he was locked in a bank vault. But they're lucky, because when you see them together it is obvious that this tall, tanned leggy brunette and the hairy, burger-necking, beer-sniffing oilman were made for one another.

'May as well make the most of the time here,' Gav said, raising his bottle at me. Gav is the original workaholic, he puts in massive hours, rig-hopping all over the place. This was the first time I'd seen him relax properly; generally he has a phone pressed against his ear. We'd usually plan to do something on a weekend, but then the phone would ring, and within a few hours Gav would have his head shoved up a tool joint in some oilfield pipe yard.

Together we explored the town as far as my groin would let me. I'd heard all the disparaging NT—'Not Today'—comments, but Darwin is actually a lot of fun and feels like it would be a relaxed, balmy kind of place to live. Every day could be a Sunday; every night could be Saturday night. It's packed with good-looking young people, packed like a Melbourne tram in rush hour during Fashion Week. There are manicured avenues lined with chic apartment buildings, and developments all over the place.

Every morning, I'd hobble to my physiotherapy appointment down streets sparking to life, past cafés frothing milk, and tourists looking for crocs. Every day the hobble back got closer to a walk, and every day my pain backed off a little more and my mood improved. By the end of the week I was feeling confident, and it was almost a pain-free stroll back to the hotel. I was dishing out my smiles to strangers and my change to the bums.

That night we went out on the town; the girls bailed after dinner, sensing the evening was headed for a boys-drinking-their-body-weight session. Gav and I bar-hopped about, looking for a place that suited us.

First was a slick, overdone, neon open-plan place that reeked of air-conditioned people under twenty. After that came a series of bars that just blurred together, ending in your standard every-Western-country-on-the-fockin-planet-has-one Instant Ye Olde Irish Fockin Pub, your very own slice of the Emerald Isle. Is there a factory somewhere punching out all the old Guinness signs and fake memorabilia? But the place was alive, the music was good, the beer was cold, and to Gavin's delight you could smoke inside without a bouncer dragging you out and shooting you in the head.

Donald Millar, the man originally slated to get me to Darwin, called us while we were at the pub. Gav waved his phone at me, yelling, 'It's Millar time.' Donald had just arrived in Darwin on his way out to his rig. While we had been on the road, every time we turned on the telly the news was all about the West Atlas rig. Donald was in fine form as usual, though he'd been through a lot in the past month. He sat down and gave us the whole story. With a 6 a.m. chopper booking he didn't jump into the beer pool with us; instead we made plans to catch up in Perth after it was all done and dusted.

I've never known a man to put in the kind of hours he did over the next few months trying to kill that well, and he was truly shattered when he lost his rig to an ignition and fireball that completely destroyed her. He took it hard, feeling deeply the impact of losing the rig, as well as the impact it would have on the ocean, the life in it and around it. All of this weighed heavily on his mind, you could see it in his eyes. His ability to bounce back is remarkable, and I'm proud to be his friend.

The next day we got the call that Betty was almost ready and the truck was serviced, so Dan and I grabbed a cab out to pick up the truck and then went straight over to check out Betty. We ended up spending the whole day out there; we replaced the tyres, tubes, brakes, bars, levers, tank, front guard, rear brake line, chain, sprockets and CVT belt; we welded the pegs back on, changed the filters, lines and injectors, and refuelled her. Finally she was ready. There was nothing else to do but get back on.

This was the moment of truth. Almost two weeks had passed since the accident. I slowly dragged my leg over the bike, the torn muscles firing bolts of sharp pain into my spine. I put all my weight onto the seat and started her up. She coughed, rattled for a while and began ticking over, *catonk*, *catonk*, *catonk*, sounding like she was chewing a steel mint.

I pulled out into the Berrimah back streets, my confidence flaking off my bald head like dandruff, the hot road no longer a path to enlightenment but a giant black belt sander whistling by underneath me, ready to grind my arse into failure if I made another mistake. A few k's later I came back and gave Dan the nod to follow me back in the truck over to the hotel. My rotator cup was really giving me problems—the old vibration rattling down my arms made my shoulder sting on every turn—but this was it. Tomorrow we were due to leave. I had made my decision. Clare and I had already talked over the options. She was behind me, but not too happy about it. I would have to overcome my fear: if I backed out now, it would be months before I could pick it all up again and finish.

We pulled into the hotel car park. Dan parked the truck and tentatively walked over with his camera. I gave him the nod. It was painful but I knew I could keep going; tomorrow was on.

19 STAGE FIVE: UNEASY RIDER

Our final morning in Darwin started with some last-minute shopping. Gav and I went into town to get water, food and gas refills for the portable stove. We wandered into a fishing tackle and camping supply store and came out with two compound crossbows, as you do.

I went back to the hotel to pay the bill and explain to my wife why our bank balance was missing some digits—the perfect time to also explain my purchase of the totally-useless-in-the-suburbs-of-Perth crossbow. As you can imagine, she wasn't impressed with either explanation, but Clare is cool; she was still behind my decision to continue and backed me up all the way. Without her I would have been lost.

The hotel's business development manager came over and introduced herself while I was turning page after page of the hotel bill. 'Mr Carter, how do you do, I'm Nikki Wright. I hope your stay was comfortable.' She looked good; formal, but not too serious. I wasn't sure what was coming—had Lola been hurling plasma TVs into the pool and setting off all the fire alarms?

What came next was completely unexpected. 'The hotel would like to extend a discount on the bill. How does half price sound?'

'Sounds wonderful, Nikki,' I said, smiling broadly.

She smiled, and nodded to the reception staff. 'Good luck with the rest of your journey.' She shook my hand, swivelled on her high heels and went back to doing good deeds. Again, the universe had come to my aid—in the nick of time, too.

With our wives and kids lined up out the front waving, we had to say goodbye again. This time was more painful than before. Lola's little face looked slightly confused. 'DADDY,' she yelled out as we pulled away. I couldn't look back; her plaintive cry hurt more than my sore body.

While I was in Darwin, I had done another ABC Radio interview. I had also done several phone interviews roadside along the way. We had been lucky with the media on this trip, and now the interest was really picking up. Random people were starting to recognise the bike. 'Is that the veggie burner?' some would ask. Others had me posing in photos. A lot of people seemed really enthusiastic about what we were doing. 'Wow, is that the bike? Good on ya.' Rather than kebabs in the face, I was getting the thumbs-up from overtaking cars. And the truckies went from something to be feared and avoided to princes of the highway. They got on the radio to talk about the bike; I sat there listening to the chatter. 'Looks like a cunt of a way to get around,' said one. 'Our washing machine's got more grunt,' said another. But now they gave me a heads-up and a wide berth, always with a honk and a nod. On ya, fellas.

We burbled out of Darwin's lush green setting, back down to Katherine and then on to the Victoria Highway, towards our first night's stop in Victoria River. I was now over two weeks behind schedule, two bike rebuilds over budget and too far gone with an increasing obsession with the horizon. Night came but we pushed on. Through my pain I became incredibly focused and ready. I dodged the occasional blown truck tyre and everything else that came out to get me that night: cattle, donkeys, roos, all having a surprise midnight street party. However, I did trade places with the truck and let Gav take the lead: he had the bull bar.

When we finally pulled into Victoria River late that night I was beyond any stuffed I'd ever been. I fell off the bike and into a deep donga sleep, waking up with a start at three in the morning, rising slowly and painfully in need of a toilet. Gav and Dan were still up, running about in the dark with flashlights and freaking out at all the cane toads. There were thousands of them; wherever Dan shone light the ground was hopping. Gav appeared to have some sort of inherent fear of the toad. 'Fuck.' He jumped. 'Oh, shit.' He ran for the porch. 'They're everywhere.' I found that fascinating; here's a guy who will wade into a fistfight in a crowded bar without blinking an eye, but he was running for his life from a toad. But then again, I react the same way to cockroaches and spiders, so I can't talk.

Perhaps it's got something to do with what you were exposed to as a kid. After all, back in Scotland where Gav grew up, the amphibians don't get this big, the wildlife rarely eats you and the road kill is usually a squirrel or a hedgehog, not a bloated, 300-pound blowfly-maggot-infested cow with a 50-pound giant eagle sitting on it giving you its best 'fuck off, it's mine' look.

After having a good laugh at Gav, I stumbled back to bed for three hours. When I woke again at sunrise, I thought I was still dreaming. Overnight the harsh, sun-blasted dusty brown earth had been replaced by lush monsoonal shades of green. The difference was startling, just beautiful. Mother Nature had clearly also pulled in last night for a donga and a sandwich. Cue flocks of NapiSan-white cockatoos flying past. Cue friendly wave from the truck driver next door. Cue the smell of real coffee and an egg-and-bacon roll.

'This place is a welcome sight,' said Gav. He was standing out the front of his donga, bollock-naked with a fag dangling from his bottom lip. The chatty truck driver next door explained why the place was so fertile. 'It's the Wet, mate.'

I had heard people in Darwin talking about 'the Wet'. Apparently, for six months a year up here it rains Noah's Ark kind of rain. 'The new bridge should make a difference,' the truckie said; seemingly, before the bridge was built this place would be cut off from the rest of the world for months due to flooding. Years back, the volume of water hurtling down the Daly River every seven minutes during the monsoon was measured as equal to the entire contents of Sydney Harbour.

The people up here are very hardy and adaptable. I would have thought the Wet must put a terrible strain on everyone, but apparently not. In fact, the general reaction to the Wet was: 'Good, no more tourists for a while—we can have the place to ourselves for a bit.'

We pulled over in Timber Creek, where we had to phone Bullo River Station, our accommodation for the night, and let them know we were on the way. Sounded simple enough, only Gav's work phone rang while we were there, and he was on it for ages. I threw water over him, pleaded with him, abused him, but nothing gets Gav off the phone before he's ready. Finally we set off on the last 100 k's of blacktop we'd see for a while.

Bullo River is one of those places you get to experience only once in a lifetime, a full-on working cattle station planted in some of the most awe-inspiring country on earth. We found the gate just off the highway, and Dan jumped from the truck, camera in hand, to get the obligatory entrance shot, when we heard a horn. A big BMW GS pulled in behind us, and the rider strolled up and introduced himself as Simon. I recognised him straightaway: we'd been passing each other on the road for weeks; or rather, he went past me at light speed, got to where he was going and stayed for a few days. By the time he was ready to leave, I would finally hit town. We'd seen each other at a series of service stations too; the boys would be filling up the truck and he would blat past, waving. Now he had been about to zap past me again, until he saw us pull over so he'd stopped to say hello at last.

He was a nice guy. We stood there in the heat sweating and swapping road tales for a good hour, until it was Gav's turn to start hurrying me up. Simon and I made a plan to meet in Broome for beers and bullshit, and then we set off on the unsealed road to Bullo.

There is no easygoing, laid-back Territory introduction to offroad riding. For a conventional rider the usual deal would be to have plenty of armour and hit the track at speed. If you hit corrugations or deep sand, well, you flogged it, and the bike would plane over the top. I didn't have the sudden burst of power to dial up or unlimited amounts of torque, thanks to Betty's smaller rear sprocket. The CVT belt would start to spin and smoke under too much of an incline.

The 75 k's to Bullo was a mix of everything. It started as corrugations, formed by years of trucks passing over the dirt. These buggers were punctuated by sudden, deep tennis-court-sized holes full of soft bull dust. Hitting them was terrifying because I instantly lost all my torque and speed. Thump! The front wheel would sink; it took all my strength to avoid a flight over the handlebars while the bike snaked wildly left to right. Back to the c-c-c-c-c-c-c-corrugations until I picked up enough speed to get over the top. My shoulder and leg were throbbing. My kidneys and liver were starting to jiggle their way out of my mouth. Another patch of bull dust, and BANG, I went down.

The first fall didn't hurt at all, the second only made me drug-dependent, but the third had me on my knees. It wasn't much to look at; I was only doing about ten kilometres per hour when the front wheel just dug in once again and stopped. I just didn't have the upper body strength to rake back the handle bars; I went over on my side, my cracked ribs recracked, my whole face creased in pain as though I'd got a noseful of wasabi.

Betty's impeller hoovered in bull dust, the whole right side of the handlebar was buried in the ground, her throttle wide open. The engine screamed as she choked down dirt-filled air and spewed out thick white smoke.

Gav rushed over. 'What can I do?' he yelled over the squealing engine. Betty's back wheel was spinning, throwing out oil and dirt. I was too winded to answer, so he bolted to the back of the truck and came back with a pair of pliers to cut the throttle line. I knew the bike couldn't take much more, so I sat up, grabbed the buried handlebar and pushed the heavy machine up. The back wheel bit into the dust. I twisted the throttle back and she stopped. I fell back, my ribs and shoulder burning, spasms of white-hot pain in my lungs.

Gav helped me up and lifted my leg over the bike for me. We had to push on; we were so close. I was sore, but by now I was getting better at blanking it out.

Bullo appeared at dusk through magnificent ghost gums decorated like Christmas trees with thousands of cockatoos preparing to roost. Wallabies and grey kangaroos scattered in their hundreds at our arrival, bounding in every direction. It was an explosion of life, nature and beauty like I've never seen before. I fell off the bike in the front yard of the station house. Ruth, one of the staff, came over to greet us with an esky of cold beer; it tasted like the best beer I'd ever had.

We met Marlee, the owner of this magnificent piece of heaven. Her husband Franz was away at the time. Marlee runs the place; she's one of the most capable people I've ever met—there's nothing she can't do. She sat down to dinner with us that night and went through the list of activities we could try on the property. We didn't know where to start. The sun slowly faded on Bullo that first night, sending wave after wave of deep orange and red across the sky. I wished Clare was there to see this place.

In the morning a full breakfast was waiting, and we met two more staff members, Trevor and Evan. Rollie-smoking, beer-drinking men in their sixties, they were the nicest fellas to explore this place with. Both men had spent a lifetime in the bush, and had incredible stories and fascinating snippets of information, as well as a fantastic sense of humour.

We jumped in Evan's Landcruiser and drove into the bush then into a valley, past wandering buffalo and bubbling billabongs. We pulled up next to a steep red rock face jutting a few hundred feet out of the earth, and climbed up into the cliff via a track only Evan could have found.

'This place is a sacred site for the Aboriginal people who lived here.' Evan walked us into a deep shaded section only a few metres wide where the cliff wall had split open over the centuries. We were stunned: it was an art gallery, stretching some 30 feet or so along the wall all the way to the top. The rock art was beautiful: the artists had used their mouths to blow pigment over their hands and outstretched fingers and made handprints. The paintings nearer the top dated back some 16,000 years; you could clearly see the image of a Tasmanian tiger. As the cliff section slowly split open, the floor had lowered, and the images nearer the base dated back just 300 years. I've visited art galleries and museums all over the world, but there and then, listening to Evan's soft voice talking about this sacred place, I was mesmerised and felt at peace.

On the ground there were several large boulders that didn't match the other rocks—they looked like polished glass. 'That's thousands of years of human skin and sweat polishing the rock,' Evan said. I was looking at this with my city eyes—of course, it was a table, with chairs at one side; there was a perfectly round bowl worn into the rock and next to it lay the mortar. 'That's where the different pigments were made. We've left it exactly as we found it.' Apparently Franz was out in his chopper one day rounding up cattle when completely by chance he looked down into the split cliff and noticed the colours. He landed to investigate and walked straight into this amazing place.

Gavin was quietly climbing around snapping away with Dan's stills camera; later that day, while Dan and I jumped into a billabong for a swim—only after Evan promised I would not get taken by a croc—he was again busy with the camera. That night after dinner he went off again, crawling around under bushes and hanging off trees like a big deranged Scottish primate, snapping away.

At breakfast the next morning he announced that he was going to get his own camera. Gav had discovered a real passion for photography, and Dan showed him how to use different lenses and change effects. For the rest of the leg, all the way to Broome, Gav was one snap-happy Scotsman. I was pleased to see the change in him, as he went from sizing up everyone in the room to taking their photo.

That morning Trevor took us fishing in the Victoria River. Our little tinny slid down a ten-foot mud bank into the brown water. During the Wet, this place would look amazing. Trev was patient with us; he needed to be, as not one of us had been fishing before. He fired up the outboard and we shot off downstream towards a huge mud bar. 'Gotta get the bait,' he said, leaping out of the boat with a net and a bucket, and running at the edge of the mud bar. When he got to the water thousands of tiny fish scrambled to get away, Trev just threw his net in the water and came back with a bucketful. We all had a go, then noticed the tide had gone out so we had to push the boat out into deeper water. My leg and shoulder were starting to hurt by the time we were waist-deep in the brown water.

'Hop in the boat, Paul.' The tone of Trev's voice and the constant knowledge that the river was teeming with big crocs was enough; I was out of that water so fast I was dry when I landed in the boat.

We started to fish. I didn't know how to cast, or hold the reel, or fish while drinking beer, or bait my hook and drink beer, or any of the man skills everyone up there seemed to be born with. For Trev it must have been like fishing with a kindergarten group; he's used to serious professionals who go up there to do Olympic fishing. He was having a good chuckle at the three of us fumbling about. The second my line landed in the water and I got a bite, I would go into this panicky flap like my mother at a Chanel counter in Paris: 'Oh, oh, Trevor, what do I do, what do I do?' He was pissing himself after the first ten minutes. Gav was loving it, Dan was loving it, I could have sat there all day. Every time a line went in a big fish came out.

Trev pointed over to the trees on the bank some 30 yards away. 'See that eagle, fellas?'

'Er, no.'

He picked up a small catfish he'd pulled out of the river earlier and casually tossed it into the water a few feet from the boat. We sat there gobsmacked as Batman launched out of a treetop, flapped his massive wings a few times and banked hard, turning down for an effortless glide across the surface before extending his talons and snatching the fish from under our noses. 'Good fishin, mate,' said Trev. Amazing. I was back in the mesmerised state I had been in the previous day at the rock art. 'That sea eagle has been following us since we got on the river; I've been treating him for years.' Trevor chuckled.

Evan and Trevor ran rings around our pale sweaty city-boy antics. Their mindset is so different from ours; I wanted to spend more time there than we could. You have to travel this far out to meet people like this. I had so much to learn from them; one day I'll go back to Bullo.

The muster was kicking off the next day. It was done by Marlee in a 'bull catcher'—basically a big old four-wheel drive that looks like it just rolled out of Matt Bromley's *Mad Max* workshop—and a man in a chopper. She normally did all her own flying, but her chopper was out of service.

At dinner we asked Marlee if Dan could go up with the pilot to film the muster. Marlee got on the phone to ask him. 'Sorry guys, he said no, too dangerous.'

However, the next day there was a problem and the chopper couldn't make it, so Marlee had to find another pilot. 'Dave Henry's coming,' she said, smiling. 'You guys are very lucky. If there's anyone who'll take Dan up, it's Dave—ask him tomorrow.' Turned out Mr Henry had more flying hours in the R22 than anyone in the world.

The muster started slowly, moving the cattle down a fence line; we were in the bull catcher with Marlee. She made it all appear so easy, while Dave displayed helicopter aerobatics that simply stunned me. I've spent twenty years crew-changing in choppers, but in comparison to Dave's antics, that's like a city bus next to a racing car.

As Dave expertly manoeuvered through the bush targeting the strays, we moved the herd towards the gate. At lunch I asked Dave if Dan could go up with him. 'Sure,' he said. We asked if he would take the quintessential bike-chasing chopper shot of Betty going flat out across the open paddock. 'Sure,' he said. Marlee had told us that if Dave agreed to do some flying for us, the charge for an hour's flying would be $1000. I was just happy he didn't mind.

Dan climbed into the R22 and got the ride of his life, while I raced Betty all over the place as hard as she would go, Dave buzzing past me like a giant mosquito. I was having a great time. Dave was talking to me over the radio the whole time, as calm and relaxed as if he was on the porch at lunch. He knew exactly what we wanted.

Afterwards he strolled back to the house for a cuppa, while I went off to get my cash stash. I offered it to him, but he refused.

'No worries, Paul, it's on the house.'

I couldn't believe it.

'Are you sure, Dave?' I protested.

'Nah, mate, it was fun. Are you doing anything for charity?' he asked me. I told him my intention was to donate the proceeds of the sale of my support truck when the trip was over.

'Well,' said Dave, 'add it to that.'

Bullo River was something I'll never forget, a huge experience for me—an oasis of natural beauty and peace in the middle of Australia, and right when I needed some serious R&R from the bike. When I can I'm going back with my family; it's just one of those places.

20 STAGE SIX: NUMB

Back to the blacktop, another state, another time zone, another stinking hot day. Fifty degrees and I was cooking. I'd lost ten kilos in the last two months. Strangely enough, it didn't make much difference with Betty; I wasn't moving any faster.

We kept going, all day and half the night. We'd stop at roadhouses to eat and drink and get straight back on the road. Cattle met me for wide-eyed close calls, as did every other critter out looking for a late-night game of dodge-bike. Emus were the best. They have the whole continent to run about in, they can go in any direction that pops into their head, but every time they chose to: a) run alongside the loud funny-smelling bike, overtaking it, or b) dash out into the bush, and then double back, rushing out into the road right on top of the bike to ask the hysterical rider, 'Hey mate, is that thing diesel?'

We pulled up at Halls Creek, then Fitzroy Crossing, finally lumbering, malodorous and sore, into Broome. What an amazing, beautiful place; for anyone arriving from the city it's on super slow mode. It has pristine beaches, pearls, a melting pot of Asian, Aboriginal and European cultures. Everyone I met had a smile and time for a chat.

We found Carrie, who would be my support driver for the Perth leg, absorbed in a book outside her room at the motel. Like everyone in the Downey clan, she's small, but, like Matt, she's a real character. Did I mention she's a physical training instructor with the Australian Navy? That means she's fit—got-muscles-in-her-shit fit.

Gav, Dan and I spent the rest of the day doing our washing and I went through my bike ritual, then we had beers. I met up with Simon, my BMW pal, who had been soaking up the Broome thing for over a week, lucky bastard. We jabbered on into the night. The next day Gav was walking up to the entrance of Broome Airport; he was gonna be missed.

I called Erwin before we left. He was very quiet and I knew something was up. 'I'm sorry mate, I have to go offshore.' Bugger, the last leg was looming and I was down a driver.

There was nothing we could do about it then; we had to hit the road. Carrie was organised, and took care of everything. I was really impressed; she is seriously on the ball. We made incredible time, stopping at the Sandfire Roadhouse halfway to Port Hedland off the Great Northern Highway. We took in the view at Eighty Mile Beach. I stopped to change a CVT belt while Dan watched an electrical storm brewing inland. As we got ready to pull off, lightning hit the ground a few k's away and kicked off a bush fire. So Dan broke out the long lens and did some filming while Carrie brewed up some tea.

I was glad for the break; the vibrations were playing havoc with my hands and arms. I was having trouble just holding on to my mug. Carrie suggested we rig up some sort of grip cover. I had a bit of foam in the back of the truck so we tried that, but it didn't really do anything except make the handlebars look like I had a big rubber dildo over each grip.

Next was Port Hedland for an entree, followed by the main course: oily, overcooked Karratha with extra salt please.

Karratha is all about salt production, mining, oil and gas. More trucks passed me on the way into town than on the entire trip so far; it was just never-ending road freight. I phoned an oilfield mate, Nigel, and went out for a few beers with him that night. In the pub I ran into my friend Brad who works for Chevron; Brad noticed I was having trouble holding a beer. 'Come by the warehouse tomorrow,' he said. 'We've got spare rubber and foam, you can rig up some grip covers.' Another guy there, from Schlumberger, said he had some high-density neoprene as well, and would drop it off with Brad in the morning.

The next day we found the warehouse and set to work. I fiddled with different setups for two hours until I had something that worked. My grips were twice as thick now and the vibration was considerably reduced. Again my mates had helped me through.

Back once more to the blacktop, and more flat-chat roadhouse- and donga-hopping to Carnarvon. This time we rode through endless scrub, which made me feel like I was in preparation for the Nullarbor. We had a great stay in Geraldton, the African Reef Beach Resort; I pulled Betty up right in front of the Indian Ocean and dipped my toe in salt water for the first time in nine weeks. Cleansed, weightless relief. I bobbed about in the water till the sun went down; I was super tired but my hands felt better, and the seafood dinner was sensational.

Our run down the coast into Perth saw the landscape change; the countryside was greener, and the closer I got to my home the more I could feel Clare and Lola pulling me on.

One by one, the familiar landmarks started to appear. Soon we hit the outskirts, then my suburb, and finally my street.

The front lawn looked good; as he'd promised, Nick had looked after the place for me, I heaved my weight off the bike and opened the front gate and there they were, my girls. Even Ossy had a hint of recognition for me. I held my wife tight; the warmth of her skin and her familiar laugh put me in a wonderful, restful cotton-wool space. Lola held on to me for much longer than usual. That night I watched her sleeping face for a while, my little girl, happy and safe. I had been gone for ten weeks. I was home, and all I wanted to do was stay. But now, as hard as it seemed, I had to do the last leg, ride from Perth back to Adelaide. I fell into bed that night full of home cooking and deep in-your-own-bed slumber. Even my body was feeling better.

At 2 a.m. I woke with a start: 'MMMMMAWWW.'

Carrie stayed in our spare room, eating fruit and doing one-armed push-ups; Dan stayed over at Gav's, hoovering down beer and salty snacks. I got the truck off for another service, and spent two days trying to find a support driver to replace Erwin. Everyone I called was tied up or offshore. Clare stuck her head in the garage while I paced about with my address book and a glass of whisky. 'Call Matt, he'll do it.'

She was right: Matt was up for it. 'Oh good, I need to eat more salad rolls and hot fuckin chips.' He flew in the next day; I dropped Carrie off and picked Matt up. Dan sobered up and came over looking worse than he had on the day we got into Perth. Betty and the truck were both serviced and polished, and for the last time I kissed my girls, climbed on to Betty and reluctantly made my way out of town.

21 STAGE SEVEN: HARDER THAN YOU THINK

Retracing the trip Clare, Lola and I had done as a family ten weeks earlier was harder than you might think. I would ride past some spot where we'd stopped to brew up all those weeks ago and all my emotional triggers would go off. The very Plain Nullarbor was waiting down the road.

Dan was very quiet; I suspected he was rediscovering the horror of being stuck in a truck cab with Matty endlessly taking the piss and spinning yarns. For Dan it must have felt a bit like being stuck in an elevator with someone poking your brain box with a big stick twelve hours a day.

Southern Cross was right where we left it. Matt started to lose it that night at dinner; the buffet displayed several different types of salad, none of which he could eat. I stood next to him with my plate piled high, pointing at each one in turn. 'What about that one?' 'Got cheese in it.' I'd point at another. 'Mayo.' Another. 'Fuckin egg.' The last one. 'Ham, Pauli, dead pig.'

I went back to the table. Dan was starting to look a bit like a junkie: he hadn't shaved for a few weeks, he was pale and his cheeks were drawn. The waitress came over. 'Anything else, gentlemen?' Dan ordered a beer, I asked for a Coke.

'Water,' said Matt. 'And a bowl of your finest dust.' She went blank.

'He means a plain salad, no meat, no egg, no cheese, just lettuce, tomato, cucumber, no dressing and a plain bread roll, no butter.'

'Extra dust though,' said Matty. Poor bugger. 'And a bowl of chips.'

The next morning we had coffee sitting outside a small place on the main street. Dan announced through a blocked nose and runny eyes that he was sick. He ran to the toilet, came back for ten minutes, then ran in again.

Matt had his head in the paper. Since the last leg of the trip, he had redone his hair. It was now jet black with a bright pink strip down one side. This made for the odd interesting double take by locals. I was watching a big man in a sleeveless shirt stare at him from inside the coffee shop while he waited for his morning latte.

A gaggle of early-retirement red Ducati roosters showed up with matching $1000 lids and no wear on their tyres. They strutted about pecking at each other's bikes for a bit, then mooched over to take a morbid but sympathetic curiosity in Betty's plumage. To them it no doubt appeared she was just a nasty twenty-dollar crack whore with a university sticker on her tank. Then they started scanning for the rider. We got pinged on the far table. The head rooster squeaked over in his leather Ducati pants. 'I hope they're paying you to ride that thing.' He pulled out a cigar and manned up, nipping the end off with his teeth. What a tinea of a human.

'Good morning.' I smiled and finished my coffee.

'So.' Rooster One was not giving up. 'Is it part of some experiment?'

IS THAT THING DIESEL?

I just couldn't be fucked. 'Sort of.'

Dan, who had returned from the toilet looking paler than before, looked at his camera on the table. *He's thinking about picking it up, no, don't touch the camera, Danny, or this punisher will puff up his feathers and start making an even bigger ponce of himself.*

Rooster One fired up his Romeo and tried to think of something to say. 'It looks like it couldn't pull the skin off a rice pudding.' He grinned.

Matty was apparently ignoring all of this, hiding behind the newspaper, but I just knew he was going to say something soon. Dan was looking really bad. After three months of living in each other's pockets I knew him well now. He was sitting there clenching and sweating; too polite to just walk off, he'd rather sit there and shit himself.

Rooster One was still not sure who the rider was; I wasn't in my gear yet and the helmet was sitting under the table.

'You haven't come all the way from Adelaide on that thing have you?' said Rooster One.

He's going to engage . . . oh no, Dan, don't engage—DAN.

'Are they all Ducatis?' Aw fuck.

'Yup,' said Rooster One, visibly preening. 'We're on a run for the day, you know, throw them into a few corners and hammer the adrenalin.'

Dan looked like Rooster One had just pulled out his cock and pissed in his face.

'Is that thing diesel?' Rooster One asked at last.

'Fuck off, mate.' Matt finally let go.

'Excuse me?' Rooster One was clearly not a fighting cock, you could see it in his eyes.

'Leave us alone.' Dan jumped up and Rooster One jumped back, dropping his $100 cigar.

'He's sick.' I smiled. Poor Danny. 'Sorry, we're just tired. Enjoy your ride.'

Rooster One went back to the gaggle. They glared at us for a bit then roared off. The big guy with no sleeves came out with his latte. 'What a fuckwit,' he said. 'Good luck on the chip burner, Paul.'

I love it.

We detoured off the highway to Kalgoorlie for lunch; Dan found a chemist and parked himself outside a coffee shop with a muffin. Matt and I wandered up the main street and back down the other side. Typhoid Danny was not feeling any better, so we kept going. That night we were in Norseman. Dan crashed early, full of Lomotil and flu night meds, and I sat up with Matty watching old horror films. The couple in the room next door had a fight; Matty was about to go over and join in but then they started shagging, though at first I thought he was murdering her. Together Matty and I got drunk and took it in turns to fart on Dan's head. Childish? You betcha.

Then before I knew it, it was 6 a.m., and I was back on the Eyre Highway, about to start Australia's longest, straightest, dullest bit again. Dan staggered into the cab, looking like he'd just spent the last three months living underground. As I rode I was thinking about Lola; I wondered what she was doing—would she be out at playgroup with Clare? I was miles away in the cotton wool, thinking about my girls, when BANG!—a punch in the head. I swerved, looked back; I couldn't believe it, a bird had clocked me. A wind-blown line of blood tracked across my visor. Right, I thought, pay attention; worry less, ride more, and watch out for air traffic.

The road ahead was an agonising hollow motorcycle shaker into scrub emptiness. We stopped so Dan could shoot the big open nothing, and then got on the road again. And so we continued: shoot again, go again.

'Dan's freaking out about the lack of footage.' Matt came over on the radio while Typhoid Danny stumbled into a mud flat with his camera. 'He's panic shooting mud now.' I think Dan was developing Stockholm Syndrome; in his weakened state, Matt had devoured him.

At the halfway mark across the Nullarbor, Madura Pass made for a hilly bit, a nice change, and we spent the night there. I tried to get Dan to eat the quiche.

I'd done all this before with the girls, and it didn't feel much different on the bike. The road was just mind-numbingly boring, an endless unrolling of blacktop, a long line of nothing. Those three days across the Nullarbor were a seamless blur of one long road punctuated by a sick cameraman, a demented driver, and a border crossing. We were burnt out.

On the morning we left Ceduna, it suddenly got cold, and the wind picked up as the day wore on. We just kept going; by nightfall I was a wreck, the road was slippery and I needed to refuel. 'Pulling over, mate.'

Matty swung over to the side of the road and killed the engine. Dan was asleep in the cab and Matt fell asleep at the wheel before I'd finished doing my bio thing. I turned off the fuel pump, stowed the line and zipped shut the flap. The truck's lights caught the rain starting to fall: gently at first, then it bucketed down. I changed the CVT belt, checked the oil, and then I just stood there looking through the truck's windscreen at the guys, both fast asleep. The wind whipped past me, flapping the tarp covering the truck's cage. Water was cascading down the glass, and I knew that inside the boys had the heater on. I was so tired; it was like my internal bike had just gone down through its gearbox from fifth to neutral while I was standing there: *wwwhm, wwwhm, wwwhm, wwwhm*. I pictured myself getting motivated. Harden up, I said to myself. I thought about pushing on to Adelaide, when suddenly there was a rhythmical squeak and a little Japanese guy on a bicycle loaded like a Pakistani mule pulled up beside me.

'Good evening.' He cut a big smile.

'Where did you come from?'

'Sydney.' He beamed. 'On the way to Perth.'

He had to be 50. If he could do it, so could I. Would I give up? Would I fuck. 'Would you like some tea?' I asked.

I like the pub in Kimba, the Community Hotel. We had a feast in there that night. One more day on the road and we'd be done. A few people came up with words of encouragement. Matt looked rested and ate well for once, and Dan was on the mend too, chatting up a blonde at the bar. My phone rang. It was a guy called Jock from the Australian Motorcycle Association; he'd been following the ride online and asked if a few of the members could join up with me in Port Wakefield the next day and ride with me into Adelaide. I was chuffed; I never thought anyone would want to join up and ride with me.

The next morning, riding into a feral head wind, we rounded into Port Augusta and found our rally point. There were eight bikes waiting, a really nice group of men and women. Those last 100 k's were wonderful. I stopped just outside the city and called Colin.

'The press are here, you on time?' He sounded excited.

'I'll be there in twenty minutes mate.'

'See you then.'

The plan was to ride back to exactly the same spot from where I had left three months ago. I left Dan and Matty behind; riding through the last set of lights and into the university grounds felt surreal. I couldn't believe the bike and I had made it. Then I looked around, bewildered: there was no sign of any media. Colin, Rob, Phil, Steve and the mechanical engineering students were all standing on the far side. As we all pulled up, Colin ran over.

'You're never going to believe this.' He rubbed his hand over his face. 'Everyone just bolted down the road on foot, five minutes ago. Apparently the Premier of South Australia just called a press conference to deny shagging a parliamentary waitress in his office.'

I was gobsmacked. 'You're kidding.'

'Sorry mate, bigger story.'

'Let's have a drink.'

I looked over to see a familiar face. It was Rob Egan, my biggest sponsor, all the way from Singapore. He shook my hand. 'Well done, mate.'

It was weird standing there surrounded by people after spending so much time alone with my thoughts on the bike. Now I was getting bombarded with questions and going blank. It was over. I was so familiar with Betty that I just expected to get back on her, ride off and keep going. But it was done. Now, weirdly, I didn't want it to be over. I didn't want to leave Adelaide and leave that bike behind.

Finally, Dan and Matty pulled up. In the morning they were flying back to Sydney. Poor Dan's job wasn't over, though; he had nearly 200 hours of footage to go through and turn into a DVD.

Rob took us all out to dinner in a great Italian place close to the uni. The drinking went on all night. Quaily shouted me a flash hotel suite in the city—what a guy. My plan had been to get back in the truck in the morning and, you guessed it, drive it back to Perth. However, as we all went our separate ways that night Rob handed me a business class ticket back home, and told me Ashley Taylor and Ron Currie—two other sponsors—had chipped in to pay for the truck to be freighted back to Perth. I could have kissed him.

I slept the happy sleep of the righteous and woke feeling energised and newly alive. I walked into the uni workshop that morning and started unloading a mass of spare parts, then wandered about looking for Betty like an anxious parent. She had already been stripped; I found her, in the same spot where I'd first laid eyes on her, now just a frame, surrounded by her parts, her wiring splayed out over the floor in an empty room. She was looking very sad indeed, I felt like what identified me with her had been pulled out before I got a chance to say goodbye. We had a connection; after all, she tried to kill me once.

'Don't worry, mate.' Rob came round the corner. 'She's getting rebuilt again. Nice work on the frame and brakes, by the way.'

'That was Matt Bromley,' I said.

Betty was getting a new engine, a new paint job, a new start. The engine I had used was getting mounted on a stand and sent to the National Motorcycle Museum in Nabiac as an exhibit, the first bio-fuelled engine to power a motorcycle round Australia—nice one.

In the meantime, though, Betty's bigger, badder high-speed sister sat out in the main workshop somewhere, waiting for me. I hoped we would get on better than Betty and I had.

Colin came over while I was talking to Rob. 'You're gonna want to see this.'

IS THAT THING DIESEL?

The last time I saw the High Performance Diesel Motorcycle it was just an engine on a table. I rounded a corner, anticipation rising, and the first thing I saw was Dan picking up his camera. He moved aside and there it was: long, low, and very mean. Now it was a weapon.

Colin started going all rocket scientist, talking about gearing, thermal dynamics, piston acceleration. But I was long gone. That bike had me at hello. I climbed on, lay over the beast and grabbed the bars.

'You ready for this?' Colin looked buzzed.

I could feel prickles of adrenalin run through my body. Was I ready? Was I fuck.

The current land speed record for a bio diesel motorcycle is 267 kilometres per hour . . . Well, not for long.

EPILOGUE

Betty and I did 14,500 k's around Australia.

We did two complete bike rebuilds, chewed up sixteen CVT belts, 600 litres of bio-fuel, four tyres, and two of everything else.

Twelve thousand dollars went to charity and education in Western and South Australia.

I got my bike trip and something to write about.

I sit here now in comfort; nothing's sore or broken, my seat is not vibrating and I can feel my hands again. I wanted another adventure and I got it, but more importantly I realised that I'm not at all what I thought I was. I look at the footage Dan shot and think, 'Wow, you're actually a complete muppet'—but I hope to improve on that.

I'm not a hard-faced, hard-core, well-financed professional traveller, I'm just a regular bloke trying to do something with his fleeting existence on this earth other than just plod through life paying bills. The road trip—this road trip—was to be as much a journey into the darkest reaches of my soul as it was a turning point in my life. I wanted to know if I could do it, all of it. And I did, but only with the help of family, friends and colleagues.

At 40 I'm constantly looking to exorcise my ghosts of respectability in the pursuit of another journey. But now I realise that can't happen anymore. My girls are the real journey I couldn't see through the dream of dust and bio-diesel. It wasn't until I got my first real look at Australia, not until I was thousands of empty miles away from them, that I understood that at last. I set out on the trip wanting to feel like I used to on a bike miles from anywhere, but I didn't, I couldn't. Everything has changed. The internal road that plays out in Clare and Lola's world is where I'm headed.

Well, as soon as I crack 300 on the salt.

ACKNOWLEDGEMENTS

It's with much pride and heartfelt gratitude that I try to start the thank-yous without writing another book in the process. So before I start saying thanks I'll remind you why it's so important that I do say thanks, especially when you consider the global financial market I was lucky enough to get sponsorship from. If I missed you out, I was on drugs.

My wife Clare for the leave pass, for backing me up, for putting up with my madness. Lola for shoving those dummies up my tail pipe. Peter West and Craig Voight for letting me take the time off and for doing my job while I was gone, especially the part when you let me come back even after realising how little I do. Dr Colin Kestell for his unwavering support and total commitment to helping me get this off the ground; his brilliant students; the guys in the workshop—Rob, Steve and Phil; and all the team at the University of Adelaide—thank you! My drivers for not running me over, for putting things right; in the right order, 'Drug Free' to 'Free Drugs' Howard Fletcher, Shane Edwards, Phil Downey, Mathew Downey, Gavin Kelly and Carrie Downey: you all did me proud. Dan Stevenson for his support, brilliant camera work and ability to drink and shoot at the same time. My dad Alan for so much help along the way. And the outstanding team at Allen & Unwin, especially Catherine Milne for her patience and advice all the way from San Francisco.

My sponsors, all good people who thought I was mad but backed me anyway:

Rob Egan,
Rig Inspection Services

The whole team at
IKM Testing

John Duncan,
Tubular Leasing
Australia

Ashley Taylor, Pentagon
Freight

IS THAT THING DIESEL?

 Greg Quail, Quail Television

 Greg Cooper, Jet Lube

 Thomas Reinbold, Bestolife

 Ross Luck, Tasman Oil Tools

 Dare Jennings, Deus Ex Machina

 Dr Colin D. Kestell, PhD BSc (Hons) CPEng MIEAust MSAE, University of Adelaide

Thanks to the following firms and individuals for their assistance:

Graeme Barton for a great paint job, Ross Luck for so much advice, Paul Bettles, Donald Millar, Neil Boath, Stephen Digby, Ron Currie, Charlie Morgan, Shaun Southwell, Dare Jennings, Ben Monroe, Matt Bromley, Taka Aoyama, Peter Keegan, Arthur Palmer, Anthony Black, Jordan West, Bob Hicks, Lou Amato, Steve Hudson, Siggi Buba, Paul and Christina Blair, Peter Gerrand, Eleanor Collins, Rick Popik, Senior Constable Ben Lavington, Detective Kent Crane, David Easton, Chris Brinkworth for the Macallan and for being a legend, Stephen Yarwood, Sky Di Pietro, Jane De La Vega, Gail Lodge, Peter Hymus, Peter Dewar, Nigel Michalaney, Leo O'Hagan, John Lloyd, James Ward for the DB9, Haydn Harper, Greg Waters, Doug Howard, Dave Sadler, Nigel Begg, Clayton Jacobson, Claire Balart, Liam Kelly, Tim Walker, Nikki Wright, Brad Neenan, Janine McBride, Mitch Elkins, Sue Hines, Christa Munns. The staff at Longreach Hospital, Mel and Kim the paramedics; Marlee, Evan, Trevor and Ruth at Bullo River Station; Dave Henry the chopper pilot; Simon the BMW guy; Rory Panetta at Gimoto Leathers; brilliant photographers Christos Doudakis and Brendan Beirne; the musical Craig Doherty; and Erwin Herczeg—see you on the salt.

Here's to the riders.